KU-532-623

LIVE & WORK IN

GERMANY

LEEDS BECKETT UNIVERSITY
LIBRARY

DISCARDED

Ian Collier

SERIES EDITORS VICTORIA PYBUS & DAVID WOODWORTH

Leeds Metropolitan University

www.

17 0364978 0

Published by Vacati... ...Street, Oxford

LIVE AND WORK IN GERMANY
First edition 1992 Victoria Pybus
Second edition 1998 Ian Collier
Third edition 2002 Ian Collier

Copyright © Vacation Work 2002

ISBN 1-85458-288-7

No part of this publication may be stored, reproduced or transmitted in any form, or by any means without the prior permission of the publisher

LEEDS METROPOLITAN
UNIVERSITY
LEARNING CENTRE
1703649780
70-B   ✓
CC- 40119   12/5/03
          31/7/03
914·3 COL   ℗

Publicity: Roger Musker

Cover design by Miller, Craig and Cocking Design Partnership

Text design and typesetting by Brendan Cole.

Printed and bound in Italy by Legoprint SpA, Trento.

CONTENTS

LEEDS BECKETT UNIVERSITY LIBRARY

DISCARDED

SECTION I
– LIVING IN GERMANY –

The publisher has every reason to believe in the accuracy of the information given in this book and the authenticity and correct practices of all organisations, companies, agencies etc. mentioned: however, situations may change and telephone numbers, regulations, exchange rates etc. can alter, and readers are strongly advised to check facts and credentials for themselves. Readers are invited to write to Vacation Work, 9 Park End Street, Oxford OX1 1HJ, with any comments, corrections and first hand experiences. Those whose contributions are used will be sent a free copy of the Vacation Work title of their choice.

SECTION II
– WORKING IN GERMANY –

FOREWORD TO THE THIRD EDITION

*L*ive and Work in Germany is one of the successful *Live & Work* series of books which identify the opportunities for living, working, starting a business, or retiring in another country. The book is divided into two sections, *Living in Germany* and *Working in Germany* respectively, which between them cover all aspects of such a venture, from how to find accommodation or a removal firm, what school to send your kids to, to ideas and the procedures for setting up a small business. Apart from having been posted to Germany there are many good reasons to take advantage of the opportunity to live and work in another country either for your employer or in your own business; aside from the novelty of a new experience. In Germany these reasons include pleasant working conditions, an excellent integrated transport system, a generous social welfare system and the high standard of living. There is also the opportunity to make new friends and develop new interests and while the hard working Germans in your office, factory or shop may seem aloof at first, once that German formality has been cracked, durable friendships will blossom.

For those wishing to study in Germany, there is a guide to the higher education system and a section on *Temporary Work* for you to make money either in part time work or over the summer. Germany has recently completed agreements with the governments of Australia and New Zealand that allow their citizens to take 'working holidays' in Germany.

Americans and Canadians will be happy to note that where possible the book has been expanded to meet their need for information that applies to them.

The EU has beaten down the barriers between Member States unleashing an array of opportunities for those seeking jobs and business opportunities. Germany, one of the cornerstones of the EU, has set an example to the rest of Europe with its highly trained workforce and patronage of small businesses. The country's geographic position coupled with the Single Market, the open borders of the Schengen Agreement, the Euro (see note below) and the opening of new markets in Eastern Europe all mean one thing: for those wishing to do business in Europe the place to be is Germany.

Ian Collier
Oxford, April 2002.

ACKNOWLEDGMENTS

*I*would like to thank the following (in no particular order) for their invaluable help in compiling this book: Anke Büttner; Joy Coulton; Andre de Vries; Inge Kempfer; Hans-Willi, Evi, Maike, Almut and Clemens Büttner; Cathy J. Matz, Alaistair Heron, Sarah Sierra, Andrew Faulds, Marina Zvetina, Bob Harrison, Scott Adams for Dilbert and not forgetting Victoria Pybus for the first edition.

Section I

TELEPHONE NUMBERS

Please note that the telephone numbers in this book are written as needed to call that number from inside the same country. To call these numbers from outside the country you will need to know the relevant international access code; these are currently 00 from the UK and Germany and 011 from the USA.
To call Germany: dial the international access code + 49 + the number as given in this book minus the first 0.
To call the UK: international access code +44 + and as Germany, the complete number omitting the first 0.
To call the USA or Canada: international access code +1 + the complete number as given in this book.

THE EURO

On January 1st 2002 the Euro became the legal currency in Germany replacing the Deutschmark at the unromantic rate of 1.95583 DM to the Euro. The value of the Euro against the UK £ and the US $ varies from day to day: at the time of going to press one Euro is worth UK £0.62 or US $0.87.

GENERAL INTRODUCTION

CHAPTER SUMMARY

○ Germany is one of the largest European countries.

○ Its population of around 82 million includes many non-Germans.

○ Bargain flights are available with low-cost and Star-Alliance airlines to major and regional airports across Germany making most areas practicably accessible to expatriates.

○ **History:** Up until the mid 19th century Germany was a collection of separate kingdoms and principalities.

○ Divided after World War II, East & West Germany reunited in July 1990.

○ Modern Germany only gained full sovereignty over its territory with the ratification of the reunification treaties by Britain, France, the USA, and Russia.

○ **Government:** The German political system of two elected houses of representatives has more in common with the American one than the British one. But the election system is radically different.

○ The German President is selected by the Federal Convention and not directly elected, the President maintains balance between all political parties and so acts as a figurehead for the nation.

○ **Economy:** Germany is the third largest economy in the world after the USA and Japan.

DESTINATION GERMANY

Given the rantings of Britain's tabloid newspapers and the decline of the US military presence in Germany, one would think that emigrating to Germany held little interest except to refugees and asylum seekers. However, recent figures put the number of British expatriates in Germany at over 110,000. This may be down from the figure used in the last edition, but no doubt the natural down turn in the construction industry as projects were completed and the government moved into its new buildings and offices in Berlin has had a large part to play in that. The number of American citizens resident and working in Germany is somewhat larger at 112,000 plus, but both these figures have also dropped as a result of the 'peace dividend' of the early 1990s, the reunification of Germany and its effect on the NATO military presence in Germany.

Despite the above points, the economic and developmental burden of re-unification followed by a recession, a change of government, and now monetary union Germany still has much to offer in terms of career and business prospects for non-Germans.

After all it is still one of the most industrialised countries in Europe with one of the highest standards of living. Along with Denmark, Germany shares a higher element of social welfare in the workplace and the community than any of the other EU countries. Labour and employer relations are amongst the best in Europe with workers having the chance to sit in on committees overseeing negotiations on wages and conditions.

Undoubtedly, given the high rates of unemployment especially amongst the young, in the 'new' Länder in the East a number of problems still need to be solved. But the tax and social security system has recently been restructured to benefit everyone. It may be that these elements also account for Germany's popularity with asylum seekers, 88,365 of whom arrived in 2001 (one wonders if they are excluded or included in unemployment statistics).

Despite the problems associated with introducing any new currency, problems which should soon pass, the miraculous economic recovery of the Fifties and Sixties should be taken as an indicator of how well the Germany economy can roll with the punches and come out a winner.

As most readers of this book are likely to be moving for sound employment reasons either to build up a CV/résumé, 'the boss told you', or with your partner then economic woes are less of a worry. Compared to the UK Germany has a much lower cost of living and the US$ is likely to remain high against the Euro.

PROS AND CONS OF MOVING TO GERMANY

Those intent on living and working in Germany will find that Germany is not only a major player in the European Union but is also home to many multinational companies, allowing the potential expatriate, who isn't being transferred in by their employer, to choose from a wide range of employment and career possibilities. From the employee's point of view there are distinct advantages to working in Germany: high wages; generous fringe benefits and salary related social security payments (see Chapter 6, *Employment*).

So while you may pay a lot for your benefits, you can still take a lot home with you secure in the knowledge that you'll have a decent safety net too. Many Germans in the engineering and electronics industries now work a 35 hour week, thus achieving an old aim of the trade unions to develop a leisure society. Although some of these shorter working weeks are made up of shift work in an attempt to prevent job losses, the practical upshot is that the workers have a good job, good wages and a good part of the week to themselves and their families. Two standard additions to pay packets across Germany are the payments of *Urlaubsgeld* and *Weihnachtsgeld*, the former is an extra months pay for one's summer holiday, while the latter is for Christmas presents.

Even before re-unification Germany was not generally considered to be a country of stylish expatriate living in the manner of France's Provence or the Italian 'Chiantishire'. However, as can be seen from the above, the Germans enjoy one of the most uniformly high living standards in Europe combined with the shortest working week in Europe, and a generous amount of annual leave. Even if the 'ossie' of the eastern länder still feel left behind by their more worldly 'wessie' western cousins, the German government is determined to unify the country in as many ways as possible.

Setting up home in another country will always cause problems even for proficient linguists as the newcomer gets to grips with slang terms or variations in dialect, in amongst the various logistical and bureaucratic tasks relevant to setting up a new home, not forgetting the occasional bout of home-sickness or even culture shock. The German language is perceived as a bigger problem than most due to its many rules, exceptions and regional variants. However, be comforted by the knowledge that most urban Germans are more than proficient at speaking English (who will generally relish the opportunity to practise or 'fine-tune' their grasp of English) and 'neu-Deutsch' has a growing number of English words in it (even if some aren't what they might seem). As most expats work and settle in the same urban conurbations (eg Berlin, Frankfurt, Hamburg, or Munich) then you won't be too far from other migrants if it all gets too much, but anyway you shouldn't be heading for Germany if you only wish to speak English!

For those seeking an expatriate life in Germany, there is much to recommend it. 82.1 million people are spread across 357,000 square kilometres, so the population density (230 per square kilometer) is relatively high. Despite this, perhaps because of the draw of urban conurbations such as Berlin, Frankfurt, or the Rhur valley, one is never far from an extraordinary variety of charming landscapes. Driving on the *autobahn* between Nürnberg and Frankfurt one winds through wooded valleys and vineyards perched on steep sided hills.

Public transport is well laid out, often with integrated networks of trains, trams and underground systems in the larger cities. While the German winter is generally colder with more snow than in Britain but similar to America's Northeast and Midwest, due to its continental location, the Germans have houses and heating systems built to cope with it. Not only that but they have both staff and an individual's public duty to help keep the paths and streets clear of snow. German efficiency and social responsibility may be viewed askance by more relaxed cultures, but it means that when snow falls, things do not come to a grinding halt because of it.

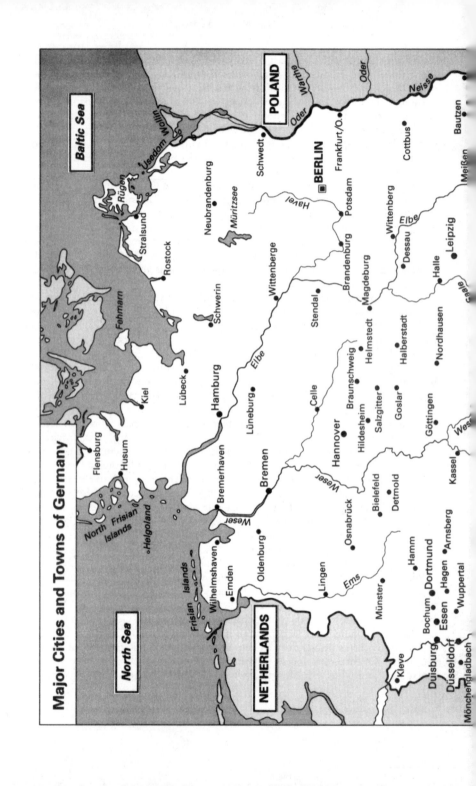

Major Cities and Towns of Germany

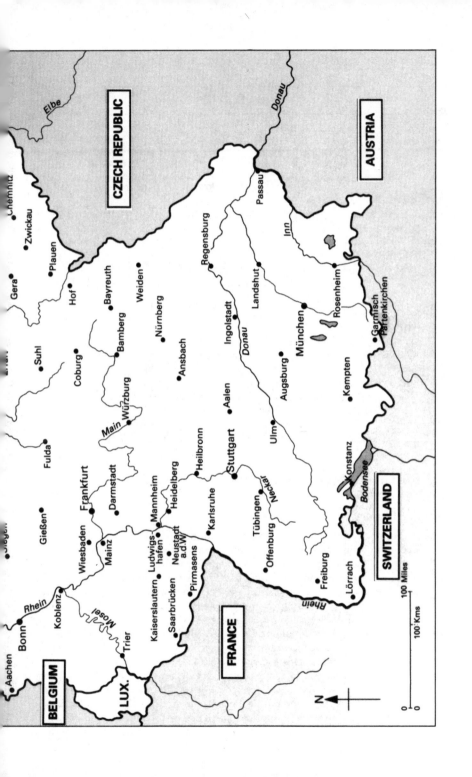

The following is a summary of the main pros and cons of living in Germany:

PROS AND CONS

Pros:
- Germany is one of the most developed countries in Europe.
- Germany has one of the strongest economies in the EU.
- The welfare system is one of the most generous in Europe.
- German labour laws are amongst the most employee-friendly in the West.
- Germany has a pleasant and civilised environment for living and working.
- Most cities and large towns have efficient bus and tram networks which reach into the surrounding countryside.
- Many Germans speak English.
- A cost of living which makes food and necessities cheap.

Cons:
- German is a difficult language to learn.
- Unemployment has risen in the run up to the Euro.
- The German wage deductions are quite high.
- Moving to any new country is always going to be awkward especially if it means leaving family behind, if only temporarily.
- The Germans can be very formal, and thus distant, socially.
- Some Germans are still keen to mind other people's business for them.

POLITICAL AND ECONOMIC STRUCTURE

Economic History

The recovery of Germany from the destruction of World War II was one of the economic miracles (*Wirtschaftswunder*) of the twentieth century. As the modern appearance of many parts of Germany's historical cities testifies, they were rebuilt from the rubble resulting from the Allied bombing campaign. In 1945 the defeated Germany could not have been in a worse state: amongst the rubble of some of their finest cities, the people of Germany were faced with a ruined infrastructure and chronic food shortages.

Under the agreement of the London Protocol of 1944, Germany was divided up by the Allies. This partition was originally to have been into three zones, but after the surrender in 1945 this was expanded to four occupation zones. The British took charge of the industrialised north-west, the Americans policed the south including Bavaria, Württemberg and Hessen, while the French, oversaw territories adjacent to their borders: the Saarland, Baden and areas in the Rhineland and Palatinate, which appropriately perhaps, included some of the finest wine-growing regions. These zones including the western zone of the partitioned city of Berlin, were democratised in about four years. The whole process began immediately after the fall of the Nazi regime when democratic forces emerged under the auspices of the Western powers and were transmuted into the BRD (*Bundesrepublik Deutschland*). The Russians had control over East Berlin and those parts of Germany east of a line running from Lübeck on the north coast in a rough curve to the Czech border, from which the GDR (German Democratic Republic) or East Germany was born.

With the descent of Churchill's *iron curtain* and the sovietising of the recently liberated Eastern Europe the West was obliged to shore-up the financially shattered BRD as an integral part of the policy to create a new stronger Europe in order to counterbalance the threat of communism from the east. Thus they did not exact war reparations in the crippling way that occurred after World War I, and which many experts agree was one of the major factors that allowed the rise of Nazism. Instead West Germany was allowed to go straight back into manufacturing. Stalin however, wanted reparations in payment for Soviet losses after the invasion of 1941 and proceeded to move all the available industrial equipment back to Russia. Despite the picture of devastation conjured up by descriptions of post-war defeat, the fact remains that most of Germany's industrial production plants were unscathed by the devastation that afflicted the civilian populations of the great cities. Germany thus had a solid base from which to recommence manufacturing. Germany was also permitted to benefit from the Marshall Aid Plan and by 1947 this much needed injection of capital was producing a modest economic improvement.

The other linchpin of economic recovery was the currency reform of 1948. The brainchild of the German economist Ludwig Erhard, the reform involved the creation of a new bank which was to become the Deutsche Bundesbank. The inflationary *Reichsmark* was abolished overnight and replaced with the new *Deutsche Mark*. Germans were allowed to exchange their Reichsmarks for the new currency at the rate of 60 Reichmarks for one new mark. On the face of it perhaps a bad deal, but with the increasing stability of the Deutsche Mark it turned out to be a blessing in disguise as the reform spurred an economic revival.

In Berlin the signs of success of the post-war economy in West Germany served only to heighten the discrepancy between the Allied and Russian zones. In June 1948 Stalin used the introduction of the Deutsche Mark as a pretext to blockade Berlin, the Russians sealing the exits from east to west with a view to swallowing up the whole city into East Germany; which they then demanded be recognised as the capital of East Germany. The Allies countered with the famous Berlin airlift, which kept the citizens of West Berlin from starvation and finally forced the Russians to abandon their siege of West Berlin in April 1949. This show of solidarity forged a partnership between the western powers and their former enemies.

The tensions between the western powers and the soviets had been building since 1945 and while the siege of Berlin was one symptom another was the re-drawing of boundaries. As eastern Poland and the pre-war German region of Könisberg were absorbed into Russia a large chunk of pre-war Germany east of Stettin and Frankfurt/Oder was given over to Poland. This coupled with the expulsion of ethnic Germans from Czechoslovakia and Hungary saw over seven million people deported into West Germany. These coupled with the numbers of Germans fleeing communism or trying to rejoin families in the west saw the population of West Germany swell by an estimated thirteen million which provided Germany with an almost inexhaustible supply of cheap labour which was a vital element in the recovery of the economy. With cornerstones of the recovery in place Germany was ready to accept a challenge that few nations have ever had to face: to rise from the debris of utter defeat in a new form – a challenge that was taken up with unparalleled zeal.

Germany's post-war economic recovery was on a scale unmatched by any other European nation. From 1950 to 1964 GNP tripled. By 1960, the BRD was producing 50% more steel than had the larger pre-war Germany. Germany had few reasons for gratitude to Hitler, but the Volkswagen car, pioneered under the Nazis, became the greatest symbol of the German post-war export boom.

Other factors contributing to the success of the post-war economy were the self-imposed wage restraints practised by the workers and the relatively small number of unions (sixteen) which avoided the demarcation disputes that so hampered the British post-war industrial relations, and thus the economy.

By the 1960's recession, slight by today's standards, had crept into the German economy producing an unemployment figure of 700,000. By the 1970's Germany's economy suffered like others in Europe from its reliance on imported energy sources and the oil price rises occasioned by various Middle East crises including the Iranian revolution of 1979. Meanwhile, expenditure on social welfare had risen from 38% of GNP to 51% by 1980. Unemployment reached 8.5% in 1982 and inflation 6.5% in 1981. By 1986, thanks to the widespread boom of the eighties, Germany's budget deficit had fallen from 4.5% in 1982 to an astonishing 1.5%. Inflation was zero.

However, the unemployment figure has grown over the years, in part through the acquisition of the former East Germany and the need to reorganise a command economy to match the western 'social market economy' and make it economically competitive. This led to workforces being trimmed to bring the factories into line with western working practices, however, the high wage deals of West Germany were then applied to companies in the new länder causing many to fold quite soon after. Despite a change in government in 1998 to a coalition of SPD and Greens, unemployment has only dipped and risen again in the intervening 4 years despite their promises to cut the jobless figure to less than 3.5 million. Currently 4.29 million German workers are unemployed (roughly 19% in the Eastern länder but less than half that figure in the West) and the strain on the economy of this coupled with the introduction of the Euro and other recent events (eg BSE in German farm animals and the knock-on effects of the New York terror attacks) mean that at the time of writing the German economy is teetering at the edge of a recession.

Recent Political History

In modern times, unlike Britain and France, Germany has not enjoyed a continuity of government or even borders. Before 1815, Germany was a jigsaw of little states and principalities ruled by an absolutist aristocracy, the names if not all the boundaries of which are echoed in some of the sixteen present day Länder such as Bavaria, Thuringia and Saxony. In 1871 the first unification of Germany was orchestrated by Bismarck and dominated by a cohort of aristocrats and the legendary army of Prussia, a state which ceased to exist after the end of 1939-45 War. Around Prussia, the smaller satellite states clustered, as if seeking protection. This Imperial period lasted until the end of the Great War when having lost all credibility in the eyes of ordinary Germans it was replaced by the Weimar Republic. This lasted until 1933 when Hitler was elected Chancellor and shortly after created a one-party state. It was a tragedy for the Western world that the experimentally democratic Weimar republic proved so weak and unstable, thus allowing the demonic forces of Nazism to wreak so much havoc across Europe. The political vacuum left by the obliteration of Hitler and the Nazis was filled by the Allied occupational forces who oversaw the democratization of Germany. The short-lived so-called 'denazification' whereby the Allies supposedly rooted out from public institutions many of those who had held power in the Nazi era was in fact limited to those well-documented cases where people could be proved to have carried out their duties in a particularly brutal way. It is truer to say that a large percentage of Germans holding office were not Nazi fanatics, they had merely gone along with Nazism until it proved a total failure. It became quickly apparent to the Allies that if they barred all former Nazis from holding office, there would be no-one left to run the country. A compromise was reached whereby those with dossiers against them were penalised and the rest were able to retain their posts after the war.

Between 1945 and 1947 the Russians and the Allies set about re-organising their respective zones into Länder. The commanders of the Russian and Allied zones permitted the formation of four main political parties, the KPD, CDU, SPD (see *Political Parties* below) and the Liberal Democratic Party. As the Cold War became an increasing reality, the Allies concentrated their efforts on rapid stabilisation of West Germany as a bulwark against the spread of Communism.

In 1946 the Russians forced a merger of the KDP and SPD in their zone into the SED (*Sozialistische Einheitspartei*, Socialist Unity Party) hoping to prompt a similar merger in the Western zone, thus producing a ruling party strong enough to carry out a re-unification of Germany which would remain in the Russian sphere of influence. In the event the attempt was a failure and the Russians' interest in a re-united Germany declined thereafter. Until in the late 1980s political unrest and dissatisfaction with their way of life lead to free elections followed by the fall of the Berlin Wall and reunification in July 1990. As soviet influence in Eastern Europe collapsed after this the 'Iron Curtain' fell with it.

GOVERNMENT

On May 23rd 1949 under a new constitution (the Basic Law), the liberal and democratic Federal Republic of Germany was inaugurated. Full sovereignty was not achieved until May 5th 1955 as the interim occupation regime had to be dismantled in stages. Under the Basic Law Germany is a democratic republic made up of federal states based on the rule of law and social justice. Germany as a whole is governed by a Parliamentary system comprising an upper house, the Bundesrat and a lower house, the effective legislature of the country, the Bundestag. While its Federal status means that Germany, is made up of the sixteen German Länder which reflect features of the political and legislative framework of the nation in their regional administration. So each of the Länder has its own legislature elected by popular vote on the same terms as the Bundestag.

An elected Federal President (*Bundespräsident*) is the Head of State, while the Government is led by the Federal Chancellor (*Bundeskanzler*). The office of Federal President is elected by a Federal Convention made up of members from the Bundestag and others elected by the state parliaments. The Presidential term of office is five years, with re-election allowed only once. It is the President who suggests to the Bundestag a candidate for the office of Federal Chancellor taking into account the party political majority in the Bundestag, the Chancellor is nominated by the President and elected by the Bundestag. In effect the Chancellor is the elected government as it is the Chancellor who creates a Cabinet by proposing members of the Bundestag for the various ministerial posts, their appointment as Federal Minister is the decision of the President. The Federal President at the time of writing is Johannes Rau, while the post of Chancellor is currently held by Gerhard Schröder as head of a coalition government which has been in power since 1998.

Following the reunification of Germany the Bundestag voted by a small margin to move the parliament and government from Bonn to Berlin, the Bundesrat foolowed this with its own vote on moving. In recompense for this decamping, Bonn was named a Federal City and six federal ministries are still located there.

The Bundesrat

The Bundesrat represents the sixteen federal states, and has a part in the legislative process as more than half of all bills need its formal approval especially those concerning the financial or administrative affairs of the states. The senators are not directly elected to this house by the people but are usually cabinet members of the Länder governments. Voting in the Bundesrat is made up of 69 votes split between the various states according to their population (see the *Regional Guide* for particulars). The Bundesrat can object to a particular bill, but this can be overruled by the Bundestag, if an agreement can not be reached then a mediation committee made up from both houses will attempt to resolve the problem. The President of the Bundesrat, elected annually is in effect a deputy to the Federal President.

The Bundestag

The Bundestag, the lower house of 656 seats, is elected every four years by universal suffrage (although the number of seats may vary to reflect the electoral situation). The electoral system is a combination of proportional representation and direct election of the candidates nominated by their respective parties. In order to ensure that government can function properly, only parties which poll at least five per cent of the vote or, win three seats under the first-past-the-post system may have representatives in the Bundestag. It is the Bundestag which provides the main check on government affairs as it is this chamber that draws up most legislation. While the Federal Government generates most of the bills, the others being introduced by ordinary members of the Bundestag or Bundesrat, each bill has to face three readings before a vote is taken to pass it or not. Of the 7,500 bills put before the German parliament since 1949 4,600 have been passed into law.

THE ELECTORAL SYSTEM

The conversion to democratic rule, has proved more traumatic for Germany than other European nations. Germany's first attempt at rule by political parties was the Weimar Republic (1919-1933) which was undermined by the iniquitous terms of the Versailles treaty, aggravated by the French occupation of the Ruhr and the crippling burden of war reparations, which left many people sceptical of government. The combination of these factors made a democratic consensus difficult and instead favoured the rise of extremist factions. For all its problems, the Weimar Republic did work for the first ten years. Its fate was ultimately sealed by the world economic crisis which proved to be the last straw. The recession gave rise to the situation where the small National Socialist German Workers Party (NSDAP) from Bavaria could gain votes in northern Germany due to the dissatisfaction of the voters. Eventually this party grew in strength and Hitler came to power, initially as Chancellor of a coalition, President Hindenburg remained distrustful of this undemocratic process which saw the other parties disbanded. On Hindenberg's death Hitler promptly merged the roles of president and chancellor. The Third Reich benefited by contrast with the turmoil of the Weimar years from a period of economic stability, until Hitler's dreams of an empire plunged Germany into World War.

With the demise of the NSDAP or Nazis, it was left to the Allied Powers to nurture the seeds of German democracy which had lain hidden or imprisoned and from their efforts emerged an extremely stable system. The German political system has several checks to prevent a repeat of the instability of the Weimar period. One of these is the five percent clause, by which only parties gaining at least five per cent or three constituency seats can be represented in parliament. Although this hurdle is waived for national minorities in the länder elections, such as the Danish minority which has a seat in the Schleswig-Holstein parliament.

Anyone in Germany who is 18 or over and has held German nationality for at least one year may vote or stand for election in parliamentary elections. Bundestag elections are based on a system of personalised proportional representation, each voter has two votes. The first vote is for a constituency candidate, and election is on a first-past-the-post basis from the number of votes cast, the second vote goes to a candidate picked from a list put up by the parties. The votes from constituency and state lists are offset so that the party political composition of the Bundestag reflects the votes for the parties across the constituencies.

Political Parties

The last general elections were in 1998 and saw a change in the political landscape. Listed below are the political parties which make up the current Bundestag, with the numbers of seats held in brackets.

Alliance 90/The Greens. (47). The Green movement which began in Germany in the 1970's developed a higher profile in Germany than in any other European country. Some pundits attribute this to the greater need of younger Germans to rebel against the excessive materialism and industrial success of their over orderly nation. The Green Party was formed in 1980. After several victories at Länder level they achieved representation in the Bundestag in 1983 and the European Parliament in 1984. The Greens failed completely at the polls in 1990 only gaining representation by sharing with Alliance 90, the eastern civil rights campaign with whom they merged in 1993. At present they are led by Joschka Fischer who is also Deputy Chancellor and Federal Foreign Minister. For further information see www.gruene.de.

Christian Democratic Union (CDU)/Christian Social Union (CSU). CDU (198) & CSU (47). Formed after the war the Christian Democratic Union operates in all the Länder bar Bavaria where its sister party, the Christian Social Union, operates. The CSU led by Edmund Stoiber, operates solely in Bavaria, although the CDU and CSU act as joint parliamentary group in the Bundestag, and therefore this pair is the largest party. In contrast to the Catholic Centre Party of the Weimar years, these parties draw support from Catholics and Protestants. A former CDU leader was Adenauer the first post-war chancellor, and its current leader is Angela Merkel, although in the run-up to the 2002 general election Stoiber is the candidate for the Chancellorship. For further information see www.cdu.de and www.csu.de.

Free Democratic Party. FDP (43). The Free Democratic Party (*Freie Demokratische Partei*) a small but influential centre party which has formed coalitions with both the CDU/CSU and the SPD during its history. A firm supporter of liberalisation of criminal law and pro-abortion, the FDP was also committed to the support of Ostpolitik. Although a small party the FDP has been in coalition with the CDU/CSU in many previous governments. For further information see www.liberale.de.

Party of Democratic Socialism (PDS). PDS (36). The successor to the Socialist Unity Party (SED) which once ruled East Germany although it hasn't been able to establish itself very well in a united Germany. In the 1990 election it only gained seats through the exception to the five percent clause given to the eastern länder. However in the 1994 elections they gained four constituency seats in Berlin, they built this in 1998 to pass the 5% hurdle. For further information see ww.pds-online.de.

Social Democratic Party (SPD). SPD (298). The German Social Democratic Party (*Sozialdemokratische Partei Deutschlands*) is currently the senior partner in a coalition government (in partnership with the Greens/Alliance 90). Originally a radical left-wing party its origins go back to 1875 and the formation of a Socialist Labour party compounded from the German General Workers' Association and the Social Democratic Workers Party. After the Second World War the SPD shifted towards the centre in order to court popularity amongst the electorate, and the election success of 1998 may be in part due to this ideological change. The SPD was the party of the much venerated foreign minister of the sixties, Willy Brandt who pioneered the concept of *Ostpolitik* (detente with the East). The SPD leader and *Bundeskanzler*/Chancellor, at the time of writing, is Gerard Schröder. For further information see www.spd.de.

Other Parties

The current Bundestag is made up of 669 seats due to the share of direct votes within the proportional system. There are other parties which can be found holding seats in the länder parliaments which can climb to greater prominence given the rules of the German political system, these include:

DVU: (Deutsche Volksunion). In common with France, Germany has experienced the worrying phenomenon of a rise in popularity of extreme right-wing politics. The DVU won six seats in the Bremen state parliament in 1991. Campaigning on a platform of clamping down on fake asylum seekers of which Germany has had more than its fair share, the success of the DVU has so far largely been at the expense of the SPD.

Republicans: The Republicans are Germany's right wing radical party of the south and in the April 1992 Land elections they polled nearly 11% of the vote at the expense of the CDU. This result was viewed as a protest vote against liberal government policy toward asylum seekers.

GEOGRAPHICAL INFORMATION

Germany occupies an area of 137,777 sq miles/356,844 sq kms, geographically, almost at the heart of Europe. Germany is bordered on the west by the Netherlands, Belgium, Luxembourg and France; on the south by Switzerland and Austria, on the east by the Czech Republic and Poland and on the north by Denmark. To the north west lies the North Sea while the Baltic washes the northern beaches. Generally, the north of Germany is formed of the flat North German Plain, while the Central Upland Range of hills and mountains effectively divides north and south Germany as the ground rises towards the Alps. The upland areas of south west Germany are cut by the valleys of the Mosel, the Main and Rhein (Rhine), which water the vineyards of these terraced hills. While further south the land rises again into the slopes of the Schwarzwald (Black Forest) it dips briefly into the Lower Bavarian Plain before rising into the Alps along the Swiss border. More highlands occur in the Bavarian Alps of south east Germany. There are several important navigable rivers including the Donau (Danube), the Mosel, the Rhein, the Elbe and the Weser.

Regional Divisions And Main Towns

The Federal Republic of Germany comprises sixteen Länder, six of which were formed from the former East Germany. The länder including the city of Berlin and the Hanseatic Cities of Bremen and Hamburg are (in German): Baden-Württemburg; Bavaria (Bayern); Brandenburg; Hesse (Hessen); Lower Saxony (Niedersachsen); Mecklenburg-West Pomerania (Mecklenburg-Vorpommern); North-Rhine-Westphalia (Nordrhein-Westfalen); Rhineland- Palatinate (Rheinland-Pfalz); Saarland; Saxony (Sachsen); Saxony-Anhalt (Sachsen-Anhalt); Schleswig-Holstein; Thuringia (Thüringen).

TABLE 1	THE LÄNDER AND CAPITALS		
Land	Capital	Population in Millions	Area in Sq Kms
Baden-Württemberg	Stuttgart	10.4	35,751
Bayern	München	12	70,552
Berlin	...	3.4	889
Brandenburg	Potsdam	2.6	29,479
Bremen	...	.668	404
Hamburg	...	1.7	755
Hessen	Wiesbaden	6	21,114
Mecklenburg-Vorpommern	Schwerin	1.8	23,170
Niedersachsen	Hanover	7.8	47,338
Nordrhein-Westfalen	Düsseldorf	18	34,080
Rheinland-Pfalz	Mainz	4	19,849
Saarland	Saarbrücken	1.1	2,570
Sachsen	Dresden	4.5	18,413
Sachsen-Anhalt	Magdeburg	2.65	20,445
Schleswig-Holstein	Kiel	2.7	15,729
Thüringen	Erfurt	2.5	16,171

Population

Germany's population is the largest of any European Union country with 82 million people living there. This figure divided by the area of Germany (357,000 sq km) explains why Germany is one of Europe's most densely populated countries with 230 people per square kilometre, compared to the EU average of 116. The reason for such a density of population can be attributed to the influx of 14 million German-speaking refugees who fled from Eastern Europe after the Second World War, and the high numbers of refugees and asylum seekers from Vietnam and the former Yugoslavia. Thus the population count includes some 7.2 million non-Germans. Many ethnic Germans have returned to Germany from countries which were once German territory, in the three years up to 1992, 2.3 million immigrants of German origin arrived, and this migration is still occurring, in 1996 the number of migrants entering Germany including immigrants of German origin was 252,000.

The population is not evenly distributed across Germany, as can be seen from the table below, only a few cities have more than a million inhabitants, yet the industrialised area of the Rhine-Ruhr is home to 11 million. Here though the towns and cities have a tendency to merge into one long urban sprawl making town population counts difficult. The west of Germany is the more densely populated region having 16 of the 19 towns inhabited by more than 330,000 people, while in the east one fifth of the population live on roughly one third of the land. However, only 26 million people live in the 84 cities of more than 100,000 inhabitants, the majority of Germans live in small towns and villages.

As may be expected given the methods used by Bismark to unite Germany there is a distinct North/South divide, exemplified by the Bavarian view of anything 'Prussian'. This is one example of regional difference which forms the basis for much German humour. In the cities where populations tend to be mixed and sophisticated, and the north/south stereotype tends to break down, but you'lls till find jokes about some other region's inhabitants.

As mentioned above the indigenous German population is interspersed with many foreign nationals. Some of these are guest workers (*Gastarbeiter*) or their relatives, who began arriving in the 1960's and 70's to provide much needed labour for burgeoning German industry. In 1995 the German government claimed that 'Foreigners stimulate every sector of the economy' with 28 percent of welders and 25 per cent of hotel staff being foreign given as examples. At one time welcomed for their usefulness to German Industry the gastarbeiter have never really integrated into German society. What will happen to relations between Germans and them now that the laws on citizenship have been relaxed remains to be seen.

TABLE 2	POPULATIONS OF THE MAIN CITIES		
Berlin	3,398,800	Frankfurt	643,900
Bremen	543,000	Hamburg	1,700,000
Cologne (Köln)	962,600	Hanover	516,200
Dortmund	591,700	Leipzig	437,100
Dresden	452,800	Munich (München)	1,188,900
Duisburg	523,300	Nuremberg (Nürnberg)	487,100
Düsseldorf	568,400	Stuttgart	582,000
Essen	603,200		

Climate

Germany lies on the western edge of the European continent, in the moderately cool west wind zone between the influences of the North Atlantic weather systems and continental climate of the East. Continental influences from the south also make themselves apparent with the regular appearance of the warm alpine Föhn. The driest months are April and October but otherwise precipitation is evenly distributed around the year, although as has been seen in recent years this can vary. Summers can be especially hot with July being the warmest month with average temperatures ranging between 18-20°C. Germany usually has notable Indian summers brought on by the high pressure systems which normally prevail at that time of year, and winters vary in severity depending on the area. The region crossed by the Rhine and its tributaries generally has an average winter temperature of 1.5°C while the higher points of the Bayerische Wald can drop to -6°C and in the Alps to -10°C. However, the open plains of the north are also prone to cold winters lying as they do between the North and Baltic Seas. In the higher altitudes of the German Alps snow-free periods only occur in the summer months. The snow-blanket in the highest range, the Zugspitze, is over six feet thick from December to May.

TABLE 3		AVERAGE TEMPERATURE CHART			
Area		January	April	August	November
Berlin	min	-12°C (10°F)	-2°C (28°F)	7°C (46°F)	-3°C (25°F)
	max	8°C (48°F)	22°C (72°F)	31°C (88°F)	12°C (55°F)
Frankfurt	min	-10°C (14°F)	0°C (32°F)	8°C (48°F)	-2°C (27°F)
	max	10°C (50°F)	23°C (75°F)	8°C (48°F)	-2°C (27°F)
Hamburg	min	-2°C (28°F)	3°C (38°F)	12°C (54°F)	2°C (37°F)
	max	2°C (36°F)	12°C (55°F)	22°C (72°F)	2°C (37°F)
München	min	-5°C (23°F)	3°C (38°F)	12°C (55°F)	4°C (40°F)
	max	1°C (35°F)	13°C (56°F)	22°C (73°F)	13°C (56°F)

REGIONAL GUIDE

Like the shires of England and the States of America, Germany's regional differences are defined not so much by the political divisions of the Länder, each with its own Parliament, but by historical differences, regional dialects and accents. Although the Länder all bear historic-sounding names, only a few, most notably Bavaria and the free cities and regions of Hamburg and Bremen have kept their historical boundaries intact. Others are jigsaws of former duchies and kingdoms, pushed together first by the Prussians and then the Allies. It is for this reason that local identity is strongest in the historically unaltered Länder, and that the modern German's concept of *heimat* (homeland) comes from the region they live in rather than the concept of a German fatherland. Examples of these historic and regional differences can be found in the anti-prussian jokes of the Bavarians, which are mostly aimed at Berliners, these are told in the same manner as jokes in Scotland about the English, or jokes about Californians. Not all of these differences are based on history, to many western Germans with relatives in the East, the accent of a Saxon brings back memories of the GDR's Border Guards. However, these memories appear to be fading, especially as so many physical traces of the iron curtain have been built over.

It is a myth that the greatest visible regional differences are between the north and south: the hackneyed tourist images of fairy-tale castles and medieval towns of half-timbered buildings may be found equally in the north e.g. Lemgo (Lümeberg), Hamelin (Hameln), Goslar etc; as in the heavily promoted south (e.g. Bavaria's Schloss Neuschwanstein). After the war it was probably true to say that the north-west was more industrialised than the south, but decades of development mean that both north and south now have their share of industrial areas. Likewise while the heavy industries of East Germany were a blight on the land, the eastern länder are now much cleaner and greener than in the nineties. More information about the länder of Germany, including maps, can be obtained from German Tourist offices or from a good map and travel guide shop.

The Länder and Regional Capitals of Germany

DENMARK

Baltic Sea

North Sea

Kiel
SCHLESWIG-
HOLSTEIN

MECKLENBURG-
WEST POMERANIA
Schwerin

Hamburg

Bremen

NETHERLANDS

LOWER SAXONY

BRANDENBURG

Berlin

Hannover

Potsdam

POLAND

NORTH RHINE-
WEST PHALIA

SAXONY-
ANHALT

Halle

Düsseldorf

Erfurt

SAXONY

Bonn

BELGIUM

HESSE

THURINGIA

Dresden

RHINELAND
PALATINATE

Wiesbaden

LUX.

Mainz

CZECH
REPUBLIC

Saarbrucken

SAARLAND

Stuttgart

BAVARIA

FRANCE

BADEN-
WÜRTTEMBERG

München

SWITZERLAND

LIECH.

AUSTRIA

City State

0   100 miles

0   150 km

ITALY

Useful Addresses

German National Tourist Office (UK): PO Box 2695, London W1A 3TN; ☎020-7317 0908. 24 hour Brochure Order Line 09001-600 100 (60 pence per minute); e-mail gntolon@d-z-t.com; website www.germany-tourism.de (multiingual). German National Tourist Office: PO Box A980, Sydney, NSW 2000, Australia; ☎02-9267 8148; fax 02-9267 9035. German National Tourist Office (Canada): P.O. Box 65162, Toronto, Ontario M4K 3Z2, Canada; ☎877-315-6237.

The US website seems to cover Canada too. German National Tourist Office (USA): 122 East 42nd Street, New York, NY 10168-0072, USA; ☎212-661 7200; fax 212-661 7174; e-mail gntony@aol.com; website www.visits-to-germany.com.

Edward Stanford Ltd: 12-14 Long Acre, Covent Garden, London WC2E 9LP; ☎020-7836 1321; www.stanfords.co.uk.

BADEN-WÜRTTEMBERG

Capital: Stuttgart.
Main cities: Mannheim, Karlsruhe, Freiburg, Heidelberg, Ulm, Heilbronn.
Seats in Bundesrat: 6.
Website: www.baden-wuerttemberg.de.

Baden-Württemberg is one of the two big Länder that make up the south (the other being Bavaria) and is one of the newest states having been formed in 1952. The region is made up of two distinct historical entities with divergent cultures. Baden is the region to the west which includes most of the Black Forest and whose largely Catholic inhabitants are generally more laid-back than those of Württemberg (often known as Swabians after the local mountain range), who embody more of the stereotypical hard-working, houseproud German who keeps a watchful eye on the purse strings.

The south of Germany is often referred to as the 'sunbelt' and is traditionally less industrial than the north. However this is perhaps truer of Bavaria than Baden-Württemberg whose industrial base grew up in the nineteenth century. But the modern state manages to earn its income from work and pleasure, given that more tourists visit Baden-Württemberg each year than it has inhabitants, it is Germany's third largest wine producer, yet it is also the location for the headquarters of Bosch, Daimler-Benz and Porsche. Since the 1970's a successful drive to keep up with new technology has paid dividends and Baden-Württemburg boasts no fewer than 130 research institutes and a dozen science parks where university professors work part-time for companies they have been encouraged to set up themselves. Daimler-Benz has its biggest plant in Germany at Sindelfingen just outside Stuttgart and the mighty IBM corporation has its European headquarters nearby. Publishing is also a major industry, with 40 percent of all German books being published here.

In addition to the scenic attributes of the Swabian Alps and the Black Forest Baden-Württemberg includes the northern shores of Lake Constance (Bodensee) which forms part of the border with Switzerland and Austria. It is also home to Germany's oldest university, Heidelberg and eight others, including Tübingen, which are equally at home with venerable traditions and the latest high technology research. A high speed data link is being constructed to link the universities, so it shouldn't be too long before Baden-Württemberg produces modern scholars to rival those of the past such as Schiller, Hegel or Heidigger.

The regional capital Stuttgart experienced something of a building crisis in the early nineties, brought on by the unsuitability of its hilly environs for building on. This forced prices for land and property in Stuttgart to an all-time record for anywhere in Germany, however, Munich has since taken this lead. As a consequence of this, people in their thousands and industries in their hundreds have been relocating to smaller towns nearby.

Mannheim in the northwest corner of the region is a masterpiece of seventeenth century town planning; it was laid out in 1607 on the grid pattern (later exported to America), which admirers of Lisbon in Portugal, will appreciate. Throughout the nineteenth century, Mannheim became steadily industrialised. It is the home of the Benz automobile company whose founder demonstrated his prototype here in 1886 and named the car after his daughter, Mercedes. Heavily bombed, Mannheim has unfortunately lost much of its original charm. This cannot be said of Heidelberg, 18 kms distant, which was spared the attention of the bombers it is said, largely because of its pre-war popularity with Americans.

A former state capital of Baden, Karlsruhe (Charles' Rest) is positively a neophyte in the line-up of historic German cities. It did not exist before 1715 and like Mannheim is a fascinating example of town-planning. The central point is the Schloss from which the main avenues radiate outwards like the rays of a sun. Karlsruhe is chiefly important as the seat of the two highest courts of Germany: the Federal Court of Justice and the Federal Constitutional Court.

Freiburg im Breisgau, usually referred to as just Freiburg, is a historic university town near the border with France. It has a retained a relaxed and lively atmosphere, which it owes to its Austrian overlords the Habsburgs, who held sway here for over four centuries until 1805. It's cosmopolitan atmosphere is derived in part from the university and in part from its proximity to both France and Switzerland, this atmosphere combined with its convenient position for visits to the Black Forest including the famous spa of Baden-Baden, make this city interesting enough for serious consideration as a place to live and work.

BAVARIA *(FREIESTAAT BAYERN)*

Capital: München.
Main cities: Nürnberg, Augsberg, Regensburg, Ingolstadt, Würzburg.
Seats in Bundesrat: 6.
Website: www.bayern.de.

The largest of the Länder, and home to 12 million people, the Bavarian state dates from the 6th century and its people are noted for speaking a pronounced dialect. Bavaria is also home of Germany's highest mountain the Zugspitze (2,962 metres). The clichéd view of Bavaria of jovial, beer-swilling, wurst-gorged, inhabitants and mad kings is most relevant to the south of the region around the capital Munich (München). Also found in the south are the Swabian Alps (south west), a string of lakes (Ammersee, Starnbergersee or Würmsee, Walchensee, Tegernsee and Chiemsee) and the Bavarian Alps which form the boundary with Austria. The perfection of this idyll is seldom marred except by the dreaded Föhn, a warm, dry, headache-inducing wind that blows on the German side of the Alps.

The River Danube (Donau) flows from the west right across central Bavaria and for 240kms/149 miles beside it from Ulm to Regensburg is a well-worn cycle route. To the north of the Donau lies Franconia (Franken) and the main northern city of Nürnberg. To the east lies the untamed swathe of the Bavarian Forest and ultimately the border with the Czech Republic. Until the 1950s Bavaria was primarily an agrarian state, while agriculture and forestry still play key roles over 90 per cent of the state's gross domestic product comes from the production and service sector.

The former kingdom of Bavaria was ruled by the Wittelsbach dynasty, first as Dukes then as kings, from 1180 to 1918. Bavarians are very conscious of their long history of autonomy and their national flag proclaims *Freistaat Bayern* (The Free State of Bavaria), somewhat inaccurately since they are now firmly part of Germany and separatism is not a serious issue, although Franconians will point out that they are nothing like Bavarians. Bavaria does however have a reactionary image stemming from the brief communist government of Munich in 1919, and the 1920's when it was the headquarters of the Nazi party. These tendencies were echoed in the strong electoral support in the north of the state, mainly amongst the peasantry, for the extreme right during the 1960's. Bavaria is also notable for its cultural events such as the Munich Oktoberfest, and the Bayreuth Festival with its season of Wagnerian Opera, not to mention the Passion Plays of Oberammergau, which have occured every ten years since 1634.

The regional capital could hardly be elsewhere than the important city of München which is stylish, extremely hedonistic and friendly, with a frenetic business tempo which belies the jolly rustic, Bavarian image. Despite the CSU predominance in rural Bavaria, München itself has always been, and is, staunchly 'red' (i.e. SPD voting and thus ruled). Recently however extreme right-wing movements have also made some electoral inroads in München.

During the Second World War, München endured over 70 air raids but unlike many German cities managed to adhere to aesthetic principles in its rebuilding and reconstruction, which add much to the city's appeal. Host to the ill-fated Olympic Games of 1972, Munich has splendid sports facilities. Other plus points include one of the best integrated public transport systems in Europe and a huge new airport which opened in 1992. München is popular with foreigners as a place to live and work and currently around 20% of its population is estimated to be non-German. Despite a lively cultural scene, München's most celebrated annual event remains the Oktoberfest, a two-week orgy of beer-drinking and merry-making that takes place in marquees (*Bierzelte*) on the Theresien Meadow under the gaze of a 60 foot statue, the Goddess Bavaria. This rowdy and enjoyable custom dates from 1810 though it would appear that the majority of participants these days are from Australia. It isn't all beer and pig knuckles though as München is home to six million volumes in one of the largest libraries in Europe.

Bavaria's other most famous city is the medieval city of Nuremberg (Nürnberg), sadly still inextricable in many people's minds from pre-war Nazi rallies and post war Nazi trials. Although most of the Nazi era architecture has been destroyed and built over, especially during the expansion of the city in the 1950's, some does remain and is used to teach school parties to avoid the mistakes of the past. Apart from the remarkable castle (*Burg*), the city is notable for the twin churches of St Sebaldus (*Sebalduskirche*) and St Lawrence (*Lorenzkirche*) which sit on the slopes either side of the river Pegnitz. Both of which have been restored from almost complete ruin during the war. In the fifteenth and sixteenth centuries Nürnberg was a flourishing centre of Renaissance arts and was the home of Hans Sachs and Albrecht Dürer; the lattter's house is now a museum in a street below the Burg. Modern Nürnberg has a twin city in nearby Fürth, and between them sits an industrial conurbation focusing on electrical and mechanical engineering, plastics, and toys.

Augsburg, situated on the Romantic Road, is one of the Germany's oldest cities having been founded in 15 B.C. It is renowned chiefly for its Renaissance art and architecture. It is also an important manufacturing centre for a variety of industries from textiles to automobiles.

The historic city of Regensburg is situated on the Donau and has been inhabited since Roman times when it was known as *Castra Regina*. Its main attractions are the intact medieval architecture, including the Stone Bridge dating from 1146, and innumerable beer gardens popular with the large student population.

Würzburg, a city situated on the River Main in the north west of Bavaria, is the capital of the wine district of Franconia. Wurzburg which lost much of its architectural heritage in one air raid, was once the seat of Bishop Princes and their former palace is renowned for one of the most beautiful staircases in the world (thanks to Neumann and Tiepolo). These days the city can boast a busy electronics industry and Bavaria's three largest vineyards.

BERLIN

Seats in Bundesrat: 4.
Website: www.berlin.de.

From Imperial capital to bombed-out wreck and uneasy bridge between ideologies, Berlin is a city that has seen more drama and adversity in its 125-year life than most European cities of greater lineage. So it is hardly surprising that the reunification of the two halves of Berlin has come to symbolise the reunification of Germany itself. Until November 1989 West Berlin was an isolated enclave of West Germans situated deep in East Germany with the Berlin Wall, erected almost overnight in 1961, dividing the city between Democratic West and Communist East Germany. On November 9th 1989 the GDR government abandoned all border checkpoints in the city and amidst scenes of great emotion the *Wessis* (West Germans) and *Ossis* (East Germans) danced on the Wall, the politicians, including the patriarchal Willy Brandt, arrived to shed tears at the Brandenburg Gate and the dismantling of the concrete remains of the Berlin wall began. Reducing the psychological wall is an ongoing process, as there are still tensions between east and west in this city of contradictions; flamboyant yet coy. Heartland of a dictatorship, and home to those who resisted it, East German capital while West German city, the inhabitants still take a great deal of pride in Kennedy's famous phrase '*Ich bin ein Berliner*', while pointing out that it can also be read as 'I am a doughnut'.

Modern Berlin has changed a lot over the last decade as thousands of building sites transformed what was once no-man's land into apartments and offices. A city which lost ninety percent of its buildings in the war is now a gleaming catalogue of modern architectural practices. Where Checkpoint Charlie stood on the Friedrichstrasse, is now a new business centre. In 1991 it was decided that Berlin would once again be the German capital, this provoked a flood of new building to house the ministries and accommodate their staff. Most embassies and foreign offices based in Bonn also moved here, often into gleaming new office complexes or award winning architecture.

Berlin now has twelve Technology and Business Incubation Centres, the first being created by enterprising academics, which provide advice and financial assistance for fledgling companies. Once an industrial city the home of Siemens and AEG, with Daimler-Benz and Sony developing new sites, Berlin is also rapidly developing its service sector. In addition to this it is also home to 250 research institutes and three universities (the Humboldt, Free and Technical) giving it Germany's largest student population with 147,000 students living and studying there.

Berlin is also a museum city, with an 'island' of grouped museums in rebuilt or refurbished buildings. Musically Berlin is home to several major orchestras and three opera houses, not forgetting the cultural event of the year for many young Germans; the Love Parade in the summer, arguably the world's biggest open air rave, and while some Berliners complain about the amount of rubbish it generates others happily count the millions of extra revenue it brings. Berlin may be famous for the bars and cabarets, some of which are building on the exotic club life of the twenties, but the city is also famous for its many beer halls and more than a few Irish pubs, most of which are actually run by Irishmen.

BRANDENBURG

Capital: Potsdam.
Main cities: Frankfurt an der Oder, Brandenburg, Cottbus.
Seats in Bundesrat: 4.
Website: www.brandenburg.de.

Brandenburg surrounds Berlin but has a smaller population spread over a greater area, even so they voted in the late nineties against merging with Berlin, contrary to the plans of both parliaments. This stubborn nature may go some way to explain how the people of this area came to be a major European power. Characterised by marshland and massive pine forests this area was once written off as barren and useless owing to an over-endowment of lakes. This was changed 250 years ago, at the behest of Frederick II, by the engineering skills of the Dutch who drained much of the marsh to create the Oderbruch an area which was to become Berlin's vegetable garden. Prior to the creation of Prussia, the area was the largest electoral province ruled by the Hohenzollern dynasty, in 1685 the 'Great Elector' Frederick William signed an edict granting religious tolerance and freedom from persecution to 20,00 hugenots, lutherans and jews, in contrast to later views of the state he helped create. Under Frederick II, Prussia became a European military power, his home was the magnificent Sanssouci Palace, designed by him but based on Versailles.

The main city, Potsdam is situated on the Havel river and was a royal seat of the Hohenzollern Electors of the Brandenburg March, the city still has many Baroque palaces from this period. In 1945 the Cecilienhof Palace was the site of the 1945 Potsdam Conference at which the Allies met and agreed upon the division of nearby Berlin, into four zones of occupation. Potsdam-Babelsberg, the spiritual and studio home of the German film industry once the stage for Marlene Dietrich, is once again busy as new German film-makers flock to work there.

Brandenburg's traditional agricultural output has been market vegetables for Berlin, rye and oilseed, however the economy is expanding into the electronics and optics markets, with over 120 major investors. There are many canals linking waterways across northern Germany and the world's largest ship elevator can be found on the Oder-Havel canal. Other revenues come from tourism and wildlife as there are numerous nature reserves in the woods (Uckermark, Elbtalaue, and Spreewald). The area around the lakes is a popular recreation area and tourist attraction.

Potsdam is not just a museum town for tourists, but also the centre of an industrial area of chemical, textile and clothing factories. Oil refineries and lignite-fired power stations are the major blots on the landscape, particularly the latter which claim to be the largest of their kind in the world. While Frankfurt an der Oder is home to the Viadrina University, where Kleist and the von Humboldts studied, which now specialises in German/Polish research and teaching.

BREMEN (HANSESTADT BREMEN)

Main cities: Bremen, Bremerhaven
Seats in Bundesrat: 3.
Website: www.bremen.de.

The Free Hanseatic city of Bremen is like Bavaria, Hamburg, and Saxony a political entity which existed prior to 1945. A Land in its own right, situated on the river Weser within Lower Saxony, it is, after San Marino, the second oldest city republic in the world. A bishopric since 787 and granted the rights of a free city in 1186 Bremen joined the Hanseatic League in 1358. Its subsidiary city the sheltered, deep water harbour of Bremerhaven which lies 65 kms to the north was founded in 1827 at the mouth of the Weser.

The economic life of Bremen revolves around trade and shipping, each year 10,000 ships link Bremen with 1,000 ports around the world. Bremerhaven is Europe's largest container terminal, while the Bremen Securities Exchange has been in operation for over three hundred years. In addition to this Bremen is noted for ship-building, luxury foods and also has a key role in aerospace component manufacture.

In addition to the university with its emphasis on engineering and natural sciences Bremen has five research institutes conducting work on subjects ranging from Polar Ecology to Applied Beam Technology.

With its historic squares of renaissance buildings and gothic cathedral Bremen attracts many tourists and the 960 year old Bremen Free Market on the Bürgerweide is one of Germany's largest fairs.

HAMBURG (HANSESTADT HAMBURG)

Seats in Bundesrat: 3.
Website: www.hmburg.de.

Germany's second largest city and as mentioned above a state in its own right, Hamburg is also Germany's principal seaport even though it is situated 90kms inland on the Elbe. Founded in 811 it began to flourish in the twelfth century and was one of the founders of the Hanseatic League. Hamburg has always maintained a policy of structural change, which coupled with some disastrous fires and the war has left little of the old city standing. The most notable building is the baroque St Michael's Church, locally known as 'Michel' it is the city's landmark.

Hamburg is a focus for trade with the east with around 370 firms from Asia trading here, amongst the 3,000 firms engaged in the import and export business. Hamburg also has a thriving service industry, the city is the banking and insurance capital of northern Germany. As well as trade Hamburg is famous for ship-building and the attendant port industries of refining and processing raw materials. The city is also a major media centre, being home to several publishing groups and broadcasters, employing over 50,000 people. Although some of them may move to Berlin when the government moves there, at present 15 of the largest circulation magazines are produced here and Hamburg based editions account for 50 percent of German press circulation.

New developments helped by Hamburg's own Business Development Corporation created 20,000 jobs in one five year period. The city has also benefited from reunification in regaining its traditional hinterland which now means that goods can move across north Germany for export through Hamburg. In the mid-eighties the city developed links with Scandinavia to replace this lost trade, which now means that it benefits both ways while Rostock in the east has lost out. Another development is the construction of the Transrapid levitating train to run between the city and Berlin.

Hamburg might be Germany's second largest industrial centre but it is at the same time an incredibly green city with almost half of its land area being given over to arable crops and private gardens or to public parks and heaths. Landscape and nature reserves account for 28 percent of the city's area.

The city was the site of Germany's first opera house and as well as hosting Handel's first opera, the international career of the Beatles was launched here. Brahms is another famous son and Hamburg was home to the publisher of Heinrich Heine's novels.

HESSE (HESSEN)

Capital: Wiesbaden.
Main cities: Frankfurt am Main, Darmstadt, Kassel, Marburg, Wetzlar.
Seats in Bundesrat: 5.
Website: www.hessen.de.

Hessen with its population of six million is Germany's fifth largest state and is composed of a group of formerly autonomous states. Before Bismarck's unification the region encompassed four, principalities and the free city of Frankfurt, which were absorbed into Prussia with the exception of the Grand Duchy of Hesse-Darmstadt. In 1945 the American military government merged the Duchy with the Prussian territory to form this new Land. The Land parliament occupies the former Ducal Palace of the Duchy of Nassau in the regional capital, Wiesbaden. Hessen is phenomenally prosperous thanks to a combination of industries and banking. The region is focused on the dynamic city of Frankfurt, Germany's answer to Manhattan and home to the German Stock Exchange, the Deutsche BundesBank, the European Central Bank, and more than 400 other banks. Frankfurt also has Germany's premier airport and is home to the national carrier Lufthansa.

Historians might refer to Hesse as a unity born from diversity but geographers would consider it a colourful jumble of uplands and valleys with the rivers Main, Wetter and Eder cutting through the upland ranges of the Tanau and Vogelsberg. In addition to the wide Rhine (Rhein) valley along which the state border with Rheinland-Pfalz runs. Hessians speak a marked dialect and the local cuisine has developed to be accompanied by the regional wines. The Bergstrasse and Rheingau are among Germany's best fruit and wine growing areas, as this is the home of the Rheinwein and Reisling.

With four major industries represented by Hoechst, Degussa, Volkswagen and Opel (i.e. chemical, motor vehicle, mechanical and electrical engineering) and the financial heartland of Germany it is little wonder that Hesse's gross domestic product is over €25,000 per capita. The Rhein-Main airport just outside Frankfurt employs over 60,000 and is one of Europe's busiest. Frankfurt is also famous for hosting several trade fairs of which the autumn Frankfurt Book Fair (Frankfurter Buchmesse) is the world's biggest, drawing over 9,500 companies from a hundred countries, and an estimated 270,000 visitors.

The cities of Wiesbaden, Frankfurt and Darmstadt are all clustered together in the southern corner of Hesse, while the north of Hesse is less heavily populated. Kassel is the main town here, home to the Brothers Grimm Museum while the old university city of Marburg, one of Germany's finest medieval gems lies to the south west of Kassel.

MECKLENBURG-WEST POMERANIA (*MECKLEN-BURG-VORPOMMERN*)

Capital: Schwerin.
Main cities: Rostock, Neubrandenburg Greifswald.
Seats in Bundesrat: 3.
Website: www.mecklenburg-vorpommern.de.

The Land of a thousand lakes, Mecklenburg-West Pomerania with its island of Rügen, is probably most well known through the art of Caspar David Friedrich, the state's most famous son. The state forms Germany's northern coast, the Mecklenburgische Seenplatte, on the Baltic and is noted for its scenic beauty. The many lakes set amidst gently rolling hills, forests and meadows make this an area popular with both holiday makers and wading birds. Of the large lakes (Müritz, Schwerinersee, Plauersee and Kummerowersee) the Müritz is the largest in Germany, with an area of 117 square kilometres. Off the Pomeranian coast is the large island of Rügen with its stunning white cliffs, to the west of which is the island of Hiddensee, which is popular with naturalists. Pomerania was historically Swedish territory before becoming the Prussian state Pommern, while Mecklenburg an independent part of the German Empire, spent three hundred years divided into two states; Mecklenburg Schwerin and Mecklenburg Strelitz. The region is mostly remarkable for the dialect spoken which is actually Low German (*Plattdeutsch*).

Four of the state's cities are Hanseatic towns from the period when the area dominated trade with Scandinavia, a tradition which meant that Rostock became the home of the GDR's biggest shipyards. Ship-building is still a major industry in the city, but luxury foods, engineering and construction are beginning to take larger shares in the state economy. Nonetheless agriculture has always dominated the region, with 80 percent of the land being tilled to produce grain, oilseed and potatoes.

As noted earlier tourism is a major industry with around 4 million visitors a year to the state's lakes, cliffs, reserves (there are nearly 400 nature and landscape reserves) and the three national parks.

The Land capital, Schwerin was founded in 1160 and is situated on the southern end of the Schwerinersee and was once home to the Grand Dukes of Mecklenburg-Schwerin, whose palace is now home to the länder parliament. The city is also notable for its Brick Gothic cathedral. While Rostock is a university city and is actually larger than Schwerin, it is best known for its seaside resort of Warnemünde and the festive Hanseatic Port Days. Rostock was also home to Field Marshal Blücher, who commanded the Prussian force at Waterloo.

LOWER SAXONY (NIEDERSACHSEN)

Capital: Hannover.
Main cities: Braunschweig, Göttingen, Salzgitter, Wilhelmshaven.
Seats in Bundesrat: 6.
Website: www.niedersachsen.de.

The modern Lower Saxony was based on former kingdom of Hannover with some duchies and principalities tacked on, so that it is now the second largest state in Germany. However, it is the least populated, with 7.8 million people spread across 47,388 square kilometres stretching between the North Sea and the Harz Mountains. Much of Lower Saxony is taken up by the North German Plain and is therefore rather flat and windswept. In between the sea and the mountains lie remote heathlands, the metropolitan area of Hannover, and the Hildesheimer Börde an area of the most fertile soil in Germany. The East Frisian islands, the coast, the mountains, the Teutoberg Forest (scene of Rome's worst military defeat) and the Lüneberg Heath (Germany's oldest nature reserve) provide recreation for millions of Germans who swell the population on holiday each year. Brunswick (Braunschweig) was one of the four major metropolises of the Late Middle Ages, the royal house of Hannover provided England and Wales with King George I, and it was on the Lüneberg Heath that the German surrender was signed in 1945.

The anglicised versions of some the city names of Lower Saxony should be familiar to anglophone readers, such as Hanover, Brunswick and Hamelin (Hameln) with its rodent clearing flautist.

Two thirds of the state's economy is agricultural, Lower Saxony provides one fifth of Germany's natural gas and Wolfsburg is the home of Volkswagen and the famous Beetle. Over 50 million cars have been built by Volkswagen to date, with MAN producing trucks here too. The levitating Transrapid Train route is being built across the state to run between Hamburg and Berlin, the train itself is being built and tested in Emsland. Transport figures heavily in Lower Saxony as the state has the most extensive network of cycle paths in Germany. Wilhelmshaven, which was once home to the Imperial German Navy is now Germany's deep-water super-tanker port. Brunswick is home to Central European Time at the Federal Institute of Physics and Metrology, and the Brothers Grimm, in addition to their work on folk tales began compiling the Deutsches Wörterbuch (a comprehensive German dictionary) at Göttingen University in 1838. The last volume of this was completed in 1961.

NORTH-RHINE-WESTPHALIA (*NORDRHEIN-WEST-FALEN*)

Capital: Düsseldorf.
Main cities: Münster, Dortmund, Duisberg, Bonn, Essen, Köln, Aachen, Mönchengladbach.
Seats in Bundesrat: 6.
Website: www.nordrhein-westfalen.de.

The most populous of the länder North Rhine-Westphalia has twice the population of Bavaria but only half its surface area. The Rhine-Ruhr conurbation, with no less than fifteen cities is one of the most built-up areas in Europe, in one area of the map the cities of Duisberg, Essen, Bochum and Dortmund simply merge into one urban strip 60 kilometres long by 25 kilometres wide. The Ruhr with its 30 power stations is Germany's main source of energy, and was once the heavy industrial heart of Germany. There is less heavy industry in the area since the clean up campaign of the sixties and over half the land is used for agriculture, yet despite this and the pastoral fringe of lakes and wooded valleys the area is still Europe's largest industrial area.

Modernisation and a desire to clean up industry has led to a great diversification in the state's economic structure, where once the coal and steel industry employed one in eight workers they now employ one in twenty-five. In addition to this there are over 1,600 firms focusing on environmental technology in the area. New industries such as media and culture employ 230,000 people as part of the 60 percent of the state's workforce employed in the service sector, almost half of Germany's top 100 firms have their headquarters in the region. Düsseldorf the state capital is one of Germany's banking centres, while Duisberg on the Rhine is the world's largest inland port, controlling cargo traffic from the North Sea to Switzerland. One might assume that the move of capital to Berlin would signal Bonn's decline, but Bonn has been designated the federal city for science and communication, home to Deutsche Telekom and the Centre for Advanced European Studies And Research (CAESAR). Bonn is also home to Haribo's Gummi-Bears (*Gümmibärchen*), the little jelly teddy bears which generate over a billion euros of income per year.

One of the great cities of Germany is Cologne (Köln), founded by the Romans in 33 BC, which owes much of its importance to being accessible from the North Sea via the river Rhine on which it is situated. Cologne was practically flattened by wartime bombing, but miraculously the famous cathedral (the *Dom*) survived and ironically the bombing allowed the discovery of much of the roman city beneath the medieval buildings. One of the charms of Köln is that its inhabitants (*Kölner*) are easy going and friendly, even if the Kölsch dialect is almost incomprehensible to outsiders. Düsseldorf, after Frankfurt, is a major centre of international finance and banking, while Dortmund is home to Becks beer and has overtaken München as a brewing centre. With its 99 theatres, 15 opera stages, and 390 museums any culturally minded individual would enjoy life in the region which gave birth to Beethoven.

RHINELAND-PALATINATE (*RHEINLAND-PFALZ*)

Capital: Mainz.
Main cities: Ludwigshafen, Kaiserlautern, Koblenz, Trier.

Seats in Bundesrat: 4.
Website: www.rheinland-pfalz.de.

Home to Gutenberg, Karl Marx and Martin Luther's Reformation, the Rheinland-Palatinate is used to dramatic change. The most recent being the amalgamation by the French of several disparate parts of Germany into one new länder in 1945. This picturesque landscape, crossed by the Rhein and Mosel, is probably Germany's most famous wine producing area. Many of the cities spread out along the Rhine are some of Germany's oldest: Koblenz, Mainz, Worms and Speyer can each boast 2,000 years of occupation, while Trier on the Mosel (near the border with Luxembourg) has the spectacular Roman remains of the *Porta Nigra*. At the confluence of the Rhine and Mosel stands the city of Koblenz. The stretch of the Rhine from Koblenz to Mainz cuts through slate mountains crowned with the picturesque ruins of many castles. This is the haunt of the Lorelei and other characters of German folklore. It was at Mainz that Johannes Gutenburg developed the mass printing techniques which have since had such an incalculable impact on modern civilization.

To the southwest, flows the Mosel whose banks are dotted with vineyards and villages like Bernkastel and Piesport, familiar to German-wine lovers. Unfortunately the Wine road (*Weinstrasse*) which runs from Schweigen on the French border to Bockenheim is a heavily publicised tourist industry in its own right and should therefore be avoided in high season. Although the wine festivals in September are worth braving the crowds for. Just as inspirational in its own way but considerably less trampled and less river-oriented, is the lower part of the Rhineland-Palatinate, including the modest Hunsrück mountains and the Pfalz which is heavily forested. This area enjoys a certain popularity with the Germans but few foreigners have heard about it and its wooded tranquillity makes it an ideal escape.

While the region is Germany's largest wine producer, there are other heavier industries present. Ludwigshafen with its many factories, including the chemicals giant BASF, forms an industrial belt linking up with Mannheim across the Rhine in Baden-Württemburg. While Mainz still maintains its links with the media, the land capital is home to Europe's largest television network ZDF and its rival SAT1.

SAARLAND

Capital: Saarbrücken.
Main citiy: Saarlouis, Völklingen.
Seats in Bundesrat: 3.
Website: www.saarland.de.

Of the German States Saarland is the smallest Land of all, only the three city states are geographically smaller. For much of modern history the Saarland has been fought over, like two dogs over a bone by the French and Germans. French until 1815, it then passed into German hands until the end of the Great War when in 1920 under the terms of the armistice its administration was in the hands of the League of Nations. In 1935 the people voted to return to German rule, an act which was repeated twenty years later in 1955, when the region again voted for integration with Germany having been under French administration since the Second World War. This small area which provided a prototype for re-unification in the fifties, now seems to be repeating the procedure on a

European level with the cross-border activities of the Saar-Lor-Lux mega-region. This is an initiative undertaken by the Saarland, Luxembourg and Lorraine in France to 'Think European: Act Local' in an attempt at mutual integration. In fact the area has been central to Franco-German and European politics since the Middle Ages, when the Dukes of Burgundy lived here.

The Saarland takes its name from the river Saar a tributary of the Mosel, which meanders through a picturesque countryside of sloping vineyards. Once prized for its coal and iron ore deposits the area's major exports are now the fine reislings grown along the Saar. Although cars and steel still take a share of the state's output, much of the local workforce commutes across one border or another thus clouding the employment and productivity statistics.

SAXONY (FREIESTAAT SACHSEN)

Capital: Dresden.
Main cities: Leipzig, Chemnitz, Freiburg, Zwickau.
Seats in Bundesrat: 4.
Website: www.sachsen.de.

Home to the renowned Meissen pottery in Dresden, Saxony is the most densely populated of the new Länder. The Free State of Saxony was ruled by a dynasty of Saxon kings from the fifteenth century up to 1918. Saxony has been a home to much of Germany's cultural history; Bach, Strauss, Wagner and Schumann all worked on and performed famous pieces here. During the reigns of Augustus the Strong (1694-1733) and Augustus III (1733-1763), the capital Dresden became North Europe's centre for art, music, literature, and architecture earning the title 'Florence on the Elbe'. The other great city of the east, Leipzig is also in Saxony. In the eighteenth century Leipzig was a lively commercial city with strong artistic trends, especially in music: Johann Sebastian Bach, who worked there from 1723-1750, is probably the city's most illustrious maestro.

Many of the region's factories were shut down following unification but the region is on an economic upswing and 60% of employees now work in the service sector. The former Trabant factory has been taken over by a private enterprise and now turns out autoparts for Mercedes amongst others. Dresden attracts seven million tourists a year to its architectural glories and the Meissen pottery works but it is also home to many modern innovations. The first reflex cameras were produced here and at Scharfenstein the first CFC-Free fridge was developed. Since unification Saxony has seen much investment from global operators; Shell, BP and Phillips all operate here and the electronics giant Siemens has a microelectronics centre in Dresden. Volkswagen has an automobile plant at Zwickau with an engine plant at nearby Chemnitz.

In the thirties Chemnitz, Dresden and Leipzig formed a triangle of industrial activity, and suffered immensely for it during the war. Dresden still bears many scars but the Semper Opera House and Zwinger and Taschenburg Palaces have been reconstructed and the rebuilding of the baroque Frauenkirche is almost complete. Once the most imposing Protestant church in Germany it has been a memorial in rubble for most of the last half-century.

Leipzig has always had a large book trade and it is now home to the most modern large scale mail order house in the world, while the number of banks opening branches here are likely to turn the city into Germany's third major financial centre.

The former airport has been converted into a conference and business fair centre and the annual book fair in March is a rival to Frankfurt's. Leipzig's University was founded in 1409 making it one of Germany's oldest institutions. and Chemnitz has eastern Germany's second largest Technical University.

Saxony may once have been home to some of the worst sites of industrial pollution, but much has been cleaned up, and while the region's wineries were decimated by years of neglect there are still vineyards producing some fine Weissburgunder wines.

SAXONY-ANHALT (*SACHSEN-ANHALT*)

Capital: Magdeburg.
Main cities: Halle, Naumburg, Dessau, Quedlinburg.
Seats in Bundesrat: 4.
Website: www.sachsen-anhalt.de.

Saxony Anhalt has only a brief recent history, its territory (the Altmark to the north, the Magdeburger Börde, the Harz mountains and Anhalt to the east) is a patchwork of older regions ruled by other states; Anhalt was a minor princedom founded by the Ascanian princes and flourished in the 18th Century under the Princes of Anhalt-Dessau. Ranging from the Harz mountains to the North German plains Saxony Anhalt is a region of extraordinarily scenic landscapes. The state capital, Magdeburg, on the banks of the Elbe dates from 805 and is home to the first Gothic cathedral built in Germany. Saxony Anhalt was the heart of the Reformation with Martin Luther's birthplace at Eisleben and the church in Wittenberg where he nailed up his theses, here. A major industrial city of the east, Halle has the honour of being the birthplace of Georg Friedrich Händel in 1685, and is notable for its cathedral church and Red Tower.

The south of the state was the industrial region, with Dessau being home to both the first all metal commercial airliner (in the Junkers Ju52) and the first colour film in the 1930s. Heavy machinery and vehicle construction are still dominant in the economies of Magdeburg and Dessau. The Bitterfeld chemical works were once a synonym for industrial pollution, but chemical production in the Halle-Mersburg-Bitterfeld triangle has occurred since the 19th Century and continues today, although using cleaner technology.

Agriculture has a fair share of the economy as the Magdeburger Börde and Harz foreland contain rich, fertile loess soils. Grain, sugar-beet, potatoes and vegetable crops all grow well here and Germany's northernmost vineyards are to be found along the Saale.

The state is rich in art and architectural history, apart from being the home to the Nazi's Stuka aircraft, Dessau was the home of Walter Gropius and the Bauhaus movement. They may have been thought of as degenerate by Hitler, but their work has been lauded by architects around the world; the town's Wörlitz Park has one of Europe's finest English-style gardens. In the Harz mountains Naumberg is the site of the art-historically important 13th Century statues of Ute and Ekkhard, remarkable for their life-like faces and Quedlinburg has 1,200 half timbered houses in its Old Town, making the town a UNESCO World Heritage site.

SCHLESWIG-HOLSTEIN

Capital: Kiel.
Main cities: Lübeck, Flensburg.
Seats in Bundesrat: 4.
Website: www.schleswig-holstein.de.

Bordered by the North Sea and the Baltic, Schleswig-Holstein is Germany's most northern state, and home to an ethnic mix of inhabitants. Hence one can hear conversations in German, Low German, Danish and Frisian, as the state includes the Frisian Islands off its western coast and is home to over 50,000 Danes. From the red cliffs of Helgoland, across the islands of Sylt, Föhr and Amrum and to the mud flats of Wattenmeer National Park, the region is a holidaymaker's and nature lover's paradise. Further inland are the lakes of 'Holstein Switzerland' and the open air museums of Molfsee and viking Haithabu. With such scenic beauty it is not unsurprising to find the area is home to many of modern Germany's finest authors, such as Günter Grass, Siegfried Lenz and Sarah Kirsch.

The Kiel Canal links the Baltic with the North Sea and Kiel was the pre-war home of the German Navy: hence heavily bombed. Lübeck was luckier and the 'Queen of the Hanseatic League' retains many fine medieval buildings, so that it is now a World Heritage Site.

For many years the region depended on agriculture and fishing, while Kiel's life revolved around its shipyards; these have survived by specialising in the types of ship built, while the rest of the state has embraced new technologies. Schleswig-Holstein is home to more than 1,500 wind turbines making it Germany's main supplier of 'wind' electricity, while 4,000 firms are involved in information and communications technology. With three universities and four polytechnics employers in the area can draw upon a skilled workforce.

THURINGIA *(FREIESTAAT THÜRINGEN)*

Capital: Erfurt.
Main cities: Weimar, Gera, Jena, Ilmenau.
Seats in Bundesrat: 4.
Website: www.thueringen.de.

The geographic heart of Germany, The Free State of Thuringia is a land of forests and mountains crossed by the rivers Saale, Werra and Weisse Elster. This is a fairy-tale land, perched on the Harz mountains and covered by the Thuringian Forest. The capital Erfurt, reinforces this image with its perfectly preserved medieval and renaissance town houses in a pedestrianised centre. Apart from Erfurt and the forests of the Thüringen Wald, the main attractions of the Thuringia region are the two historic cities of Eisenach and Weimar. Eisenach is overlooked by the ancient fortress of the Wartburg, where Luther translated the New Testament into German and which was also the inspiration for Wagner's opera Tannhauser (based on a troubadours' singing contest that took place in the Middle Ages). The Wartburg also gave its name to the sister automobile to the GDR's Trabant. Eisenach itself is the birthplace of Johann Sebastian Bach. In 1919 Weimar was the seat of the constitutional assembly of a briefly liberal republic, and also the first home of the Bauhaus movement, but its golden age was earlier; when in the 18th century it was the home of Goethe, Schiller and Wieland.

Sadly only ten kilometres from Weimar is Buchenwald, the antithesis of German enlightenment. An infamous Nazi concentration camp where over 50,000 Jews, gypsies, homosexuals and communists were incarcerated or killed; Buchenwald is now a national monument to the victims of fascism.

Industrialisation in Germany began in Thuringia, with the mining of Potash, followed by gunsmithing, glass making, and machine tool manufacture. The famed German optics industry is based upon the Zeiss and Schott works in Jena. Eisenach once home to the laughable Wartburg now turns out cars for Opel. Half of Thuringia is agricultural land producing grain, rape, potatoes and sugar beet.

Germany's oldest hiking path winds through the Thüringen Wald, and the region has a wealth of mineral springs and resorts for the footsore traveller. The 'Thuringian Classical Route' is a 300 kilometre long tour of the state's beauty spots, palaces and cultural history, remembering the period when the region was the centre of German intellectual life, not just the geographical centre.

RESIDENCE AND ENTRY REGULATIONS

CHAPTER SUMMARY

O Entry and settlement for EU nationals and some other nationalities is easy.

O However, everyone will need to register with the local authorities where they settle.

O Registering requires you to bring a variety of documents, photocopies of same and notarised translations if necessary.

O Moving within Germany means de- and re-registering with the old/new local authorities, and you are advised to always register with your nearest embassy or consulate.

O IT skills are in demand and a 'green card' easy entry scheme has been set up.

O Australians and New Zealanders can visit on Working Holiday Visas.

THE CURRENT POSITION

A large workforce of immigrant *gastarbeiter* (guestworkers) and liberal immigration laws have been the power behind German reconstruction since the early fifties. However, times have changed and the German economy has been under pressure since the early nineties. Unemployment and economic sluggishness may be causing some problems but a skills shortage in Information Technology and a developing generation gap have opened up new possibilities for immigration into Germany. UK citizens are entitled to live and work there and many opportunities exist in addition to those in IT. Recent bilateral agreements now open up the temporary work market to Australians and New Zealanders, who can now visit on a Working Holiday Visa.

So recent problems paint a grimmer picture of the opportunities to live and work in Germany than is actually the case. If anything immigration into Germany may get easier in the future as plans have been discussed to bring in a points system along similar lines to those of the US, Australia and New Zealand. There have also been changes regarding naturalisation so of the 7 million plus non-Germans living there over half could, if they wished and satisfied the language, income, and residence tests, become German citizens.

Settling in Germany is as much about getting all the paperwork sorted out as finding a job there. To register as a citizen, obtain your tax card, health insurance and a residence permit all takes time. While the EU may seem to be a scary network of civil servants trying to legislate against everything, being a citizen of an EU state has many benefits. Not least of which are the rights of work and residence in any EU state.

The most important factor to note is that while attempting to get a job and register yourself in Germany might seem like being asked to climb a bureaucratic mountain, the officials of the German authorities are very thorough, and they will try to make it as painless as possible; unfortunately they are also very busy. It helps if you have done your homework first and this book and your local consulate in Germany can help. The offices in the cities with most applications (e.g. Berlin) tend to open early, to help speed things up. So sit back and be patient, the Germans may not be quite as bad as the clichés make out but they are very efficient and you can be sure all paperwork will be dealt with as quickly as possible. Of course if you feel you are being shuffled between offices by unfriendly officials then it always helps to ask the name of the person you are dealing with. If they know that you will say who sent you when you get to the next office, then they will be more helpful, but on the whole, German civil servants tend to be just that.

Please note that all the competent diplomatic authorities emphasise that you need to be able to speak German if you intend to find work in Germany.

Registering with Your Embassy

All embassies and consulates recommend that their nationals register with their embassy or the consulate thereof responsible for the region where they reside. This helps with notification in the event of an emergency, renewal of lost documents (passports), voting from overseas, and may also prove useful in the event of marriage in Germany. Registering will also allow the migrant to obtain details of the full range of services (such as tax assistance for US citizens) offered by their foreign service.

The Schengen Agreement

Austria, Belgium, Denmark, France, Finland, Germany, Greece, Iceland, Italy, Luxembourg, the Netherlands, Norway, Portugal, Spain, and Sweden are all signatories of the Schengen Agreement which allows free movement across national borders within the territory of signatory countries. EU nationals and the holders of residence permits entitled to stay in an EU country, may travel on a valid passport, without requiring a visa, for up to 90 days per six-month period to any of the other countries. Holders of visas with no territorial restrictions (visitor's or business visa allowing the holder to stay up to 90 days per six-month

LEEDS METROPOLITAN UNIVERSITY LEARNING CENTRE

period, transit or airport visas) may enter freely with the proviso that the visit is for the same duration and purpose as their visa. Norway and Iceland have also fully implemented the Schengen regime since 25 March 2001.

RESIDENCE PERMIT

Anyone planning to stay in Germany for longer than three months need to obtain a residence permit; these have different names depending upon the type required, but *Aufenthaltsgenehmigung* is the umbrella term. If you are entering to work then you should obtain one as soon as you begin work. These are issued free of charge. While you can stay for up to three months whilst looking for work, you are effectively a tourist, so it helps if you are looking for work while living there to clarify your position by registering as an 'Alien' with the local citizens administration (*Einwohnermeldeamt, Landeseinwohnermeldeamt, Bezirksamt,* or *Ortsamt*) who will issue a Certificate of Registration (*Anmeldebescheinigung*). Ideally you should obtain this certificate within seven days of arriving in Germany, you will need to take it and your passport with you when you need to obtain a residence permit, and you can apply for that as soon as you have a job offer. You can then take this certificate to the local office of the Foreign Nationals Authority (*Ausländeramt*) where you will be issued your *Aufenthaltsgenehmigung.* It should be noted that the system as described is based on the entry regulations for citizens of EU States and the USA, and this is easier than for citizens of other countries, also some municipalities (eg Düsseldorf) have set up seperate offices for EU citizens. You will also find it very helpful to take these documents with you when setting up bank accounts and utilities. While registering yourself within the municipality you should also acquire a tax card *Steuerkarte,* which should be given to your employer. Note also that if you want to be exempt form the 8-10% Church Tax you should be sure declare that you are not a churchgoer, doing it later is time consuming.

At the Einwohnermeldeamt

The local office will also be listed in the telephone book under the heading *Stadtverwaltung.* They will give you a registration application form (*Anmeldung, Anmeldformular,* or *Meldeschein*) which must be completed with proof of residence (i.e countersigned by a landlord, hotel manager or estate agent). The *Meldeschein* must be presented to the registration authority, who will issue the *Anmeldebescheinigung.* It should be noted that any change of address must be reported to the registration authority within one week, you should also inform them if you leave Germany permanently. With this, some passport size photos and your passport you can now obtain your residence permit. **Note** if you move within Germany you will have to deregister before moving and register at your new residence, likewise if you leave.

At the Ausländeramt/Ausländerbehörde

To obtain your residence permit take the Certificate (*Anmeldebescheinigung*) to the local Foreign Nationals/Aliens Registration Authority (*Ausländeramt*) which can be found in the Town Hall (*Rathaus*) or the Area Administration Centre (*Kreisverwaltung*). In smaller towns the Rural District Office (*Landratsamt*) is usually located in the town council building (*Stadverwaltung*). Residence application is free of charge and must be accompanied by evidence of means of subsistence and/or that employment has been taken up (se *Useful Terms*) or proof of enrolment at a university, two passport photos, proof of identity (a passport will suffice) and proof of medical insurance. For non-EU citizens it may also be necessary to undergo a medical examination. The German authorities will issue a temporary residence permit, valid for two months, if an applicant has not secured employment at the time of request. The residence permit lasts for three to five years and is renewable. The permit is no longer endorsed in passports but instead separate cards are issued by the registration authority. These are not identity cards and therefore are not valid for crossing frontiers. However, they should be carried with your passport when you are entering or leaving Germany. Further information on the application procedures is available from the German Embassy in your country, and your country's consulates in Germany.

Note that it is an offence to remain in Germany for over three months or to take employment without first obtaining a residence permit.

ENTRY FOR BRITISH AND EU NATIONALS

British nationals or citizens of other EU member states wishing to visit Germany for three months or less require only a valid passport endorsed with the words 'Holder has the right of abode in the UK', 'UK Citizen' or 'European Community'. Under EU agreement these regulations also apply to an individual's family members (spouse and children up to 21 years of age), irrespective of their nationality. However your passport should be valid for at least four months after your arrival in Germany.

ENTRY FOR NON-EU NATIONALS

US, Canadian, New Zealand and Australian citizens do not require a visa for visits of up to three months. It is possible to extend such a visit to a maximum of six months by application to the local Authority for Foreigners (*Ausländerbehörde*) when in Germany. However the validity of the traveller's passport should exceed the length of their visit by at least four months. For longer stays applications should be made in advance to the German embassy in your country of residence.

Americans visiting who decide to stay for more than 90 days or to settle naturally have to apply for a residence permit as detailed above, but may do so inside Germany, students will have to show an affadavit from whoever is financing their stay.

Canadians do not require a visa for longer stays, to work, or to study. However, they can speed up the registration and permit process by applying through the embassy or nearest consulate in Canada.

ENTERING TO WORK

European Community regulations allow for the free movement of labour within the EU, hence UK citizens do not require a work permit (*Arbeitserlaubnis*) to work in Germany. Although British nationals looking for employment can enter the country on a valid passport they must apply for a residence permit if they intend to stay and work for more than three months (see above). Job applicants should have proof that they have registered with the local authorities. To work in bars, restaurants and similar establishments it is necessary to have a health certificate (*Gesundheitszeugnis*). This can be obtained from the local health department (*Gesundheitsamt*), but can take a few weeks to be processed.

US Citizens

At present due to the treaties concluded between Germany and the USA, US citizens have practically the same status as EU Citizens when looking for work in Germany, in that they can stay for up to three months while looking for work. Temporary work permits can be obtained from a local employment office, but a residence permit should be obtained first (as above), although it may make life easier to obtain the work permit in advance through the German embassy in America. Permanent settlement or work requires that the permits be obtained in advance. Military personnel and their dependants are an exception, as are students who only need to register and obtain a residence permit using their proof of enrolment. Work permits for permanent work are usually the responsibility of the German employer. Americans with German ancestors who can prove this (e.g. birth certificate) are automatically granted a five year permit.

Other Non-EU

Australians, Canadians and New Zealanders coming to work in Germany need to obtain a visa before leaving their homeland, for which proof of employment in Germany must be provided, except in the case of working-holidaymakers (see section on *A Working Holiday*).

Non-EU nationals who intend to work or establish themselves in business (or other self-employed activities) require the permits (as above), workers also need proof that they have unique capabilities or that no EU resident was available to do the job. To apply it is first necessary to obtain a visa. This must be done before entering Germany and application forms are available from the Visa Section of the nearest German Embassy. The form must be completed in triplicate and submitted with a valid passport, three passport photos, written confirmation of work from your prospective employer and proof of medical insurance cover. If the application is approved a visa will be issued. The visa can only be issued in the country of application, and it cannot be forwarded to Germany. After entering Germany the applicant must register immediately with the Foreign Nationals Authority (*Ausländeramt*), who will issue the residence permit. The permit is valid for up to five years or the duration of employment and is renewable.

THE GREEN CARD

The rapid growth of the information technology market has led to a shortage of Information and Communications Technology (ICT) specialists in Germany, recent figures noted 75,000 ICT vacancies which could not be filled from the available labour pool. To rectify this the German government instituted the *IT-specialists Temporary relief Program*, more commonly known as 'Green card', an entry system for suitably qualified foreign ICT personnel. It forms part of an ongoing programme of retraining and opening within the German IT market, and so is only a temporary measure, where temporary means five years. The target of the project is to produce 250,000 ICT specialists by 2005, 20,000 of whom will be foreign workers enticed in by high wages, easy immigration and the beauties of Germany as a place to live and work. Specialists with U citizenship can naturally move to Germany to work, and so don't need to apply through this scheme.

The programme is aimed at qualified (from universities or polytechnics, or who are offered a job paying over €50,000) staff responding to job postings on the Online Job Fair (at www.arbeitsamt.de) or who are offered work by a German IT company (possibly in response to a direct application). Foreign students graduating from German institutions may also apply. Initially 10,000 work permits will be issued under this scheme, the scheme and market will then be reassessed and another 10,000 permits made available according to need.

The permits will be valid for the length of employment contract or up to five years. The scheme itself came onto the statute books in August 2000 and will expire in July 2008. At the time of writing over 8,000 permit places had been taken up by specialists from India, Russia, and Romania.

ENTERING AS A STUDENT

The various Student Exchange agencies can provide more detailed information and the most authoritative is the German Academic Exchange Service (*Deutscher Akademischer Austauschdienst*) which publishes a very useful guide for students as well as lists of scholarships and sources of funding. Would be students, except from within the EU/EEA or USA, will need a student visa applicable to their course of study (note a language course visa can not be converted into either a 'study applicant' or 'visa for study' visa).

In order to study in Germany you will have to prove that you are sufficiently competent in the language to make study there worthwhile, unless you are enrolling on an international degree programme taught in English. The main universities have their own Foreign Student or International Offices (*Akademisches Auslandsamt* or *AAA*), which you should contact at least 6 months, preferably a year, in advance of your planned start date for studying. These offices in conjunction with the DAAD will be able to advise you on all aspects of entering Germany to study.

While entering Germany to study is easier for EU and American nationals the basic requirements for entry are that you have documentary proof of your place at a German university, a passport which will remain valid for the entire period of your stay, proof that you have sufficient funds to cover registration costs and support you during your studies (at least €500 per month), and if necessary the correct visa. 'Study Applicant' visas are issued to applicants, obviously, and if a place is obtained must be converted to 'visa for study' as soon as possible (using your proof of enrolment). On registering at the Aliens Registration Office with your various documents and passport photos (see above) you will be issued with a Student Residence Permit (*Aufentsbewelligung*).

Students are now allowed to work for up to 20 hours per week and full-time in vacation, but don't rely on this to pay your way. Most institutions have their own student job shops, so you needn't tramp to the *Arbeistamt*.

A WORKING HOLIDAY IN GERMANY

The working holiday programme aims to enable young people from Australia and New Zealand to gain an insight into the culture and daily life in the Federal Republic of Germany. This scheme is based on bilateral agreements between Germany, Australia and New Zealand, allowing young people to travel to Germany (and vice versa) for a longer stay than is normal for tourists (up to 12 months) and take temporary jobs to help finance their stay.

Australian or New Zealand citizens between the ages of 18 and 30 years can take part in the programme. Children who are under 18 years of age are not eligible.

Working Holiday Visas are only available from the German Embassies in Canberra or Wellington, the consulates in Sydney or Melbourne, and through the Honorary Consulates in Auckland and Christchurch. You must be in Australia or New Zealand respectively, as per your nationality, at the time of application. Visas are issued free of charge in New Zealand, but in Australia a A$5 administration charge is levied.

To apply each applicant must have the following:

> ○ A passport which is valid for at least three months after the expiry of the visa.
> ○ Return air tickets (if only a single ticket is presented, you have to be able to show that, alongside the funds to cover your stay, you can finance a return fare).
> ○ Proof of sufficient funds for the stay, for Australians this is a minimum of A$400 per month, New Zealanders see note below.
> ○ Proof of health insurance valid in Germany for the duration of the stay.

Applicants should allow at least 2 weeks for their visa to be processed. Included in the visa is a document which acts as a work permit allowing a total of 90 days work in Germany during your stay.

With regard to finances, how much money you will need will be determined very much by your lifestyle. Depending on your employment prospects you must be able to prove at least €980 per month. This can take the form of credit cards, copies of account statements or by providing a guarantor.

ENTERING TO START A BUSINESS

EU Nationals are free to enter Germany on a valid passport and set up a business. The German authorities welcome new enterprises and the Federal Ministry of Economics (*Bundesministerium für Wirtschaft*) acts as a first point of contact for new enterprises. They can provide information about the correct ministries and länder development agencies to contact. The various chambers of commerce in Germany can help prospective business men as can the Legal Department of the German-British Chamber of Commerce in London, which offers help and information for prospective entrepreneurs planning to move to Germany. The procedures for officially establishing a business are detailed in Chapter Seven *Starting a Business*.

ENTERING ON A SELF-EMPLOYED BASIS

While the information above applies to any EU national seeking work in Germany there are additional formalities which a self-employed worker needs to complete **before** leaving for Germany. As most self-employed Britons seeking work in Germany are taking up work in the construction industry, it is essential, in the light of recent problems with dubious building agencies, that they have prepared the correct documents. In order to work in Germany as a self-employed worker you will need to register with the local Chamber of Handicrafts office (*Handwerkskammer*), to be registered you will need to provide a Certificate E101 and a certificate of experience.

The E101 is a document which shows that you have been paying self-employed National Insurance contributions in the UK and that you will remain in the UK NI scheme. A British worker who is normally self-employed in the UK can remain in the UK insurance scheme for up to one year while working in Germany. Current information on the regulations concerning self-employment for non-Germans can be obtained from the Embassy or the German-British Chamber of Commerce.

ENTERING TO RETIRE

Since 1 January 1992 pensioners from EU Member States have been able to live wherever they choose in the new boundary-less European Community. As stated above people intending to retire to Germany require a residence permit (*Aufenthaltsgenehmigung*), in compliance with the Foreign Nationals Act (*Ausländergesetz*). It will have to include pension details, proof of adequate medical insurance cover and supply evidence that individuals have 'sufficient' funds to support themselves without working. Under European Union regulations if you work in two or more EU states you will be able to combine state pension contributions paid in each country; for up to date information on this contact the Department of Social Security. UK pensions can be paid directly to individuals resident in Germany, and if your retirement scheme includes health insurance you should have the right to have the same cover as a retired German. To obtain these benefits you should inform your pension authorities of your planned move and obtain a form E121 from your health authority, this should be handed to the relevant authorities in your new homeland.

GERMAN RESIDENCY

The residence permit is renewable and provided you give a satisfactory reason for remaining, residence in Germany on such a permit can be indefinite. A renewal may be restricted to 12 months if the applicant has been out of work for more than one year. A permit will automatically expire if the holder gives up his or her residence in Germany for more than six months, except in the case of compulsory national service in the home state. Actually obtaining the permit should not take more than an hour or two, so long as you turn up with the right paperwork, and can speak German well enough to understand the process (and by then it should be a doddle). Should you decide to leave Germany on a permanent basis you must notify the local registration authority (*Einwohnermeldeamt*) before leaving.

People resident in Germany for more than ten years are entitled to apply for citizenship. Applicants must meet certain criteria. These include: no prior criminal convictions, and a sufficient knowledge of spoken and written German. However, German laws do not generally allow for dual citizenship. Marriage to a German national guarantees residency in Germany but does not ensure naturalisation.

Retaining Your Right To Vote

UK or EU citizens are entitled to the same rights as a German national, with the exception of voting in German general elections. As local affairs will affect all residents, any EU national living in a country other than their own can vote in municipal elections, and elections for local Members of the European Parliament. However, they may only vote in one European election, either where they currently live or where they came from. Thus British nationals retain the right to vote in UK general elections, while being able to vote in German municipal elections, although they should clarify their position with their local consular authority. EU citizens may even stand for election to municipal bodies, although you will need to confirm this with the local election regulations.

British Citizens who have not lived outside the UK for more than 15 years can maintain their rights to vote in the UK, provided that they register. Forms are available from consular offices and registration can occur at any time throughout the electoral year. Overseas electors used to only be able to vote by proxy, this has changed and they can now register for a postal vote if they wish.

American citizens wishing to register for an absentee ballot should either register thus in their home state or contact the consulate covering their area in Germany for the application form. The Consulate General will also carry out notarial services, such as notarising signatures on absentee ballot forms.

BIRTHS, DEATHS AND MARRIAGES

The British Consul in Düsseldorf, is the registry for births and deaths for British citizens in Germany. The nationality section will also process applications regarding citizenship for minors (and adults) who do not have an automatic right of British citizenship. Registration of a birth with the consul is not a legal requirement for nationality, but it does ensure that the birth is registered with the General Register Office (GRO), and that copies of the birth certificate can be obtained as necessary later on in life. The consular office will also pass details of marriages to the GRO.

American citizens wishing to register a birth should contact the nearest consulate and complete a 'Report of Birth' form which serves as birth certificate. The consulate general reccomend that parents complete the form, apply for a passport and social security number as soon as possible in case of emergency repatriation. Birth forms should be completed at the consulates, usually by appointment and parents will need to bring the German birth certifcate (*Abstammungsurkunde*), their US passports, marriage certificate and US$40. The American consulates can also assist in informing families in the event of a death overseas.

USEFUL TERMS

Einwohnermeldeamt:	Citizens Administration Office.
Akademisches Auslandsamt:	Foreign Student Office.
Anmeldungen/Abmeldungen:	Registration/De-Registration.
Arbeistvertrag:	Employment Contract.
Aufenthaltsgenehmigung:	General Residence Permit.
Aufenthaltsbefugnis:	Refugee's Residence Permit.
Aufenthaltsbewilligung:	Student Residence Permit (no paid work permitted).
Aufenthaltserlaubnis:	Residence Permit for Workers.
Auskunfte:	Information (Help Desk in an Einwohnermeldeamt).
Ausländerangelegenheiten:	Foreigner's Affairs
Bescheinigungen:	Certificates of Residence etc.
Befristet:	Temporary.
Einreisen:	Immigration into Germany.
Firmenvisa/Geschäftsvisa:	Business/Trade Visa.
Kinderausweis:	Child's Identity Card.
Kontoauszug:	Bank Statement.
Lohnsteuerkarten:	Tax Cards.
Melderegister:	Registration of Citizens.
Personalausweis:	Identity Card.
Reisepässe:	Passport.
Umzugleichtgemacht:	Information Sheets for new arrivals, essentially 'Move Made Easy'.
Unbefristet:	Permanaent.
Unterhaltsnachweis:	Proof of financial support.
Zulassungsbescheid:	Enrolment certfcate for university.

Marriage

German regulations on marriage vary across the Länder. British, American, and Canadian Consular offices can advise on local rules and some will help provide some of the paperwork such as 'certficates of no impediment' (*Unbedenklichkeit sbescheinigung, Ehefähigkeitsbescheinigung* or *Ledigkeitsbescheinigung*) to those who can provide a the necessary papers eg full passport, a full birth certfifcate showing parents names and proof of having lived in the consular district for at least 21 days. Fees are sometimes charged for this service. If a previous marriage has been dissolved then the divorce papers will also be needed. Only marriage services carried out at a registrar's office (*Standesamt*) in Germany are legally recognised.

USEFUL ADDRESSES:

The German Federal Foreign Office (*Auswärtiges Amt*) website www.auswaertiges-amt.de which has information in German, English, French, Finnish, Japanese, Russian, and Spanish can be used to find out the latest information on entry to Germany and the contact details for the nearest embassy or consulate.

Federal Foreign Office: Werderscher Markt 1, D-10117 Berlin, Germany; ☎01888-170; fax 01888-173402; website www.auswaertiges-amt.de.

GERMAN EMBASSIES AND CONSULATES

Britain

Embassy of the Federal Republic of Germany: 23 Belgrave Square, London, SW1X 8PZ; ☎020-7824 1300; fax 020-7824 1435; website www.germa n-embassy.org.uk.

Consulate General of the Federal Republic of Germany: 16 Eglinton Crescent, Edinburgh, EH12 5DG, Scotland; ☎0131-337 2323; fax 0131-346 1578; e-mail German-Consulate@ukgateway.net.

Honorary Consul of the Federal Republic of Germany: Douglas Getty c/o AVX Limited, 1 Ballyhampton Road, Larne, Northern Ireland, BT40 2ST; ☎028-7034 4188; fax 028-7034 2626; e-mail Gettyd@col.avxeur.com.

Australia

Embassy of the Federal Republic of Germany: 119 Empire Circuit, Yarralumla, ACT 2600, Australia; ☎02-6270 1911; fx 02-6270 1951; e-mail embgerma@bigpond.net.au; website www.germanembassy.org.au or www .germanembassy-canberra.com.

Consulate General of the Federal Republic of Germany: P.O. Box 76, South Yarra, Vic. 3141, Australia; ☎03-9864 6888; fax 03-9820 2414; e-mail consuger_melb@primus.com.au.

Consulate General of the Federal Republic of Germany, 13 Trelawney Street, Woollahra, N.S.W. 2025, Australia; ☎02-93 28 77 33; fax 02-93 27 96 49; e-mail consugerma.sydney@big pond.com.

Canada

Embassy of the Federal Republic of Germany: P.O. Box 379, Postal Station A, Ottawa, Ontario K1N 8V4, Canada; ☎613-232 1101; fax 613-594 9330; e-mail GermanEmbassyOttawa@on .aibn.com; website www.GermanEm bassyOttawa.org.

Consulate General, Quebec: 1250 Boulevard René-Lévesque Ouest, Suite 4315, Montreal, Quebec H3B 4XL, Canada; ☎514-931 2431; fax 514-931 7239; e-mail consulallemandmon@p rimus.ca.

Consulate General, Toronto: Postal Station P, P.O. Box 523, Toronto, Ontario, M5S 2T1, Canada; ☎416-925 2813; fax 416-925 2818; e-mail germancons ulatetoronto@netcom.ca.

Consulate General, Vancouver: Suite 704, World Trade Centre, 999 Canada Place, Vancouver, B.C. V6C BE1, Canada; ☎604-684 8377; fax 604-684 8334; e-mail gkvanc@telus.net.

Ireland

Embassy of the Federal Republic of Germany: 31 Trimleston Avenue, Booterstown, Blackrock, Dublin, Ireland; ☎+353-(0)1-269 3011; fax +353(0)1-269 3946.

New Zealand

Embassy of the Federal of Germany: 90-92 Hobson Street, Thorndon, Wellington, New Zealand; ☎+64(0)4-473 6063; fax 04-473 6069; e-mail Germ anEmbassyWellington@xtra.co.nz; website www.deutschebotschaftwell ington.co.nz.

Honorary Consul Auckland: Columbus House, 6th Floor, 52 Symonds Street, Auckland 1, New Zealand; ☎+64(0)9-913 3674; fax 09-309 3003.

Honorary Consul Christchurch: Floor 2, Harley Chambers, 137 Cambridge Terrace, Christchurch, New Zea-

land; ☎+64-(0)3-379 3193; fax 03-379 3193.

USA

Embassy of the Federal Republic of Germany; 4645 Reservoir Road, N.W., Washington, D.C. 20007-1998, USA; ☎202-298 4000; fax 202-298 4249; e-mail ge-embus@ix.netcom.com; website www.germany-info.org. Consular district: District of Columbia, Delaware, Maryland, Virginia, West Virginia.

Consulate General, Atlanta: Marquis Two Tower, Suite 901, 285 Peachtree Center Avenue, N.E., Atlanta, GA 30303-1221, USA; ☎404-659 4760; fax 404-659 1280; e-mail atlanta@germanconsulate.org; website www.germany-info.org/ newcontent/gc/consub – atlanta.html. Consular district: Alabama, Georgia, Mississippi, North Carolina, South Carolina, Tennessee.

Consulate General, Boston: 3 Copley Place, Suite 500, Boston, MA 02116, USA; ☎617-536 8172; fax 617-536 8573; e-mail boston@germanconsulate. org. Consular district:Connecticut, Maine, Massachusetts, New Hampshire, Rhode Island, Vermont.

Consulate General, Chicago: 676 North Michigan Avenue, Suite 3200, Chicago, IL 60611, USA; ☎312-580 1199; fax 312-580 0099; e-mail chicago@germanconsulate.org. Consular district: Illinois, Indiana, Iowa, Kansas, Kentucky, Michigan, Minnesota, Missouri, Nebraska, North Dakota, Ohio, South Dakota, Wisconsin.

Consulate General, Houston: 1330 Post Oak Blvd., Suite 1850, Houston, TX 77056-3057, USA; ☎713-627 7770; fax 713-627 0506; e-mail info@ger manconsulatehouston.org. Consular district: Arkansas, Louisiana, New Mexico, Oklahoma, Texas.

Consulate General, Los Angeles: 6222

Wilshire Boulevard, Suite 500, Los Angeles, CA 90048, USA; ☎323-930 2703; fax 323-930 2805; e-mail LosAngeles@GermanConsu late.org. Consular district: parts of southern California, Arizona, Colorado, Nevada, and Utah. *Consulate General, Miami:* 100 N. Biscayne Blvd., Suite 2200, Miami, FL 33132-2381, USA; ☎305-358 0290; fax 305-358 0307; e-mail gc@gcmiami.de; website www.gkmiami.de. Consular district: Florida and Puerto Rico.

Consulate General, New York: 871 United Nations Plaza, New York, NY 10017, USA; ☎212-610 9700; fax 212-610 9702. Consular district: New York, New Jersey, Pennsylvania, and Bermuda. *Consulate General, San Francisco:* 1960 Jackson Street, San Francisco, CA 94109, USA; ☎415-775 1061; fax 415-775 0187; e-mail gksf@pacbell.net. Consular district: Alaska, parts of California, Hawaii, Idaho, Montana, Oregon, Washington, and Wyoming.

EMBASSIES AND CONSULATES IN GERMANY

Britain

British Embassy: Wilhelmstrasse 70-71, D-10117 Berlin, Germany; ☎030-204570 (consular enquiries ☎030-2045 7563); fax 030-609 3938; e-mail info@britischebotschaft.de; website www.britischebotschaft.de or www.britbot.de.
Consulate General, Düsseldorf: Yorckstrasse 19, D-40476 Düsseldorf, Germany; tel. 0211-94480; fax 0211-488190; e-mail info@duesseldorf.mail.fco.gov.uk; website www.british-consulate-general.de or www.british-dgtip.de.
Consulate General, Frankfurt am Main: Triton Haus, Bockenheimer Landstrasse 42, D-60323 Frankfurt am Main, Germany; ☎069-170 0020; fax 069-729553; e-mail info@frankfurt.mail.fco.gov.uk.
Consulate General, Hamburg: Harvestehuder Weg 8 a, D-20148 Hamburg, Germany; ☎040-448 0320; fax 040-410 7259; e-mail infohamburg@fco.gov.uk.
Consulate General, Munich: Bürkleinstrasse 10, D-80538 München, Germany; ☎089-211090; fax 089-2110 9166; e-mail info@munich.mail.fco.gov.uk.

Consulate General, Stuttgart: Breite Strasse 2, D-70173 Stuttgart, Germany; ☎0711-162690; fax 0711-162 6930.

Australia

Australian Embassy: Friedrichstrasse 200, 6. Etage, 10117 Berlin, Germany; ☎030-880 0880; fax 030-8800 88210; e-mail info@australian-embassy.de; website www.australian-embassy.de.
Consul General: Grüneburgweg 58-62, D-60322 Frankfurt am Main, Germany; ☎069-905580; fax 069-9055 8109.

Canada

Embassy of Canada: Friedrichstrasse 95, 23rd Floor, D-10117 Berlin, Germany; ☎030-203120; fax 030-2031 2590; e-mail berlin@dfait-maeci.gc. ca; website www.kanada-info.de.
Consulate, Düsseldorf: Benrather Strasse 8, D-40213 Düsseldorf, Germany; ☎0211-172170; fax 0211-359165; e-mail ddorf@dfait-maeci.gc.ca.
Consulate, Hamburg: Ballindamm 35, 5. OG., D-20095 Hamburg, Germany; ☎040-460 0270; fax 040-4600 2720; e-mail: HMBRG@dfait-maeci.gc.ca

or hamburg@consulates-canada.de.
Consulate, Munich: Tal 29, D-80331 München, Germany; ☎089-2199 5700; fax 089-2199 5757; e-mail munic@dfait-maeci.gc.ca.
Honorary Consul, Stuttgart: Lange Strasse 51, D-70174 Stuttgart, Germany; ☎0711-223 9678; fax 0711-223 9679; e-mail hcons.stuutgart@consulates.de.

Ireland

Embassy of Ireland: Friedrichstrasse 200, D-10117 Berlin, Germany; ☎030-220720; fax 030-2207 2299.
Honorary Consulate, Hamburg: Feldbrunnenstrasse 43, D-20148 Hamburg, Germany; ☎040-4418 6113; fax 040-410 8050.
Honorary Consulate, Cologne; Frankenforster Strasse 77, D-51427 Bergisch-Gladbach, Germany; ☎02204-609860; fax 02204-609861.
Honorary Consulate, Munich: Denninger Strasse 15, D-81679 München, Germany; ☎089-2080 5990; fax 089-2080 5989.

New Zealand

New Zealand Embassy: Friedrichstrasse 60, Atrium, 4. Stock, D-10117 Berlin, Germany; ☎030-206210; fax 030-2062 1114; e-mail: nzemb@t-online.de; website www.immigration.govt.nz.
Consulate General, Hamburg: Domstrasse 19, Zürich-Haus, D-20095 Ham-

burg, Germany; ☎040-4425550; fax 040-4425 5549.

South Africa

Embassy of the Republic of South Africa: Friedrichstrasse 60, D-10117 Berlin, Germany; website www.suedafrika.org.

USA

Embassy of the United States: Neustädtische Kirchstrasse 4-5, D-10117 Berlin, Germany; ☎030-238 51 74; fax 030-238 6290.
Embassy Consular Section: Clayallee 170, D-14195 Berlin, Germany; ☎030-832 9233; fax 030-831 4926.
Consulate General, Düsseldorf: Willi-Becker-Allee 10, D-40227 Düsseldorf, Germany; ☎0211-788 8927; fax 0211-788 8938.
Consulate General, Frankfurt: Siesmayerstrasse 21, D-60323 Frankfurt am Main, Germany; ☎069-75350; fax 069-7535 2277.
Consulate General, Hamburg: Alsterufer 27/28, D-20354 Hamburg, Germany; ☎040-411 7100; fax 040-411 7222.
Consulate General, Leipzig: Wilhelm Seyfferth-Strasse 4, D-04107 Leipzig, Germany; ☎0341-213840; fax 0341-213 8471.
Consulate General, Munich: Königinstrasse 5, D-80539 München, Germany; ☎089-28880; fax 089-280 9998.

OTHER USEFUL ADDRESSES

Ombudsman for Foreigners There are various offices in each land, their addresses can be found in the phone book under *Ausländerbeauftrage* or online at www.bundesauslaenderbeauftragte.de.

American Chamber of Commerce in Germany: Rossmarkt 12, D-60311 Frankfurt am Main, Germany; ☎069-929 1040; fax 069-9291 0411; website www.amcham.de.

American Chamber of Commerce in Germany: Luisenstr. 44, D-10117 Berlin, Germany; ☎030-2887 8921; fax 030-2887 8929.
Austrade: Grüneburgweg 58-62,

D-60311, Frankfurt am Main, Germany; ☎069-905580; fax 069-9055 8119.

British Chamber of Commerce in Germany: Severinstrasse 60, D-50678 Köln, Germany; ☎0221-314458; fax 0221-315335; website www.bccg.de.

German Academic Exchange Service/Deutscher Akademischer Austauschdienst: Kennedy-allee 50, D-53175 Bonn, Germany; ☎0228-8820; fax 0228-882444; e-mail postmaster@daad.de; website www.daad.de.

German-British Chamber of Industry and Commerce: Mecklenburg House, 16 Buckingham Gate, London SW1E 6LB; ☎020-7976 4100; fax 020-7976 4101; e-mail mail@ahk-london.co.uk; website www.germanbritishchamber. co.uk.

German Chambers of Industry and Commerce/Deutscher Industrie-und Handelstag: Breite Strasse 29, D-10178 Berlin, Germany; ☎030-203080; fax 030-2003 08 1000; website www.diht.de.

The German Information Centre: 34 Belgrave Square, London, SW1X 8QB; ☎020-7824 1300; fax 020-7824 1566; e-mail infoctr@german-emba ssy.org.uk; website www.german-em bassy.org.uk.

The German Information Center: 871 United Nations Plaza, New York, NY 10017, USA; ☎212 610-9800; fax 212 610-9802; e-mail gic1@germany-info.org; website www.germany-info.org.

SETTING UP HOME

CHAPTER SUMMARY

○ Moving to Germany is much easier given the large number of specialist relocators and international removal firms.

○ Most accommodation is Germany is rented, not just by expatriates and students. Buying a home is an expensive option so most Germans rent.

○ Tenants have much more security of tenure in Germany, and may decorate or add shelves as they please.

○ Although some locations are more expensive to rent in than others, renting a house or flat is often cheaper than in the UK or USA.

○ All tenants will have certain shared maintenance tasks within their apartment building, that are carried out weekly or monthly (eg washing down the stairs, or hall windows).

○ Specialist mortgage banks and home loan societies exist to help finance house purchases.

○ When arranging a house purchase contract the legal services of a notary *Notar* must be engaged to drawing up an checking all the legal documents of the sale/purchase. Notars work for both parties as the even handed representative of the state.

○ Pets can be imported to Germany, provided they have been innoculated against rabies.

Culture shock and the hassles of moving aside, some of which are dealt with in this chapter, while the former is dealt with in the next, Germany is an excellent place to move to given the generous size of available accommodation and its setting. As for the problems of moving, most workers sent on a foreign assignment can expect to have the company help with setting up a new home, given the costs involved. This may involve a relocation company retained by the employer taking on the work, or financial help to assist the employee who is arranging their own move. Relocators are listed later on in this chapter, but the golden rule for expatriation is to research your destination throughly, this book will help either by giving you the names and addresses or by pointing you in the right direction.

One reputable research organisation that many companies use is *Economist Intelligence Unit* (☎020-7830 1000; fax 020-7491 2107; www.eiu.com), part of the business group that includes *The Economist* magazine, which carries out worldwide cost of living surveys. These carefully researched reports make statistical comparisons of various facets of living in one country or another and give an accurate indication of the likely costs or savings to be faced by an employee if transferred to another location. Their website has much useful information in addition to articles taken from the magzine which will provide background to the employee or business owner. Another resource can be found on the expat website www.expataccess.com, where there is a table of cost of living indices which can be applied to work out the difference between home and Germany for emigrés from around the world.

While the Germans are much like the British and Americans in wishing to own their own homes, relatively high property prices make this an expensive option. This fact coupled with the probable reasons for being in Germany mean that most expatriates will rent their accommodation while there. However the high prices of property and the costs of borrowing mean that most Germans rent their houses and flats for a very long time.

The biggest problem with much accommodation in Germany is in its externals, the flats are generally airy and spacious to live in, and even a two-bedroom council flat is likely to have storage space in the attic or basement, possibly both. However, because of the need to house people quickly after the devastation of the war many apartment blocks and housing schemes from the fifties and sixties are rather drab and uniform looking when seen from the outside. Unlike similar schemes dating from post-war Britain or inner city 'projects', the Germans had the room and sense to plant lots of trees and grass around them to enhance the area, and some cities encourage the painting of colourful murals on end walls to brighten things up.

Property buying and renting procedures are bound to be unfamiliar to the majority of expatriates and this chapter outlines the main processes involved. It is essential to take expert professional and local advice before any financial commitments are made. Such advice is easily obtainable from relocation agencies, many of whom will happily research possible houses and flats for you as part of the service. Other possibilities are estate agents (*Makler*) property agents (*Immobilien*), other expatriates, building societies (*Bausparkassen*) and of course the mortgage banks (*Hypotheken*).

HOW DO THE GERMANS LIVE ?

There are over 37 million dwellings in Germany, ranging in size from single rooms to mansions through the usual range of flats and family houses. Of these, roughly 43% in western and 31% in eastern Germany, are owner occupied with the remainder being rented. While flats have traditionally been rented out privately, 14% of those in western Germany are subsidised by the Federal government, this 'social housing' is mostly for the elderly, disabled and low income families. The German population increased by over four million between 1989 and 1998, consequently the demand for housing, and therefore the prices of real estate and accommodation rose sharply. Even with a record expansion in house building prices rose, and the search for affordable property increasingly resulted in a shift to satellite towns and villages.

In east Germany the standard of accommodation was poorer than that in the west, for a variety of reasons, mostly due to the hasty construction of the post-war years and a lack of maintenance since. The focus of effort was on new building rather than looking after the existing stock. Unlike western Germany, eastern Germany did not tear down buildings left standing after the war and more than 51% of east German housing stock pre-dates 1948, compared with 19% in western Germany. The average available living space per individual is smaller in the east than the west 29.8 square metres compared to 37.4. Since the fall of the wall, over half the housing stock has been repaired and modernised (at government expense), new buildings have gone up and in some places old housing has been demolished to be replaced with new. Home ownership has been promoted in the east and the owner-occupier figure has risen by 5% in the last 4 years.

Tenancy law in Germany is aimed at establishing a fair balance between the interest of tenant and landlord. Unjust or arbitrary eviction or increases in rent are not a feature in the lives of Germany's renting society.

RELOCATION AGENCIES

The increasing globalisation of industries and markets has meant an increase in the numbers of staff being sent on assignment to subsidiary or partner firms in foreign countries. This in turn has lead to a boom in the relocation business, as companies are set up to help executives and others settle in new homes in different cultures. A good relocation agency can cover a lot of ground for you, saving you time in finding a home, a good school for your children, a local medical practice and even a social life. Relocation companies are either global networks of offices or national companies providing services for trans-national clients. The companies listed below are mostly based in Germany and offer a range of service packages for the would-be expatriate. Most of them will, in addition to finding you accommodation, provide you with assistance with registering and getting through all the administrative tasks on arrival. These services are either charged for individually or included in a package offer, either way their activities on your behalf can be tailored to suit your needs and pocket, whether you are an individual or a company wishing to send staff to Germany.

Professional Associations of Relocators

There are several professional bodies for relocation and we recommend that you confirm that any company you engage is a member, as this provides you with an assured level of service and (hopefully not necessary) redress in case of problems. These bodies are the British *Association of Relocation Agents* (*ARA*), the pan-european *European Relocation Association (EuRa)* and the worldwide (but originally American) *Employee Relocation Council (ERC)*. The ARA is a professional body (founded in 1986) which requires full members to have been trading for two years and to abide by rules of conduct and professional standards for relocating clients. The ARA runs courses for accreditation and professional development and will arbitrate in any disagreements with member firms, its membership covers Britain and Europe. EuRA (founded 1998) may share a postal address with ARA, but its scope is wider and the EuRA website can provide country lists of member relocators.

The US's Employee Relocation Council (founded 1964) is a professional association and its membership includes 1,250 corporations and 10,000 individuals and small companies involved in all aspects of moving employees (eg real estate, counselling, removals, mortgage services).

Association of Relocation Agents: PO Box 189, Diss, IP22 1PE; ☎08700-737475; fax 08700-718719; e-mail info@relocationagents.com; website www.relocationagents.com.

Canadian Employee Relocation Council: 20 Eglinton Avenue West, Box 2033, Suite 1104, Toronto, Ontario M4R 1K8, Canada; ☎416-489 2555; fax 416-489 2850; e-mail info@cerc.ca; website www.cerc.ca.

Employee Relocation Council: 1720 N Street NW, Washington, DC 20036, USA; ☎202-857 0857; fax 202-467 4012; e-mail info@erc.org; website www.erc.org.

European Relocation Association: PO Box 189, Diss, IP22 1PE, UK; ☎08700-726727; fax 01359-251508; e-mail info@eura-relocation.com; website www.eura-relocation.com.

Relocation Companies

ARRIVA relocation services: Ingrid Henke, Giesebrechtstr. 10/Sybelstrasse 43, D-10629 Berlin; ☎030-882 4830; fax 030-885 4558; e-mail arriva@berlin.snafu.de or arriva@snafu.de; website www.arriva.de (in 4 languages). Arriva can arrange house purchase and sales, removals, shipping, imigration paperwork, arrangements for pets, and provide advice on schools, language courses and orientation. ARA member.

Cendant Relocation: Windmill Hill, Swindon, SN5 6PE; ☎01793-881000; fax 01793-897000; e-mail solutions@cendantrelocation.co.uk; website www.cendantrelocation.co.uk. Cendant is the world's leading provider of relocation management services (moving over 100,000 families a year), assisting organisations transferring staff at home and abroad either as part of a career move, an office move or an international assignment. Cendant Relocation is the UK subsidiary of Cendant Mobility and overseas moves are serviced by Cendant International Assignment Services operating in 300 cities around the globe.

Cendant International: UK office: Landmark House, Hammersmith Bridge Road, London, W6 9EJ; ☎020-8762 6500; fax 020-8762 6550. *Melbourne Head Office:* Cendant HWI Pty Ltd, 245 Kilda Road, St Kilda, Victoria 3182, Australia; ☎03-9536 9888; fax 03-9536 9800; e-mail getmoving@cendanthwi.com.au. *United States Corporate Headquarters:* 40 Apple Ridge Road, Danbury, CT 06810, USA; ☎203-205 3400 (Also California: 27271 Las Ramblas, Mission Viejo, CA 92691, USA; ☎949-367 2500, and Texas: 8081 Royal Ridge Parkway, Suite 200, Irving, TX 75063, USA; ☎972-870 2700).

Checklist Executive Relocation Services GmbH: Im Riesling 5, D-65760 Eschborn, Germany; ☎06173-320261; fax 06173-68065; e-mail checklist@t-online.de; website www.checklist-relocation.de. Checklist believes that its important for transferring employees to be able to settle to work on arrival and so takes the burden of moving and arranging on for them.

Directmoving.com: 11, Bd Emile Augier, F-75016 Paris, France; ☎+33-1-42 15 75 00; fax +33-1-42 15 75 05; e-mail info@directmoving.com; website www.directmoving.com Directmoving.com is a web portal launched in 2000 (part of Moving International Technologies (M.I.T.), a Paris based company). The portal is an online market place for international relocation and expatriation.

In-Lease Deutschland GMBH: Kurmainzer Strasse 83, D-65983 Frankfurt, Germany; ☎069-313130; fax 069-315034; e-mail In-lease@t-online.de; website www.in-lease.com. Specialise in furniture rental services. IN-Lease provides short and long term rental plans, rental purchase and purchase of furniture in traditional, contemporary, European and American styles, including: kitchen and home entertainment appliances, cutlery, crockery, bedding and linens, curtains, blinds, and floorcoverings.

Professional Organizing Relocation Consult GmbH: Wiesenstrasse 18, D-65843 Sulzbach/ Taunus, Germany; ☎06196-594613; fax 06196-594671; e-mail m.wagner@profe ssional-organizing.de; website www.professional-organizing.de. (Founded 1982). Having helped 15,000 professionals and their families relocate since 1982, Professional Organizing believe in individully tailored relocation solutions.

RAA Relocation & Administration Services: Max-Dingler-Strasse 3a, D-82131 Munich, Germany; ☎089-895 5580; fax 089-8955 5810; e-mail info@relocatio n-services.de; website www.relocation-services.de. (Founded 1983). Offer corporate and individual relocation assistance to 15 cities. Home searches include accompanying the client to view and assistance with purchase/rent contract negotiation and the arrangement of utilities, banking, schools and tax registration. International experience and connections allow for the door-to-door packing and shipping of effects.

RCG Relocation Consulting Group GmbH: Bavariastrasse 1, D-80336 München, Germany; ☎089-7201 7979; fax 089-7201 7978; website www.relocation-con sulting.de. RCG's services include house finding, immigration documentation, house management, office set up and recruitment, cultural adaptation, language training, and departure/repatriation services. Relocation service packages are custom designed to meet the client's requirements.

RE/MAX Relocation Europe: Marktplatz 3, D-65183 Wiesbaden, Germany; ☎0611-341 5312; fax 0611-341 5333; website www.europe-relocation.info. The european arm of RE/MAX International they provide destination, departure, moving and consulting services to individuals and companies relocating. Their services include legal documentation and immigration, languages and an award winning 'Kids Survival Guide to Moving video. Member of EuRA, ERC and CERC.

RSB Deutschland GmbH: Dreieichstrasse 59, D-60594 Frankfurt am Main, Germany; ☎069-6109 4721; fax 069-6109 4740; e-mail info@rsb-relocation.de; website www.rsb-relocation.de. In business since 1987 RSB can assist clients to settle in more than 60 German cities, and offers relocation services for transfers of staff: to Germany, within Germany, from Germany elsewhere and from one country to another. Member of ARA, ERC and EuRA.

RTS Relocation & Translation Services: Ringstrasse 187, D-22145 Hamburg, Germany; ☎040-678 1084; fax 040-678 9015; e-mail info@rts-relocationservic es.de; website www.relocation.hamburg.de. Provide a full range of relocation services to help those moving to Germany and when leaving, wherever they come from or go to. This includes translation and interpretation services, school researching, setting up utilities and bank accounts and ongoing support during the time in Germany.

UTS Deutschland: Windeckstrasse 81, D-68163 Mannheim, Germany; ☎0621-423930; fax 0621-416512; e-mail sales@uts-germany.de; website www.uts-germany.de. International Move Managers.

Welcome Relocation Centers: Start-Up Services GmbH, Stefan George-Ring 2, D-81929 München; ☎089-93 94 52 0; fax 089-930 49 14; e-mail info@start-up -services.de; www.start-up-services.de. Start-Up Services GmbH is the founder of Welcome Relocation Centers and offers complete 'Relocation Services', 'Subsidiary Start Up', and 'Self-Managed Relocation' programmes for employees and their families, groups, and companies. Welcome Relocation Centers can be found in Ingolstadt, the Frankfurt area, and Düsseldorf/Cologne; other destinations in Germany and repatriation relocation are covered by partner companies within the TIRA organisation. For a free relocation checklist telephone 089-9394 5213.

PURCHASING PROPERTY

Given that most readers of this book are most likely only going to be in Germany for a few years it may seem odd to suggest buying property. However, while expensive it can be a good investment, and who knows maybe you'll be seduced into settling permanently. In Germany the method of buying a house is radically different from the system known to Britons. For a start is that German property buying is not predicated on the concept of getting onto any 'ladder' whereby you trade up in size and cost as you move from flat to house to mansion. However, the 'buy for life' attitude of the German house buyer means that there is less upward movement of property prices compared to other locations.

Another difference is that German estate agents (*Immobilien-Makler, Haus-Makler,* and *Wohnungsvermittler* are the German equivalents of estate agents.) are a lot harder to find, and speculative browsing of houses on the market is likewise more difficult; you can't just stroll down the high street looking in office windows at potential purchases. While there are some British firms who deal in the German property market such as Knight Frank these firms often specialise in commercial property rather than residential, unless you fancy a castle or vineyard. The *European Confederation of Real Estate Agents* are a useful resource for the prospective tenant or purchaser as there membership is made up of 25,000 estate agents across 14 countries, their website allows you to start hunting for property in advance of travel. Another hurdle for the prospective house buyer is of course the cost, in buying a house the deposit at around 40% excludes all but the well-off from taking out a mortgage until they have spent several years saving towards it (see the section on *Bausparkassen* below).

Most German estate agents are either independent brokers working from home or they operate from very office-like offices, rather than the office cum shop of their British counterparts. Finding them is more a case of searching the press and yellow pages. If anything the German estate agent could be regarded as secretive, but this is due to the way that houses are sold. If you buy a house, through them you will pay them an introduction fee (*Nachweissgebühr*), so they do not particularly wish to risk losing sales by giving out information willy-nilly, after all for all they know you could be another *Makler.* However, once you have arranged an appointment to discuss buying a house and the type of house you're looking for they can be quite professional. But be very wary of signing yourself up as an exclusive customer, that will prevent you finding property through any other source, unless you like the idea of paying out lots of money for the sake of bypassing the makler you signed up with. What you should expect is a very large bill on top of the house purchase price for all the expenses of the house buying process. As stated above the estate agents charge a fee and this can range from 5-7% of the purchase price of the house, so it is prudent to ask what the rate of commission (*Provisionssatz*) is before engaging their services. You may find that this fee is split between buyer and seller, and sometimes the makler's fee comes solely from the seller's pocket.

Once you have found a property that you wish to buy and have been introduced to the seller, the sale process begins; you have to instruct a notary (*Notar*). Unlike the solicitors engaged by both parties other countries, the Notar works for both parties, at the same time. The Notar's role is to be the fair and even handed representative of the state, overseeing the legal side of the house sale (registering change of ownership and updating the land registry). So while this can be very fair, you do not have the security of having a legal representative who is definitely working on your behalf. The Notar is responsible for drawing up and witnessing the legal document (*Urkunde*) containing the sale and purchase details. As stated the house purchaser engages the Notar, and thus pays their fees, these are between ½ to ¾% of the house price, this is on top of the agent's fees for introducing you to the seller. Added to which is the Land Purchase Tax (*Grunderwerbsteuer*), 3.5% of the house price. So by the time you have completed the formalities of buying a house you can expect to have to add on roughly 10% of the house price to cover the fees and taxes.

It is possible to cut out the makler by consulting the property and classified pages of your local German newspaper, and dealing with the house sellers directly, these will be marked *von privat.* However, many of these adverts may have been placed by makler, so you'll have to ask around. Your country's embassy and consulates across Germany are also a useful source of information on local housing conditions, and which local newspapers are the best for adverts.

Association of German Estate Agents (Verband Deutscher Makler für Grundbesitz, Hausverwaltung und Finanzierungen e.V.): Riedemannweg 57, D-13627 Berlin, Germany; ☎030-38302528; fax 030-38302529; website www.vdm.de.
European Confederation of Real Estate Agents (Confédération Européenne de l'Immobilier): 4 rue de Stockholm, F-75008 Paris, France; ☎+33-1-42 93 79 86; fax +33-1-42 93 79 80; website http://web-cei.com.

FINANCE

It is a hard life for the expatriate worker who wishes to purchase property overseas as most of the information aimed at expatriates seeking properties or mortgages appears to have been written under the misapprehension that all expats are only concerned with buying houses to return home to, or as investments to be rented out in your absence abroad. Financing the purchase of a property in another country is harder to arrange than you might expect, given that most expatriates are earning very good salaries. However, the mortgage situation for overseas residents is now improving and details of how one can go about arranging a mortgage locally follow.

German Home Loan Societies (Bausparkassen)

Unless they have sufficient funds so that they can afford to buy outright, any foreigner wanting to enter the German property market will have to consider taking out a loan with a German home loan society (*Bausparkasse*). There are 34 Bausparkassen across Germany, 21 private and 13 public, the public ones are operated by the Länder banks, while the private bausparkassen are run by share groups (*Aktien Gesellschaft*) and so have the AG suffix. Of the 13 Landesbausparkassen 4 are legally independent operations, the remainder are subsidiaries of the state banks. In practice this division means that you may find offices of all 21 private Bausparkassen in your home town, with the only apparent competition for them coming from the offices of the Landesbausparkasse. However, while each Landesbausparkasse can only operate in its home state, contracts with them can be arranged through any local *Sparkassen* bank office (*Sparkassen* are a variant of Landesbanks in that they are backed by city or regional councils).

Bausparkassen are credit institutions which have developed from the same roots as the British building society system, however, they operate in a different manner to the British model, and the two should not be confused. Where British building societies operate on the 'open' system; taking savers deposits as a 'float' to trade in stocks and shares in order to finance loans and mortgages, the Bausparkassen utilise the 'closed' system. This entails the collection of savers to form a pool of funds from which loans can be drawn. Over 20 million Germans hold a *Bauspar* savings agreement, and two-thirds of German homes are co-financed by this method.

Unlike in Britain where you start savings accounts as soon as you wish, with only a vague notion of when you might want to buy a home, the German Bauspar system is geared towards buying right from the start. Unlike banks Bausparkassen will only lend money to savers, and these loans will only be made for the purchase of houses, flats, building land or the business extras required in building properties for accommodation. The Bauspar system works by identifying members as savers (creditors) or borrowers (debtors), as you are either saving money with them or paying back an amount borrowed. The potential home buyer enters into a savings contract (*Bausparvetrag*) with the Bausparkassen, this sets out how much they wish to borrow to finance their purchase and how much they need to save each month and for how long, until they will be issued the loan. While Bausparkassen will lend up to 80% of the purchase price, the typical amount the saver needs to build up before receiving the loan is 30%-50% of the amount required.

The benefits of this system are that the interest rates tend to be low on the loans (varying between 5% and 6.5%), though the Bauspar savings do not attract very good interest rates, typically being around 4%. The amounts you can borrow, and so the amounts you need to deposit each month will vary according to the individual Bausparkasse and the tariffs and loan periods that they offer. In some respects the modern Bausparkasse is a more customer friendly institution than in the past, and you can obtain loan agreements which are much more tailored to your needs should you wish to, and waiting times for loans have come down in recent years. The differences between Bausparkassen and mortgage banks (*Hypotheken*) are that as a saver you have a legal right to the loan, it being part of your Bauspar contract, the interest rates of the loan do not vary with market fluctuations, and as a Bauspar saver you obtain certain safeguards through the land registry.

The main types of Bauspar agreements are Fast, Standard, Long-Term and Options. The Standard tariff is aimed at medium level savings for 7 years with interest accruing at 2-3.5%, with a loan repayment period of 11 years, with interest on the loan of around 4.5%. The Long-Term agreement involves a longer savings period with lower monthly deposits at 4-4.5% interest, followed by a longer repayment period where interest is at 6-6.5%. The Options tarif is tailored to the individual customer's requirements and the Fast agreement speaks for itself as an option for those with sufficiently high income. According to the Association of Private Bausparkassen (*Verband der Privaten Bausparkassen e.V*; Klingelhöfer Strasse 4, D-10785 Berlin, Germany; ☎ 030-5900 91500; fax 030-5900 91501; e-mail bausparkassen@vdpb.de; website www.bausparkassen.de.) the upper and lower time limits on loans are 6.5 and 18 years respectively. In all these cases however, there will be differences between individual tariffs and the interest and repayment levels they will operate at.

There are also facilities available to those customers wishing to purchase or renovate property at short notice, and whose bauspar agreement has not yet 'matured'. It is possible to provide funding for saving or pre-financing of an agreement with a loan from another credit institution (eg a *hypothek* or bank loan), this loan is free from redemption payments until the allocation date of the Bauspar loan, which is then used to repay the other loan. This is also the most advantageous financial mixture for housing purchases; the combination of bauspar loan and mortgage. It is not uncommon now for banks, Bausparkassen and Hypotheken to work together, so that the procedure from application to redemption is simplified by package services, often including insurance policies.

Mortgages With German Banks

In addition to the loans offered to savers in the Bauspar system, mortgage banks (*Hypotheken*) exist in Germany as well as the German version of the standard bank. The range of services available from either of these institutions with regard to the prospective house buyer, will vary from bank to bank. At present there are some 35 mortgage banks with offices across Germany. Unlike the Bausparkassen they will lend money for any purpose, but only to a maximum of 60% of the purchase price. The mortgage banks give mortgages and municipal loans by raising funds through the issue of bonds, therefore, the rates and terms will vary according to market conditions.

Offshore Mortgages

Many expatriates would like to be able to obtain mortgages with the institutions that they are used to dealing with, however, for any expat being a non-resident often makes it very difficult to obtain mortgage funding. This is especially the case should you apply for a mortgage to buy a property outside of the your home country, something most mortgage lenders are chary of. For the British expat some building societies do arrange financing for properties in France, Spain or Italy, but this is not yet the case for Germany, and indeed there are restrictions on the amount of information that can be given on this subject in publications available in the UK. On this subject it is really a case of asking around within the expat community for a referal to a lender or asking your home bank if they can give any advice.

Most of the information aimed at expatriates about obtaining a mortgage, has the purchase of a home property in mind, either for letting out to obtain income, or as a home to move into on your return. Hence the lender can accept that as security for the loan, because in the event of your defaulting they can easily dispose of the property. However, this does not necessarily preclude you from using your assets, a domestic or foreign property to help secure finance for a house purchase and advice on these matters can be sought from financial consultants.

In Britain one such firm is *Conti Financial Services*, who can advise you on foreign purchases. It should be noted that as well as risking your home if you can not maintain repayments on any mortgage or loan secured on it, you are also at risk from exchange rate variations with foreign currency mortgages, except for EU expats who are now protected by the adoption of the euro. Conti are based at 204 Church Road, Hove, BN3 2DJ; ☎ 01273-772811; fax 01273-321269; e-mail simon@conti-financial.com; www.overseasandukfinance.com. They have over 20 years experience of arranging finance for clients in Britain and abroad wishing to purchase property around the world and are also an independent mortgage broker and can arrange financing in several currencies. As members of the Federation of Overseas Property Developers, Agents and Consultants, and an affiliate member of the Association of Relocation Agents this firm is a specialist in overseas residential mortgages.

Housing Incentives

The German government provides assistance for homeowners through various schemes which either pay a grant or supplement to homeowners, or which pay a premium on savings held by would-be homeowners (to encourageg working people to develop assets to build or buy their own home). The laws incorporating these bonuses also contain an ecological element in the promotion of energy efficient homes. These savings premiums vary according to location west or east and amount saved per annum. Amounts less than around €1,600 receive between 20-25% and the maximum of approximately €1800 per annum receives 10%. There is also an income related element in working out the actual premium paid. The owner-occupied home premium is paid for eight years and is paid irrespective of income and is around €9,750 for new buildings and half that for existing property.

There are also housing supplements available for those who can not afford to cover their rent or housing costs but obviously you have to be below certain income thresholds.

RENTING PROPERTY

Given the rent-control and tenancy laws which are very fair to tenants and the costs involved in buying, most German accommodation is rented. Generally this accommodation is rented unfurnished, so that tenants can furnish it how they wish with their own stock of furniture and decorate it how they please. This is especially true with regard to the kitchen, more than a few expatriates have been surprised to move into their new flats only to find that the kitchen is an empty concrete box without even a sink or any taps. Furnishing and decorating the flat or house are entirely the domain of the tenant, except that the tenants must redecorate to the landlord's wishes, or return the accommodation to the decorative state current at the start of their tenancy when they move out. This includes removing shelves and cupboards and making good the walls and plasterwork.

It is always wisest if your company is not arranging accommodation to take a few days holiday well in advance of your new posting to make the arrangements for renting a flat or house. More often than not you will be able to find temporary furnished accommodation to last you until you can get a flat or apartment of your own.

Tenants in Germany also have their own local, state and national associations *Mieterverein* or *Mieterbund*. These, very active, tenants associations in return for an annual subscription will help negotiate for you in disagreements with landlords and advise on rent rates and leases. Rent rates are published in booklets *Mietspiegel* and usually sold for around €5 (£3/$4).

Some of the rent figures noted in the *Housing Reports from the Main Cities* have been taken from either the relevant *Mietspiegel* or The Economist Intelligence Unit's *Worldwide Cost of Living Survey* carried out in the Autumn of 2001. Mieterverein/Mieterbund addresses for the länder and some of the larger towns have been included at the end of this section so that readers can contact them for information on current rents. As an example of rents current at the time of writing a 2 bedroom unfurnished apartment in London will range in cost between £1,300 ($1,912) and £2,300 ($3,382) to rent per month and have between 210-690 square feet (or 20-64 square metres) of floorspace, while a similar apartment in Düsseldorf would cost between €665 (£407/$582) and €1,022 (£626/$896) and have around 100-120 square metres of floorspace. Hence while much is made of accommodation being expensive in Germany, on the whole it is reasonably large and priced.

Apart from the Mieterverien listed on the following pages the Ring Deutscher Makler, the Association of German Estate Agents, and the European Confederation of Real Estate Agents are all able to put enquirers in touch with estate agents, or help find properties. Not forgetting the ever useful store of knowledge to be found in the expat community, which can be accessed online or through clubs and societies, and that can put you in touch with either landlords or tenants with property coming onto the market.

The Costs of Becoming a Tenant

There is considerable capital outlay involved in renting an apartment. If the apartment has been located by an agency, the agency commission will be at least two months rent. According to the Economist Intelligence Unit's report the fees charged by agencies vary from two to three months rent, or even 25% of the annual rent (Berlin).

Once the prospective tenant (*Mieter*) has located a flat he or she will have to sign a contract with the landlord (*Vermieter*) or owner (*Hausbesitzer*). Leases are generally for one or two years, but can be for up to five. Tenants have to pay at least a month's rent in advance, plus a refundable deposit the *Kaution* (usually equivalent to three months rent) against damages. The damages deposit must be paid into an account and the tenant receives it back, plus interest if there are no damage charges on departure. Then there are the *Nebenkosten* or charges for rubbish/garbage disposal, utilities, service charges and suchlike, followed by VAT and of course insurance. If you add up all these expenses before you even move in, then it works out that you will have paid at least four to seven months worth of rent without actually spending a night in your new home. And of course you will have had to conclude a deal with the previous tenants with regard to the such items as cupboards, wardrobes and kitchens, unless you have a sink unit and cupboards of your own to fit or other furnishings. 90% of the time the previous tenants will take the kitchen with them. Do not bank on being able to pop down to Ikea either, although this chain exists in Germany, the waiting time for kitchen units can be long (a matter of months in some locations).

Note that rent figures are usually advertised as *warm* or *kalte* (cold), the former meaning that the figure incudes rent, nebenkosten (heating, water, etc) and other costs, while cold rent is for the accomodation space alone.

Tenancy law is based on freedom of contract and is aimed at establishing a fair balance between the interests of tenants and landlords. No tenant need fear unjust and arbitrary eviction or excessive rent increases. A landlord can only give notice to a tenant who is meeting their contractual requirements in the event that 'justified interest' can be proven (eg if they need the accommodation for themselves). Rents may rise at the end of each contract providing it does not rise above that charged for comparable housing in the same area. It is always worth having a German friend, the mieterverein, your relocator or your company's legal department take a look at any tenancy agreement as they will spot any dodgy clauses, and it only takes about a quarter of an hour to read through the lease. Most leases are fair, but occasionally landlords will try and get you to sign a lease with a clause adding 8% to the rent each year, or one that states that if you don't notify them two years before the contract expires it will run on for another five years automatically. It is also useful to check the contractual notice required from the tenant, as with lease running for up to five years it is not unusual for contracts to stipulate three to six months notice of termination should you want to move, for whatever reason. However, if at the end of a five year contract the landlord wishes to sell the property, the tenants have first option on buying it.

Occupants' Obligations And Hausordnungen

In many parts of Germany, tenants of apartment buildings are obliged to participate fully in the maintenance of the common areas (e.g. grounds, paths, cellar/basement, corridor, landing etc). Legal requirements include that the occupant of a house with a chimney, should engage the services of a chimney sweep two or three times a year. The occupant is also required to keep the public pavement outside the dwelling, clear of ice or snow during winter. There are alos often restrictions on noise levels outdoors and on bonfires.

Being a tenant in Germany involves adhering to a set of fairly strict indoor *Hausordnungen* (house rules). These may include such unfamiliar restrictions as how late or early you can take a bath, restrictions on the decibel level of televisions, music centres etc. and a precise time for locking outside doors.

USEFUL ABBREVIATIONS AND TERMS

Abstellr. (Abstellraum):	storeroom (for hoover etc.).
Altb.(Altbau):	old building.
App.(Appartement):	apartment.
Atelierwhg. (Atelierwohnung):	studio flat.
Aufzug:	lift.
Bad (pl. Bäder):	bathroom(s).
Baugrundstück:	building estate.
Bes. (Besichtigung):	viewing.
Bj. (Baujahr):	year of construction.
Blk. (Balkon):	balcony.
beziehb.(beziehbar):	ready for occupation.
bzf.(bezugsfertig):	ready to occupy.
Dachgarten:	roof garden.
DG (Dachgeschoss):	attic floor.
Dachgeschosswohnung:	attic flat.
3-Zi-Komf-DG-ETW (Dreizimmer-Komfort- *Dachgeschoss-Etagenwohnung):*	three-roomed, luxury attic flat in an apartment block.
EBK(Einbauküche):	fitted kitchen.
EG (Erdgeschoss):	ground floor.
EFH (Einfamilienhaus):	family home.
eig. (eigen):	own.
Ein-zimmer-wohnung mit Bad/Dusche:	single-room flat with bath/shower.
Esszi.(Esszimmer):	dining room.
ETW (Etagenwohnung):	flat (in an apartment block).
excl.(exclusiv):	exclusive
Fahrstuhl:	lift.
Fertigst.(Fertigstellung):	to be completed.
freist. (freiestehend):	free standing/detached.
Gehmin. (Gehminuten):	minutes walk.
gepfl. (gepflegt):	well maintained.
Gge.(Garage):	garage.
gr.(gross):	large.
Grd.(Grund):	ground.
he. (hell):	light, airy.
Hzg.(Heizung):	heating.
die Kaution:	security deposit against damage. Usually two months rent.
Kaltmiete:	rent minus heating.
Keller:	cellar/basement.
kl.(klein):	small.
kompl.einger.(komplett eingerichtet):	fully furnished.
Kü.(Küche):	kitchen.
Lage:	site, situated.
langfristig zu vermieten:	long-term let.
leer:	unfurnished.
Maklercourtage:	agent's commission.
die Miete:	rent.

die Mietdauer:	period of lease.
die Mieteinnahme:	revenue from rent.
die Mieterhöhung:	rent increase.
der Mietvertrag	tenancy agreement.
möbliert:	furnished.
Monatsmiete:	monthly rent.
nähe/nh.:	near/close to.
Nebenkosten:	maintenance charges (for a block of flats).
Neub.(Neubau):	new building.
Nfl.(Nützfläche):	usable space.
OG (Obergeschoss):	upper floor.
reizv.(reizvoll):	charming.
renov.(renoviert):	renovated/newly decorated.
ruh./rhg. (ruhig):	quiet.
Schlafzi.(Schlafzimmer):	bedroom.
sep.(separat):	separate.
Spitzenlg.(Spitzenlage):	prime site.
S-Lage (Südlage):	south facing.
Stellpl.(Stellplatz):	parking place.
Stck. (Stock):	floor (storey).
Terr. (Terrasse):	terrace/patio.
TG (Tiefgarage):	underground parking.
überd. (überdacht):	roofed.
UG (Untergeschoss):	cellar/basement.
VB (Verhandlungsbasis):	guide price.
Verkehrsgünstig:	convenient location.
voll einger. (voll eingerichtet):	fully furnished.
von Privat:	private let/sale, i.e. no agent's fee.
Warmmiete:	rent including heating (e.g. €1400 Warm).
Wfl./Wohnfl.(Wohnfläche):	living area.
Wokü/Wohnkü. (Wohnküche):	kitchen/diner.
Whg.(Wohnung):	flat/accommodation generally.
Wohnzi.(Wohnzimmer):	sitting room.
zentrale Lage:	central situation.
Zhg. (Zentralheizung):	central heating.
das Zimmer:	room.
2-Zi-Whg (Zweizimmerwohnung):	two-roomed flat; (also *Zimmerige Wohnung*).
zzgl.(zuzüglich):	plus, including.

HOUSING REPORTS FROM THE MAIN CITIES

As stated earlier tenants associations (*Mieterverein*) operate in most towns, in return for an annual subscription they will help negotiate for you in disagreements with landlords and provide information on current rent rates. Other than a search through the classified adverts you can also try to find accommodation through an estate agent (*Makler*). In Germany these are office based rather than at street level with pictures of properties in the window, and you will need to make an appointment first. The prospective tenant should also clarify the terms for the agent's fees as it is the party renting who pays the agent's commission.

Berlin

As the German Government moved here from Bonn it was inevitable that prices and rent rates would soar as the demand for accommodation went up. A large building programme to provide new housing and renovate old apartment blocks helped but demand is still high. In some areas of Berlin the older accommodation stock has been converted for arts and business uses. Information on accommodation can be obtained from the accommodation office (*Wohnungsamt*) for the district where you plan to live, or from the *Mitwhonzentralen* agencies, one of which has women only apartments available. General accommodation information can be obtained from the Senatsverwaltung für Arbeit und Frauen. The best local German newspaper in which to look for property adverts is the *Berliner Morgenpost*. The Berlin equivalent of the Citizen's Advice Bureau, the *Verbraucherzentrale* may also be able to advise foreigners looking for accommodation.

A two bedroom apartment can cost between €700 and €1,200 for 75 square metres of floorspace; typical advance payments are three months rent upfront and a similar figure for the *kaution*.

Useful Addresses
Berliner Mieterverein e.V: Wilhelmstrasse 74, D-10117 Berlin, Germany; ☎030-226260; fax 030-2262 6161; e-mail bmv@berlin-mieterverein.de; website www.berlin-mieterverein.de. Office hours are Monday-Wednesday 9am-5pm, Thursday 9am-7pm, and Friday 9am-3pm.
Senatsverwaltung für Arbeit und Frauen: Storkowerstr. 97, D-10407 Berlin, Germany; ☎030-4214 3713.
Verbraucherzentrale: Bayreuther Strasse 40, D-10787 Berlin, Germany; ☎030-214850; fax 030-211 7201; website www.verbraucherzentrale-berlin.de.

Bonn

Bonn always had a shortage of accommodation because of its huge population of diplomats, bureaucrats and politicians, this has eased with the move of half of the government ministries to Berlin, and the attendant move of most foreign embassies and their staffs. The most exclusive areas (e.g. Bad Godesberg, Venusberg) are understandably very expensive. Cheaper houses, both to rent and buy may be found in Meckenheim 40 minutes west of the city by bus. The local tenants' association (*Mieterverein Bonn/Rhein-Sieg/Ahr e.V.*) *produce a list* (*Mietspiegel*) of local rent rates as well as assisting with tenancy problems. The current edition of the Mietspiegel dates from 2000 but a new edition is to be produced in mid 2002. According to the last figures a good quality flat in a good area would cost between €13 and €15 per square metre, according to the age of the building.

The local daily newspaper *General Anzeiger* (Wednesday and Saturday editions) is the main source of advertisements for accommodation to let.

Useful Address
Mieterverein Bonn/Rhein-Sieg/Ahr e.V.: Berliner Freiheit 36, D-53111 Bonn, Germany; ☎0228-9493 0912/090; fax 0228-9493 0922; e-mail info@mietervere in-bonn.de; www.mieterverein-bonn.de. Office hours are Monday-Thursday 9am-Noon and 2-5pm, Friday 9am-Noon.

Düsseldorf

Accommodation in Düsseldorf is often difficult to find, flats are snapped up as soon as they are advertised so it is advisable to do your house hunting on the spot, use a Makler or consider looking in the smaller surrounding towns. The Cost of Living Survey estimates that current Makler fees in Düsseldorf are around the equivalent of two months rent, while the British Consulate General's information sheet, estimated it at between that an three months worth. Accommodation is publicised in the local daily newspapers, with the peak days being Wednesday and Saturday. The main daily is the: *Rheinische Post.* Other widely read local newspapers include the *Westdeutsche Zeitung, Neue Rhein-Ruhr Zeitung* and the *Westdeutsche Allgemeine Zeitung.* Furnished temporary accommodation is sometimes available.

At the time of writing the average rent on a two bedroom flat was between €700 (£430/US$620approx) and €1,000 (£615/US$890 approx.) for roughly 100-120 square metres of floorspace.

Useful Addresses
The British Consulate General: Yorckstr. 19, D-40476 Düsseldorf, Germany; ☎0211-94480. Produces a leaflet *Living in Düsseldorf* which contains hints on residence permits and accommodation.
Mieterverein Düsseldorf Beratung & Schutz: Oststrasse 47, D-40211 Düsseldorf, Germany; ☎0211-169960; fax 0211-351511; e-mail info@mieterverein-dues seldorf.de; website www.mieterverein-duesseldorf.de. Office hours are Monday-Tuesday 8.15am-5.30pm, Wednesday-Thursday 8.15am-4.30pm and Friday 8.15-11.30am.

Frankfurt

The centre of Frankfurt is primarily a banking and commercial area, and therefore contains limited accommodation. Most accommodation is in the suburbs and surrounding area. According to the British consular information for Hesse unfurnished accommodation currently costs between €6-€10 per square metre. They also give approximate figures for small and medium flats: one room, bath and kitchen annex costs between €300-€400 (£185-£246/US$265-$355approx) and a two-room flat, plus bath and kitchen, would cost about €500-€800 (£310-£495/US$455-$710 approx) per month, plus around €50 for bills. The time taken to move in can be from ten days to a month, although only a month's rent is required in advance. Frankfurt also offers furnished accommodation. Areas where accommodation prices are likely to be lower, are Bochenheim (near the university) and Bornheim (north of the centre). The best newspaper for accommodation to let advertisements is the *Frankfurter Rundschau* and in particular the Saturday edition which comes out at 2pm on Fridays, but all the adverts are quickly followed up.

Short term accommodation may also be obtained through the *City Mitwohnzentrale* or other agencies of which a few are listed below. There is also other temporary furnished accommodation which can be from €500 to €1,500 per month. The Frankfurt Tenants' Protection Association *Mieterschutzverein Frankfurt a.M. e.V.* Eckenheimer Landstrasse 339, D-60320 Frankfurt am Main, Germany; ☎069-560 10 57; fax 069-56 89 40. Frankfurt's biggest tenants' association, with over 20,000 members, gives legal advice to its members regarding all problems over rents and leases. Annual membership costs €72 and includes legal costs cover for all legal proceedings between tenants and landlords. The office hours are Monday-Thursday 2-6pm, Friday 2-4pm.

Useful Addresses

Allgemeine Mitwohnzentrale Frankfurt: Jahnstrasse 49, D-60318 Frankfurt/Main; ☎069-9552 0892; fax 069-9552 0891; e-mail info@allgemeinemitwohnzentral e.de; website www.allgemeinemitwohnzentrale.de.
City Mitwohnzentrale: Hansaallee 2, D-60322 Frankfurt/Main, Germany; ☎069-299050; fax 069-289477; website www.city-mitwohnzentrale.de.

Hamburg

Hamburg is the most Anglophile city in Germany with a large British population and many British expatriate clubs. German unification put port of Hamburg at the centre of trade with eastern Europe. Evidence of this can be seen in the record number of traders and companies in Hamburg. This influx caused an unprecedented demand for business and residential premises and pushed up property prices. Buying property is therefore likely to be out of the question for most expatriates, unless they go at least one hour from Hamburg city centre.

According to the Mietenspiegel produced by the Hamburg Tenants' Association (*Mieterverein zu Hamburg*), 'cold' rents will range between €3-6 (approx £1.80-£3.70/ US$2.65-$5.35) and €6-10 per square metre in the 40-90 square metre space range (the low end of the two bedroom flat size range in Germany), according to the age of the building. Some of Hamburg's accommodation stock is pre-1918, but this tends to be less than 65 square metres. Luckily the advance rent and kaution only add up to four month's worth but moving in takes between ten and thirty days. The temporary furnished accommodation that is available is not cheap either.

The best newspaper for accommodation advertisements is the *Hamburger Abendblatt,* which is published daily around mid-morning. The Wednesday and Saturday editions carry extra property supplements.

Anyone having difficulties with their landlord or in need of preliminary advice about renting accommodation, could contact the Hamburg Tenants' Association. As well as the *Living in Hamburg* brochure the British Consulate General in Hamburg produces brochures for Bremen, Kiel and Hannover.

Mieterverein zu Hamburg: Glockengiesserwall 2 (Wallhof) II, D-20095 Hamburg, Germany; ☎040-879790; fax 040-8797 9120;e-mail info@mieterverein-ham burg.de; www.mieterverein-hamburg.de. Office hours are Monday-Thursday 8.30am-6pm, Friday 8.30am-1pm.
Verbraucherzentrale: Kirchenallee 22, D-20099 Hamburg, Germany; ☎040-248320; fax 040-2483 2290; e-mail info@vzhh.de; website www.vzhh.de.

Munich

Small to medium sized flats are difficult to find and so are expensive, with rents being expensive. A one room unfurnished apartment will cost upwards of €400 (£245/US$355), while a three bedroom apartment will be in the region of €900-1,000. While moving in can take as little as two days, the kaution is usually three month's worth of rent and makler fees almost as much. There is some temporary accommodation but at a price, a quick look at the München row in the table of house rents/prices will indicate that the city is probably the most expensive place in Germany for accommodation.

The main newspapers for accommodation advertisements are the *Süddeutsche Zeitung* (Wednesday and Friday editions) and the *Münchener Merkur* (Thursday and Saturday editions), 95% of these will be placed by estate agents. Other useful publications include a leaflet produced by the British Consulate in Munich and the English-language newspaper *Munich Found*.

Useful Addresses

Mieterverein München: Sonnenstr. 10, D-80331 München, Germany; ☎089-552 1430; fax 089-554554; e-mail postmaster@mieterverein-muenchen.de; website www.mieterverein-muenchen.de.

Ring Deutscher Makler: Landesverband Bayern e.V., Theatinerstrasse 35, D-80333 München, Germany; ☎089-29 08 20 13; fax 089-226623; www.rdm-bayern.de.

MIETERVEREIN ADDRESS LIST

Included in this list are the Land offices of the *Deutscher Mieterbund* (Littenstrasse 10, D-10179 Berlin, Germany; ☎030-223230; fax 030-2232 3100; e-mail info@mieterbund.de; website www.mieterverein.de), the umbrella organisation for *mieterverein*; these offices will be able to provide contact details for organisations in smaller towns. Those listed in the previous section on housing in major cities aren't repeated here to save space, please note also that addresses, especially e-mail addresses may change over the life of this edition. The mieterverein in the larger cities often have websites packed with useful (although a few listed here were being built while the book was researched) information but at the time of writing only a few had pages in other languages.

Baden-Württemberg

Deutscher Mieterbund Landesverband Baden-Württemberg: Olgastr. 77, D-70182 Stuttgart, Germany; ☎0711-236 0600; fax 0711-236 0602; e-mail info@mieterverein-bw.de; website www.mieterverein-bw.de.

Mieterverein Baden-Baden und Umgebung e.V.: Lange Str. 13, D-76530 Baden-Baden, Germany; ☎07221-25512; fax 07221-392831; e-mail Mieterverein-Baden-Baden@t-online.de.

Mieterverein Heidelberg und Umgebung e.V.: Poststr. 46, D-69115 Heidelberg, Germany; ☎06221-20473; fax 06221-163418.

Mieterverein Karlsruhe e.V.: Ritterstr. 24, D-76137 Karlsruhe, Germany; ☎0721-375091; fax 0721-378125;

e-mail info@mieterverein-karlsruh e.de; website www.mieterverein-kar lsruhe.de.

Mieterverein Stuttgart und Umgebung e.V.: Moserstr. 5, D-70182 Stuttgart, Germany; ☎0711-210160; fax 0711-236 9223; e-mail info@mieterverein-stu ttgart.de; website www.mieterverein -stuttgart.de.

Mieterverein Ulm/Neu Ulm: Fischergasse 16, D-89073 Ulm, Germany; ☎0731-62762; fax 0731-610116; e-mail info@mieterverein-ulm.de; website http://mieterverein-ulm.de.

Bayern

Deutscher Mieterbund Landesverband Bayern: Am Antritt 15, D-83727 Schliersee, Germany; ☎08026-606 6910; fax 08026-4000; website www. mieterbund-bayern.de.

Mieterverein Augsburg: Hallstr 11, D-86150 Augsburg, Germany; ☎0821-151055; fax 0821-151252; e-mail mieterverein.a ugsburg@t-online.de.

Mieterverein Ingolstadt: Paradeplatz 5/iii, D-85049 Ingolstadt, Germany; ☎0841-17744; fax 0841-17734; e-mail mieterverein-ingolstadt@gmx.de.

Mieterverein Nürnberg: Schlehengasse 10, D-90402 Nürnberg, Germany; ☎0911-22029; fax 0911-226009; e-mail info@mieterverein-nuernbe rg.de; website www.mieterverein-nu ernberg.de.

Brandenburg

Mieterbund Land Brandenburg e.V.: Schopenhauerstr. 31, D-14467 Potsdam, Germany; ☎0331-951 0890; fax 0331-951 0891; e-mail Mieterbund-Brandenburg@t-online.de.

Hessen

Deutscher Mieterbund Landesverband Hessen: Adelheidstrasse 70, D-65185 Wiesbaden, Germany; ☎0611-308 1719; fax 0611-378070; e-mail lv@mieterbund-hessen.de; website www.mieterbund-hessen.de.

Mecklenburg-Vorpommern

DMB Landesverband Mecklenburg-Vorpommern: Dr-Külz-Strasse 18, D-19053 Schwerin, Germany; ☎0385-712460; fax 0385-714669; e-mail information @mieterverein-schwerin.de; website www.mieterverein-schwerin.de.

Mieterverein Rostock: Kirchenplatz 4, D-18119 Rostock, Germany; ☎0381-51174; fax 0381-51175; e-mail post@mieterverein-rostock.de; website www.mieterverein-rostock.de.

Niedersachsen & Bremen

Deutscher Mieterbund Landesverband Niedersachsen-Bremen: Herrenstrasse 14, D-30159 Hannover, Germany; ☎0511-121060; fax 0511-121 0616; e-mail info@mieterbund-nieders-bremen.de; website www.mieterbund-nied-ers-bremen.de.

Mieterverein Bremen: An der Weide 23, D-28195 Bremen, Germany; ☎0421-320209; fax 0421-337 9208.

Mieterverein Bremerhaven: Fritz-Reuter-Str. 5-7, D-27576 Bremerhaven, Germany; ☎0471-954 9999; fax 0471-954 9940; e-mail info@miet erverein-bremerhaven.de; website www.mieterverein-bremerhaven.de.

Mieterverein Celle: Jägerstr. 24, D-29221 Celle, Germany; ☎05141-214404; fax 05141-214110; e-mail info@mie terverein-celle.de; website www.mie terverein-celle.de.

Mieterverein Hannover: Herrenstrasse 14, D-30159 Hannover, Germany; ☎0511-121060; fax 0511-121 0616; e-mail info@mieterverein-hannover.de; website www.mieterverein-hannover.de.

Nordrhein-Westfalen & Rheinland

Deutscher Mieterbund Nordrhein-Westfalen e.V.: Luisenstrasse 12, D-44137, Germany; ☎0231-149260; fax 0231-162722; e-mail mieter@deutscher-mieterbund-nrw.de; website www.deutscher-mieter-bund-nrw.de.

Rheinischer Mieterverband e.V.: Mühlenbach 49, D-50676 Köln, Germany; ☎0221-246118; fax 0221-240 2537.

Mieterverein Aachen und Umgebung e.V.: Oppenhoffallee 9-15, D-52066 Aachen, Germany; ☎0241-949790; fax 0241-949 7915.

Mieterverein Dortmund: Kampstr. 4, D-44137 Dortmund, Germany; ☎0231-557 6560; fax 0231-5576 5616; e-mail info@mieterverein-dortmund.de; website www.mieterverein-dortmund.de.

Mieterverein Köln: Mühlenbach 49, D-50676 Köln, Germany; ☎0221-202370; fax 0221-240 4620; e-mail mieterverein@netcologne.de.

Rheinland-Pfalz

Deutscher Mieterbund Landesverband Rheinland-Pfalz: Walramsneistrasse 8, D-5429 Trier, Germany; ☎0651-994 0970; fax 0651-994 0974; e-mail dmb-rhpl@gmx.de.

Mieterschutzverein Mainz: Kurfürstenstr. 8, D-55118 Mainz, Germany; ☎06131-613154; fax 06131-613152; e-mail info@mieterschutzverein-mainz.de; website www.mieterschutzverein-mainz.de.

Saarland

Deutscher Mieterbund Landesverband Saarland .e.V.: Karl-Mar-Strasse 1, D-66111 Saarbrücken, Germany; ☎0681-32148; fax 0681-32107; e-mail msaar@saarnet.de.

Sachsen

DMB Landesverband Sächsischer Mietervereine e.V.: Fürstenstr. 10, D-09130 Chemnitz, Germany; ☎0371-402 4097; fax 0371-402 4095.}

Mieterverein Dresden: Schäferstr. 42-44, D-01067 Dresden, Germany;

☎0351-866450; fax 0351-866 4511; e-mail mvd@arcormail.de.

Mieterverein Leipzig: Rosa-Luxemburg-Str. 19-21, D-04103 Leipzig, Germany; ☎0341-213 1277; fax 0341-213 1278; e-mail mieterverein-leipzig@t-online.de.

Sachsen-Anhalt

DMB Landesverband Sachsen-Anhalt e.V.: Alter Markt 6, D-06108 Halle, Germany; ☎0345-202 1467; fax 0345-202 1468; e-mail dmblvsachsa nhalt@aol.com.

Mieterverein Halle: Alter Markt 6, D-06108 Halle, Germany; ☎0345-292966; fax 0345-292 9689; e-mail mieterverein.ha lle@t-online.de.

Mieterverein Magdeburg: Otto-von-Guericke-Str. 6, D-39104 Magdeburg, Germany; ☎0391-561 9155; fax 0391-561 9156; e-mail mv.magdebur g@t-online.de.

Schleswig-Holstein

Deutscher Mieterbund Landesverband Schleswig-Holstein e.V.: Eggerstedtstr. 1, D-24103 Kiel, Germany; ☎0431-979190; fax 0431-979 1931; e-mail info@mieterbund-sch l e s w i g - h o l s t e i n . d e ; website www.mieterbund-schleswig-holstein.de. For Kiel's own mieterverein, the same address and phone details apply but use info@ kieler-mieterverein.de as the e-mail address.

Thüringen

Deutscher Mieterbund Landesverband Thüringen e.V.: Schillerstrasse 34, D-99096 Erfurt, Germany; ☎0361-598050; fax 0361-598 0520; e-mail MieterbundThuer@aol.com.

RENT AND PROPERTY PRICES

Below is the 2001 table of rent and purchase prices put together by the Association of German Estate Agents (*Verband Deutscher Makler für Grundbesitz, Hausverwaltung und Finanzierungen e.V.*: Riedemannweg 57, D-13627 Berlin; ☎030-38302528; fax 030-38302529; website www.vdm.de). This lists prices for flats and houses from a variety of cities and towns across Germany. These give some indication of the likely cost of housing and, on careful analysis, some clues as to how much accommodation is actually available to rent or buy. The table is divided fairly obviously into columns according to the type of accommodation available. The last two columns deserve special attention as they list the prices for building land **(A)** indicates building land for a family house, while **(B)** is building land for the construction of an apartment block or business premises which can then be rented out.

TABLE 4   RENT AND PROPERTY PRICES

City/Town	Flat Rental 70-80m² (€/m. sq.)	Flat Purchase 60-90m² (€/m. sq.)	Terraced House c. 100-140m² (in thousand €)	Detached 1 Family House 150-220m² (in thousand €)	Building Land (A) incl. service mains	Building Land (B) incl. service mains
Berlin	3-11	766-3,325	120-425	128-1,075	92-1,073	179-1,430
Dresden	2.5-7.67	770-2,810	122-255	175-410	50-410	50-410
Düsseldorf	5-10	1280-3,325	179-434	230-970	255-510	255-560
Frankfurt/Main	5-12	1,483-3,451	225-353	297-997	410-665	460-920
Hamburg	4-10	1,310-3,998	159-384	297-997	410-665	460-920
Köln	6-9	1,125-3,064	230-420	305-765	230-419	189-562
Leipzig	4-7	970-2,198	102-255	92-358	40-194	76-306
München	7-14	2300-5,625	203-767	460-1,790	511-920	511-1,227
Stuttgart	5-13	1,483-5,880	280-818	409-1,763	435-1,482	435-1,482

INSURANCE

In Germany it is vital to insure yourself and family with third party liability insurance (*Haftpflichtversicherung*). This is because under German law, should you or any member of your family be found guilty of 'ordinary negligence' you could lose everything, because there is no ceiling on the damages that could be awarded. Ordinary negligence can vary from someone falling on an icy pavement outside your building to the damage caused by a falling roof tile. The absence of a damages ceiling means that it is vital to take out *Haftpflichtversicherung* while living in Germany whether in rented or purchased accommodation. Apart from the insurance possibilities offered by the main German insurers, or any relocation agency that you engage, you can engage an insurance broker (*Versicherungsmakler/ in*) to obtain the best deal for you, one such is *Cathy J. Matz*: Hainstrasse 2, D-61476 Kronberg, Germany; ☎+49-(0)700 INSURE ME or 0700-46787363; fax 06173-4497; e-mail matz@insure-invest.de; www.insure-invest.de. An independent international insurance and investments advisor who's offices are based near to Frankfurt am Main. Full services available in English and German and a wide range of high quality products covering health, disability, life, liability, household, car and legal and animal insurance.

Apart from this 'damage limitation' insurance you will still need to cover your property and goods against theft, damage or loss, and likewise maintain the insurance on any property that you leave behind. If your goods are in storage then your storage company will probably have some form of liability cover against damage, or you may wish to save yourself this trouble by engaging a house-sitter, or letting your property out (see below) in which cases these options may well pay you while looking after anything that you don't take with you. One of the problems of leaving your home empty while you are away is that many insurance companies exclude water damage from policies in cases where property is empty for more than 30 days. While the insurance market has been soft in the past the climate variations that make storms or floods more frequent means that many companies are taking a harder line. The only way around this is to take out insurance with a specialist firm.

HOUSE SITTERS

Many families with homes who have to move abroad for work purposes find that one way of ensuring that their home and possessions are safe, is not to store them but to pay for house-sitters or even rent out their home and make some extra cash (see below). This certainly means that if you can not take furniture with you then at least you don't have to sell it or worry about it mouldering in storage. House sitters are also a useful bargaining tool when discussing your new situation with your insurers. Even if you empty all your furniture into storage and leave your own home empty while renting accommodation abroad, you run the risk of burst water pipes, squatters or vandals causing damage in your absence. Housesitters can save you money, Aylesbury based Homesitters have arranged up to 10% discounts on home insurance policies, and have a list of insurers and brokers with reductions available to their clients. Fees are usually calculated by the house sitting company on a daily basis. The house sitters are usually middle aged and have had extensive background checks carried out on them by the agencies.

However it is still necessary to exercise caution in this matter, any company which does not accept responsibility for its employees actions should be avoided, fidelity bonding which protects owners from rogue sitters is an assurance of risk cover and is offered by the best agencies.

For house sitting in America and Australia the situation is a little vaguer. In Australia house-sitters are arranged on a more personal and informal level, so it is up to the homeowner to screen sitters once they have found someone suitable. Many house-sitters are people looking to swap homes from one end of the continent for a holiday, while others are looking for short-term rent-free accommodation. The companies listed below are listed for information only and the author does not imply any approval or reccomendation by their inclusion.

Absentia: Little London, Berden, Bishop's Stortford, CM233 1BE; ☎01279-777412; website www.home-and-pets.co.uk. A national and international house-sitting company. Although the main operation is holiday house-sitting, arrangements can be made to look after your property should you have to move abroad before selling it, or if a property becomes vacant in your absence overseas. The sitters taken on to watch your house in these circumstances will therefore, remain until all the legal procedures of sale or probate are completed, giving you the reassurance that all is well in your absence.

The Australian House Sitters Directory: Southern Dynamics, PO Bo 2280 Gateshead, DC NSW 2290, Australia; ☎1800-502002; fax 1800-502003; website www.housesitters.com.au. This directory includes a guide to the house-sitting system with information on houseswaps and a directory of would-be sitters.

GlobalSitters: ☎1-800-682 5762; website www.globalsitters.com. This service provides an online directory of sitters to be contacted by homeowners, with listings arranged by zip/postal code.

Happy House Sitters: PO Bo 449 Caulfield East, Victoria 3145, Australia; ☎03-8500 2184 (local rate from other states 1300-780809); fax 03-9532 9837; website www.happyhousesitter.com.au.

Homesitters Ltd: Buckland Wharf, Aylesbury, HP22 5LQ; ☎01296-630730; fax 01296-631555; e-mail admin@homesitters.co.uk; website www.homesitters.co.uk. Homesitters was established in 1980 to provide a nationwide live-in housesitting service, available throughout the year, to care for homes, possessions and pets. The Homesitters, who are responsible mature homeowners, are carefully matched to clients' individual requirements and the company is well used to assisting at very short notice. The sitters are meticulously vetted and personally interviewed before being employed by the company; on sits they operate under the company's direction, with 24 hour backup and comprehensive insurance cover – including fidelity bonding. Norwich Union, Axa and Chubb are some of the insurers who will reduce policy premiums if a house sitter is used.

House Sitters: 1049 Terrace Drive, St Louis, MO 63117, USA; ☎314-781 4722; e-mail info@housesittersinc.com; website www.housesittersinc.com. Offer house, pet and plant care.

Sitterbyzip: website www.sitterbyzip.com. This is an online directory listing house and pet siiters by postal area, it offers support in five countries. However, the sitters post their own details and references.

Universal Aunts: PO Box 304, London, SW4 0NN; ☎020-7738 8937. In operation since 1921, this company will arrange sitters as necessary, depending on the owners requirements, for up to a year and possibly longer by arrangement. Their sitters will only leave the house for two hours a day to shop or walk any pets, and light garden maintenance (eg watering plants) is included in the daily rate. Sitters will undertake actual gardening on your behalf, and look after larger pets, even livestock, subject to negotiation.

LETTING YOUR PROPERTY

One way of helping towards the cost of your new accommodation in Germany is to rent out your own home; this has the added benefit of also covering your current mortgage costs without putting you to the time and trouble of selling before you leave and gives you somewhere to come back to when your assignment ends. If at the end you don't wish to return home then you can think of it as an investment, although of course you should check with the tax authorities with regard to your liability with regard to taxes in your home country.

In Britain if you are looking to let your property then you should check that the agent is a member of *ARLA* (*Association of Residential Letting Agents:* Maple House, Woodside Road, Amersham, HP6 6AA; ☎0845-345 5752; e-mail info@arla.co.uk; website www.arla.co.uk). ARLA members are required to employ ARLA qualified staff, hold separate client accounts and professional indemnity insurance and are covered by the unique ARLA bonding scheme. They will normally offer a full management service to landlords in addition to letting and rent collection. ARLA have an information hotline (01923-896555) which will help find an agent in a particular area of the UK, or there is a search engine on their website.

At present if an owner is not registered for UK taxes the agents have to retain funds as a provision for tax at source, but any interest on this money should be forwarded to the owner. Agency fees are usually around 10% for supervising letting and 15% for full property management. The differences between the two services are that the former is really just administering the collection of rent and arranging contracts, so that should there be any problems the tenants would be passed on to the landlords to deal with them. Full management essentially means that the agency acts as the landlord's representative, ideal for those landlords overseas. If any problems arise the agency will deal with them, hiring contractors or repairmen as necessary.

Chesterton Residential: 40 Connaught Street, London, W2 2AB; ☎020-7262 5060. Have 17 offices around London dealing with London area properties. Their Landlord's Information Pack contains details of services (including property management), rates and a London area rent guide.

Finders Keepers: Head Office, 226 Banbury Road, Oxford, OX2 7BY; ☎01865-311011; e-mail oford@finders.co.uk; website www.finders.co.uk. This property management agency has been specialising in quality property rentals for over 30 years. They are a member of the National Approved Letting Scheme and are bonded for lettings through the *National Association of Estate Agents*. They have a comprehensive property list and advice for tenants on their website. There are also offices in Swindon (☎01793-886200), Banbury (01295-27666), Abingdon (☎01235-535454), and Witney (☎01993-700150).

UTILITIES

It is important for anyone looking for accommodation in Germany to note that most rents do not include charges for water, gas, oil and electricity which are expensive commodities, all of which are metered so you only pay for what you use (or what you think you use, see below). In addition to natural gas, Germany also has substantial reserves of coal and lignite (*Braunkohle*). Oil accounts for 40%, Lignite supplies around 10% of the primary energy consumed and coal around 13%. However, coal is no longer a competitive resource and Germany subsidises its coal industry quite heavily, much of this subsidy comes from a levy on electricity consumers, the subsidy will continue until around 2005 and is set to drop over the years. Nuclear energy production is being discontinued and the plant are being slowly shut down.

Most local supply companies will have application forms (available at the *Einwohnermeldeamt*), so that new residents can inform them as quickly as possible, in order to maintain supplies. If this isn't the case look up *Stadtwerke* in the telephone book. The cards produced by one such local company in Nürnberg allows those moving in and moving out to arrange their supplies, not to mention reporting meter readings for billing. On the subject of which, it is worth noting that most Germans pay their domestic debts by a monthly debit direct from their bank accounts. These come under the general heading of *Nebenkosten* in most household accounts. These payments cover municipal rates for street sweeping and rubbish collection, as well as monthly payments to cover energy, water and sewerage bills. Of course some towns will have more expensive utilities than others. Thus in Berlin the average monthly expenditure on energy alone will be around €200 (these figures are based on moderate usage by a family of four, in a survey taken by the Economist Intelligence Unit), while in Frankfurt electricity, gas and water will cost €39.49 (£24.18/$34.62), €36.81 (£22.54/$32.26) and €35.79 (£21.91/$31.37) respectively; totalling €112.09 (£68.63/$98.25). Compared to these large cities, Nürnberg would appear to be nearer the average for a German town in its cost of c. €75 per month for all the services (this figure is based on the Nebenkosten of a family of five). Although the charges are deducted on a monthly basis, these deductions are based on an estimate of your usage, these estimates are either derived from meter readings or extrapolated from the size of your house and family calculated against use patterns. How often your meter is actually read will depend upon the practices of your local supplier, however, if you undershoot their estimates, you will either receive a rebate or be charged less for the next year.

Electricity

Electricity is supplied by regional networks which enjoy lucrative local monopolies, these can be small city based companies or big regional concerns of which *Eon, Bewag (Berliner-Kraft-und-Licht AG), RWE, Preussen Elektra* and *Bayernwerk* are examples; EU legislation also means that the energy market is open to non-German suppliers. Germany's electricity is 80% generated from conventional sources and 13% nuclear, with an increasing ratio of supplies (2.5%, up from 1.4% in 1990) coming from 'green' technologies. Around 19 nuclear power stations are currently in operation in Germany, and around 8,000 wind turbines.

Consumers can request free wiring checks and also buy recommended appliances from the company supplying their area. The electrical current is 220 volts AC, 50 cycles, two phase, and so only a little different to the UK's 240 volt supply but radically different to the 110 volt supply of the US & Canada. This means that appliances from the UK will work, albeit slightly sluggishly, while American ones won't. However, since there is a risk of damaging sensitive equipment designed for UK electrical specifications, it is important to seek the manufacturers' advice before importing such equipment for use in Germany. There is also the added hassle of having to change all your plugs or buy adapters for those items where the plug is integral with the power cable. Since German electrical equipment is renowned for its durability and high safety standards, it is better to buy your equipment once you are there. In Germany, electrical goods come with a plug of the continental two-pin type attached. Electric light sockets are for screw-type bulbs only.

Electricity is measured by an electricity meter which is usually black in colour and measures usage in kilowatt hours.

Gas

Germany has enough natural gas (*Erdgas*) to supply about a third of domestic needs. The rest is piped in from Holland and Russia. Like electricity, the gas market is run by private companies. Two of the largest are BASF and Ruhrgas. It was a consortium of gas companies with various European investors which began the Russo-German gas pipeline project in the 1980s. Gas is metered by the cubic meter and your gas meter will either be painted yellow or have yellow connections to the supply pipe.

Water

All German houses have water meters fitted as standard and water is charged for each month by the cubic metre used. In addition to this there is a separate charge for sewerage, the rates for which are charged as a set annual fee per person. The costs are per cubic metre for water, plus 7% VAT, without VAT for sewerage.

Telephones

Obtaining a phone line from Deutsche Telekom involves an installation fee of around €50 including VAT. If you take over the previous tenant's telephone number the connection charge drops to about half that. Private lines can usually be installed within two weeks of application in most parts of western Germany, with basic rental and bills rendered monthly. More details can be found in the next chapter. To arrange a phone line or buy a new unit drop in to the *T-Punkt* in the nearest shopping centre or post office.

REMOVALS

While those readers moving to Germany for only a short while can get by with renting a furnished apartment, those beginning long term settlement and employment, especially those taking their family with them will have to ship or store almost all their goods, unless they can afford to run two homes, or wish to rent out their home and furniture.

However much of your furniture and household goods you wish, or can afford, to take with you to Germany you will need a good removal firm to ship them for you. Lists of these can be obtained from professional associations such as AMSA (*American Moving and Storage Association*), AFRA (*Australian Furniture Removers Association*), BAR (*British Association of Removers*), FEDEMAC, or FIDI (*International Federation of International Furniture Removers/Fédération Internationale des Déménageurs Internationaux*). FIDI is a network of over 750 companies worldwide, with membership criteria covering financial and operational structure, members have trained staff (with an emphasis on overseas moving) and specialist insurance cover. Nearly all moving companies displaying the FIDI logo are members of an approved national moving association. *FEDEMAC e.V.* represents around 3,460 professional moving companies in 13 European countries, working towards the harmonisation of working methods, quality standards, training and co-operation within the Moving industry. *The British Association of Removers* have an International

Removers list (also available online), if you contact them with an outline of what you'd like to move they will send you a list of up to 3 companies in your area who are capable of meeting your requirements, which you can then contact for an estimate or more detailed discussion. Or you can pick a company by studying advertisements or surfing the internet.

Professional Associations

American Moving and Storage Association: 1611 Duke Street, Alexandria, VA 22314, USA; ☎703-683 7410; fax 703-683 7527; e-mail amconf@amconf.org; website www.mover.org.

Australian Furniture Removers Association: P.O. Box 7104, Baulkham Hills Business Centre, NSW 2153, Australia; ☎1800 671 806; e-mail admin@afra.com.au; website www.afra.com.au.

The British Association of Removers: 3 Churchill Court, 58 Station Road, North Harrow, HA2 7SA; ☎020-8861 3331; fax 020-8861 3332; e-mail info@bar.co.uk; website www.bar.co.uk.

FEDEMAC e.V./The Federation of European Movers Associations: Schulstrasse 53, D-65795 Hattersheim, Germany; ☎06190-989811; fax 06190-989820; e-mail fedemac.troska@web.de; website www.fedemac.com.

International Federation of International Furniture Removers/Fédération Internationale des Déménageurs Internationaux: 69 Rue Picard B5, B-1080 Brussels, Belgium; ☎+32-2-426 51 60; fax +32-2-426 55 23; e-mail fidi@fidi.com; website www.fidi.com.

Movers

Allied Pickfords: Heritage House, 345 Southbury Road, Enfield, Middlesex EN1 1UP; ☎0800-289 229; www.allied-pickfords.co.uk (UK) www.alliedintl.com (USA). Can arrange storage and shipment of all types of personal effects, including moving furniture and pets to all parts of Germany. Shipping requirements are discussed in a personal visit and a full packing service is offered.

Capital Worldwide: Kent House, Lower Stone Street, Maidstone ME15 6LH; ☎01622-766380; website www.capital-worldwide.com.

Classic International Inc.: 1674 Broadway, Suite 802, New York, NY 10019, USA; website www.classicinternatio nal.com.

Crown Worldwide Movers: Security House, Abbey Wharf Industrial Estate, Kingsbridge Road, Barking Essex IG11 0BT; ☎020-8591 3388; fax 020-8594 4571.

Crown Worldwide Moving & Storage: 2070 Burroughs Avenue, PO Box 5577, San leandro, CA 94577, USA; ☎800-669 3869 or 510-895 5080; fax 510-614 4100; website www.crownms.com.

Interdean Interconnex: Central Way, Park Royal, London, NW10 7XW; ☎020-8961 4141; fax 020-8965 4484; e-mail id.icx@interdeaninterc onex.com; website www.interdeanin terconex.com.

Interdean Interconnex Inc.: 17120 Vally View Avenue, La Mirada, CA 90638-5828, USA; ☎562-921 0939; fax 562-926 0918; website www.inte rdeaninterconex.com.

Marlog USA Inc.: 1800 W. Walnut Parkway, Los Angeles, CA 90220, USA; ☎310-669 9138; fax 310-669 9108;

e-mail usa@marlogcargo.com; website www.marlogcargo.com. Marlog have offices across the USA and world.

Trans International: 9 Goulburn Street, Kings Park Industrial Estate, Kings Park, Sydney, NSW 2148, Australia; ☎02-9671 1166; fax 02-9671 1666; website www.transInternat ional.com.au. Melbourne Office: 202-228 Greens Road, Dandenong, Melbourne, VIC 3190, Australia; ☎03-9797 1414; fax 03-9797 1449.

Trans International (New Zealand): 8 Lockhart Place, Mt Wellington, P O Box 12355, Penrose, Auckland, New Zealand; ☎09-276 7999; fax 09-276 1149.

Customs Regulations Regarding Household Effects

Since 1993 British and other EU citizens have been able to move household effects around Europe without any customs documentation, although just in case you are stopped on a spot check it is always handy to have proof that you are taking up residence or beginning a job in Germany.

For non-EU nationals the requirements are more stringent. You will have to prove that:

O You have actually given up your usual residence abroad (e.g. by means of documents showing the sale of your home or contract of employment with a German employer).

O You are establishing a new residence in Germany (e.g. lease agreement)

O You have lived outside Germany for at least 12 consecutive months Exemption from custom duties is granted only for those goods you have been using abroad, personally or professionally, for at least 6 months and which you will continue to use in Germany for another 12 months.

Redirecting Post

If you are moving house to Germany then there is unlikely to be anyone to forward your post for you, should you accidentally forget to inform anyone of your new address. Or if your stay is not for very long you may find it easiest to just have your post redirected. This option solves both long and short-term mail forwarding problems and saves you having to send out lots of change of address notes to friends, family, book clubs etc. British readers can have their post forwarded to them by the Royal Mail's Redirection Service, this service can be arranged either by filling in the leaflet available at Post Offices, which includes a pre-paid envelope; or you can apply on 08457-777888 (calls charged at local rate), if you wish to pay by credit card. Redirection is available for one, three or twelve months (costing between £12 and £60 at time of writing) and will begin from one week after your application.

CARS & MOTORCYCLES

Importing or Buying Locally

If you are intending to live in Germany for longer than one year you may import a motor vehicle that has been registered in your name for at least six months in your previous country of residence duty free, EU nationals are exempt from duty anyway. However, German safety and anti-pollution laws for motor vehicles are some of the most stringent in Europe and, depending on the vehicle, may necessitate costly modifications.

Bear in mind that Germany and Europe drive on the right. The left lane is for passing/overtaking, the right lane is for driving. There is more information on driving in Germany in the next chapter.

Apart from registering the vehicle with the local authorities it must also be inspected within 90 days by the Technical Inspection Authority (TÜV). Seat belts are mandatory for all passengers, although exceptions have been made for older makes of vehicle; if you find that seat belts can be retro-fitted to your car you should do so. It is also illegal for under-12s to sit in the front of any motor vehicle and child seats should be of an approved make. Compulsory items such as warning triangles and first-aid kits should ideally be purchased in Germany to ensure that they are of the required specifications. For instance the German first-aid kit must include impermeable gloves as an anti-HIV precaution.

American readers can contact (in writing) an office of the TÜV in Michigan for information on conversions (*TUV Rheinland of North America Inc.:* Automotive Technology, 32553 Schoolcraft Road, Suite 100, Livionia, MI 48150, USA; website www.us.tuv.com). You will need to provide the make and type, (for cars include body form) and year of the vehicle and a check to cover a processing fee.

Another reason for buying locally is that there are considerable savings to be made on the prices of a BMW, Mercedes or Porsche, especially with the current state of the Euro against Sterling and the US dollar. Sales tax is 16% in Germany against the 17.5% of British VAT. Buying a German model also means that your car has the driver's seat on the correct side of the car for driving on German roads. The prices on the cars themselves may not look 'cheap', but despite German trading law they can be reduced somewhat. Cash payment means a 3% reduction in the price and trading in your old car in will help too. The used car market may actually have a lot of high-quality stock, not just because most Germans are keen to look after their cars. Car manufacturers allow staff to buy at a discount and sell on after a year (hence the term to look for is *Jahreswagen*) alternatively you may find that the dealer has a test drive vehicle *Vorführwagen* which will be in nearly new condition. Cars can be bought used through dealers or privately via the adverts in specialist magazines or the classified columns of the local paper. If buying through a dealer they will usually handle all the registration paperwork but if buying privately from a small ad. then it is up to you; registering is dealt with in the next section.

Finally readers should note that a second-hand/used beige Mercedes may seem like a bargain, but as these provide the bulk of the German taxi fleets unless you get it repainted you'll have people flagging you down.

Licensing, Car Tax and Vehicle Inspection

If your residence in Germany is temporary (less than one year) British readers may drive on a British registration for that period. Others may import their car using a German translation of their registration documents, although the cost of shipping a vehicle from the US or Australia make this an expensive luxury. Cars in Germany should be licensed by the German licensing authority (*Zulassungsbehörde*). Motor vehicle tax (*Kraftfahrzeugsteuer* shortened to *KFZ-Steuer*) will also need to be paid. The local vehicle registration office (*Kfz.-Zulassungsbehörde*) will be listed under local council offices in the phone book and will advise you on the papers you will need to re-register your car for German licence plates. These will usually be proofs of ownership/vehicle log-book (*Kraftfahrzeugbrief*) and insurance *Kraftfahrz eugversicherung*; third party liability insurance is mandatory. The registration charge (*Zulassungsgebühr*) is currently €30, while the motor vehicle tax varies according to engine size and emissions levels. Licence/registration plates stay with the vehicle until it is sold or the owner moves out of that particular registration area. The letters and logos on the plates indicate the city or district of registration and the TUV inspection date (see below).

Some new cars entering Germany may need to pass type-approval tests, to ensure that it complies with EU safety and technical regulations. For information on whether or not your vehicle needs type approval contact the Federal Motor Transport Authority (*Kraftfahrt Bundesamt*), Fördestrasse 16, D-24944 Flensburg.

Every two years (if not a special vehicle), the vehicle must have a mechanical inspection carried out by a Technical Supervisory Agency (eg *Technischer Überwachungsverein* TÜV or DEKRA). The same agencies are now required to perform an anti-pollution vehicle emissions test (*ASU*) which is carried out yearly, ideally in the same month as the TUV is due even though it is a separate examination of the car. Before taking your car for its TÜV its wise to have it checked by a reputable garage; make sure that you have the approved first aid kit and safety equipment in the car, and don't forget your papers (*Fahrzeugschein*). Once inspected, if passed, a disc will be placed on the rear registration plate, which will note the expiry date of the certification.

Driving Licences (Führerschein)

Drivers entering Germany are allowed to drive on their current licence for up to six months, after which they must obtain a German licence – a process which involves written and practical examinations at an approved driving school before obtaining a licence from the issuing office (*Stadtverwaltung: Führerscheinstelle*) for the region. Driving exams can be taken in German or English, but this is a case of finding the right driving school. There are exceptions to this requirement for EU citizens and drivers who obtained their licences in certain parts of the USA and Canada. If you will only be staying for up to 364 days you may also continue driving on your current licence, proof of the length of your stay should be shown to the licence office at the sixth month point.

In Germany it is also a requirement that you carry your drivers licence and vehicle registration documents/log book (*Fahrzugschein/Kraftfahrzeugbrief*) with you when driving. Further information on driving in Germany can be found in Chapter Four (*Driving*).

Licences for EU Nationals. Since 1996 a standardised pink driving licence has been adopted across the EU/EEA, drivers holding this who change their residence within the EU no longer have to exchange their licence for the local version after 12 months. Licences issued in one member country will be valid in all the others until expiry (even if it is an old national licence). The new EU licences are divided up into categories according to which type of vehicle you are licenced to drive, in Germany some of these categories require the driver to undergo a medical examination in order to qualify, and this will apply to expatriate drivers even if their home state does not require a medical for that category of licence.

Licences for Americans and Canadians. Drivers from those parts of the USA and Canada that have reciprocal agreements with Germany are exempt from the requirement to pass German driving exams, although they will have to apply for the German licence. To do so they will need a certified translation of their current licence, these can be obtained at ADAC (the main German automobile club; see the motoring section in the next chapter) and insurance offices and other documents (see box). A list of states that issue driving licences acceptable to German driving law can be obtained from embassies, consulates and websites such as www.fuehrerschein.net, http://berlininfo.com and the American Chamber of Commerce. The only Canadian province without such an agreement with Germany is Manitoba.

Those Americans and Canadians who obtained their licences in states or provinces without reciprocal arrangements may have to take either one or both tests before applying for a German licence.

To obtain a German licence the following documents will need to be taken to the *Führerscheinstelle*:

> ○ Passport or identity card
> ○ Residence registration certificate
> ○ Original driving licence with certified translation
> ○ Two passport photos (signed on reverse)
> ○ Sometimes you may also need to provide a statement that the licence
>   is still valid, or the results of a recent eye test.

Other Nationalities

Drivers from the rest of the world will find it more difficult to obtain a licence. First they will have to enrol at a driving school and then apply to transfer their licence. For this they will need the documents, translations and copies of the documents listed in the box below.

> ○ Passport
> ○ Residence registration certificate
> ○ Original driving licence with certified translation
> ○ Passport photo (signed on reverse)
> ○ Proof of an eye test taken within the last two years
> ○ Proof of completion of the *Sofortmassnahmen am Unfallort* first-aid course

The licence office will (after a period of a month or so) confirm that you may take the driving exams. Once these are passed you should take the exam certificate and your passport back to the licence office to have your *Führerschein* issued.

Car Insurance

Car insurance in Germany is expensive. The various premiums are calculated using the following criteria:

- ○ The period for which the driver has held a licence and for how long he or she has been accident-free.
- ○ The classification of the car into a class (*Typentarif*) according to the average frequency of damage to that car model.
- ○ The area in which the owner of the car resides.
- ○ The proportion of each claim which will be paid by the owner.

These points mean essentially that young drivers in cities may pay up to eight times as much as older drivers in rural areas (according to the drivers' age, make of car and 'no claims bonus').

In Germany, it is compulsory to have third party insurance. Fully comprehensive insurance also covers fire, theft and damage, but this and other types of insurance are optional. No-claims bonuses accrued with British car insurance companies will be taken into account by German insurance companies when setting premiums for UK citizens resident in Germany. The same is true for drivers from the USA and Canada as good driving records can be transferred over when arranging insurance: if the agent says they can't then find another agent. You should therefore obtain confirmation of any such bonuses or credit from your insurer. Cars registered in Germany have to be insured with a third-party liability insurer 'registered' in Germany. On the plus side insurance premiums are a tax deductible expense.

IMPORTING PETS TO GERMANY

Most removal firms and relocators can give you all the help and advice needed to take pets with you to Germany. The base guidelines can be found in EU Regulations 92/65/EC and 90/425/EC which have been passed into German Law as the *Binnenmarkt-Tiersüchen-Schutzverordnung* and these also cover the import of American pets into Germany.

Dogs and cats being imported to Germany must be vaccinated against rabies at least 30 days and not more than 12 months before landing. In the case of dogs and cats vaccinated before the age of three months the validity of the rabies vaccination certificate is three months. Re-vaccinations must have occurred within 12 months of the previous vaccination. Vaccination certificates supplied by a veterinarian, or International Vaccination certificates should be provided and accompanied by a certified translation, seals and stamps should include the veterinarian's address. Full details of the requirements can be obtained from the Land veterinary ministry you are travelling to.

You can bring your pet back into the UK without entering quarantine as long as you follow the rules laid down by the UK *Department of Food, Environment and Rural Affairs* (DEFRA) in the Pets Travel Scheme (PETS). It does, however, take at least seven months from the initial insertion of a microchip and rabies injection before you can get a re-entry certificate from your vet.

With birds and other animals certificates of good health are needed. The UK Department of Food, Environment and Rural Affairs (DEFRA) can provide forms for specific countries. If you are thinking of exporting animals other than cats and dogs the PETS Helpline will give you the number of the section you need to call.

If you are bringing a pet from the United States, then vaccination against rabies is necessary, unless it is under three months old. There is an online club (www.takeyourpet.com) for US residents who want to take their pets abroad.

Independent Pet and Animal Transportation Association International Inc members around the world can arrange for transportation of animals and advise on local rules. The *International Air Transport Association* rules on animal transport can be found at: www.iata.org/cargo/live.htm.

DANGEROUS DOGS

Before travelling with your pet you are advised to that 47 breeds are regarded as generally or potentially dangerous in Germany. Four breeds: Pitbull Terriers, Bull Terriers, American Staffordshire Terriers and Staffordshire Bull Terriers are banned outright. Details of the breeds considered dangerous can be obtained from embassies, consulates, and the Land *Innenministerium* or *Staatsministerium des Innern*. The latter can advise on specific local regulations and lists. An example is NordRhein-Westfalen where dogs that reach a shoulder height of over 16 inches/40cm or a weight of over 44 pounds/20Kg at maturity are subject to dangerous dog regulations.

Useful Addresses

Department for the Environment, Food and Rural Affairs: Nobel House, 17 Smith Square, London, SW1P 3JR. PETS Helpline ☎0870-241 1710; ☎020-7238 6000 (switchboard); fax 020 7238 6591; website www.defra.gov.uk.

Bundesministerium für Verbraucherschutz, Ernhrung und Landwirtschaft (BMVEL) (Federal Ministry of Consumer Protection,Food and Agriculture): Rochusstrasse 1, D-53123 Bonn, Germany; ☎0228-5290; fax 0228-529 4262; website www.verbra ucherministerium.de/.

The Independent Pet and Animal Transportation Association International, Inc.: Holly Lake Ranch, Route 5, Box 747, Highway 2869, Big Sandy, Texas 75755 USA; ☎903-769 2267; fax 903-769 867; e-mail info@ipata.com; website www.ipata.com.

Takeyourpet.com: Net Publishing LLC, 9612 E Aspen Hill Cir, Littleton CO 80124, USA; ☎(toll-free) 800-790 5455; fax 303-662 1241; e-mail general@takeyourpet.com; website takeyourpet.com.

Dogs in Germany

Once in Germany, dogs have to be kept on a lead in parks or wherever signs indicate that this is necessary. As a general rule, fighting dogs must be muzzled in public places, and most Germans 'poop-scoop', and will expect you to do so too, in built up areas. For dogs, an annual registration at the Town Hall is required. This *Hundesteuer* is similar to the Dog Licence in Britain, except that rates are set by individual town or city councils. These are generally higher in more built up areas, and while the fee increases with the number of dogs you have the increases are less than you may expect and some cities charge a single flat rate. Vetinary Surgeons (*Tierärzte*), can be found through the yellow pages, but many people prefer personal recommendation.

Dog & Cat Health Insurance

Should your pets be in good health and under 5 years old it may be advantageous to purchase pet health insurance, as the cost of veterinary bills is relatively high in Germany.

Dog Liability Insurance. When you bring a dog(s) to Germany, it is essential to purchase separate dog liability insurance as it is not included in your regular family insurance. 'Fighting dogs' are uninsurable in Germany. To help you to get an idea of the costs of insuring your pets whilst in Germany, you can obtain a quote ahead of time from insurers such as Cathy J. Matz (Hainstrasse 2, D-61476 Kronberg, Germany; ☎0700 INSURE ME or ☎0700-46787363; fax 06173-4497; e-mail matz@insure-invest.de; website www.insure-invest.de) an independent, international insurance advisor offering a service in both English and German.

DAILY LIFE

CHAPTER SUMMARY

- Anyone intending to live in Germany will find speaking some German essential even though English is taught as a second language in German schools.

- **Education:** German school and university places are provided free of charge.

    - There are a large number of international schools catering for the expat community.

- **Transport:** Germany's road network is one of the world's best.

    - By reputation speed limit free, the *autobahnen* do in fact have areas of speed restriction based on road conditions and there is a recommended maximum of 130kph.

    - Germany has an impressive network of urban and rural trains, trams and buses.

    - There is also an excellent high speed cross country train network, the ICE.

- **Taxation:** almost half a worker's gross pay is deducted at source to pay for public services, church upkeep, medical and pension insurance.

- **Banking:** The network of banks and financial institutions is extensive but charges are levied on accounts.

- **Shopping:** Shop opening hours are restricted by law to protect staff from overwork, and observe religious holidays.

    - Shopping with credit/debit cards is still quite rare, even in large city stores; the EC debit card is accepted more than any other.

    - Sales Tax or VAT is 16%.

Moving to a new country gives rise to one set of problems: the red-tape, finding a home, moving your goods. Living there presents the newcomer with another, subtler, set. The little nuances of daily life and the habits and rituals of shopping, banking and even catching the bus are now a challenge. This chapter is intended to supply sufficient practical information for the reader to get to grips with their new home as quickly as possible. However as Germany is a nation of federal states regional variations will occur, and things may change over the life of this book, so not all the information is uniformly applicable. As in any endeavour being properly prepared will make life easier, whether this means attending a training course, or immersing yourself in all things German at your local library, or by surfing German related websites. However, there are other ways to deal with this and the Embassies and Consulates will have an information office from which you can find out more about Germany if the other options are closed to you.

BE PREPARED

INFORMATION RESOURCES

A good starting point for information is the German Tourist Office in your home country for a supply of maps, transport information and brochures. The German National Tourist Office in London has a premium rate phone line for ordering brochures. German maps are of a very high standard and are widely available through specialist stores and bookshops, amongst the most widely stocked are Kümmerly and Frey whose range includes a very detailed 1:500,000 one sheet map. In the UK Stanfords in London have an up-to-date selection of maps ranging in price according to the publisher and scale.

Alternatively you may want to visit one of the *Goethe Instituts* who have many centres around the world, and whose aim is to disseminate information about Germany and German culture (see below).

Other useful information to prepare you for your new life can be found on the internet, either specific information relevant to your new home from the various Federal or Länder government websites (see the *Regional Guide*), these are the best for raw data, but there are many informal ones which give an 'on the ground' view of life there and the expat ones are obviously full of information pertinent to your experience. The latter range from sites full of factual and experiential essays to newsgroups where you can hook up and 'chat' with those who've gone through the hoops already.

Many German newspapers and magazines are available outside Germany at larger newsagents, airport newsstands, college libraries, or even online (in German that is). So it is worthwhile checking out the availability of papers to prepare yourself for the presentation of news in Germany. Some are available on by subscription. In the UK this can be arranged through your local newsagent (and their supplier, probably WH Smith) while in the US, *German Language Publishing Inc*, can arrange subscriptions to three magazines and seven newspapers, details of which can be found in the section on *Media & Communications*. Full details of cost

and which daily issues can be supplied are obtainable from GLP's website.
The German publication *Deutschland* is a useful read providing news and information on Germany society and culture in a bi-monthly magazine published in 14 languages and distributed in 180 countries.

Useful Addresses:

Deutschland Frankfurter Societäts-Druckerei GmbH, Frankenalle 71-81, D-60327 Frankfurt/Main, Germany; ☎069-7501 4274; fax 069-7501 4502; e-mail vertrieb.deutschland@fsd.de; website www.magazine-deutschland.de.

German National Tourist Office (UK): PO Box 2695, London W1A 3TN; ☎020-7317 0908. 24 hour Brochure Order Line 09001-600 100 (60 pence per minute); e-mail gntolon@d-z-t.com; website www.germany-tourism.de (multilingual).

German National Tourist Office: PO Box A980, Sydney, NSW 2000, Australia; ☎02-9267 8148; fax 02-9267 9035.

German National Tourist Office (Canada): P.O. Box 65162, Toronto, Ontario M4K 3Z2, Canada; ☎877-315 6237. The US website seems to cover Canada too.

German National Tourist Office (USA): 122 East 42nd Street, New York, NY 10168-0072, USA; ☎212-661 7200; fax 212-661 7174; e-mail gntony@aol.com; website www.visits-to-germany.com.

German Language Publishing Inc: 153 South Dean Street, Inglewood, NJ 07631, USA; ☎800-457 4443; e-mail info@glpnews.com; website glpnews.com.

Edward Stanford Ltd: 12-14 Long Acre, Covent Garden, London WC2E 9LP; ☎020-7836 1321; website www.stanfords.co.uk.

SOME USEFUL WEBSITES:

AcrossFrontiers: www.acrossfrontiers.com. Engaging 'new media' products deliver the culture, country and business knowledge epats need to successfully travel, do business and live overseas.

American Citizens Abroad: www.aca.ch ACA is a nonprofit association dedicated to serving and defending the interests of individual US citizens living worldwide. For only $35/year you can become an individual member and get the latest print and electronic information on taxes, citizenship, voting and the census.

EscapeArtist.com: www.escapeartist.com. Expatriate resources and resources for Americans fleeing America, or anyone moving abroad, in a database of expatriate resources, embassies, international jobs and offshore financial services. Has a magazine on moving to other countries covering Jobs Overseas – Lifestyles – Opportunities – Homesteading – and Investments for anyone running away to home.

Expatica: www.epatica.com. The number one English-language news and information source for epats living in France, Germany and Holland.
Expat Access: www.expataccess.com. A very useful resource.
Expat Exchange: their peer network is www.expatexchange.com. Founded in 1997, this network has become the largest online community for English-speaking expatriates. Comprised of over 140 country and topic networks that can be accessed for FREE, the community has supported over 500,000 expats through all phases of the expatriation and repatriation process. Their goal is to build the most useful online pool of resources for individuals living outside of their country.
Expat Forum: www.expatforum.com. Expat chat.
Expatnetwork www.expatnetwork.com An expatriate community web site with overseas jobs, international contract news and an online magazine.
Homesick: www.homesick.com.au. The site for expat Australians.
Overseas Digest: www.overseasdigest.com. Articles on living abroad from an American perspective.
TCK World: www.tckworld.com Dedicated to the support of 'third culture kids' the children of expats whether their parents be businesspeople, missionaries, civil or military service.
The Voyage: www.the-voyage.com. A bi-lingual website aimed at the children of British expats.

TRAINING COURSES

Another option to prepare yourself for your new life is to attend a training course; there are many of these available, some run by educational charities, or organisations engaged in promoting Germany, while others are run by businesses.

One such is Farnham Castle International Briefing & Conference Centre, which provides a comprehensive range of programmes in support of international business people and their families. Programmes include scheduled and customised country briefings for individuals, partners and children for any destination, providing up to date information and practical advice on every issue faced when moving to a new country; business briefings for all major countries and regions; cross cultural awareness workshops; cross cultural communication and negotiation skills and intensive tuition in any language.

Farnham Castle, International Briefing & Conference Centre: Farnham Castle, Farnham, Surrey, GU9 0AG; ☎01252-721194; fax 01252-719277; e-mail info@farnhamcastle.com; website www.farnhamcastle.com.

THE GOETHE INSTITUT-INTERNATIONES

The main German cultural society worldwide is the Goethe Institut a non-profit organization with 128 institutes in 76 countries and 15 institutes in Germany. Its task is to promote the German language and to foster international cultural cooperation. The Head Office is located in Munich, the New York office functions as the regional institute for the United States, Canada and Mexico coordinating the 11 institutes in the North Americas. The Institut supports a wide range of international cultural exchange and educational programmes in the arts, humanities, sciences and technology.

Teaching German as a foreign language involves learning about German life and culture as an integral part of the language course.

The information centre and libraries provide comprehensive information about contemporary Germany with access to about thousands of books, numerous newspapers and periodicals as well as audio-visual materials.

Addresses:

Goethe Institut Inter Nationes (UK): 50 Princes Gate, Exhibition Road, London SW7 2PH; ☎020-7596 4000; fax 020-7594 0240; e-mail mail@london.goethe.de; website www.goethe.de/london.
Glasgow: 3 Park Circus, Glasgow, G3 6AX, Scotland; ☎0141-332 2555; fax 0141-333 1630; e-mail mail@glasgow.goethe.de; website www.goethe.de/glasgow.
Manchester: Churchgate House, 56 Oxford Street, Manchester, M1 6EU; ☎0161-237 1077; fax 0161-237 1079; website www.goethe.de/manchester.

Goethe Institut Inter Nationes (Australia):
Melbourne: 448 St. Kilda Road, Melbourne, VIC 3004, Australia; ☎3-9864 8999; fax 3-9864 8988; e-mail pfranz@goethe.edu.au; website www.goethe.de/melbourne. The Melbourne office covers Victoria, Tasmania, South Australia and Western Australia.
Sydney: PO Box 37, Woollahra, NSW 1350, Australia; ☎2-8356 8333; fax 2-8356 8314; e-mail gi-syd@goethe.org.au; website www.goethe.de/sydney.
The Sydney offices serve New South Wales, ACT, Queensland and Northern Territory.

Goethe Institut Inter Nationes (Canada):
Montréal: 418, rue Sherbrooke Est, Montréal, Québec, H2L 1J6, Canada; ☎514-499 0159; fax 514-499 0905; e-mail goethe-institut.montreal@ uqam.ca; website www.goethe.de/ montreal.
Ottawa, (Branch of Montréal): 47 Clarence Street, Suite 480, Ottawa, Ontario, K1N 9K1, Canada; ☎613-241 0273; fax 613-241 9790; e-mail goethe@storm.ca. These institut offices serve the provinces of Québec, New Brunswick, Newfoundland, Nova Scotia, and Prince Edward Island.
Toronto: 163 King St. West, Toronto, Ontario M5H 4C6, Canada; ☎416-593 5257; fax 416-593 5145; e-mail mainoffice@goethetor.org; website www.goethe.de/toronto. The Goethe-Institut in Toronto serves Ontario, Manitoba, and Saskatchewan.

Goethe-Institut Inter Nationes (Ireland):
Dublin: 37 Merrion Square, Dublin 2, Ireland; ☎01-661 1155; fax 01-661 1358. Language Department: 62 Fitzwilliam Square, Dublin-2, Ireland; ☎01-661 8506; fax 01-676 2213; e-mail admin@goethe.iol.ie; website www.goethe.de/dublin.

Goethe Institut Inter Nationes (New Zealand):

Goethe-Institut Inter Nationes Wellington: 150 Cuba Street, PO Box 9253, Wellington, New Zealand; ☎4-385 6924; fax 4-385 6883; e-mail wellington@goethe.org.nz; website www.goethe.de/an/wellington.

Goethe Institut Inter Nationes (USA):

Atlanta: Colony Square, Plaza Level, 1197 Peachtree Street, NE Atlanta, GA 30361-2401, USA; ☎404-892 2388; Language Department 404-892 2316; fax 404-892 3832; e-mail goetheatlanta@mindspring.com; website www.goethe.de/atlanta. The Goethe-Institut Atlanta serves the following states: Alabama, Florida, Georgia, Mississippi, North Carolina, South Carolina, and Tennessee.

Boston: 170 Beacon Street, Boston, MA 02116, USA; ☎617-262 6050; fax +1-617-262 2615; website www.goethe.de/boston. The Boston institute serves: Connecticut, Maine, Massachusetts, New Hampshire, Rhode Island, and Vermont.

Chicago: 150 North Michigan Avenue, Suite 200, Chicago, IL 60601, USA; ☎312-263 0472; Language Department 312-263 0474; fax 312-263 0476; e-mail gibibl@interaccess.com; website www.goethe.de/chicago. Chicago serves the states of Illinois, Indiana, Iowa, Kansas, Kentucky, Michigan, Minnesota, Missouri,

Nebraska, North Dakota, Ohio, South Dakota, and Wisconsin.

Los Angeles: 5750 Wilshire Blvd. £100, Los Angeles, CA 90036, USA; ☎323-525 3388; fax 323-934 3597; e-mail gila@artnet.net; website www.goethe.de/losangeles. The Goethe-Institut Los Angeles serves Arizona and Southern California.

New York: 1014 Fifth Avenue, New York, NY 10028, USA; ☎212-439 8700 (Language Department 212-439 8684; Language Courses in Germany 212-439 8685); fax 212 439-8705; e-mail admin@goethe-newyork.org; website www.goethe.de/newyork.

San Francisco: 530 Bush Street, San Francisco, CA 94108, USA; ☎415-263 8760 (Language Department 415-263 8761); fax 415-391 8715; e-mail language@goethe-sf.org; website www.goethe.de/sanfrancisco. The Goethe-Institut in San Francisco serves the states of: Northern California, Colorado, Hawaii, Nevada, Utah. In addition the language department covers Southern California.

Washington: 814 Seventh Street, NW Washington, DC 20001-3718, USA; ☎202-289 1200; fax 202-289 3535; e-mail info@washington.goethe.org (Language Classes in Germany lnaumann@washington.goethe.org); website www.goethe.de/washington. Washington's institute covers the following states: Delaware, District of Columbia, Maryland, Virginia, and West Virginia.

ANGLO-GERMAN SOCIETIES

If you haven't been able to prepare using the previous options, then before actually leaving for Germany it is a good idea to find out if any German clubs and societies exist in your country or even area as these organise various social events and seminars will help to soften the blow of culture shock on your arrival in Germany, allowing you to develop potentially useful contacts in the expat community before you get to Germany. Addresses of such societies can be found in your local library or information centre or you can contact the Cultural Department of the German Embassy which should be able to supply a list of such societies.

The *British-German Association* (34 Belgrave Square, London SW1X 8QB; ☎020-7235 1922; fax 020-7235 1902; e-mail BGALondon@compuserve.com; website www.britishgermanassociation.org) exists to promote friendship between the two countries. They arrange social events, seminars and study trips to Germany. There are 60 affiliated organisations in the UK which you can contact through the association or its quarterly magazine *British German Review*.

For businessmen and students there is also the *Anglo-German Foundation for the Study of Industrial Society* (17 Bloomsbury Square, London WC1A 2NH; ☎020-7404 3137; fax 020-7405 2071; website www.agf.org.uk), which aims to support bi-lateral research and links between academics and industry.

THE GERMAN LANGUAGE

The main drawback of moving to Germany is having to learn a new language, and German has a fiendishly complicated grammar with many variations and exceptions. Some of the main hazards include gender and case endings of nouns (similar to Latin) and immensely long sentences or compound words. One famous and often cited opinion on this trait of the language is Mark Twain's essay of 1880 'The Awful German Language' which claims that *only the dead have time to learn it* a full text of this essay is available to read on the web and ironically is recommended by several of the language sites on the net, you can find it at www.bdsnett.no/klaus/twain/. However do not be put off by such comments about these facets of the language, it is not that bad really. While German can create long compound words to give a clear definition of something (e.g. *Donaudampfschiffahrtsgesellschafts kapitänsmütze* meaning Danube tourist steam boat Capitain's hat) such long words are usually paraphrased or avoided, by native speakers. Even the more widely used term *Geschwindigkeitsüberschreitung* (breaking the speed limit) might look like a long winded way of saying it, but the policeman saying it will take no longer to say it as would an English speaker their version.

Pronunciation is less of a problem than grammar. The vowels and vowel combinations can be learned quite quickly. The umlaut (two dots) used above the vowels a, o and u, represents an e. Thus *ä*, is a combination of a and e pronounced like the e in pet, *ö*, is a combination of o and e like French *eu* and *ü* is a combination of u and e as in the French 'tu'. This added 'e' is quite an easy way to get into pronouncing umlauts and is used as a shorthand on the internet, where technology works against the use of accented vowels.

The above refers to Standard German or *Hochdeutsch* which is taught in all German schools and used in the media. There are two main dialect groups: *Plattdeutsch* (Low German) and *Hochdeutsch* (High German). Standard German is a form of High German which means that it is mutually intelligible with other German dialects (e.g. Bavarian, Franconian, Swabian, Hessian, and Saxon). The differences in the dialects are mostly related to regional or cultural oddities and accents. It is very much like the differences in English between a Geordie and a Cockney, both speak English but that doesn't mean that they pronounce it the same way. All of this means that when you arrive in Germany you will not understand the occasional dialect term in any given conversation, but within a few months you'll have picked them up because every time you gave someone a quizzical look they would have explained in Hochdeutsch.

Low German on the other hand has no standard form (other than Dutch) and is a lot less intelligible to someone who only knows Standard German. As a result, these dialects (spoken in the Northern Plains and in the Rhineland) owing to the advance of Standard German, are a lot less thriving than their High German counterparts (although 8 million north Germans speak them) having lost a lot of ground since the Middle Ages when it was the official commercial language of northern Germany. One 1994 debate in Bonn was held almost entirely in *Platt* to prove a point that the language needed more support. However, practically everybody who speaks them will also know good Standard German and will speak that to anybody they do not know. Which means that anyone living and working in northern Germany is unlikely to have problems understanding people face to face.

Language Manners

The biggest hurdle to watch out for as you learn German and interact with locals is the **Sie/Du** divide. The different forms of 'you' are a trap for the unwary; how do you address those you don't know, those you've known for a few months and children?

> ○ Du is the familiar form of 'you', used amongst family, friends and by adults to children.
> ○ Sie is the formal you to use with people you don't know.

Just because you live next door to someone and have had dinner together a few times, do not use 'Du' with them until they do. Otherwise you can be perceived as over familiar or at least to be flighty and not willing to take life seriously. Essentially it springs from the long-standing formality of the Germans. Younger Germans are becoming freer about using 'du' between casual acquaintances, but its best to keep to the rules.

Remember that bit above about 'du' being used by adults to children? Nobody likes being talked down to and using 'du' on a shopkeeper comes across like that. As an unlearned foreigner you can just about get away with it, if you don't mind being thought of as stupid. If it takes several months or years, then it means that when your German 'friends' use 'du' it means you really are friends.

The main problem for the learner is that German is currently a language in flux, as the researchers of the *Duden* the main German Dictionary needed to find a standardised way of writing and spelling modern German. This reform would standardise the spelling of various new words and would ease teaching and learning of written German, by removing such oddities as the 'b' shaped squiggle for double 's' or 'sz'. 1996 saw the German Government's decision on 'the spelling reform of the century' after many discussions with the cultural ministries of the other German language states, Austria, Liechtenstein and even parts of Switzerland and Italy.

A couple of final points on the subject of German orthography is the numbering system. While the numbers when written by hand show a similarity between 1 and 7, the 1 has a longer downstroke at the top of the stem than in English usage, thus resembling a 7. The 7 being differentiated by a horizontal stroke across the middle of its stem. In multiplication where English speakers use **x** to denote the action of multiplying Germans schools use a dot, set at half letter height, around the cross point of the x (so it looks much like a semi-colon where the comma hasn't printed).

The most noticeable difference that you'll see daily is the use of the decimal point; in German mathematics and the prices of goods or services the system used in English numbering is reversed thus the decimal point . is actually a comma , until one reaches the level of thousands when it switches around again. Thus one euro and fifteen cents (1.15) will be written 1 , 15 and four thousand, five hundred (4,500) will appear 4 . 500.

Self-Study Courses

The advantage of self-study courses is that they allow the student to absorb material at their convenience and own learning pace, thus you can fit in some study while working rather than having to arrange your life around a course timetable. The disadvantages are, that a lot of self-motivation is required and it is not possible to practice spontaneous conversation and your pronounciation may suffer. However, these methods are popular, relatively cheap and would not still be available if they were ineffective. Almost all self study courses are available from bookshops and most include tapes to help you train your ear for the sound of German.

The BBC offers learning language materials for adults in fifteen languages and these range from simple survival guides to comprehensive courses. In German this range includes phrase-books, tapes, grammar guides and travel packs which are available in all good bookshops or direct from the BBC, with prices ranging from £2.99 to £12.99. The BBC has also produced some very fine language learning programmes for radio and television. As well as *Deutsche Direkt !* and *Ganz Spontan* for which the books, tapes and videos are still available, there is the latest offering, *Deutsche Plus* which has programmes on BBC2 and Radio 4. The language programmes are designed as multi-media packages, of television and radio programmes coupled with study books and audio tapes. The course *German Means Business* is accompanied by a course book and audio tapes and a special video pack is aimed specifically at those who already have some German and wish to survive in a business environment. Based on location recordings it is aimed to help the business person dealing with German business contracts including cultural differences and the business meal. For the casual visitor or complete beginner there is also the *Get By In* course which consists of a book, two audio cassettes, a video and video handbook.

All the books and tapes can be ordered direct from the BBC from BBC Books (Book Service By Post Ltd, PO Box 29, Douglas, Isle of Man, IM99 1BQ; ☎01624-675137; fax 01624-670923). Overseas readers can order through the BBC Shop in Newcastle, (☎0191-222 0381; fax 0191-261 9902), however the shop does not offer an enquiry service. Further details and queries about the BBC's language courses can be obtained from BBC Information (PO Box 1116 Belfast, BT2 7AJ; ☎08700-100222; website www.bbc.co.uk/education/languages).

Deutsche Welle the German broadcast station offers language courses over the internet via its website www.dw-world.de.

Linguaphone (111 Upper Richmond Rd, London SW15 2TJ; ☎020-8333 4898; www.linguaphone.co.uk, www.linguaphone.com/usa) distribute self-study courses with cassettes, CDs, Videos, CD-Roms and On-line courses with prices ranging according to type and size of course purchased.

Language Courses

Goethe Institut Inter Nationes: 50 Princes Gate, London SW7 2PH; e-mail germa n@goethe.london.org; website www.goethe.de/london. 1014 Fifth Avenue, New York, NY 10028, USA; ☎212-439 8700; e-mail languageservice@goet he-newyork.org; website www.goethe.de/. The Goethe Institut Inter Nationes offers language courses in the UK and USA at its centres in London, Glasgow, Boston, New York and Washington for details contact the Language Course Offices (London: ☎020-7596 4004; fax 020-7594 0210. Glasgow: ☎0141-332 2555; fax 0141-333 1630; e-mail language@glasgow.goethe.org) or find your nearest office via the website www.goethe.de.

Berlitz (U.K.) Limited: Lincoln House, 296-302 High Holborn, London WC1V 7JH; ☎020-7611 9640; fax 020-7611 9656. Another international organisation, Berlitz offers language courses in the UK which can then be continued at any of its 450 centres overseas. The Berlitz method involves tailoring the course to the individual's requirements as far as the level and course intensity is required. The cost varies depending on these factors. Further details may be obtained from the above address.

CESA Languages Abroad: Western House, Malpas, Truro, Cornwall, TR1 1SQ; ☎01872-225300; fax 01872-225400; e-mail info@cesalanguages.com; web-site www.cesalanguages.com. Arranges German and other European courses in language colleges, with accommodation, in the countries concerned, and also South American Spanish, Arabic, Russian, Chinese and Japanese tuition abroad.

EF International Language Schools: EF Education London, 74 Roupell Street, London, SE1 8SS; ☎020-7401 8399; fax 020-7401 3717; website www.ef.com. EF Edu-cation East Sussex, 1-3 Farman Street, Hove, East Sussex; ☎01273-201410; fax 01273-748566. **USA** EF Education Cambridge, One Education St, Cambridge, MA 02141, USA; ☎617-619 1000; fax 617-619 1001. *Australia* EF Education Sydney, Level 3, 44 Miller, Sydney 2060, Australia; ☎02-9957 4699. EF run schools with a mix of students of all ages, nationalities and abilities to create a relaxed and enjoyable learning environment. Teachers use a balanced combina-tion of written work, role-play, conversation and language laboratory work to develop your fluency. Courses are matched to individual requirements and the fees include accommodation with a local family to help you practice outside your course. EF's courses can last from two weeks to an academic year, and students can prepare for internationally recognised language qualifications.

Euro Academy: 24 Clarendon Rise, Lewisham, London, SE13 5EY; ☎020-8297 0505; fax 020-8297 0984; website www.euroacademy.co.uk/. Offer courses for young people and adults across Europe, with 10 sites in Germany alone. They believe that the most stimulating learning method is to 'learn the language on location'. Crash, Intensive and Business courses are available all year and last from two to four weeks.

Eurolingua European Corporate Offices, Eurolingua Institute sarl, 5 rue Henri

Guinier, 34000 Montpellier, France; tel/fax +33-467 15 04 73.
UK: Eurolingua House, 61 Bollin Drive, Altrincham, WA14 5QW; tel/fax 0161-972 0225; website www.eurolingua.com. Provides unique opportunities for people of all ages to learn languages in the country where they are spoken. Combined language learning, study, activity and holiday programmes are offered including one-to-one homestay programmes.

Part-Time Courses

Most local colleges of further education run evening courses in German, these can be of a formal nature for complete beginners to 'A' level standard; or of a more conversational type for students of varying standards. Information about these courses and costs can be obtained from your local library or college of further education, which usually have a large advertising drive in June or July for courses starting the following September. While most of these courses run along the same timetable as the academic year, some have start up dates in January or are re-run each term. In addition many colleges of further education and local adult education organizations offer personal language tuition on a one-to-one basis which can be very useful if you want to brush up your business vocabulary. Course lengths and prices vary according to the local authority and funding. Another way of finding a private tutor is to check the classified advertisements in the press or through local Anglo-German clubs or societies, although you should make sure of your tutor's qualifications to speak English and German, before you part with any cash.

Courses In Germany

In almost all large German towns, and some smaller historical ones, facilities exist whereby foreigners can attend German courses. Some of these will be run by the German equivalent of a local college of further education (*Volkshochscvhule*) these may be run all year round based at a permanent language institute, e.g. the Goethe Institute, EF etc. (see above), or by universities during the summer vacation. Many of the language courses are run parallel with others on the history and culture of Germany and thus a combined course can provide excellent access to a deeper understanding of the country.

SCHOOLS AND EDUCATION

The problem of deciding how and where to send children to school is a perennial one for parents and arises wherever they live at home or abroad. Moving abroad with young children need not cause a lot of disruption to their education, since in many ways younger children are far more adaptable when it comes to picking up foreign languages and ways, than older, teenage children. If your offspring are already at boarding school in the UK or USA, it is tempting to leave them there in order to avoid unsettling them. However, this may pass up an exciting opportunity to broaden their horizons (and bring them geographically and emotionally closer to you) by sending them to an international or a German school; with the added benefits of developing international connections and the chance to become fluent in another language. It is however important to maintain continuity in the type of education: thus a child who has already embarked on GCSEs, 'A' level courses or SATs in the UK or USA should ideally attend a British or American school in Germany, where the same curriculum is pursued. Unfortunately with the decline of the military presence in Germany there are fewer such schools around. A child of primary school age, whose education has not begun in earnest could be sent to a German primary school for one or two years and could then be switched into the UK or American system without any long-term adverse effects which would be likely to result from a later changeover between two curricula. They would also benefit from getting extra tuition in German so that they could mix with the other children. Many parents favour sending their children to an international school, where the emphasis on languages within a rounded education may prove beneficial, especially given the good pupil teacher ratios of classes in these schools.

GERMAN SCHOOLS

British parents living in Germany on a long-term basis who have put their children through the German state education system have been impressed not only with the range of subject matter, especially in international politics, and foreign languages, but with the high quality of teaching. The main differences between the German and British state schools are that unlike in British schools where the emphasis is on developing the whole person, the object of German schooling is only to train the mind; secondly most German schools operate lessons between 8am and 3pm (this can vary according to school and region) after which most children return home to do their homework. In this respect German schools are perhaps closer to their US counterparts. School attendance is compulsory for all children between the ages of 6 and 18, based around nine years of full time schooling followed by a further three years of either full-time academic or part-time vocational study (*Berufschule*). As schools are subject to state laws there will be regional differences between the attendance, areas of study and homework required from pupils. In the state education sector, after primary education, children are streamed into three types of secondary education depending on ability and aims; these are Secondary Generals, Intermediate and Grammar schools (*Hauptschule, Realschule* and *Gymnasium*), each offering a different type of school leaving certificate according to academic prowess. There are also a few Comprehensive Schools (*Gesamtschule*) which offer the same school leaving certificates as the other three types of secondary school. Nearly 13 million pupils study under 720,000 teachers at more than 52,000 schools across Germany and state education is free. The state system accounts for the education of most German children; 625,000 attend the 3,793 private general education and vocational schools, these being divided between Grammar (*Gymnasium*), Waldorf and special schools.

Secondary Education and Qualifications

After Primary school children attend an observation level of the various secondary schools or if available an orientation level of a Gesamtschule. Whatever type of school the child enters the observation stage (school years five and six) is a phase of special encouragement to ensure that the child is helped to make the right choices for themselves regarding their future educational path. These school years are taught by a mixture of teachers from each school type to allow for a fair assessment of the pupil on one side and the different schools on the other. Hauptschule and Realschule aim to give children a general basic education with the standards of Realschule being higher, with the Gymnasium being higher again. Hence the different school leaving qualifications (*Abschluss*) or the higher education entrance qualification (*Abitur* or *Zeugnis der allegemein Hochschulreife*) awarded by the different types of school. An important point to note is that like Britain and America schools operate within a catchment area, and all children in this area must attend that school, until they reach Gymnasium level. At this level the child and parents can choose which establishment to attend, for example if the nearest school does not emphasise French as much as another more distant school, the Francophone child may attend the latter for preference.

THE GERMAN EDUCATION SYSTEM

Pre-School

Kindergartens are not strictly part of the education system being run by the Länder or city Child and Youth Services offices, private firms, churches, or charitable organisations. In 1996 a child's right to a kindergarten place became enshrined in law, although attendance is purely voluntary. This meant that the difference in the number of places available and the number of children didn't become critical and since then more kindergartens have been set up. According to the last figures available 78 per cent of all eligible children attend a kindergarten, although generally they only offer morning care for the child.

Primary School (*Grundschule*)

Grundschule cover the first four years (six in Berlin and Brandenburg) of schooling and begins at age 6. Apart from reading and writing, children receive a grounding in the subjects they will be studying at secondary school namely *Sozialkunde* (social affairs), *Geschichte* (history), *Erdkunde* (geography), *Biologie*, *Physik* (physics), *Chemie* (chemistry), *Mathematik*, *Religionslehre* (religion), *Musik* (music), *Kunsterziehung* (art), *Handarbeit* (needlework) or *Werken* (crafts) and Sport. All subjects are compulsory and the number of weekly lessons varies depending on the year from 20 to 30.

Secondary Schools

Hauptschule Around a quarter of German children attend Hauptschule for years five to nine of schooling, although a voluntary tenth year is offered in most of the Länder. The subjects studied correspond to the Primary School subjects with the addition of a foreign language (usually English) and *Arbeitslehre* (Working World Practices). In Bavaria *Haushalts und Wirtschaftskunde* (Domestic Sciences) are also studied. In Bavaria, Grundschulen and Hauptschulen are amalgamated into one unit, the *Volksschulen* (Elementary Schools). Hauptschulen are designed for children to begin vocational training after nine or ten years at school, once they have their school certificate (*Hauptschulabschluss*) they can go on to part-time vocational study at *Berufschule*.

Realschule: The aim of the Realschulen is to provide the basis for careers in middle-management and positions at a similar level. In 1994 about 40 percent of all pupils obtained the Intermediate school certificate (*Realschulabschluss*). This enables the holder to go on to full-time vocational school (*Berufsfachschule*) or a vocationally orientated upper secondary school (*Fachoberschule*). The latter allows the student to study for the Polytechnic (*Fachhochschule*) entrance certificate (*Fachochschulreife*). The subject matter and extent of the Realschule curriculum varies between Länder. Learning foreign languages and the general overall higher level of study marks the difference between the Hauptschule and the Realschule, as students are taught a second foreign language (usually French) from year eight.

Gymnasium: Are for the most academically promising and are geared to providing a general education leading to the Abitur for university entrance. The Abitur is generally reckoned to be more rigorous than the UK 'A' levels as it is aimed at achieving a high level in a range of subjects, but is still less difficult than the infamous French baccalaureate. There is also a seven stage Gymnasium for those children who's aptitude only becomes noticeable at the observation level of the other schools. Subjects are divided into three categories: language, literature and art; social sciences; and mathematics, science and technology. For their Abitur, students must take four examination subjects. The Abitur entitles the holder to study the subject of their choice at university or an equivalent institution, subject of course to availability.

German Private Schools

Those Germans who wish their children to attend private schools (*Ersatzschulen*) have a choice of anthroposophical schools (*Waldorfschulen*) based on the system of education founded by the Austrian scientist and humanist, Rudolph Steiner, which looks at the child as a whole rather than a mind to be developed. There are about 80 Waldorfschulen, as well as Montessori schools, where the ideology is 'Help me to help myself', (in fact some state schools have classes based on the Montessori principle) and some private schools run by churches. In general the private schools tend to be patronised by the offspring of German intellectuals and professionals, who can afford the fees. There are also around 20 *Internate* (boarding schools) run along English public school lines. The academic reputation of the private schools is however considerably lower than that of the Gymnasien, which are the only places where a child can take an Abitur.

GERMAN UNIVERSITIES

The academic traditions of many German universities reach back several centuries (eg Heidelberg was founded in 1386 and Leipzig in 1409), while others are more recent; to cope with expanding demand more than 20 have been founded since 1960. In the sixties only eight percent of each age group went to university, nowadays it is closer to thirty; more than 1.9 million students are enrolled at universities and *Fachhochschulen* (polytechnics) across Germany. However, even with over 344 institutons and 400 disciplines, many lecture theatres are crammed and courses are over-subscribed by eager students.

Until the middle of the 20th century the academic style of German universities was based on the principles of Wilhelm von Humboldt, who believed that universities should be purely for academic research. So that students were not taught with any future profession in mind. This has changed to reflect the needs of modern society and the individual student, thus traditional universities rub shoulders with technical universities, colleges of education and Fachhochschulen.

The modern German university is owned by the regional government but self-governing, headed by a Rector or President. The governing bodies should be comprised of 50% professors and by law, a selection of representatives from all categories including: academic tutors, students and employees.

As in most other European countries it is a constitutional right in Germany, that everyone who attains the university entrance qualification is entitled to enter higher education. However, the employment circumstances of the 1990s and recent years meant that an increasing number of *Abiturienten* reached the conclusion that a university degree was not necessarily a guaranteed career-ticket and consequently, many pursue apprenticeships instead. Every third student enrols at a Fachhochschule for a practical related study course, which is of shorter duration than at university. These courses cover such areas as business studies, engineering, design and social work, and while the degree awarded used to be a Diplom. now bachelors and masters degrees can be studied for at a fachhochchule.

It should be noted that with the overcrowding of classes, a high drop out rate and a general dissatisfaction with the length of studies, many changes have been discussed. These changes included making institutions more responsible for selecting the students they enrol and introducing more three or four year first degrees, as opposed to the situation where it could take seven years or longer to obtain a first degree.

There are also a few private institutions, which naturally charge high fees. For €15,500 you can study medicine, or for €4,100 a semester you can study at the European Business School, so while the latter course does result in excellent job offers, only 2% of students study at these private institutions. There is also a German equivalent of the UK's *Open University* at Hagen,for those who wish to study from home or while working (*FernUniversität GesamtHochschule Hagen*), as well as distance learing courses arranged by many universities.

Costs

University tuition is free and students are covered by the institution's health insurance, so the only costs to students are social contributions (€20-50 per semester), living expenses, books and stationery, which are usually met by their families. There is a little help with this as a child in higher education still qualifies for the German child benefit (*Kindergeld*) until they are 27, however this is not necessarily a large sum. Under the Federal Training Assistance Act students have the legal right to public funding, half of which comes in the form of a grant and the rest as an interest free loan re-payable within five years of the end of the entitlement period.

Period of Study

The German academic year consists of two semesters which run from October to March (*Winter Semester, WS*) and April to September (*Sommer Semester, SoSe*). Most study programmes have two stages, general preparatory studies (*Grundstudium*) followed by specialisation (*Hauptstudium*) but their duration is not fixed: you are supposed to obtain a certain number of course credits and pass exams in whatever time it takes you for both stages. Examination entry often requires proof of attendence at a requisite number of lessons, these are measured in SWS (*Semesterwochenstunde*) of 45 minutes duration eg a 90 minute lecture counts for 2SWS, the SWS requirement for any given course and other exam/study decrees can be found in the institution's *Studienordnung* or *Prüfungsordnung*. Apart from certain subjects including teaching, law, and medicine it is possible to perpetuate your studies almost indefinitely. This length of study coupled with increased overcrowding has led to a rise in the number of students dropping out of their courses. The average time for completing a degree is now seven years. What is more, many students are commencing their studies late, after an apprenticeship or compulsory military service.

Degrees

The degrees awarded in Germany are the *Magister Artium*, the *Diplom* or *Diplom Ing.* and the *Staatsexamen* according to the course studied. The Magister is a Masters level degree in Arts and Humanities which is taken by those students who wish to continue their studies as research students and eventually become academics. The Diplom is also at Masters level and is awarded within the Social and Natural Sciences to those subjects which have a practical or professional bent such as psychology, with the Diplom Ing. as an engineering graduate qualification. While the Staatsexam is a professional qualification set and invigilated by the länder governments, it applies to law, teaching, medical degrees and those taken by civil servants. Since the last edition was published students have been able to pursue courses resulting in Bachelor's (BA or BSc) or Master's degrees as found in the UK and US; these can be followed up to doctoral level. International degree courses are now available for undergraduate and postgraduate study which lead to Bachelor and Masters qualifications. Many of these courses are held in English.

Admission

The Federal and State governments are keen to attract foreign students, around 174,000 studied there in the winter semester of 1999. For students wishing to study in Germany admission to a German university depends on a thorough knowledge of German, in addition to the Abitur, or its foreign equivalent. An exception being those international degree programmes noted above. The language proficiency test *DSH* (*Deutsche Sprachprüfung für den Hochschulzugang ausländischer Studienweber*) is carried out at the instituion that you are applying to, exemptions to this are based on language qualifications or if you will only spend one semester in Germany. The

Deutscher Akademischer Austauschdienst (German Academic Exchange Service) listed below can supply the relevant information outside Germany, including details of its German preparation course. Would-be foreign students need to contact the *Akademisches Auslandsamt* of the university or college they wish to attend, ideally a year or so in advance. The DAAD can supply all the information and literature needed to start applying, the bilingual blue book *Destination Germany: guide for international students* is a pocket sized resource that students should find worth its weight in gold.

At present tuition is free for both first and postgraduate degrees to both native and foreign students but living expenses need to be met by the student. For postgraduates there are various grants, details of which can again be obtained from the DAAD. Another organization useful to students wanting to study at German universities as part of their UK course is the UK Erasmus Socrates (address below). Although they cannot actually arrange placement with a German university they can supply information leaflets on the processes involved. The other branches of ERASMUS in Britain can arrange teacher exchanges anywhere in the EU.

Alternatively a budding engineer can study at the Technical University of Braunschweig which has a teaching agreement with the University of Rhode Island, this rewards engineering graduates with a D. Ing. and an American Master's degree.

STUDYING IN GERMANY

At present there are around 174,000 foreign students studying at German universities, with courses ranging from mining, media studies and applied cultural studies to the typical courses offered by universities. In order to study in Germany you will have to prove that you are sufficiently competent in the language to make study there worthwhile (unless you are doing an international degree as these are taught in English), and have carried out sufficient research on the course you wish to study and where it is available. The easiest way to do this is to contact an educational exchange organisation, either one run by your own national authorities, e.g. the British Council, German Academic Exchange Service, Fulbright Student Programme, or a multi-national enterprise like the EU's Socrates/Erasmus scheme. Within the EU, the encouragement of student mobility means that periods of study at a foreign university are fully recognised as modules towards your final degree and you may well be eligible for a grant.The German Academic Exchange Service (*Deutscher Akademischer Austauschdienst*) publishes a very useful guide for students as well as lists of scholarships and sources of funding. It assists people enrolled full-time at an institute of higher education to study or do research in Germany. The London office also publishes a list of summer language and music courses in Germany. In addition to their offices in other countries, the DAAD can also be contacted through the offices of the cultural departments of German embassies. Any place that is not for a whole degree course will only be open for the duration of one semester rather than an academic year as German universities, unlike those in Britain, work on the semester system, although you can apply to extend your study.

Useful Addresses

DAAD: Main Office, Kennedyal-lee 50, D-53175 Bonn, Germany; ☎0228-8820; fax 0228-882444; e-mail postmaster@daad.de; website www.daad.de.

DAAD (UK): 34 Belgrave Square, London SW1X 8QB; ☎020-7235 1736; fax 020-72359602;e-mailinfo@daad.org.uk; website www.daad.de/london.

DAAD (USA): 871 United Nations Plaza, New York, NY 10017, USA; ☎212-758 3223; e-mail daadny@daad.org; website www.daad.org.

DAAD (USA): DAAD Consulting Center, Dr. Eckhard Schröter, c/o Goethe-Institut Inter Nationes, 530 Bush Street, San Francisco, CA 94108, USA; e-mail eschroet@socra tes.berkeley.edu.

DAAD (Australia): Study Information Centre, Dr. Susanne Scharnowski, c/o Goethe-Institut Inter Nationes, 448, St. Kilda Road, Melbourne, VIC 3004, Australia: ☎+61-3-9864 8916; fax +61-3-9864 8988; e-mail daadmelb@ozemail.com.au.

DAAD (New Zealand): Study Information Centre, Dr. Sabine Fischer-Kani, c/o Department of Germanic Languages and Literature, University of Auckland, PB 92 019, Auckland, New Zealand; ☎+64-9-373 7599; fax +64-9-373 7447; e-mail daad@auckland.ac.nz.

UK Erasmus-Socrates: R&D Building, The University, Canterbury, Kent CT2 7PD (☎01227-762712; www.erasmus.ac.uk).

FernUniversität GesamtHochschule Hagen: Dez. 2.4, D-58084 Hagen, Germany; website www.fernuni-hagen.de.

In addition to the information available through the DAAD and its websites there is information on DAAD's literature at:

- ⟳ www.germany-opportunities.de/literature
- ⟳ *Hi!Potentials* www.campus-germany.de which has multilingual pages on all aspects of moving to study in Germany.

The main universities have their own Foreign Student Offices (*Akademisches Auslandsamt*), which you should contact at least six months, preferably a year, in advance of your planned start date for studying. These offices in conjunction with the DAAD will be able to advise you on all aspects of entering Germany to study.

While entering Germany to study is easier for EU and American nationals the basic requirements for entry of all nationalities are: that you have documentary proof of your place at a German university; a passport which will remain valid for the entire period of your stay; proof that you have sufficient funds to support you during your studies and if necessary the correct visa. The DAAD recommend that you arrive with at least €200 (£125) on you to cover the various expenses of the first few weeks of term., They also recommend that you should allow between €540 and €665 (£340-£420) a month for living expenses. Non-EU nationals registering at the Aliens Registration Office with their various documents and passport photos will be issued with a Student Residence Permit (*Aufenthaltsgenehmigung*) which is valid only for study and does not permit the holder to take up any temporary work between semesters.

The EU operates a series of study programmes, aimed at developing educational and cultural links across Europe. The SOCRATES schemes enable students to study at universities abroad, and grants funding to universities to develop joint courses across EU borders. Candidates for a SOCRATES-ERASMUS placement and bursary may need to show a sufficient knowledge of the language of the country they wish to study in so that they can communicate with fellow students although some institutions offer courses in English. However, many universities offer language study programmes for those wishing to take part in the exchange programme. The deadline for applications depends on the institution. The schemes are administered by national agencies and the *Socrates, Leonardo & Youth Technical Assistance Office* in Belgium (59-61 rue de Trèves, 1040 Brussels, Belgium; ☎+32-2-233 0111; fax 2-233 0150; website www.socleoyouth.be). Please note that this office does not deal with grants. A list of national agencies can be found online at http://europa.eu.int/comm/education/socrates/download.htm. UK students in higher education can apply for bursaries intended to help with costs, depending on the location and length of the placement from the UK Erasmus-Socrates Council (Research & Development Building, University of Kent, Canterbury, Kent CT2 7PD; ☎01227-762712; e-mail erasmus@ukc.ac.uk; website www.erasmus.ac.uk or www.erasmus-k.net). The Department for Education and Skills (DfES) also publishes information about studying on the continent called 'The European Choice.' It explains how Erasmus operates, where to find funding and recommendations on where to study. The site also provides information about studying in each individual country of the EU.

Citizens of the USA can apply for grants to assist studying in Germany by applying to the US Department of State's Fulbright Program (website www.iee.org/fulbright). These study programmes and grants are designed to give American graduates opportunities for personal development and to gain international experience, based on cross-cultural interaction. The full grant covers travel and maintenance costs, health and medical insurance, book grants and if necessary language orientation, while the travel grant speaks for itself. Most university campuses will have a Fulbright Adviser, but applicants no longer enrolled in an establishment can contact the address given above for application details. Candidates are selected on their academic record, language preparation and the extent to which their project will promote mutual understanding. For those wishing to study in Germany there are 91 full grants available and 10 travel grants, the full grant is given for a ten-month period beginning in September. Applications for awards should be submitted by October of the year prior to the year you wish to spend overseas.

There are some special schemes for Americans hoping to obtain work experience in Germany: see the end of the *Temporary Work* section in the *Employment* chapter.

VOCATIONAL TRAINING IN COLLEGE & WORKPLACE

Vocational schools are mandatory for anyone under 18 who is not at some other type of school and youth vocational training in Germany is generally acclaimed as the best in Europe. It consists of a variety of apprenticeships, work and part-time study, and full-time vocational study.

Apprenticeships last from two and a half to three years, but are only available in recognised occupations. The apprentice is paid a training allowance which increases annually, and is taught and examined according to regulations laid down by federal ministries, business associations, trade unions and chambers of crafts and trades.

While some teenagers are still taking up apprenticeships the trend in youth training is towards a more formal qualification that blends theory and practice. The State decides the conditions under which vocational training may be provided, but the financial support is largely provided by individual firms from the mega-corporation to the single employer. Vocational training generally occurs under the 'dual-system' whereby practical training on the job with one of 500,000 firms (*Betrieb*) is coupled with theoretical training at a part-time school (*Berufsschule*). Around 1.65 million young people were training in one of the 356 occupations for which recognised training is required.

Trainees are known as *Auszubildende* (or 'Azubis'). Trainees attending a Berufsschule must be in the process of undergoing their initial job training or already have a job. The contract for a two or three-year course involves the Azubi receiving general education and specialised instruction in a variety of skills at the Berufsschule for up to two days per week. In addition up to three days a week are spent in a firm learning a specific job or trade. The instruction received at the Berufsschule is closely related to the training received in firms. Vocational skills acquired in this way may include hairdressing, car mechanics and clerical skills. During the training period, the Azubi receives a small wage from the employer which rises significantly upon the completion of the training period.

In addition to apprenticeships and Berufsschule, there are the options of full-time vocational school (*Berufsfachschule*) and vocational secondary school (*Fachoberschule*). Of the two, the former offers vocational courses lasting between one and three years, which can count as part of an apprenticeship or replace it entirely. While the Fachoberschule with its theory classes, workshops and on-the-job training qualifies students for entry to the polytechnics (*Fachhochschule*) which offer practice-related study.

SCHOOLING FOR EXPATRIATE CHILDREN

Although the state schools of Germany are very good it is understandable that parents who are not making a permanent move will prefer their children to be educated in an English language school, especially one that teaches the same syllabus as the children will be returning to, or at least that will provide an internationally accepted leaving qualificaction. Naturally there are only a few schools offering either UK or US syllabi in Germany, so many parents will find their choice is between the more prevalent International Schools which offer a range of curricula and end of school qualifications, and the local German schools. With luck they may be able to get their children into one of the European Schools, which have been founded to educate the children of EU staff on placements outside their homeland. On the following pages are details of several schools in

Germany offering of interest to expatriates with school age children. New comers to Germany or would be expatriates can also obtain information about schools in their intended settlement area from the consulate offices of their national embassy in germany responsible for the region they intend to settle in, addresses for these can be found in the chapter on *Red Tape*.

INTERNATIONAL AND EUROPEAN SCHOOLS

There are many international schools in Germany each one offering a variety of curricula including the British National Curriculum, the International General Certificate of Secondary Education and the International Baccalaureate, some also offer American School programmes or programmes which lead to SAT assessment. For more information about the International Schools in Germany contact The European Council of International Schools (21 Lavant Street, Petersfield, Hants GU32 3EL; ☎01730-268244; fax 01730-267914; e-mail ecis@ecis.org; website www.ecis.org), this independent professional organisation is made up of 500 international schools and prepares printed and electronic listings of schools and colleges. Their directory publications can be obtained via their website either as the *On-Line Directory* or in print form (*ECIS Schools Directory* costs around £35). These directories are updated annually and provide useful information on schools including details of curricula, intake and fees, the web edition includes links to useful websites for expatriates.

Information on international schools in Germany can be obtained from the *US Department of State's Office of Overseas Schools* (Office of Overseas Schools, US Department of State, Room H328, SA-1, Washington DC 20522-0132, USA; ☎202-261 8200) and its website (www.state.gov/m/a/os) which lists some of the schools with details of their fees in US dollars.

In addition to the above resources 14 of the international schools in Germany have banded together to form *AGIS: The Association of German International Schools e.V* (Sigmaringer Strasse 257, D-70597 Stuttgart, Germany; ☎0711-7696 0073; fax 0711-7696 0012; e-mail info@agis-schools.org; websitewww.agis-schools.or g), this professional support network requires members to adhere to standards regarding admissions and employment policies, small class sizes and the provision of programmes for second language learners.

European Schools

The European schools, of which there are two in Germany at Karlsruhe and München, are operated by the EU to provide native language teaching for the children of EU employees wherever they may be employed. There are a limited number of places available each year for children of non-entitled families, application for these is by writing to the Head of the School. These places are fee-paying although some help can be given in cases of hardship. Each school teaches from Primary through to University entrance level, following the syllabus of the International Baccalaureate. Teaching includes one foreign language from the first year of primary school, with another language to be learned from the second year of Secondary school (languages are taken from the range available at each school). More information on the European Schools can be obtained by writing to them directly (addresses below) or from The Central Office of the Representative of The Board of Governors of The European Schools (Rue de la Loi 200, Batiment Belliard 5/7 1er étage, B-1049 Brussels, Belgium; ☎+322-295-3746/47/48).

The EU's Eurydice network can also be used to obtain information on schools across Europe, although this resource (the *Eurybase* database, www.eurydice.org) is primarily aimed at education ministries, as its available online in the national langauge and English it can also be used to compare educational systems when migrating between countries.

NATIONAL SCHOOLS

However, whichever school you choose for your children, you will need to notify the local authorities in order to obtain the neccesary exemption from attendance at a German school. This can be sorted out at the local school authority *Amt für Schule* for the area you live in, and they or the youth education office (*Behörde für Schule, Jugend und Berufsbildung*) can also provide details of local German state schools. Certainly the Hamburg office can provide an English language leaflet giving details of school types and the information offices which can help a child decide which educational direction they wish to go in (Freie und Hansestadt Hamburg, Behörde für Bildung und Sport, Amt für Schule, Postfach 76 10 48, D-22060 Hamburg, Germany). It should also be noted that some consular information sheets carry information regarding state schools where bi-lingual education is offered. There are at least two of these in Berlin itself and eight across Hessen, Baden-Württemberg and Rheinland-Pfalz.

LIST OF SCHOOLS

Fees

The schools listed below except where stated will charge fees for either day or boarded schooling, there may be additional fees to cover the costs of ensuring children are matched to the academic level that suits them best or bus travel to the school site. At the time of writing fees varied between €1,300-€13,500 for day schooling and €4,275-€9,675 for boarding (or US$ 6,100-12,405 for day schooling according to the Office of Overseas Schools) and so are not generally noted below except where supplied by the school concerned. Readers are advised to obtain fee information from the school directly.

Note on the entries. 'IGCSE' is the International General Certificate of Secondary Education, 'IBPYP' is the International Baccalaureate Primary Years Program, 'IB' is the International Baccalaureate and SAT is the American College Board Entrance Exam.

Playgroups/Kindergarten

It's A Small World: International Kindergarten and Day Care, Kaiserwerther Markt 10, D-40489 Düsseldorf, Germany; ☎0211-400321; e-mail khart_de@yahoo.com; website www .itsasmallworldinternational.com. A small (20 children) pre-school establishment.

Ladybirds pre-school/kindergarten: Verein zur Förderung der englischen Sprache e.V.: Haus der Jugend, Bebalallee 22, D-22299 Hamburg, Germany; ☎040-511 4256. This offers 4 hours of quality day care and pre-school education, five mornings per week; for children aged 3 and over and operates afternoon reading/writing sessions for children aged 7 upwards.

Lucy Bell's Early Learning Center: Georg-Wilhelmstrasse 12, D-10711 Berlin, Germany; ☎030-2529 3777. Ages 2-5. Provides pre-school care and instruction in English, between 8am-4.30pm.

Nightingale Pre-School: Düsseldorf-Kalkum, Germany; ☎0211-404412. For ages 2-6.

Noah's Ark Children Center: Am Bauenhaus 30, D-40472 Düsseldorf, Germany; ☎0211-965 3685.

The Kids Club: Pastor-Fliedner-Weg 31, D-45329 Essen, Germany; ☎0201-329980; website www.the-kids-club.de.

British Schools

Berlin British School: Dickensweg 17-19, D-14055 Berlin, Germany; ☎030-304 2205; fax 030-304 3856; e-mail bbs.enq@t-online.de; website www.berlinbritishschool.de. Ages 3-16. Opened in 1994 in a former British Services School, the school teaches the UK's National Curriculum leading up to the IGCSE.

St George's: The English School of Cologne: Raderthalgürtel 3, D-50968 Köln, Germany; ☎0221-341778; fax 0221-934 9442; e-mail st.georges -school@netcologne.de; website www.stgeorgesschool.de. Ages 4-18. Prepares pupils for UK GCSE and A Levels, and IGCSE.

American Schools

John F. Kennedy School: Teltower Damm 87-93, D-14167 Berlin, Germany; ☎030-6321 5701; fax 030-6321 6377; e-mail school@jfks.de; website www.jfks.de. Ages 5-19. This German-American community school offers teaching in English and German from Kindergarten or 'Vorschule' up to High School Diploma or 'Abitur'. Tuition is free but waiting lists are long.

European schools:

Europäische Schule: Albert-Schweitzer-Strasse 1, D-76139 Karlsruhe, Germany; ☎0721-680 090; fax 0721-680 0950. Kindergarten to sixth-form. An international, co-educational school with a European curriculum leading to the European Baccalaureate.

Europäische Schule München: Elise-Aulinger-Strasse 21, D-81739 München, Germany; ☎089-630 2290; fax 089-630 22968. A European School in Germany – places are limited to children of EU staff.

International Schools:

Bavarian International School: Schloss Haimhausen, Hauptstrasse 1, D-85778, Haimhausen, Germany; ☎08133 9170; fax 08133 917115; e-mail admissions@bis-school.com; website www.bis-school.com. Age 4-18. A co-educational day school in purpose built buildinga and an 18th century castle to the north of Munich. It offers IBPYP, IGCSE, SAT and IB programmes, currently representing 14 nationalities. The school is recognised and supported by the Bavarian government.

Berlin International School: Körnerstr 11, D-12169 Berlin, Germany; ☎030-7900 0370; fax 030-7900 0379; e-mail office@berlin-international-school.de; website www.berlin-international-school.de. The newest independent branch of the Private Kant Schools e.V., which opened in August 1998 in the Berlin district of Steglitz. A bilingual educational program (German/English) is offered for 320 children from the ages of 3-18. The school offers all German school examinations including Abtiur and the IB Diploma. There is also a Primary section at Lentzeallee 8, D-14195 Berlin-Dahlem.

Berlin/Potsdam International School GmbH: Am Hochwald 30/2, Kleinmachnow, D-14532 Berlin, Germany; ☎033-2038 0360; fax 033-2038 03621; e-mail office@bpis.de; website www.bpis.de. A non-profit, co-educational day school which serves the needs of the international community in metropolitan Berlin. Admission is open to all nationalities and students representing 27 countries are enrolled. The school offers the IBPYP, IGCSE and IB.

Black Forest Academy: Postfach 1109, D-79396 Kandern, Germany; ☎07626 91610; fax 07626 8821; e-mail admissions@bfacademy.com; website www.bfacademy.com A private residential Christian school providing both an elementary and secondary education. Most students are North American, but 16 nationalities are represented amongst the 340 students. Instruction is in English and the North American university-entrance curriculum is followed, university places have been gained by students taking AP exams.

Bonn International School e.V.: Martin Luther King Strasse 14, D-53175 Bonn Germany; ☎0228-308540; fax 0228-3085420; e-mail admin@bis.bonn.org; website www.bis.bonn.org. Age 3-19. Located ten minutes from the center of Bonn, the school serves the English speaking expatriate community from Koblenz to Cologne as it is the result of the merging of three schools (the Bonn American High School, the British High School Bonn, and the Bonn American Elementary School). Three IB scheme programmes are offered. Students are accepted throughout the year provided places are available.

Independent Bonn International School: Tulpenbaumweg 42, D-53177 Bonn, Germany; ☎0228-323 166; fax 0228-323 958. Ages 3-11. Formerly British Embassy Preparatory School, the school has some 150 pupils from 25 nationalities which represent the local and international community from the Cologne/Bonn area. The school now also has German accreditation as an *Ersatzschule*. The teaching programme was based on the British National Curriculum modified for the current pupil population, and also incorporates the requirements of the German primary school programme. Classes currently average 15 pupils and annual fees start from €6,995. The school also offers a variety of extra-curricular activities.

International School of Bremen: Thomas-Mann-Strasse 6-8, D-28213, Bremen, Germany; ☎0421-337 9272; fax 0421-337 9273; e-mail isbremen@aol.com; website www.isbremen.de. Ages 4-14. ISB offers an American/International curriculum with all instruction in English except for foreign language classes.

Dresden International School: Goetheallee 18, D-01309 Dresden, Germany; ☎0351-340 0428; fax 0351-340 0430; e-mail dis@dresden-is.de; website www.dresden-is.de. Age 3-16. 100 studentsform 8 countries. Opened in 1996 to serve the expatriate community in Dresden and its environs. English is the main language of instruction, with a strong German bilingual focus. There is full provision for students for whom English is not the first language and new students are accepted throughout the year.

International School of Düsseldorf e.V.: Niederrheinstrasse 336, D-40489 Düsseldorf, Germany; ☎0211-94066; fax 0211-408 0774. Ages 4-20. The international curriculum and IB are offered to pupils from Kindergarten to High School Grade 12/13.

Franconian International School (FIS): Christoph-Dassler-Strasse 1. D-91074 Herzogenaurach, Germany; ☎09132-797910; fax 09132-797912; e-mail mail@franconian-international-school.de. Serving the communities of Herzongenaurach, Nürnberg, Fürth and Erlangen. The school opened in September 1998 with Grade 1 and 2. Since then one Grade level has been added each year. The plan is to continue like this until the school can offer IB after Grade 12.

Frankfurt International School: An der Waldlust 15, D-61440, Oberursel, Germany; ☎06171-2020; fax 06171-202384; website www.fis.edu. Ages 4-19. Teaching is in English but mothr tongue programme is offered in Dutch, Swedish and Japanese. 1,300 pupils are taught within a range of international syllabi leading to IGCSE, SAT and IB. The school is accredited by ECIS and NEAS. The school itself is 15 km from Frankfurt and offers transportation to it and the branch site at Wiesbaden.

International School Hamburg: Holmbrook 20, D-22605 Hamburg, Germany; ☎040-883 0010; fax 040-881 1405; e-mail info@international-school-hamburg.de; website www.international-school-hamburg.de. Ages 3-18. Founded in 1957, the first such school in Germany, the school offers the IGCSE, IB and SAT, to over 500 pupils in classes of between 10 and 20 pupils. The school is accredited by ECIS and NEASC. There is also an Early Learning Centre attached to the school for Pre-Kindergarten, Kindergarten and Reception classes. German is offered from grade two onwards.

International School Hannover Region: Bruchmeisterallee 6, D-30169, Hannover, Germany; ☎0511-270 41650; fax 0511- 270 41651; e-mail IntSchH@aol.com; website www.ishr.tsx.org. Age 3-19. Founded in 1996 to serve the international community in Lower Saxony, the school offers programs from kindergarten through grade 12 based on the IB Primary and Middle Years and the IB Diploma. Lessons are taught in English with German and French taught as foreign languages. Students are accepted from expatriate families and local applicants, applications beng accepted throughout the year.

Leipzig International School: Koenneritz Strasse 47, D-04229 Leipzig, Germany; ☎0341-421-0574; fax 0341-421 2154; e-mail admin@intschool-leipzig.com; website www.intschool-leipzig.com. This is an independent, coeducational day school with a boarding section. It offers an educational program from kindergarten through grade 12 for students of all nationalities. The age range of students is 3 to 19 years. The academic curriculum is compatible with that in U.S. public and private schools as well as other international schools with international examinations in grade 10 IGCSE and grade 12 the I.B.

Munich International School: Schloss Buchhof, D-82319 Starnburg, Germany; ☎08151-3660; fax 08151-366129. Ages 4-18 An independent, co-educational, comprehensive-type day school based on an international curriculum incorporating elements of both the British and German educational systems. Curriculums taught include IGCSE, American High School Diploma (including SAT Preparation), and IB. Pupils are admitted throughout the year according to class space and ability.

International School of Stuttgart e.V.: Sigmariner Strasse 257, D-70597 Stuttgart, Germany; ☎0711-7696 000; fax 0711-7696 0010; e-mail info@international-school-stuttgart.de. 450 students, ages 3-18. Teaching an international syllabus with IB Primary Years Programme and IB Diploma.

Taunus International Montessori School: Altkönigstrasse 110, D-61440 Oberursel, Germany; ☎06171-91330; fax 06171-913317; e-mail taunus.montessori @rhein-main.net. Age 3-6.

Thuringia International School – Weimar: Gutenbergstrasse 32, D-99423 Weimar, Germany; ☎03643-776904; fax 03643-776905; e-mail this-weimar@t-online.de; website www.this-weimar.de. Age 4-11. Founded in September 2000 the school offers an international curriculum to students up to Grade 6. As the school expands to age 18 it plans to implement Primary, Middle Years and Diploma International Baccalaureate Programmes.

International School Wiesbaden: Rudolf-Dietz-Strasse 14, D-65207 Wiesbaden/ Naurod, Germany; ☎06127-99400; fax 06127-994099; website www.fis.edu. Age 3-12. Oened originally as a branch of the Frankfurt International School, this school offers English language IBPYP instruction and first language tuition in Dutch and Swedish.

DEPARTMENT OF DEFENSE SCHOOLS/SERVICE CHILDREN'S EDUCATION

In addition to the above schools there are stil schools operated by the British and American military which are primarily for the education of servicemen and other entitled personnel working abroad. These are run by the Service Children's Education (SCE) and Department of Defense Dependents Schools (DoDDS) respectively; DoDDS acts under the auspices of the Department of Defense Education Activity (DoDDEA).

The British Service Children's Education schools, while primarily for the children of service and civillian support families, do sometimes accept fee paying children of non-service families (strictly on a case by case basis). However, with changes in defence budgeting and the amalgamtion of service schools it is best to contact the SCE for confirmation of this point. The offices of SCE serve their specified areas, but SCE (UK) also offer advice to service personnel regarding children with special educational needs.

Department of Defense Education Activity: 4040 N. Fairfax Dr., Arlington, VA 22203, USA; website www.odedodea.edu.

HQ Service Children's Education: Building 5, Wegberg Complex, BFPO 40.
HQ Service Children's Education (UK): Trenchard Lines, Upavon, Pewsey, Wilts, SN9 6BE.

MEDIA AND COMMUNICATIONS

NEWSPAPERS

Germany does not have a large array of national daily papers: *Bild, Frankfurter Allgemeine Zeitung* (usually shortened to *FAZ*), and *Die Welt* are the only three that can claim a national readership, but 78 per cent of Germans read a paper every day. The traditional basis for the German daily press is the regional or local subscription paper, as can be seen from the table below. German newspapers are generally regional in nature, though in the cases of one or two readership may spread over a wide area. This is reflected in the circulation rates, where the big three do not fare as well as one might expect. For instance the *Süddeutsche Zeitung* based in Munich enjoys wide popularity across southern Germany, while the devoted readership of the sharp-shooting *Frankfurter Rundschau* extends similarly deeply into the Frankfurt hinterland. In addition to the dailies, there is one major weekly newspaper *Die Zeit.* Unlike Britain and North America there is no tradition of hefty Sunday papers, so while *Bild, FAZ,* and *Die Welt* put out Sunday editions (eg *Welt am Sonntag*) there is little chance of a German news vendor getting a hernia compared to his British and American compatriots.

Many of the papers and periodicals listed below (and on the following pages) can be obtained from newsagents (such as WH Smith in the UK) or by subscription. In the USA, *German Language Publishing Inc,* can arrange subscriptions to the following: *Berliner Zeitung, Die Welt, Handelsblatt,* Süddeutsche Zeitung, *Die Zeit, Die Woche, Welt am Sonntag, Der Speigel, Focus,* and *Stern.* Full details of cost and which daily issues can be supplied are obtainable from GLP's website.
German Language Publishing Inc: 153 South Dean Street, Inglewood, NJ 07631, USA; ☎800-457 4443; e-mail info@glpnews.com; website glpnews.com.

Bild: website www.bild.de. A massively popular daily its 4 million plus readership makes it Europe's largest selling daily paper. Its somewhat sensational in content is more akin to a tabloid than the broad sheets it is printed on and it probably goes beyond the bounds of what might be considered good taste. *Bild* being the German for 'picture' of which there are more than a few, often of young women, in large format. Despite its lurid style, Bild has an element of acute political reporting. Because of its large circulation, politicians have to take notice of Bild, and many of them grant interviews to it. Cover price 40 cents.

Die Welt: website www.welt.de. Germany's second largest national daily newspaper, and flagship title of the Axel Springer Group. It is published in Berlin but available in 130 countries across the world, making it a useful daily for those preparing themselves for the move to Germany. In Berlin and Hamburg the paper also has extensive local sections. Cover price is €1.

Frankfurter Allgemeine Zeitung:(FAZ) This is a hefty daily broadsheet. Cautious and balanced, it reflects the opinions of the business world and deals with a range of subjects: political, business and cultural, on a worldwide basis. The business section makes it the business person's favourite newspaper. Like *Die Welt* this broadsheet is popular with libraries, businesses and individuals around the world. The daily circulation figure is around 393,400. There is also an eight page English language edition. Cover price €1.10 in Germany, €1.50 across Europe.
Frankfurter Allgemeine Zeitung: Postfach D-60267 Frankfurt, Germany; ☎069-75910; fax 069-7591 1743; website www.faz.de.

Die Zeit: Die Zeit, published in Hamburg is Germany's largest weekly newspaper, not counting Sunday editions of dailies. Regarded as broadly liberal, it allows different shades of opinion on major issues to be voiced in its columns, its circulation figures have dropped over the last few years. The cover price is €2.80.
Die Zeit Kommanditgesellschaft Zeitverlag, D-20079 Hamburg, Germany; ☎040-32800; fax 040-327111; website www.zeit.de.

TABLE 5   MAJOR PRINT MEDIA CIRCULATIONS

Title	Place of publication	Editions sold
Daily Newspapers		
Bild	Hamburg	4,248,000
Westdeutsche Allgemeine Zeitung	Essen	1,124,000
Hannoverische Allgemeine Zeitung	Hannover	559,900
ZTG Thüringen	Erfurt	480,000
Sächsische Zeitung/Morgenpost	Dresden	474,700
Süddeutsche Zeitung	München	427,300
Freie Presse	Chemnitz	425,700
Kölner Stadtanzeiger/Kölnische Rundschau	Cologne	423,900
Rheinische Post	Düsseldorf	419,900
Frankfurter Allgemeine Zeitung	Frankfurt/Main	407,100
Augsburger Allgemeine	Augsburg	368,900
Südwest Presse	Ulm	345,400
Ruhr Nachrichten	Dortmund	275,000
B.Z.	Berlin	266,600
Hessiche/Niedersächsische Allgemeine	Kassel	262,900
Die Welt	Hamburg	242,600
Berliner Zeitung	Berlin	203,800
Frankfurter Rundschau	Frankfurt	190,400
Handelsblatt	Düsseldorf	167,400
Der Tagesspiel	Berlin	146,000
Weekly/Sunday Newspapers		
Bild Am Sonntag	Hamburg	2,436,800

Die Zeit	Hamburg	446,900
Welt am Sonntag	Hamburg	434,300
Bayernkurier	Munich	145,700
Die Woche	Hamburg	130,300
Rheinischer Merkur	Bonn	110,400
Magazines		
Der Spiegel	Hamburg	1,051,600
Focus	Munich	810,900

MAGAZINES:

The buoyant market for illustrated magazines in Germany (there are some 20,000 titles in circulation) probably reflects the affluence of the Germans. Magazines range from the weekly news magazines such as *Der Spiegel* or *Focus* via the sometimes lurid but topical *Stern* and its rival *Bunte* to the women's and teenage press.In the same market are the even more trivial, gossipy magazines e.g. *Neue Revue*, *Quick* and *Weltbild*.

Der Spiegel: website www.spiegel.de. Spiegel is Germany's most influential weekly news magazine renowned for its investigative journalism and in-depth articles. Its adherents point out that it has good contacts with the movers and shakers of the political world, and through them, humanises politics. The cover price is €2.80 (£2.95, US$6.50) and circulation hovers around 1 million in Germany and 5 million worldwide. A year's subscription in the USA costs $310.

Focus: website www.focus.de. A competitor to *Der Spiegel*, this magazine has a slightly more conservative approach, but its in depth articles cover modern trends in German life, business and international politics as well as advances in science and technology. Although only a recent addition to the press market it is reaping a large circulation. Cover price €2.50.

Stern: website www.stern.de. Germany's most popular news weekly. Stern is renowned for its pictorial coverage and has content from around the world. Cover price €2.50.

Women's magazines (*Frauenzeitschriften*) account for an additional, combined magazine readership of around ten million. The main ones are *Bunte*, *Bild der Frau*, *Neue Post*, *Tina*, *Freizeit Revue*, *Brigitte*, *Für Sie* and *Freundin*.
    Another market area is the Television guide magazines which have a very wide readership, especially Hörzu which has 6 regional editions. Apart from the various channel listings these weekly titles have a good range of articles from the standard interviews with the stars, behind the scenes reportage and reviews of films, to in the case of *TV Hören und Sehen* articles and advice on family issues. The top five circulation magazines are *Prisma*, *TV Movie* priced €1.45, *Hörzu* priced €1.40, *TV Hören und Sehen* priced €1.40 and *Fernsehwoche* priced €1.

ENGLISH-LANGUAGE PUBLICATIONS

Major international English-language newspapers and magazines like *International Herald Tribune*, *Time*, *Newsweek*, *The Financial Times* etc. are all readily available on German news-stands. Most of them have production facilities in Germany, both the 'Trib' and the 'FT' are printed in Frankfurt. British newspapers are available on a daily basis at news-stands and bookshops in major cities. English-language publications available across Germany, or by subscription include:

The Times: The Times is available on a daily basis in Germany although the time of arrival at news-stands will depend on location as it is produced in London and Belgium. Readers in Frankfurt can get copies as early as 7 am, but those in München or Berlin will have to wait until late morning or lunchtime. An alternative is to take out an annual subscription, the current rates for the Monday-Saturday issues is £210 (for 3 months) or £700 (for 12 months) and the Sunday Times costs £110 and £360 respectively, but it is cheaper without the magazine. For subscriptions contact *Direct News Delivery*, 4th Floor, Montrose House, 412-416 Eastern Avenue, Gants Hill, Ilford, IG2 6NQ; ☎020-8709 6666.

The Guardian: Subscriptions Department, 164 Deansgate, Manchester, M60 2RR; ☎0870-066 0510. *The Guardian International* is the overseas daily version of the Guardian, and is produced in Frankfurt, and is available at news-stands across Germany. However, it lacks the supplements found in the British version. Die hard readers who don't want to lose out will have to obtain a subscription which costs £762 per year due to the weight when posted. *The Guardian Weekly* is an internationally available round up of the week's events as reported in The Guardian, the cover price for the weekly edition is £1.20 or £71 for a year. There is also the *Guardian Europe* for which a year's subscription costs £270.30.

The Economist: This highly regarded weekly magazine offers broad international perspectives on business and political affairs, as well as analysing new trends in science and technology. The German edition goes on sale on Fridays with a cover price of €4.35, although an annual subscription is €111.50. Circulation in Germany is 30,000 and subscriptions can be arranged by contacting The Economist Newspaper Ltd, PO Box 471, Haywards Heath, RH16 3GY; website www.economist.com.

Financial Times: Number One, Southwark Bridge, London SE1 9HL; ☎020-7873 4200; website www.ft.com and Financial Times (Europe) GmbH, Nibelungen Platz 3, D-60318 Frankfurt am Main; ☎069-156850; subscriptions ☎020-7873 4200. Financial Times, World Business Newspaper, has a print site and editorial department in Frankfurt, the circulation in Germany is 28,974, worldwide 487,263.

Forces Echo: Is a service oriented English-language weekly, produced in Britain for Germany, covering service news sporting fixtures and results. Copies are available at British base shops and service clubs.

International Herald Tribune: 40 Marsh Wall, London; ☎020-751 0570 (subscriptions UK 0800-895965, Europe 00800-44 487 827); e-mail (subscriptions) subs@iht.com; website www.iht.com. Edited in Paris and printed in partnership with newspapers across Europe, this independent English language daily combines news from around the world with local perspectives. Subscriptions in Germany are €380 for twelve months or €115 for three months.

MunichFound: MunichFound Verlag, Lilienstrasse 3-5, D-81669 München, Germany; website www.munichfound.com. The oldest and only English-language magazine for Munich and Upper Bavaria is a monthly publication offering articles on culture, politics, useful tips for expatriates and English-speaking tourists and an extensive event calender. Circulation in Bavaria is 35,000 and the readership includes the whole English-speaking business community and guests at Munich's international hotels.

Sixth Sense: Catterick Barracks, BFPO 39. A weekly publication aimed at service personnel and their families, serving in Germany; with a circulation of 14-17,000 copies. It contains radio and television details, articles about Germany, situations vacant and classified adverts.

Transitions Abroad: PO Box 1300, Amherst, MA 01004-1300, USA; ☎413-256 3414; fax 413-256 0373. Is a bi-monthly magazine with articles on living and working abroad, and active involvement as a guest in the host community rather than as a tourist. An annual subscription presently costs $28.00 in the USA, $32.00 in Canada and $46 around the world.

USA Today: 7950 Jones Branch Dr., McLean VA 22108, USA; ☎703-854 3400; website www.usatoday.com. 69 New Oxford Street, London, WC1A 1DG; ☎020-7559 5859; fax 020-7559 58805. America's largest daily general interest newspaper available across Germany. The cover price is €1.50 or €250 for a year's subscription.

The Wall Street Journal Europe: Freephone customer service number on 00 800 9753 2000; e-mail subs.wsje@dowjones.com; website www.wsj.com. The European edition of the American business and finance daily, printed in Brussels. More American-oriented than The Financial Times, and with even less non-business news. At the time of writing you could get a 4-week trial subscription to at the special price of EUR 15, saving 65% off the regular newsstand price.

Woman Abroad: Postmark Publishing, 1 Portsmouth Road, Guildford, GU2 4YB; ☎01483-571730; website www.womanabroad.com. The magazine for women expatriates from around the anglophone world.

TELEVISION

As with education, television and radio broadcasting (*Fernsehen*) is a mixture of public and private enterprise, the public stations are controlled on a regional basis by the Länder. Eleven channels are available, in addition to cable and satellite. German television has over the decades been characterised by its self-imposed censorship which has resulted in it trying to broadcast only what the public will find acceptable. Unfortunately, this, combined with a conscientious objectivity on political issues and an excess of public service broadcasting, has led to accusations of dullness, uniformity and parochialism. However, on the creative side German television has some highlights: arts programmes and documentaries covering the international scene are of high quality.

Americans can benefit from AFN's transmissions if they live close to a base, AFN licence agreements with European governments mean that their signals have to target 'pockets' of US citizens and military personnel so terrestial signal reception is weaker the further you are from a base. Military personnel including retirees residing in Germany are eligible for cable/satellitte reception of AFN broadcasting, which includes TV and radio and thus should negate reception problems.

The largest public channel, **ARD** (short for *Arbeitsgemeinshaft der öffentlich-rechtlichen Rundfunkanstalten der Bundesrepublik Deutschland*) is a group of eleven regional radio and television companies: Westdeutscher Rundfunk (WDR), Norddeutscher Rundfunk (NDR), Mitteldeutscher Rundfunk (MDR), Ostdeutscher Rundfunk Brandenburg, Radio Bremen (RB), Hessicher Rundfunk (HR), Südwestfunk (SWF), Süddeutscher Rundfunk (SDR), Sender Freies Berlin (SFB), Saarländischer Rundfunk and Bayerischer Rundfunk (BR). This television channel is *Erstes Deutsche Fernsehen* (Channel One). In addition to this the regional companies transmit their own television programmes (Channel Three in each region). The second national public channel is ZDF (*Zweites Deutsches Fernsehen* Channel Two) unlike the ARD consortium, it does not also operate a radio network. It is however, like ARD in that it is run by a consortium of Länder, and is effectively a public service broadcaster, even sharing weekday morning programming with ARD. In fact *ZDF* is the largest TV-station in Europe. The programmes broadcast by both stations are broadly similar in content. The largest elements are Plays and Films (23%), News (11.3%), Children's and Youth Programmes (10%) and Sport (7.6%). Financing comes in part from advertising (20% for ARD and 40% for ZDF) and a licence fee.

Licences are required for television and radio equipment in Germany. These fees go towards the running costs of the public broadcasters. Usually in a private household only one radio or television set has to be licensed, at the moment the fee is €16.15 per month, made up of a basic €5.32 fee plus €10.83 per TV; if you only have a radio the licence fee is much lower. The licence only covers one household property so if you live in Frankfurt and have a holiday home in Gelsenkirchen then you will need two licences. Licences can be paid for by direct debit or through post offices, where you will also find application forms and information (but only in German). The administration of licence fees is carried out by the *Gebühreneinzugszentrale* (GEZ, Postfach 108025, D-50656 Köln, Germany; ☎0180-501 6565; fa 0180-551 0700; e-mail info@gez.de; website www.gez.de). The fees are gathered by GEZ and distributed among the various companies according to listener and viewer density; hence Westdeutscher Rundfunk receives a larger share compared to Radio Bremen. Members of NATO forces or their families stationed in Germany are exempt from this fee.

In addition to the 'public' channels available in Germany Deutsche Welle broadcasts in Germany and around the world via satelitte. Originally the German radio equivalent of the BBC 'World Service' or 'Voice of America', the service expanded into TV with the 1999 launch of *DW-TV* (DW-TV: Voltastr. 6, D-13355 Berlin, Germany; ☎030-464640). This provides worldwide transmission of news and information about Germany; alternating between German, English, and Spanish, 24 hours a day. At the time of writing DW-TV was about to launch German-TV in the USA as a subscription service, in partnerships with ARD and ZDF.

Cable television (*Kabelhaushalte*) is now available as are several satellite channels: SAT 1, 3 SAT, PRO7 etc. 3 SAT is a culturally weighted programme broadcast by a consortium of ARD, ZDF and the Swiss and Austrian broadcasters. In any television listings magazine the daily programme guide can be expected to cover from five to eight pages due to the availability of around 22 terrestrial, cable and satellite channels. Much to the consternation of the public broadcasting concerns, new private channels are rapidly augmenting their audience ratings. ARD and ZDF at present each have around a 30% rating. In areas with cable television, the private channels have a fifty per cent rating. The attraction of the private and satellite channels over public broadcasting is a more adventurous style of programme. In addition to serious discussions of hot political issues like abortion, there are less serious programmes with mass appeal e.g. games and quiz shows. However even if you watch pay-tv, you'll still need a licence from GEZ for your equipment.

RADIO

Germany has an expanding array of radio stations; currently the number is around fifty, as each of the eleven public broadcasters operates four or five regional radio stations, these broadcast a variety of news, light music and entertainment programmes.

English-speaking radio stations include *The World Service*, Radio Luxembourg and Radio E; a consortium of 4 national broadcasters (including the BBC and Deutsche Welle) across Europe with English-language programmes. The British Forces Broadcasting Service (BFBS) and the American Forces Network (AFN) are obviously operated by the military for the benefit of service staff. In addition Radio Stuttgart and Deutsche Welle regularly put out programmes in English. Deutsche Welle is Germany's international TV and radio broadcaster transmitting programmes in twenty-nine languages around the world as well as German for Germans living abroad, it is also useful for those wishing to find out about Germany before they move there. Programmes are transmitted in short wave, on sub-carriers from satellite tv, radio satellite rebroadcasters, and via the internet. In addition to the shortwave broadcasts some programmes, such as concerts are recorded for broadcast via satellite to radio stations across the United States.

In addition to the website page (www.dw-world.de) listing programmes and frequencies including broadcasts in English (of which there is a weekly schedule) they produce a monthly magazine with times and frequencies which is available from:

Television & Radio Stations:

Arbeitsgemeinschaft der Öffentlich-Rechtl. Rundfunkanstalten Deutschlands (ARD): Appellhofplatz 1, D-50667 Köln, Germany; ☎0221-2201; fax 0221-220 4800; website www.ard.de.

Bayerischer Rundfunk: (Bavaria) Rundfunkplatz 8, D-80335 München, Germany; ☎089-590001; fax 089-5900 2375; website www.br-online.de.

Hessischer Rundfunk: (Hesse) Bertramstrasse 8, D-60320 Frankfurt, Germany; ☎069-1551; fax 069-155 2900; website www.hr-online.de.

Mitteldeutscher Rundfunk: (Eastern Germany) Springerstrasse 22-24, D-04105 Leipzig, Germany; ☎0341-56630; fax 0341-566 3544; website www.mdr.de.

Norddeutscher Rundfunk: (Northern Germany) Rothenbaumchaussee 132-134, D-20149 Hamburg, Germany; ☎040-41560; fax 040-447602; website www.ndr.de.

Norddeutscher Fernsehen: Hugh-Greene Weg 1, D-22504 Hamburg, Germany; ☎040-41560; website www.ndr.de.

Ostdeutscher Rundfunk: (Eastern Germany) August-Bebel-Strasse 25-53, D-14482 Potsdam, Germany;

☎ 0331-723600; fax 0331-77395; website www.orb.de.

Ostdeutscher Fernsehen: Marlene-Dietrich-Allee 20, D-14482 Potsdam-Babelsberg, Germany; ☎ 0331-7310; fax 0331-731 3571; e-mail orbfernsehen@orb.de; website www.orb.de/fernsehen/tv/.

Radio Bremen: Bürgermeister-Spitta-Allee 45, D-28329 Bremen, Germany; ☎ 0421-2460; fax 0421-246 1010; website www.radiobremen.de.

Saarlaendischer Rundfunk: (Saarland) Funkhaus, Halberg, D-66121 Saarbrücken, Germany; ☎ 0681-6020; fax 0681-602 3874; e-mail info@sr-online.de; website www.sr-online.de.

Sender Freies Berlin: D-10046 Berlin, Germany; website www.sfb.de.

Suedwestfunk: (South-Western Germany) Hans-Bredow-Strasse 6, D-76530 Baden-Baden, Germany; ☎ 07221-920; fax 07221-922010.

Westdeutscher Rundfunk: Appellhofplatz 1, D-50667 Köln, Germany; ☎ 0221-2200; fax 0221-220 4800; website www.wdr.de.

Zweites Deutsches Fernsehen (ZDF): Postfach 4040, D-55127 Mainz, Germany;

☎ 06131-701; fax 06131-702157; website www.zdf.de.

DW World: Raderberggürtel 50, D-50968 Köln; website dw-world.de.

Deutsche Welle: Washington Bureau, Suite 335, 2000 M Street NW, Washington DC 20036, USA; ☎ 202-785 5730; fax 202-785 5735.

DW-Radio/English Service: D-50588 Cologne, Germany; ☎ 0221-389 4155; e-mail english@dw-world.de.

AFN: website www.afneurope.army.mil/Program/afnradio.htm. Broadcasts, via satellite and cable, radio and TV programming to US forces. There are now six locations in Germany serving US military and retirees, with two radio broadcast services 'Power Network' and 'Z-FM' details of programmes and frequencies can be found on the website (above).

BFBS: BFBS Herford, BFPO 15. Has seven transmitters across Germany broadcasting programmes between 93 and 106 Mhz, 24 hours a day. The aim of the service is to entertain and inform British Forces, while maintaining a link with events in Britain.

POST AND TELECOMMUNICATIONS

The German *Bundespost* monopoly on postal and telephone services was several years ago and the seperate parts have slowly been privatised. The three new companies *Deutsche Telekom, Deutsche Post* and *Deutsche Postbank* all have AG status. In fact *Deutsche Post World Net* (the newly privatised post office) aims to be a world player. Under EU competition regulations the German government may scrap its monopoly on post delivery (only for letters weighing over 50g) towards the end of 2002, however, this is dependent on the rest of the EU opening up their postal systems. To keep ahead of the game post offices now offer a range of services including the sale of stamps, postage, mail packaging, banking and even mortgages and insurance.

Post

Post Offices (Postämter) are normally open from 8am to 6pm Monday to Friday and 8am to 1pm on Saturdays. Post boxes are yellow and bear the post horn symbol. Large towns also have special airmail (*Flugpost*) boxes which are blue. There are stamp machines outside most post offices, in railway stations etc. and stamps (*Briefmarken*) can be bought in hotels as well as post offices. At the time of writing the cost of sending an ordinary letter to Britain from Germany began at 56 cents. A Poste Restante (*Postlagernde Sendungen*) service is provided free at the main post office (*Hauptpostamt*) of every town. You should ensure that all mail to be collected thus is clearly marked *Postlagernde Sendungen* by the sender, as Poste Restante is not a familiar term in Germany. Radio and television licence fee application forms can be obtained from post offices.

When addressing mail for Germany, it should be noted that the German address order may differ from what the reader is used to: the name of the recipient on line one, followed on line two by the name of the street and then the building number (on the right), and on line three by the postal code (*postleitzahl*) and then the name of the town or city. An example being:

Maike Büttner,
Lorenz Str. 29,
90422 Nürnberg.

Within Europe, outside Germany, it is helpful to insert a capital D before the postcode. Bear in mind that a sender's address should always be added, for Germany this is usually in the top left corner of the front of the envelope. You can expect next day delivery of 95% of post and parcels can be delivered in a day to a 400km radius and nationwide within two.

Telephones

Deutsche Telekom lost its monopoly on the German telephone system in 1998 in the deregulation of phone systems across Europe. However, it is still the largest phone provider in Germany, and Europe, even though there are around 1,700 telecomms provider companies registered with the regulatory authority *RegTP*. At present to obtain a phone line from Deutsche Telekom the installation fee is around €50, unless you are taking over an existing line number. Phones can usually be installed within two weeks of application in most parts of western Germany and bills are rendered monthly. The basic monthly rental varies according to the type of contract signed up to (an ISDN/DSL link would be €30 plus VAT). Telephone calls are still charged for by the unit at a base rate of 1-6 cents per minute plus VAT (VAT is currently 16%), the cost of your call depends on the time of day and distance involved. The cheapest standard rate is between 10pm and 6am daily, which is why long distance calls were usually made late at night; however these days many Germans use prefix codes which route calls via cheaper provicers. Information on phones can be obtained at 'T-Punkt' shops. To research telephone costs and tariffs the website www.teltarif.de is very useful.

The mobile, cellphone, or '*handy*' as the Germans call them, is prevalent, currently nearly 50 million users are subscribed to mobile phone systems in Germany. Deutsche Telekom's mobile subsidiary *T-Mobile* is doing its best to retain its monopoly (23 million subscribers), but it is facing some very stiff competition in this market from *D2* (*Vodafone-Mannesmann*), *E-Plus Mobilfunk*, and *E2 Mobilfunk*. The GSM system is used in Europe so many US made cellphones won't work in Germany, but the services are much the same the world over, and you can easily find a mobile dealership in most towns. However, please note that it is illegal to use a 'handy' while driving unless you're using a 'hands-free' set, which are naturally available from phone shops. In Germany, as elsewhere across Europe most public phone boxes are no longer payphones but need phonecards (*Telefonkarte*) for use. Telephone cards are available at post offices and railway stations and cost €6 for 40 units or €25 for 200 units. Telephone calls are still charged for by the unit, the cost of your call depends on the time of day and distance involved, as these factors affect how much phone time you actually get per unit.

The older telephone booths are easy to spot by their bright yellow colour, newer models are being installed across the country. However you would be hard put not to realise what they were, especially given the label *Telefon*. You can also telephone from main post offices where there are banks of telephones: after being allotted a booth at the counter, you make your call and return to the counter to pay. If dialling abroad, go to the counter marked *Auslandsgespräche*.

The German yellow pages are known as *Gelbe Seiten*. Listed at the front are the emergency services' numbers, directory assistance numbers and the current postal rates. The ordinary telephone directory (*Fernsprechbuch*) contains personal and business subscribers' numbers. While to call Directory Enquiries you ring 01188 (directory calls are charged for at a premium rate), International Enquiries are on 00118, there are also English language directory services which will connect you to the number you're seeking: 11837 for German numbers and 11834 for others.

To telephone Germany the International code is 49, prefixed by whatever the international access code is for your location (in Britain and Germany the access code is 00). To call the UK or the USA and Canada from Germany the international access codes are +44 (0044) for the UK, +1 (001) for the USA and Canada, and +61 (0061) for Australia; this is followed by the subscriber's number minus the first 0. For example to call Vacation Work (01865-241978) from Germany would be: 0044-1865-241978. From Germany you can direct dial most countries around the world.

Emergency Service Telephone Numbers. For the police call 110; for the fire brigade call 112 (this is also the number to call for emergency ambulances).

MAIN GERMAN TELEPHONE CODES

Aachen	0241	Krefeld	02151
Augsburg	0821	Leipzig	0341
Berlin	030	Leverkusen	02171
Bayreuth	0921	Lübeck	0451
Bielefeld	0521	Ludwigshafen/Rhein	0621
Bochum	0234	Magdeburg	0391
Bonn	0228	Mainz	06131
Braunschweig	0531	Mannheim	0621
Bremen	0421	Mönchengladbach	02161
Bremerhaven	0471	München	089
Celle	05141	Münster	0251
Chemnitz	0371	Neuss	02131
Cottbus	0355	Nürnberg	0911
Darmstadt	06151	Offenbach/Main	069

Dortmund	0231	Oldenburg	0441
Dresden	0351	Oranienburg	03301
Duisburg	0203	Osnabrück	0541
Düsseldorf	0211	Paderborn	05251
Eisenach	03691	Passau	0851
Erfurt	0361	Potsdam	0331
Essen	0201	Regensburg	0941
Frankfurt/Main	069	Reutlingen	07121
Frankfurt/Oder	0335	Rostock	0381
Freiburg-im-Breisgau	0761	Saarbrücken	0681
Gelsenkirchen	0209	Solingen	0212
Gera	0365	Starnberg	08151
Hagen	02331	Stuttgart	0711
Halle	0345	Suhl	03681
Hamburg	040	Trier	0651
Hannover	0511	Ulm	0731
Heidelberg	06221	Wiesbaden	0611
Karlsruhe	0721	Wilhelmshaven	4421
Kassel	0561	Wuppertal	0202
Kiel	0431	Würzburg	0931
Koblenz	0261		
Köln	0221		

The Internet

The global electronic data network is popular with German computer users, schools and students. The T-Online internet service provider, a subsidiary of Deutsche Telekom, has 10 million subscribers making it Germany's largest network operator, other internet providers operating in Germany are America Online (AOL), Compuserve, and germany.net. Most major cities and municipalities have their own websites, in addition to those operated by the government ministries, transport operators, universities and newspapers. The content of German websites is unsurprisingly in German, however, (unlike many websites in Britain or America, which are only in the native language) many sites do have an English language version often running to several pages, even some sites where you might not expect it have a one page summary in English. Schleswig-Holstein's website has a links page where links to sites with English pages are indentified. Around 35% of all businesses employing more than ten staff have access to the internet, and around 13% would no longer be able to do business without it.

The main problem with 'surfing' for German users is the high cost of the telephone connection from their PC to the internet. Part of the reason why T-Online's subscriber base is so large is that it is an off-shoot of Deutsche Telekom, who also provide most of the connections and phone services used for internet access, and who until recently have had a monopoly on telecommunications and thus the prices charged. The opening up of the telecommunications market has seen prices drop and many internet users are happily signed up to the *T-DSL* flat rate broadband service, which allows multiple users to surf and make phonecalls from one line.

CARS AND MOTORING

DRIVING IN GERMANY

Germany has one of the most up-to-date and extensive motorway systems in Europe, so it comes as a pleasant surprise that, unlike Italy, France etc, there are no tolls. However the *Autobahnen* (motorways) have another scourge: there is no speed limit, although this is actually a bit of a myth. **Bear in mind that Germany drives on the right.** The left lane is for passing/overtaking, the right lane is for driving.

Driving Licences

Drivers entering Germany are allowed to drive on their current licence for up to six months, after which they must obtain a German licence – a process which involves written and practical examinations at an approved driving school before obtaining a licence from the issuing office (*Stadtverwaltung: Führerscheinstelle*) for the region. There are exceptions to this requirement for EU citizens and drivers who obtained their licences in certain parts of the USA and Canada, details of these exemptions can be found in the previous chapter.

In Germany it is also a requirement that you carry your drivers licence and vehicle registration documents/log book (*Fahrzugschein/Kraftfahrzeugbrief*) with you when driving.

Speed Limits

The government recommends that drivers should restrict their speed to 130 kph (78 mph), but this is widely regarded as a joke. Consequently, German executives are inclined to give vent to their killer instincts when behind the wheels of their powerful BMW's, Mercedes and Audis by bearing down on anything in the fast lane. At speeds in excess of 200kph (125mph), lights flashing furiously, they clear the way, before accelerating into the distance. However, just because somebody does this to you, does not mean that it is accepted road etiquette in fact its illegal.

From time to time motorway speed limits are imposed by the use of light up number boards when the weather is wet, foggy or construction/repair work is in progress, and these should be adhered to. The speed limit for cars pulling a caravan is 80 kph (50 mph) on ordinary roads and motorways.

As more and more gantries for variable speed limits are erected so more speed camers are fitted, so it may be fun to do 200kph, but a few weeks later you'll find a speeding ticket in your post box. At any given time a small percentage of Autobahnen have a speed limit in operation but on the whole it seems unlikely that the Germans will bring in a general speed limit in the foreseeable future. The arguments against a speed limit include the fact that only 6% of fatal accidents occur on the motorways, making them the safest roads in Germany. However this probably says more for the high safety standards of German cars than for German driving.

SPEED LIMITS

- ○ Autobahn; 130 kph
- ○ Other major roads; 100 kph (cars with trailers 80 kph)
- ○ Urban roads 30-50kph

According to the American Chamber of Commerce a 'ready-reckoner' for working out kph in mph is to drop the 0 and multiply by 6: eg 100kph (becomes 10 x 6) equals 60mph approx.

Traffic Violations

The police have a tendency to arrest anyone acting in an agressive fashion, especially with the growing incidence of 'road-rage' in Germany; the government recently initiated a 'Drive Happy' campaign to calm traffic. Excessive vehicle speed and arrest usually result in a combination of 'penalty-points' on your licence and fines. Fines and points are added together if you're more than 20 kph over the limit, less than that and there is a scale of fines according to how fast you were travelling. Three points and a stiffer fine are added for being up to 30kph over the limit and the fine rates and points climb from there up. Fines may be collected on the spot if you have sufficient cash to hand, otherwise you'll be sent a ticket and payment slip. Repeated failure to pay will result in imprisonment, collecting 14 points will get you pointed in the direction of a driving school and amassing 18 will lose you your licence. Penalty points are only annulled after two years or so, provided you haven't collected anymore in the meantime, points accrued as a result of an accident take ten years to clear.

In a drive to stamp out aggression at its source, the licence penalty-points and fines can be imposed by the police on drivers considered to be acting in an aggressive manner. Acts which are considered likely to initiate aggressive behaviour include spitting, gesturing and shouting obscenities. Fines and points can also be obtained for parking violations.

Oh and high speed accidents often nullify your insurance.

ACCIDENTS

In the event of a traffic accident the driver must remain at the scene for a minimum of 30 minutes. Insurance and contact information must be exchanged. Even bumping a car while parking can be considered an accident and a note on the windscreen is not sufficient.

If you are first to come upon an accident scene Germany's *Good Samaritan* laws require you to render assistance, and that means more than just calling the police or ambulance.

Road Rules

At crossings and traffic junction's vehicles coming from the right have priority unless otherwise indicated by road signs. Children under 12 years old must be secured by special seats or seatbelts, and the wearing of seatbelts in both the front and back of the vehicle is obligatory. Drivers should always bear in mind that most cities have bicycle lanes and these often cross the roads at junctions, so keep your wits about you. You should also bear in mind that bus lanes are strictly for buses and taxis, the exception being when making a right turn, but only at the turn. Added to these hidden dangers are the pedestrian-only zones that some cities are enforcing, as if one-way streets and parking restrictions don't make life difficult enough. The problem is that unless you have kept up with German news and bought the latest street maps, you are likely to blunder into a problem.

Drinking and Driving. Just don't even think about it, the limit for blood alchohol in Germany is 0.5 milligrams, a blood test can be imposed and even a first offence will result in you licence being impounded for 3 months.

ROAD SIGNS WORTH NOTING

Umleitung (detour).
Fahrbahnschäden or *Strassenschäden* (damaged road surface).
Kreuzung (crossroads).
Strasse gesperrt (road closed).
Steinschlag (falling rocks).
Hupverbot (no hooting).
Einbahnstrasse (one-way street).
Halten Verboten/Halteverbot (no parking).
Give Way/Yield sign is a white inverted triangle with a red border.
Stop signs are hexagonal.
Priority signs are yellow diamonds with white borders.
White stripes across the road surface are pedestrian crossings and these are not always accompanied by traffic lights.
Buses have right of way when pulling out.
Overtaking or passing can only happen on the left, and can occur at junctions (so be careful)

Ever pollution conscious, Germany has enforced the fitting of three-way catalytic converters on all new motor cars (except very small ones) since 1986, and leaded petrol is no longer available, unleaded (*bleifrei*) petrol is rated at 91 octane and *super bleifrei* is 95. A free booklet (*Tanken & Rasten*) on the German motorway network is available at all autobahn service areas, or from *Autobahn Tank & Rast* the leading service station operator in Germany.

The German equivalent of the AA is ADAC, the AvD and AvD, are other motoring associations, all three run a breakdown service (*Strassenwacht*) on all motorways and main roads. The emergency police service can be summoned by dialling 110 or 112. There are automatic telephones situated at regular intervals along all motorways.

Useful Addresses

Allgemeiner Deutscher Automobil Club e.V.
(ADAC): Am Westpark 8, D-81373
München, Germany; ☎089-76760;
website www.adac.de.

Autobahn Tank & Rast GmbH & Co.
KG, Andreas-Hermes-Str. 7-9, D-53175
Bonn, Germany ☎0228-9220; website
www.tank.rast.de.

Automobilclub von Deutschland e.V.(AVD):
Lyonerstrasse 16, D-60528 Frank-
furt-Niederrad, Germany; ☎069-66060;
website www.avd.de.

Auto Club Europa (ACE): Schmidener
Strasse 233, D-70374 Stuttgart, Germany; ☎0711-530 3266; website
www.ace-online.de.

Automobile Association (AA): Overseas
Department, PO Box 2AA, Newcastle-upon-Tyne, NE99 2AA; ☎0870
606 1615; www.theaa.com.

RAC Motoring Services: Travel Services,
PO Box 1500, Bristol BS99 1LH;
☎0800-550055; www.rac.co.uk.

PUBLIC TRANSPORT

Y ou may find that it is possible to do without a car in Germany as the transport
system is one of the best in Europe. In many of the larger towns and cities
you'll find an excellent integrated local transport system of buses, trams and
trains (underground and regional). Since 1991 the Federal Ministry of Transport
(www.bmv.de) has spent vaast sums upgrading the rail system, roads and
waterways under the 'German Unity' transport scheme.

RAILWAYS

D eutsche Bahn runs more than 33,000 trains daily (1,200 of them
long-distance), carrying over 4.6 million passengers. Long-distance and
local train timetables are co-ordinated to allow optimal connections. Many
airports are also integrated into this system.

Standard tickets covering journeys up to 100 kilometres are valid for one day.
On longer journeys single tickets are valid for four days while return tickets are
valid for a month. It is recommended, especially on the long distance services, to
make a reservation well in advance to ensure your seat on the more popular travel
days and trains. This costs €2.60, but it's well worth it.

Tickets are designed to make things easier for you and offer you more flexibility.
Apart from our regular fares, Minigroup, Twen, Weekend, and Saver Tickets help
you to make the most of your budget. There are also some Land tickets which act
in the same way as a weekend ticket, these allow two or more to travel for one
fixed low price, so long as you don't use ICE or IC trains.

For the frequent traveller in Germany, the BahnCard (for adults and children) allows
travel on the entire Deutsche Bahn network for a year at up to 50% off the regular
fare. Bahncards retail for €130 (£/$) a year and are well worth the investment.

TYPES OF TRAINS

Long Distance

InterCityExpress (ICE): Deutsche Bahn's flagship with its modern interior design offers comfortable, reclining seats with plenty of legroom in both seating classes, and an onboard audio system with headset access. Seating is arranged in either compartments or open-plan style carriages with panoramic windows and air-conditioning. The journey time between Cologne and Berlin is just under 4 1/2 hours. The ICE3 carries its passengers at speeds of up to 205 mph. First class passengers can sit in a lounge directly behind the driver, from where they can enjoy a view right through the cockpit onto the track ahead. The ICE T tilting train uses new technology to save even more time, taking bends at speeds of up to 138 mph.

InterCity (IC): Express trains which provide a regular service across Germany between major towns and cities which are not served by the ICE. Open-plan carriages or compartments provide comfortable seating, and trains are fully air-conditioned. All trains have restaurant or bistro cars.

EuroCity (EC): An international high quality train usually integrated into the IC network.

InterRegio (IR): Similar to the IC but the network is larger and they stop at more stations, on most lines there is at least one an hour.

DB NachtZug (NZ): Quality night train services for an undisturbed rest on numerous routes within Germany and further afield to Europe. There is a choice of three categories of travel: couchettes, modern sleepers or reclining seats.

Short Distance

Eilzug (D): A semi-fast train service which stops at more stations than the long distance services on the same route.

Regional Express (RE): Regional fast train which services major stations.

Regional Bahn (RB): Slower versions of the RE stopping at more stations.An example of the difference is that the RE from Nürnberg to Bamberg takes 45 minutes compared to the 61 of the RB.

Stadt Express (SE): Urban express service.

S-Bahn: Urban trains which service the suburban areas and hinterlands of major towns and cities.

Tickets and price information in Germany can be obtained from railway stations, travel agents and regional tourist offices with a DB licence or call the DB Reiseservice in Germany (☎ 0180-599 6633). Deutsche Bahn also has its own UK Booking Centre for those who wish to make their travel arrangements before they leave (*Deutsche Bahn UK* Booking Centre: PO Box 687A, Surbiton, KT6 6UB;

☎08702-435363). Those with an Internet connection can check train details and timetables on the Deutsche Bahn web site (www.bahn.co.uk or for German speakers www.bahn.de).

Another new development planned for commuter use is the electromagnetic, levitating *Transrapid* service (www.transrapid.simplenet.com). This is planned to run between Hamburg and Berlin at up to 500 kph, with six services an hour.

CITY TRANSPORT

Most German cities and large towns have a well integrated public transport system, consisting of trams, buses, trains and cycle paths seperate from the road.

U-Bahn. Those who live and work in the cities (especially Hamburg, Frankfurt, München, Bonn, Düsseldorf, Berlin, Stuttgart, Nürnberg and Hannover), will find excellent underground railway (*U-Bahnen*) networks. As with the Paris métro it is cheaper for regular users to buy a book of tickets or multi-ride pass (*Mobikarte*) the latter are especially useful as they allow two people to travel together. The U-Bahn closes down between 1am and 5am.

S-Bahn: Many of the city underground routes are supplemented and overlapped by regional railway routes. These S-bahnen are either operated by the municipal authority or Deutsche Bahn, and serve both the town centres, urban fringe and the surrounding area.

Trams and Buses: In the larger cities bus, tram and U-Bahn tickets are interchangeable and buying a book of tickets or mobikarte is a useful economy measure if you are a regular user of city transport. Confusingly, in all city centres, trams go underground. In some towns there are 'pure' underground lines, but most are mixed surface and underground and go subterranean for only short stretches. Bus services are also useful for reaching the suburbs and bus stops (*Bushaltestellen*) are easy to find.

Be warned that larger cities like München, Hamburg and Frankfurt have an array of fare structures depending on which zone your destination is located in. Fares are graded by the number of zones through which you pass. Having worked out the correct fare, you must not forget to get your ticket cancelled by machines located at platform entrances or inside buses and trams. Machines are generally marked E for *Entwertung* (cancellation). This must be done on each stage of the journey. An oversight can result in a hefty on-the-spot fine.

Taxis. Can be hailed, booked by telephone or picked up at taxi stands. Fares vary between cities and extra is charged for luggage and dogs. Taxis are easy to spot by the regulation off-white paintwork, and in Frankfurt you can even find a few of the famous London cabs (although with a new paint-job of course). Hailing these is probably harder as at the time of writing they are rather a novelty for locals to ride in, and so there is a waiting list in operation.

Municipal Transport Authorities

Hamburger Verkehrsverbund GmbH: Steinstrasse 7, D-20095 Hamburg, Germany;

☎040-325 7750; e-mail hvv.gmbh@hvv.de; website www.hvv.de. Operates 3 U-Bahn, 9 S-Bahn., 3 A-Bahn, and 245 bus routes throughout the whole Hamburg area (roughly 40 km across). Buses and trains run every five minutes in the inner city except between midnight and 5 am, when a night bus service operates.

Münchener Verkehrs-und-Tarifverbund GmbH: Postfach 260154, München, Germany; Call-Center ☎089-4142 4344; website www.mvv-muenchen.de. Ten S-Bahn, eight U-Bahn and a vast number of bus lines and trams connect places in the city and the surrounding areas, forming a transportation network, which covers about 500 square kilometers. Daytickets for single persons and groups of up to five people are available for €4.50 and €7.50, covering the city area of Munich. For the whole network, the daytickets are €9.00 and €15 respectively. Further (and more specific) information in English can be found on the MVV website especially under MVV-Service – Broschüren – Schatzplan mehrsprachig.

Rhein-Main-Verkehrsverbund: Alte Bleiche 5, D-65719 Hofheim, Germany. RMV is a regional transport authority covering 15 counties and 11 cities in south-middle Hessen. RMV has integrated regional trains and busses as well as local busses, trams and underground. All devices can be used with one single ticket. The price for a single-ride ticket in Frankfurt is about €1.90.

BUS

Unlike Britain or America there is no nationwide network of bus routes. The rail network is supplemented and overlapped by regional buses run by the local transport authorities. In part this is the result of the extensive rail network. On the whole if a town or village is not served by a train or s-bahn regional train line then a bus will run to it, albeit on a limited time-table. Having said that, there are some coach companies running cross-country services on routes such as Berlin-München. However these are not part of any extensive network and so your ability to use them instead of the train is limited.

BOATS

Cruising on the great rivers of Germany, the Rhine, the Mosel, the Danube, the Weser and the Elbe, or along the shores of the larger lakes like the Bodensee, can be a very pleasant way to unwind. Ships of the Köln-Düsseldorfer Rheinschiffahrt AG (KD Lines), sail from Rotterdam in Holland through the west of Germany down to Basel on the German-Swiss border as well as the shorter scenic stretches between Köln and Mainz/Wiesbaden and along the Mosel. KD has also operates on the Elbe (see below), and holders of Deutsche Bahn rail cards can get discounts on tickets. On the Danube cruisers go from Regensburg or Passau. The Weser boats take passengers from Hannoversch-Münden to Hameln. For a west east trip, start at Hamburg and cruise the Elbe from Hamburg or Lauenburg to Bad Schandau, south of Dresden. On all these cruises stops are made at various places of interest. The German tourist board can supply further details.

AIR

The German national carrier is Lufthansa, with its home at Frankfurt; the busiest airport in continental Europe. Over 100 international airlines offer flights into Germany. As well as international flights Lufthansa operates on the main routes between German cities including Berlin, Erfurt, Leipzig, München and Dresden. Some of these flights are in conjunction with British carriers like British Midland and British Airways (who also operate within the German domestic flight market with its subsidiary Deutsche BA).

There are frequent flights to and from major German cities to the main UK and US airports, with either Lufthansa, BA, BM or any of the trans-Atlantic American carriers. Lufthansa itself has joined the *Star-Alliance* of airline companies based in the USA, Canada, Scandinavia, Brazil and Thailand, hence entering partnership deals for transatlantic and transglobal flights. So you may be booked with Lufthansa but fly in a British Midland plane.

The main German airports for travellers arriving from outside Europe are Frankfurt/Main, Düsseldorf and München. Other major airports are Cologne/Bonn, Leipzig/Halle, Dresden, Berlin-Tegel and Berlin Templehof.

GETTING THERE

Apart from the various airlines offering flights to Germany, more traditional and cost effective means of getting to Germany from Britain are available, especially if you wish to travel with more than twenty kilos worth of luggage and personal effects. One route is the car ferry, thus allowing you more control over how fast you get to Germany and with what personal affects. Most ferries from Britain to Germany travel in to Hamburg, so if you are relocating there this is a cost-effective option. Most non-Europeans will have to have their goods shipped in or pay very expensive airfreight costs, but a relocation company can probably get you a good deal in this area (see Chapter 2 *Setting Up Home*). Another alternative for those who like driving is to take the Eurostar, through the channel tunnel to France and then drive on to Germany.

Students on the other hand travelling with either a study abroad period or a summer job in mind will need less luggage, as will those planning a short hop to scout out a new home. In which case the cheap flight offered by low-cost operators such as *Ryan Air* or *Go* are worth the hassle of getting to Luton or Stanstead. Even so planes and ferries can be expensive and you still have to arrange train tickets from your arrival point in Germany; Go fly to Dresden, Frankfurt or Munich while Ryan Air hop into the Frankfurt subsidiary at Hahn. If you aren't looking in those areas then you'll have to fly with a major, and so more expensive, carrier. A relatively inexpensive alternative is coach travel from Britain, the major coach firms such as Eurolines run long-distance coaches from Britain to the continent.

DFDS Seaways: DFDS Seaways, Scandinavia House, Parkeston, Harwich, Essex, CO12 4QG. *Germany Direct* from Harwich with a new route in 2002 to Cuhaven. Telephone 08705-333000 for the latest discounts, offers, and sailing schedules to suit your travel needs.

Eurolines: 4 Cardiff Road, Luton, LU1 1PP; ☎08705-143219; e-mail welcome@eurolines.co.uk; www.eurolines.co.uk.. One of Europe's major coach operators, services are operated from Victoria Coach Station in London to cities across Germany. Connections with National Express services to London from across Britain can be arranged as one ticket purchase. Prices vary according to the destination required and there are discounts for children and those under 26 or over 60. Contact Eurolines for more information or a copy of their brochure.

BANKS AND FINANCE

The organisation of the banking system in Germany is to a large extent dictated by the principles on which the economy is run and the country is governed. Compared with Britain, the USA etc. only a small percentage of Germany's industry is in public ownership. Both the national government and the Länder dole out billions in subsidies and regional aid packages. To facilitate the distribution of funds on a regional basis, all the Länder governments own large banks. The Deutsche Bundesbank has handed its role as central bank to the European Central Bank since the introducton of the Euro. But it still acts as banker to the federal government, issues German euro notes and coins, acts as intermediary for financial transactions and controls the money supply and supervises the banking system.

Germany has universal banking, which means that all financial services are available in one place. Savings, checking, credit cards, loans, stock brokerage, mortgages, investment banking, and in some cases insurance, are all handled by the universal banks. Unlike American banks, German banks can also have business ties to their customers, with most major companies having at least one banker on their board of directors.

PAYMENT SYSTEMS

The main way of paying for goods and service in Germany is still hard cash, while almost all employees are paid by bank transfer into their accounts, when they spend it, on the whole they'll use bank notes and coins. Payment by cheque is rare, and while credit/debit cards are growing in use they still have yet to gain the widespread use that they have in Britain and America (recent figures estimated that while every American alive has more than one credit card only one in eight Germans has one). The main card in use with Germans is the Eurocard, which is more akin to the UK's 'Switch' card and so debits your bank account in the retailers' favour, 45 million Germans have an EC card. Mastercard, Visa and American Express are accepted, however, often only in large stores, although in the last 20 years the number of people holding such cards has leapt from 580,000 to around 18 million. Deutsche Bahn has a joint credit card rail discount card. However if you're willing to pay the interest you can obtain cash using a credit card from most bank cash machines/autotellers *(Geldautomat)*. Certainly at the moment holders of Britih bank debit cards carrying the Maestro or Cirrus logos can use German bank cash machines.

THE 'GIRO' SYSTEM

Three types of cashless transfer from your bank account to another or vice versa:
- *Transfer Uberweisung*
- *Standing Order Dauerauftrag*
- *Direct Debit Lastschriftverfahren*

Payments systems (cashless money transfers) are highly sophisticated and automated in Germany. In addition to the major banks' internal systems for payment and data processing, the *Gesellschaft für Zahlungssysteme* (established in 1982) administers all Eurocard and cheque transactions. The main methods of paying for bills in the absence of cheques are the cashless transfers which should be familiar to most Britons reading this. The simplest of these is the Transfer (*Uberweisung*) where you simply fill in the transfer form with the relevant details and hand it in to the bank. Regular payments for bills or rent can be covered by a Standing Order (*Dauerauftrag*) which deducts an agreed sum on an agreed date each month and deposits it in the recipient's account. These payments will continue until cancelled by you in writing. Should your regular debits vary in size then you can arrange a Direct Debit system (*Lastschriftverfahren*) with the organisation that you are paying. The authorisation for deductions from your account is an *Einzugsermächtigung.* As these arrangements and sums will all appear on your statement so that you can check that all is well, you also have the security of being able to contest these payments up to four weeks after deduction.

THE EURO

In January 2002 12 states within the EU switched their currencies for the Euro €. Although it had run in parallel for the previous two years for business and non-cash transactions, it has now replaced entirely all pre-eisiting currencies. Euros can be used across the 12 nations so you may find in your change at a mix of German, French and even Irish Euro coins. All notes and coins are the same size, colour and design, local national variations occurring only on one side of the coins, currency notes are standard across the 'eurozone'. Edges of coins have milling or grooves so as to be distinguishable to the the blind.

At the time of exchange the Euro was set at a rate of exchange to the Deutsche Mark of €1 = DM 1.95583, so if you see anything marked as DM just divide by two to get the rough € price.

This new currency unites Europe and should allow price transparency, at the time of writing inhabitants of eastern France were travelling to Germany to buy cheaper petrol. But not everyone is happy, most ordinary Germans don't mind the new currency, what they **do** mind is that the prices have gone up. In the run up to Euro introduction, prices were paralleled on shop shelves. Since the replacement though, prices have crept up, not just by the simple rounding of price points making €1.87 up to €1.95 (the beloved price-point of the retail analyst). In some cases prices seem to have been switched from DM to € with something added for luck. This is what makes people grumble.

OPENING A GERMAN BANK ACCOUNT

Opening a bank current account/checking account (*Girokonto*) in Germany is a remarkably straightforward and swift procedure needing only the completion of a bank account application form, the presentation of your passport as proof of identity and an initial deposit to open the account. It is recommended that you have the sum ready in cash, as cheques or drafts from your home bank will take a while to be processed, and so hold things up. The whole process need take only a few minutes. The 'big three' banks (Deutsche Bank, Dresdner Bank and Commerz Bank which are privately owned) between them have thousands of branches in Germany. If possible, it is advisable to choose one of their main city branches, rather than a smaller sub or rural branch as the former are more clued-up when it comes to transactions and advice. Many foreigners remark on the high quality of German banking services and the user-friendly environment of most German banks. It is quite usual for clients to have their own personal advisor on whom they can drop in for financial advice or even for a chat. Surprisingly for a country with such a reputation for tight controls on credit lending to companies, clients with personal accounts will be automatically granted an overdraft up to a limit decided by the bank. Generally Germans are far more wary of being overdrawn than the average Briton, especially as overdraft interest even on agreed facilities can be up to 18%. The main differences between UK and German personal current accounts is that German banking like America's, even if you are in credit, is not free. Banks are generally open from 9am to 4pm, with smaller branches closing between 1 and 2.30 for lunch.

Although the system varies from bank to bank, there is normally a monthly charge for maintenance of the account (*Kontoführungsgebühren*). In addition there are charges for withdrawal of funds from both the cashier or the cash machine, for payment of standing orders etc. Although it may pay to shop around for the best deals, be warned that, like the excellent German health service, the first class banking system is subsidised by the consumer.

For most personal banking services it is wise to shop around for the best deal for your money against the cost of maintaining accounts. There are several types of bank, the private banks, of which the big four; Deutsche, Dresdner, Commerzbank and HypoVereinsbank are the best known outside Germany. The state savings banks (*Sparkassen*) which are owned by the regional authorities, guild banks (*Genossenchaft*), credit co-operatives (*Volksbanken* or *Raiffeisenbanken*) and *Deutsche Postbank AG* post office savings accounts. All types of banks are able to transfer money abroad in Deutsche Marks or other currencies which is probably an essential service for most expatriates.

Electronic banking is proving very popular in Germany, Deutsche Bank launched the first internet branch *Bank 24* (www.bank24.de) in late 1996 and in one year had 80,000 customers.

USEFUL TERMS

die Bürgschaft/Garantie:	guarantee.
das Depositenzertifikat:	certificate of deposit.
die Hypothek:	mortgage.
der Inhaber:	bearer.
der kurzfristige Überziehungskredit:	short-term overdraft.
Persönliches Konto:	a personal account.
der Saldo:	balance.
Scheckheft: a	cheque book.
Scheckkarte:	cheque card.
die Überziehung des Kontokorrentkredites:	an overdraft.
der verbürgte Kontokorrentkredit:	overdraft secured by a guarantee.
der Wechsel:	bill.

The three main German banks have branches around the world, these are generally branches of their corporate investment arms, so you may not necessarily be able to gain any assistance with private bank accounts. Because of the simplicity of the procedure for opening an account, it is not normally necessary to open an account in advance of going to Germany. However these branches should be able to provide the address of the nearest local branch in Germany.

Useful Addresses
Dresdner Bank AG: International-Center, Jürgen-Ponto-Platz 1, D-60301 Frankfurt am Main; ☎ 069-263 4343.
Dresdner Bank AG: Riverbank House, 2 Swan Lane, London.
American Express: Postfach 11 01 01, D-60036 Frankfurt am Main.

OFFSHORE BANKING

British citizens who live and work abroad are only required to pay UK tax on income arising in the UK. There is thus an incentive for them to move their assets and savings to an offshore tax haven where they will earn interest gross of UK tax. For those habitual expatriates who move from one foreign land to another for work, there can be considerable advantage in maintaining assets offshore. Anyone living and working abroad should seriously consider this option as it not only allows easy access to their funds, no matter which foreign country they find themselves based in, but can also ensure the first steps towards tax efficiency.

With many banks and building societies now opening branches offshore there is an increasing range of facilities available. Expatriates will find a variety of products and services tailored to meet their specific needs: worldwide access to funds, accounts in different currencies, telephone banking, and assistance with insurance and investment to name but a few. The products available range from simple deposit account to index-linked deposits, managed funds, offshore trusts and packages of all these such as that offered by *Lloyds TSB Overseas Club*. Lloyds TSB is ideally placed to help British or other expatriates moving to Germany, with three offshore centres (see below) dedicated to providing offshore banking and investment services around the world.

One of the advantages of offshore banking is that if a British citizen leaves an account 'at home' they will be liable for tax on it for the complete tax year in the year their return occurs. If their offshore account is set up correctly, they will only be liable for income tax from the date of their return. Another issue is inheritance tax, which will affect all UK holdings, shares, accounts; however, offshore bank accounts are not liable. It should also be noted that UK banks are legally obliged to provide information on customers and the interest accrued on their UK holdings to the Inland Revenue if they live in certain countries (including Germany). This information will then be passed to the tax authorities in Germany.

Useful Addresses

Hansard Europe Ltd: PO Box 43, Enterprise House, Frascati Road, Blackrock, Co Dublin, Republic of Ireland; ☎+353-1211 2800; fax +353-1211 2850; website www.hansard.com Launched in 1995 Hansard Europe sell unit linked life assurance policies across the European Union, with variants in their products for France and Germany. These policies include Capital Builder and Retirement Programme.

Hemery Trust and Corporate Services Ltd: 31 Broad Street, St. Helier, Jersey JE4 8XN; ☎01534-502700; fax 01534-502714; e-mail enquiry@hemery.co.jc; website www.hemerygroup.com. Financial consultants who can offer a range of services including investment advice, for expatriates.

Lloyds TSB Bank (Isle of Man) Limited: Offshore Centre, PO Box 12, Douglas, Isle of Man, IM99 1SS; ☎01624-638000; fax 01642-638181; e-mail newaccs@lloydstsb.offshore.com; website www.lloydstsb-offshore.com

Lloyds TSB Bank (Guernsey) Limited: Offshore Centre, PO Box 53, St Peter Port, Guernsey, Channel Islands, GY1 4EN; ☎01481-706335; fax 01481-714295; e-mail guernseyoffc@lloydstsb.offshore.com.

Lloyds TSB Bank (Jersey) Limited: Offshore Centre, PO Box 770, Jersey, JE4 8ZG; ☎01534-284300; fax 01534-284351; e-mail jerseyoffc@lloydstsb.offshore.com.

Brewin Dolphin Ltd: 5 Giltspur Street, London, EC1A 9BD; ☎020-7246 1028; fax 020-7246 1093. Offer a variety of services, including investment management and financial planning.

TAX AND THE EXPATRIATE

As a result of the different tax regimes, which exist in different countries there are major complications involved in a move overseas. This does not just apply to tax affairs in the host country; a move will conjure up many tax implications in one's home country also. Many globetrotters simply leave home without informing the tax authorities in their own country. While the UK tax authorities have always been quite indulgent, as long as you can show that you were away for a whole tax year, the Internal Revenue Service in the US is much stricter. If you have already arranged a job in advance in Germany, then it would be advisable to obtain some information from the tax authorities in your home country before leaving, thus ensuring that no unnecessary tax is paid. If your tax affairs are complex, e.g. you own property or you have income in more than one country, then you will probably need to consult a tax adviser.

American consulates in Germany can not provide help with tax filing, but they can supply the necessary forms and some addresses of qualified tax advisors. There is an IRS office in the Berlin embassy building (☎030-8305 1140).

Income tax on wages is deducted by the employer and transferred to the federal tax authorities, if you have any other income then you will need to declare this on an *Einkommensteuererklärung*. 45% of tax revenues are from income taxes. Each year individuals subject to *Einkommensteuer* will be assessed by the tax office based on their previous payments, the German tax year runs within the calender year January 1st-December 31st, and the estimated tax notice (*Lohnsteuerjahreausgleich*) is sent out each Spring. This estimate requires you to make out a ta return and in the meantime make pre-payments at quarterly intervals, when your tax return is filed your total tax liability is determined, and any a refund or final payments are calculated based on this. This final figure is the base for the next tax year's figures.

Tax is not levied on earnings under certain set amounts and these figures usually change annually and vary according to marital status.

THE QUESTION OF RESIDENCE

Anyone who spends more than six months (183 days) per year in Germany has to pay German tax on his or her worldwide income unless they are eligible for the Expatriate Tax Regime (see below). Taxable income includes income from work, letting and leasing, trade enterprises, returns on investment, annuities and speculative capital gains. Before moving to Germany it is therefore important to consider where one's main residence will be for tax purposes. The important point to note is that one does not necessarily escape one country's income tax and become subject to another's just by moving there. It all depends on where the tax authorities consider one is resident for tax purposes, and also where one is ordinarily resident or domiciled – not necessarily the same thing. The terms resident, ordinarily resident and domiciled are not defined in the Tax Acts but are based on legal precedent.

Canada has a double taxation agreement with Germany, enquiries about

Canadian and German taxation should be sent to the *International Tax Service Office* (2204 Walkley Road, Ottawa, Ontario K1A 1A8, Canada; ☎613-952 3741; website www.ccra-adre.gc.ca).

Procedure for UK Residents

The situation is reasonably straightforward if you are moving permanently abroad. You should inform the UK Inspector of Taxes at the office you usually deal with of your departure and they will send you a P85 form to complete. The UK tax office will usually require certain proof that you are leaving the UK, and hence their jurisdiction, for good. Evidence of having sold a house in the UK and having rented or bought one in Germany is usually sufficient. If you are leaving a UK company to take up employment with a German one then the P45 form given by your UK employer and evidence of employment in Germany should be sufficient. You may be eligible for a tax refund in respect of the period up to your departure in which case it will be necessary to complete an income tax return for income and gains from the previous 5 April to your departure date. It may be advisable to seek professional advice when completing the P85; this form is used to determine your residence status and hence your UK tax liability. You should not fill it in if you are only going abroad for a short period of time. Once the Inland Revenue are satisfied that you are no longer resident or domiciled in the UK, they will close your file and not expect any more UK income tax to be paid.

If you are moving abroad temporarily then other conditions apply. You are not liable for UK taxes if you work for a foreign employer on a full-time contract and remain abroad for a whole tax year (6 April to 5 April), as long as you spend less than 183 days in a year, or 91 days a year averaged out over a four-year period, in the UK. Several part-time jobs abroad may be considered as full-time work employment. If you are considered a UK resident and have earned money working abroad then taxes paid abroad are not deductible. If you spend one part of a year working abroad and the rest in the UK you may still be considered non-resident for the part spent abroad, the so-called split tax year concession; this only applies to someone going abroad for a lengthy period of time.

Germany has a double taxation agreement with the UK, which makes it possible to offset tax paid in one country against tax paid in another. While the rules are complex, essentially, as long as you work for a German employer and are paid in Germany then you should not have to pay UK taxes, as long as you meet the residency conditions outlined above. For further information see the Inland Revenue publications IR20 *Residents and non-residents. Liability to tax in the United Kingdom* which can be found on the website www.inlandrevenue.gov.uk. Booklets IR138, IR139 and IR140 are also worth reading; these can be obtained from your local tax office or from:

Non-Resident Claims, Fitz Roy House, PO Box 46, Nottingham NG2 1BD; ☎0115-974 1919; fax 0115-974 1919; www.inlandrevenue.gov.uk.

General Services Unit, St. John's House, Bootle, Merseyside L69 9BB; ☎0151-472 6214/6216; fax 0151-472 6067.

Procedure for US Citizens

The US Internal Revenue Service (IRS) expects US citizens and resident aliens living abroad to file tax returns every year. Such persons will continue to be liable for US taxes on worldwide income until they have become permanent residents of another country and severed their ties with the USA. If you earn less than a certain amount abroad in one tax year then you do not need to file a tax return. The amount in 2001 was $7,200 for a single person; other rates apply for pensioners, married persons, heads of household, etc.

Fortunately the USA has a double taxation agreement with Germany so you should not have to pay taxes twice on the same income. In order to benefit from the double taxation agreement you need to fulfil one of two residence tests: either you have been a bona fide resident of another country for an entire tax year, which is the same as the calendar year in the case of the US, or you have been physically present in another country for 330 days during a period of 12 months which can begin at any time of the year. Once you qualify under the bona fide residence or physical presence tests then any further time you spend working abroad can also be used to diminish your tax liability.

Because Germany does not have a binational social security or totalisation agreement with the USA, US citizens will have to pay social security contributions when working in Germany, unless they are working for a foreign employer in the oil and gas sector (see below).

As regards foreign income, the main deduction for US citizens is the 'Foreign Earned Income Exclusion' by which you do not pay US taxes on the first $80,000 of money earned abroad (as of 2002; the amount of the exclusion has in recent times gone up by $2,000 every year). Investment income, capital gains, etc. are unearned income. If you earn in excess of the limit, taxes paid on income in Germany can still be used to reduce your liability for US taxes, either in the form of an exclusion or a credit, depending on which is more advantageous. The same will apply to German taxes paid on US income.

The rules for US taxpayers abroad are explained very clearly in the IRS booklet: *Tax Guide for US Citizens and Resident Aliens Abroad*, known as Publication 54, which can be downloaded from the internet on www.irs.gov.

GERMAN TAXES

Income Tax. German income tax is currently between 19.9% and 48.5%, in 2003 the basic rate should drop to 17%, dropping further to 15% in 2005 when the top rate should fall to 42%. The top rates of tax apply to incomes over €50,000. Income tax is made up of two elements:

- *Lohnsteuer:* Income taxes deducted at source from salary by employers.
- *Einkommensteuer:* Income taxes sourced from self-employment, rents, investments requiring completion and filing of a tax return *Einkomme nsteuererklärung.*

In addition to taxes on wages and unearned income, there are various other taxes including Value Added Tax/Sales Tax, Land Tax and Church Tax.

Church Tax. Church tax *(Kirchensteuer)* is compulsory unless you make a declaration that you do not wish to be a member of any church. If you do not make such a declaration you will be registered as a member of the local Catholic or Protestant Church which 90% of Germans are (at least for tax purposes). The tax is deducted with income tax and amounts to eight to ten per cent of the income tax to be paid.

Solidarity Tax Since 1995 a Solidarity Tax has been levied on income and corporation taxes, without any income limits, but there are regulations to prevent multiple taxation and to avoid overburdening those on low incomes. The tax has been levied to help cover the costs of reconstruction in the new Länder, and will be reduced in stages, initially set at 7.5% it is currently 5.5%.

Local Tax. A land tax (*Grundsteuer*) is levied on the owners of land and buildings, and is calculated on the basis of their rentable value. The level of tax varies between different regions, but is usually modest and deductible for income tax purposes. For acquisitions of real estate there is a transfer tax payable on land and buildings, which is levied on the purchaser.

Other Taxes: VAT/Sales Tax. *Mehrwertsteuer* or *MWSt* is charged at 16% on most goods and services for most foodstuffs, there is a reduced rate of 7%. The following are MWSt exempt: banking, insurance, education, library services, property sales, medical services and cultural performances. A turnover tax (*Einfuhrumsatzsteuer*) is levied on imports.

Useful Address.
Bundesverband der Lohnsteurhilfervereine e.V.: Limpericher Str. 6, D-53225 Bonn, Germany; ☎0228-472798; fa 0228-479493. The federal association of organizations offering help with wage and income tax.

HEALTH CARE, INSURANCE AND HOSPITALS

G ermany's health care system goes back to Bismarck's time when the foundations for the present system, aimed at the care of industrial workers, was the most progressive of its kind in the world. Nowadays the system has lost none of its edge. No expense it seems, is spared to equip hospitals and surgeries with the latest technology and well-trained staff. Germans enjoy, one of the highest standards of healthcare in the world, but as the system is entirely funded by compulsory contributions, citizens pay for it indirectly and heavily. Although preventative medicine, consultations and hospital treatment are free to those paying into the state health insurance scheme, beneficiaries still have to make contributions towards the cost of prescribed medicines, spectacles etc. The system involves the doctor, dentist etc. invoicing the sickness insurance fund (*Krankenkasse*) (see below), under a fixed scale of charges, for the treatment administered to the patient. This has generated probably the only complaint about the German health service, that there is a lot of formfilling involved.

USING THE HEALTH CARE SYSTEM

Germany has an extensive hospital system and there is a good availability of beds. Most recent law changes concerning how patients are charged for hospital care should make the system more competitive. Until now, hospitals have been paid by the length of a patient's stay. This has resulted in Germany having the highest number of days in hospital in Europe. However, this will change as the hospitals will be paid by the type of treatment, with a bonus for successful recovery, and not by how many days the patient is in hospital starting 2003.

Upon employment your company will require you to have a general medical examination, which is paid for by the employer. Your human resources department will then register you automatically with one of the national health insurance schemes (*Gesetzliche Krankenkasse*). The three main '*Kassen*' are *Allgemeine Ortskrankenkasse* (*AOK*), *Barmer Ersatzkasse* (*BEK*) and *Deutsche Angestellen-Krankenkasse* (*DAK*). If you wish to be privately insured you will need to inform your human resources department promptly to avoid confusion.

- O *Allgemeine Ortskrankenkasse (AOK):* website www.aok.de.
- O *Barmer Ersatzkasse (BEK):* website www.barmer.de.
- O *Deutsche Angestellen-Krankenkasse (DAK):* website www.dak.de.
- O *Techniker Krankenkasse (TK):* website www.tk-online.de (English pages).

FORM E111 AND E101.

Those of you employed by a UK employer, in Germany, for less than a year should contact the Department of Health or *International Services* department of the Inland Revenue before leaving the UK. You may be exempt from the German Government Health System and able continue to contribute to, and use the UK National Health System. They will also confirm which forms will need to be completed and how long the forms take to be processed (the forms to ask about are the E111, E101, E102, E106, E128, SA29 and T5.)

Form E111, is available in the UK at post offices the others are issued by the *International Services* department of the Inland Revenue. Details are also available on the Inland Revenue and Department of Health websites www.inlandrevenue.gov.uk/nic/intserv/osc.htm or www.doh.gov/traveladvice. Students on a year's study in Germany as part of a degree and UK workers working temporarily for a UK employer or self-employed should ask about form E128.

The E111 (allow one month for processing) entitles EU nationals to receive treatment under any EU country state health system for a period up to a maximum of one year, while the applicant still retains temporary status. Those going to Germany to look for a job on spec would be advised to apply for the explanatory leaflet T5 (*Health Advice for Travellers*) which contains the application form for an E111, or read page 12 of the leaflet SA29 (*Your Social Security Insurance, Benefits and Health Care Rights in the European Community*). Generally, the E111 covers hospital treatment, and private travel insurance (see below) will be needed to cover costs for prescribed medicines, specialist examinations, X-rays, laboratory tests, physiotherapy or dental treatment and repatriation back to the UK.

Those who are working in Germany for up to 12 months, but are being paid by a UK employer, will normally still be paying UK national insurance contributions. In such cases the employer should obtain form E101 from the Department of Work and Pensions International Services (see above). On arrival in Germany, the E101 should be presented to the relevant local authority in order to gain exemption from that country's national insurance scheme. Should the applicant find that owing to an unexpected change in circumstances they are obliged to continue their employment in Germany for up to another twelve months, he or she should apply at least one month before the expiry of the E101 for an extension (E102). It is necessary also to seek the approval of the German national insurance authorities before applying for continued exemption. The leaflet SA29 gives details of social security, health care and pension rights in the European Community.

Useful Addresses

International Services: Inland Revenue, National Insurance Contributions Office, Longbenton, Newcastle upon Tyne NE98 1ZZ (☎0845-915 4811 *or* +44-191 225 4811 from abroad; fax 0845 915 7800 *or* +44-191 225 7800 from abroad).
Department for Work & Pensions Benefits Agency: Overseas Division Medical Benefits, Tyneview Park, Whitley Road, Newcastle-upon-Tyne, NE98 1BA.

GOVERNMENT MEDICAL INSURANCE

If planning a move to Germany, you should be aware that 85% of the population are members of the Government Health System (GKV). It is financed by social security payments and this means that if you are employed and earn under €40,500 as your gross annual salary or €3,375 monthly (at the time of writing), then your membership in the Government Health System is mandatory.

Your employer will pay half of the insurance cost and coverage will include hospitals, out-patient and basic dental benefits. The present level (2002) for the costs is approximately 13.5% of your gross monthly salary (approximately €456 per month). Your dependents are insured without further cost. In addition, you and your dependents will be mandatory members of Government Long-term Health Scheme (*Pflegeversicherung*) which accounts for approximately 1.7% of your gross annual salary. This is approximately €57 per month and again your employer pays half. If you require higher coverage you can purchase supplemental policies, i.e. private doctors and hospitals.

PRIVATE MEDICAL INSURANCE

If you are coming to Germany and will earn more than €40,500 as your gross annual salary, you can choose whether you go into the government system or immediately into a private insurance plan (PKV). If you wish to go 'private', be sure to purchase a private medical insurance plan which can provide a recognised government certificate (*Arbeitgeberbescheinigung*). This allows you to take advantage of the employer subsidies up to a maximum of €227 monthly or 50% of your premium.

Generally, private health plans offer a wider choice of medical professionals, hospital treatment, more comprehensive dental benefits and geographical coverage. The private medical insurance market is well served by about 50 companies and there is a myriad of tariffs and benefits to suit every pocket book. The cost of full medical insurance is based, per person, on the benefits chosen, age, gender and pre-existing conditions. An important consideration in choosing cover is that the government insurance premium covers you and your dependents, whereas private medical insurance is paid per person.

If your insurer cannot provide you with an *Arbeitgeberbescheinigung* then your employer is not required to make any contributions to your insurance costs. Therefore, it is recommended that you choose specific German tariffs which are designed to cater for international executives – this gives you the best of both worlds.

In some large German companies the human resources department's main function is to administrate salaries. They are not expected or experienced in fully relocating international employees. Consequently, many international companies employ specialist relocation companies. Therefore, you would be wise to expect them not to understand all your requirements and to remain pleasant with them as they will process your paperwork. For this reason, many international employees contact their embassies, consulates, relocation companies or network with other foreigners via business or sports clubs to find specialist professionals and doctors/dentists who speak their own language or service the international community.

If you are self-employed and already privately insured with an international insurer before moving to Germany, your current product may still be suitable, but you will have to check that the geographical coverage is correct. You must also purchase the Government Long-term Health Scheme (*Pflegeversicherung*) and should purchase sick pay insurance with a German insurer.

If you are self-employed or are not required to work, then you may need to purchase a policy for visa purposes. The main 'watch out' here, is to be careful of short-term polices with no medical examination, as they do not usually offer an extension and do not cover pre-existing conditions. A typical policy costs less than €100 per month. The main problem occurs when you decide to stay longer than expected, the term of the contract expires and it is then difficult to get permanent health coverage.

It is not worth skimping on your health insurance if you are self-employed, as the cost is generally tax deductible. Health insurance should have the highest priority on your insurance list, if living in Germany.

Income Replacement Insurance / Sick Pay Insurance

Should you have an illness whilst in Germany, your employer will pay at least 6 weeks full salary. After that the health insurer (*Krankenkasse*), pays a certain amount of money up to a maximum of approximately €2,000 per month as 'Krankengeld'.

If you are earning more than this per month, you can purchase supplemental sick pay insurance at reasonable rates. This could be important if your fixed living costs are higher than the €2,000 per month. If you purchase private medical insurance, it is highly recommended that you also purchase sick pay insurance as a separate tariff. Please note that this insurance does not cover you for permanent disability.

Insurers

BUPA International: Russell Mews, Brighton, BN1 2NR; ☎01273-208181; fax 01273-866583; website www.bupa-intl.com. BUPA International offers a range of schemes to suit most needs. As the standard of healthcare in Germany is uniformly high, private patients' plans are not strictly necessary. However it can cut the waiting time which may otherwise be necessary for some treatments.

Expacare – high-quality health insurance cover, for individuals or families living abroad. To find out more...

For a copy of the **International Health Plan** brochure for individuals or groups (minimum of 5 employees) please email **info@expacare.net** or visit **www.expacareworld.net**

ExpaCare is a trading name of JLT Healthcare Limited. Regulated by the General Insurance Standards Council.

Expacare: e-mail info@expacare.net or visit www.expacare.net. Specialists in expatriate healthcare offering high quality health insurance cover for individuals and their families, including group cover for five or more employees. Cover is available for expatriates of all nationalities worldwide.

Cathy J. Matz: Hainstrasse 2, D-61476 Kronberg, Germany; ☎0700 INSURE ME or 0700-46787363; fax 06173-4497; e-mail matz@insure-invest.de; website www.insure-invest.de. An independent, international insurance and investments advisor offering a full service in both English and German.

Medical Evacuation

Emergency transportation is available at a fairly high level regardless of how you are insured. If you intend to take trips outside of Germany, it is strongly advised that you take out a travel health insurance including emergency medical evacuation before your journey. Please note that the government health system does not cover you outside of Germany.

Dentists

In Germany, dental care is quite expensive and very daunting. Foreign patients are often told that they need major treatment, whereas this may not be standard practice in their home country. If you are unsure of any treatment, you must get a cost estimate and present it to your insurer prior to treatment. Otherwise you could be faced with unexpectedly high bills to be paid out of pocket; whether you are government or privately insured. Tip: Get a second opinion from a recommended dentist.

Pharmacies

Germany has an extensive network of pharmacies (*Apotheke*) with branches in just about every town. The Government National Health Insurance generally includes reimbursement of 'generic drugs'; i.e non-branded. If you are privately insured, most branded medicines will be covered as long as you have a prescription. However, do not expect to be reimbursed for 'over the counter' medicines.

Tip: Should you have a chronic condition or use a lot of aspirin, it may be advantageous to bring a reasonable supply with you.

LOCAL GOVERNMENT

Operating parallel to the Federal Government are two levels of local government: the Länder and various types of Municipal Councils (*Gemeinderat, Stadtrat,* Kreisrat, *Bezugstag*) according to whether you are an urban or rural dweller. In general the Federal government works without an administrative sub-structure; only the Foreign Office, Defence Ministry and Labour Ministry have their own agencies. Thus it needs to use the administrative apparatus of local government and up to 10% of the Länder staff are employed directly by the Federation.

Länder

As stated in Chapter 1, the 16 Länder are not merely subordinate agencies. They are public entities each with their own limited form of sovereignty, a constitution and the right to self-government. The Länder each have an elected parliament (*Landtag*), a government elected by parliament, their own administrative authorities, and an independent judiciary. The administrative framework of the Länder is clearly defined and under Basic Law they have specific areas of responsibility. Thus, the fields of power that have been decentralised to the states include law and order, education, the administration of justice and measures of public assistance. All Länder have ministries of the Interior, Finance, Economy, Transport, Social Security and Education. Schooling and education provision account for nearly one-third of a Land's budget – the highest single apportionment; the police and judiciary receive 10%. Although it is the function of the national government to make the law, the Länder, through the auspices of the Bundesrat play a substantial role in the federal legislative process (see below). Each state also has its own central bank linked with the Bundesbank, and a network of savings banks.

The Länder are divided into area-states (*Flächenstaaten*)˙ and city states (*Stadtstaaten*). The three city states are Berlin, Bremen and Hamburg. Each has a Senate and senators, led in Hamburg and Berlin by a Chief Bürgermeister, and in Bremen by a Senate President. The area states, which have a Cabinet headed by a Minister-President, are Baden-Württemberg, Bayern, Brandenburg, Hessen, Mecklenburg-Vorpommern, Lower Sachsen, Nord-Rhein-Westfalen, Rheinland-Pfalz, Saarland, Sachsen-Anhalt, Schleswig-Holstein, and Thüringen.

Municipalities:

The municipalities (*Gemeinden*) form the lowest tier of public administration, but nevertheless have a special status within the Länder. They elect a council which has the right to self-government, a right that has been enjoyed since the beginning of the 19th century. Municipalities consist of rural counties (*Landkreise*) and town boroughs (*Kreisfreie Städte*), which are generally towns with a population exceeding 80,000. Among the responsibilities of the municipalities are town planning, cultural and educational affairs, public welfare, public transport and the supply of utilities (energy and water). The municipalities also play a prominent role in sports and the provision of recreational facilities accounts for more than one-fifth of a municipal council's budget. Certain tasks of the municipality governments are beyond the capability of all but the largest cities. In such instances as the supply of gas, electricity and water they can form joint undertakings with other boroughs. Revenue for these services comes from local taxation and funding from the state.

CRIME AND THE POLICE

CRIME

Germany has witnessed a dramatic rise in the number of reported crimes since reunification, which has been attributed by some social commentators to problems such as unemployment that have arisen from the merger of east and west. Other problems are more generic to the western world, such as a rise in teenage gang related crimes, such as 'tagging' trains with graffiti. However, on the whole Germany is still a safer place to live and work in than many western countries. The law abiding and orderly nature of the Germans makes the country a very safe place to live. Street crime certainly has a lower incidence than in Britain, or the US, and the busy-body manner of many Germans means that you are unlikely to be ignored if attacked. Germany's greatest problem is cutting down on the flow of illegal immigrants. While some judicial attitudes to the use of 'soft' drugs have been prominent in the media, drug use and supply is still illegal. The main focus of the media in recent years has been on the growing hard drug problem, but most of this news is misleading, rather than pampering drug-users the authorities are trying to stop them killing themselves and ensure that if they can not be weaned off the addiction then at least they won't turn to crime to feed it. The neo-nazi skinhead may grab the headlines with some obscene slogan or action, but if caught by the police he is liable to severe punishment. That the

German police do take this scourge seriously can be seen in the reactions of the yobs, arranging rallies using false names or purposes and then changing venues at the last minute to foil any action on the part of the police.

POLICE

The German (*Polizei*) police officer is little different from other European counterparts and is armed. The police are generally helpful and polite, but tend stick to the letter of the law and at times can be a bit too bureaucratic. While occasional newspaper reports show them as turning a blind-eye to neo-nazi rallies or even of treating ethnic minority groups harshly, this is down to individual officers and is no different to the situation with British or American police forces. In theory it is advisable to carry some form of ID at all times (a passport or driving licence will suffice) as if you are stopped by the police and are without personal documents, they could take you to the police station and keep you for up to six hours. In practice, few Germans, especially the younger generation, ever bother to carry any personal identification with this eventuality in mind. As already mentioned, the police are very correct and if they wish to pursue any matter they will do so with great thoroughness. If you are driving a vehicle and you are stopped you will be asked for your driver's licence and the papers for the car (*Wagenpapiere*) identifying the owner of the car, these should always be carried. If you are fined, it is advisable to pay on-the-spot fines without any debate. Apart from such encounters, you will not normally have anything to do with the police and so will not require identification. In the unfortunate event that you are arrested, you have the right to remain silent. You are also allowed to make a telephone call, and if necessary, have access to a lawyer and an interpreter. The police cannot hold an individual for more than 24 hours without charge, except for terrorist offences.

THE LAW

The German law code, the Basic Law divides the legal system into Public and Private Law. Private law governs the legal relationships between citizens and takes the form of a civil code, governing such matters as: leasing, loans, purchases and marriage and divorce. It also covers those areas of commercial law relating to tradesmen and labour law with regard to employees. Public Law regulates the relationship of the individual and public authority: central and land government, public corporations, and the relationships of the authorities to each other. *Gothe-Institut Inter-Nationes* (Kennedyallee 91-103, D-53175 Bonn, Germany; website www.inter-nationes.de/d/presse-e.html) the publishing company produce a very useful English-language booklet explaining German Law and other aspects of German life.

The Judiciary

The judiciary is accorded a powerful position of autonomy in the German legal system. Judges are independent of parliament and government and bound only by the law itself. Judges, public prosecutors and lawyers, as well as civil servants and legal advisers in industry and commerce, are required to receive the same professional training.

The Courts

The court system is divided into five different and independent branches. In addition, there is the Constitutional Court, which examines the legality of all practices carried out by the state authorities. Every German citizen has the right to be heard in a court of law and any person who is directly affected by the outcome of legal proceedings is entitled to express his or her view before a judge. The court system operates what is known as Basic Law; formal legislation set up in 1949. This covers all aspects of political and social life and created a system of values within which the protection of individual freedom is deemed to be the highest principle of law.

Regular Courts. A two-tier system of Magistrates' Courts (*Amtsgerichte*) and District Courts (*Landgerichte*) hear both civil and criminal cases. The supreme court for both is the Federal High Court (*Bundesgerichtshof*). Magistrates Courts preside over minor offences and have the power to order up to one year's imprisonment. The higher District Courts are split into two levels and generally hear more serious offences. Minor Criminal Tribunals have one professional judge and decide on crimes punishable by up to three years imprisonment. Major Criminal Tribunals (*Grosse Strafkammer*) handle the most serious crimes and are headed by three professional judges. A separate Court of Assizes (*Schwurgericht*) deals with capital offences. Juvenile Courts decide on crimes committed by youths (aged 14 to 17 at the time of the offence) and adolescents (18- and 19-year-olds).

Trials involving civil cases, such as ownership and damage claims, child maintenance and commercial matters, are settled in Civil Courts. Disputes involving amounts up to 5,000 DM are heard in Magistrates Courts. District Courts handle cases of higher value and appeals from the lower court.

Labour Courts (*Arbeitsgerichte*): These courts settle litigation arising from the breakdown of relationships between employers and employees, disputes between employers and trade unions and matters connected with the Labour Relations Act (*Betriebsverfassungsgesetz*). Appeals can be made to the regional labour courts (*Landesarbeitsgerichte*) and the Federal Labour Court (*Bundesarbeitsgerichte*).

Social Courts (*Sozialgerichte*). Social Courts act as tribunals and settle public law matters, such as those relating to statutory health, old-age and accident insurance schemes, social insurance and unemployment insurance.

The Federal Constitutional Court

The Constitutional Court is located in Karlsruhe and was established to ensure that the laws and rights embodied in the constitution are not violated. It can act only in response to appeals. The court reviews rules of law, international treaties, court sentences and decisions by public authorities, as to their conformity with the constitution. It was instituted in September 1951 and has since dealt with more than 127,000 cases, 122,000 of which have been constitutional complaints, but only 3,000 of which have lead to changes in the law.

Any court can, and must, appeal to the Federal Constitutional Court (*Bundesverfassungsgericht*) if it considers that a law which it has had to apply is unconstitutional. The Federal Government, the state governments, and the Bundestag (with the support of at least one-third of its members), may appeal to have the constitutionality of a federal or state law reviewed. The Court has two panels, known as senates, each of which has eight judges. Half are appointed by the Bundestag and half by the Bundesrat. The term of office is limited to 12 years and judges cannot be re-elected

RELIGION

The German Basic Law guarantees the undisturbed practice of religion. At present more than 55 million Germans are members of a Christian church, divided almost equally between the Protestant and Roman Catholic denominations, with both sides having around 27 million members; this may seem ironic when Germany is seen by many as the home of Protestantism. In addition to this, there are many other Christian denominations represented, almost three million Muslims and in spite of the Holocaust, Germany still retains an active Jewish community of around 100,000 people. However, of the 15 million or so inhabitants of the new länder, only a quarter are members of any organised religion, even though the democratic revolution in East Germany was hatched in the churches.

There is no State church, the Christian churches have the status of independendent public-law corporations, and are in effect in partnership with the State. The churches levy Church Tax on their members (*Kirchensteur*) to pay the Pastors' stipends, maintain the church fabric and run kindergartens and schools, but the money is collected on behalf of the churches by the State tax apparatus. Hence at present more than a few Germans are renouncing religion so as to save money. The charitable activities of the churches form a considerable part of the framework of German society. Apart from schools and kindergartens churches administer hospitals, old people's homes, and numerous other social institutions, and of course the parish ministries often provide a safety net for the poor. The churches in Germany address the public in many ways, publishing comments on topical social and moral issues, prompting widespread discussion.

The main churches are the Evangelical Church in Germany (EKD) which is an umbrella organisation for the Protestant community of 24 largely independent Lutheran, Reformed and United regional churches. Although these churches are often linked historically to the länder, only the Bayern Landeskirche follows its länder boundaries. In some areas the map of church boundaries printed by the EKD resembles a work by Jackson Pollock, rather than the patchwork quilt one might expect. The Roman Catholic Church is made up of 27 dioceses, with 70 bishops and archbishops. The Methodists joined forces with the Protestant Community to become the Protestant-Methodist Church (*Evangelisch-methodistische Kirche*) in 1968. There is also the Old-Catholic Church (*Alt-katholische Kirche*) which broke away from Rome in 1870 after the first Vatican Council, this has 58 parishes and roughly 30,000 members. The Quakers, Baptists, Mormons, Methodists, Mennonites and Salvation Army also have active ministries in Germany which make up the 280,000 members of the Association of Protestant Free Churches. Anglican churches have existed for a long time in many parts of Germany, the oldest is that of St Thomas à Becket in Hamburg (founded in 1611). Most are part of the Diocese of Europe, some belong to the Convocation of American Episcopal Churches in Europe, but all are part of the Anglican Communion and form the Council of Anglican Episcopal Churches in Germany (*Die Anglikanische Arbeitsgemeinschaft in Deutschland*). Those churches listed as hosting Anglican services below, are part of this council, members of all major Christian denominations are welcome to receive Holy Communion at Anglican services. There are also a few ecumenical and interdenominational services in English across Germany, and Anglicans enjoy a communion relationship with the Old-Catholic Church (*Alt-katholischen Kirche*).

Useful Addresses

Church Office of the Evangelical Church in Germany: *Kirchenamt der Evangelischen Kirche in Deutschland*, Herrenhäuser Strasse 12, D-30419 Hannover; ☎0511-2796460; fax 0511-279 6707; website www.ekd.de.
Secretariat of the German Bishops Conference: *Sekretariat der Deutschen Bischofskonferenz*, Kaiserstrasse 163, D-53113 Bonn, Germany; website www.dbk.de.
Central Council of Jews in Germany *Zentralrat der Juden in Deutschland*, Tucholskystr. 9, D-10117 Berlin, Germany; website www.zentraljuden.de.

ENGLISH LANGUAGE SERVICES IN GERMANY

Berlin

St George's Anglican Church: Rev Christopher Jage-Bowler, Preussenallee 17/19, Charlottenburg D-14052 Berlin, Germany; ☎030-3041280; e-mail office@stgeorges.de; website www.stgeorges.de. Anglican services at 10 am on Sundays with Roman Catholic services at noon.

Methodist Church Pastor Romesh Modayil, ☎030-341 2771 or tel/fax 030-342 0240; website www.emk-berlin.org/english. The English speaking congregation meets at Auferstehungskirche, Kaiser-Friedrich-Str. 87, D-10585 Berlin, Germany. Sunday worship at 5.30pm. 'Drop Inn' Christin bookshop and meeting place and weeknight bible study.

Bochum

International English Church in Bochum: Evangelische Pauluskirche, Grabenstrasse 9, D-44787 Bochum, Germany. Rev James Brown, Neustrasse 15, D-44787 Bochum; ☎0234-13365; fa 0234-962 1006. Worship services in English are held every Sunday at 12.30 pm.

Bonn

St Boniface: Rev. Dr Stephen Miles, Haus Steinbach, Rüdigerstrasse 92-98, D-53179 Bonn, Germany; ☎0228-269 0827 or 0221-587 9014; e-mail info@anglicanbonncologne.de. Anglican services held at 9.30 am on Sundays. For correspondence please address letters c/o The

Anglican Chaplaincy, Kaiser-Friedrich-Strasse 19, D-53113 Bonn, Germany.
St Thomas Moore Parish: Kennedyallee 150, D-53175 Bonn, Germany; ☎0228-373526; fax 0228-377 5749; e-mail St_Thomas_More_ Bonn@yahoo.de. Catholic Masses held in English at 6.30 pm Mondays and Tuesdays, 12.30pm on Wednesdays, 6pm on Saturdays and 9.30 am on Sunday. The chapel building is shared by this Roman Catholic community and the Protestant congregation below.
American Protestant Church: Stimson Memorial Chapel, Kennedyallee 150, D-53175 Bonn; ☎0228-374193/ 373393. Interdenominational Protestant services are held on Sundays at 11 am with a Sunday School at 9.30 am.

Cologne

All Saints' Church: Rev. Dr Stephen Miles, ☎0221-587 9014. All Saints Church is on Bonner Strasse at the corner with Lindenalle. Anglican services are on Sundays at 11.45 am with Sunday School throughout school terms. For correspondence contact the Anglican Chaplaincy in Bonn.
International Baptist Church: Rev David Wilson, Rheinaustr. 9, Cologne, Germany; Church Office tel/fax 0221-943 3557; e-mail wilsonibckoln@aol.com. Sunday Services are held at 2 pm with Sunday School. For midweek activities please contact the church office

Dortmund

International English Church in Dortmund: Evangelische-methodistische Kirsche, Rev Dr Rainer Bath, Weiherstrasse 3, D-44135 Dortmund, Germany (from August 2002, Gildenstr. 60. D-44263 Dortmund); ☎0231-523950; e-mail emk.dortmund@t-online.de. The Dortmund congregation invites all English-speaking Christians to services on the first Sunday of the month at 12.30 pm.

Düsseldorf

Christ Church Community: Rev Ross Buckman, Rotterdamer Strasse 135, D-40474 Düsseldorf, Germany; ☎0211-432434; fax 0211-454 2216. Anglican morning services are held at 11 am every Sunday followed by Holy Communion. On the first Sunday of the month a Family Service is held at 11am. Sunday School and a nursery are also available, and social events include meetings and lunches.
St Albertus Magnus: Father Ken McLaughlan PhL BD, Kaiserwerther Str. 211, D-40474 Düsseldorf, Germany; ☎0211-459739; fax 0211-470 8091. Roman Catholic Holy Mass is celebrated at 5 pm on Sundays and weekday services can also be arranged, as Father McLaughlan also works within the German community.
International Baptist Church: Am Bauernhaus 30, D-40472 Düsseldorf-Rath, Germany; ☎0211-965 3683; e-mail ibcd@freenet.de; website www.ibcd.de. The community meets at 11 am on Sundays in a church located in tranquil woodland. A staffed nursery and full Sunday School are provided. Church members represent 18 nationalities and many denominations

Frankfurt am Main

Church of Christ the King: The Rev Allan Sandlin, Sebastian-Rinz-Str. 22, D-60323 Frankfurt am Main, Germany; ☎069-550184; fax 069-550186; e-mail office@christ-the-king.de; website www.christ-the-king.de. Holy Communion Services are at 11 am on Sundays, 10 am June-August. Morning Prayers are held at 8.30am in the cahpel on Moday, Wednesday and Friday.

St Paul's Gemeinde: Dr Jefrey Myers, Römerberg 9, D-60311 Frankfurt am Main, Germany; ☎069-284235. This 800 year-old Lutheran church is open each day for visitors from around the world, offering materials, tours and 'Inspiration at Noon' (organ music and meditation) in English and German. The American pastor is available to answer questions and assist with the difficulties faced by foreigners.

St Leonhard's International English Speaking Catholic Parish: Alte Mainzer Gasse 8, D-60311 Frankfurt am Main, Germany; ☎069-283177; fax 069-2199 4887; e-mail email@stleonhards.org; website www.stleonhards.org. Roman Catholic Mass is celebrated at 5 pm on Saturday and 10 am on Sunday. Children's Liturgy of the Word is celebrated every Sunday. There is also a youth group for older children.

St Mary's Roman Catholic Parish: ☎06195-976670; e-mail ST_MARYS@t-online.de; website www.www.stmarys.de. Holy Mass is celebrated at 11 am on Sundays at St Marien, Wachenheimer Str.58, Leiderbach, Germany.

Mormon: Church of Jesus Christ of Latter Day Saints, Eckenheimer Landstr. 264, D-60435 Frankfurt am Main, Germany; ☎069-5480 6902.

Hamburg

The Church of St Thomas à Becket: Zeughausmarkt 22, D-20459 Hamburg, Germany; e-mail St.Thomas. Becket@t-online.de; website www .anglican-church-hamburg.de. Rev Roger White, Beim Gruenen Jaeger 16, D-20359 Hamburg, Germany; ☎040-439 2334; fax 40-4018 6735. The oldest Anglican parish in Germany, services (Eucharist) every Sunday at 10.30am with a concurrent Sunday School. Church of Scotland members and other denominations are welcomed.

Church of the Cross United Methodist Church (International English-Speaking): Röntgenstrasse 1, D-22335 Hamburg, Germany; ☎040-5004 8306 or 04-562255. Sunday School and Services at 11.30 am.

Roman Catholic Church of St Elizabeth: Oberstrasse 65, D-20144 Hamburg, Germany; ☎040-414 0630. Holy Mass is celebrated in English every Sunday at midday.

Heidelberg

Anglican Services have been held in the past at the Old-Catholic Church on the corner of Plöck and Schiesstorstrasse, D-69117 Heidelberg.

Karlsruhe

Anglican Episcopal Community Karlsruhe with Baden-Baden: The Rev Dr Hanns Engelhardt, Steinbügelstr. 22, D-76228 Karlsruhe, Germany; tel/fax 0721-28379; e-mail anglican.episcopal.karlsruhe@t-online.de. Services take place in the chapel of Luisenheim, Kochstr. 2-4 (all Sundays at 5pm) and in the Drei-Eichen-Kapelle, Rheinstr. 64, Baden-Baden (first Sunday of the month at 10.30am).

Leipzig

Leipzig English Church (Anglican): Rev. Martin Reakes-Williams, Church Hall of the Luther Church, Schreberstrass 3-5, D-04109 Leipzig, Germany; ☎0341-302 7951; fax 0341-993 8844; e-mail earwig@t-online.de; website www.leipzig-english-church.de. Services in English every Sunday at 5 pm, with Holy Communion celebrated on the first Sunday and a family Service on the second Sunday of every month, Sunday school is also available every week.

Munich

Church of the Ascension: Rev Tom Pellaton, Seybothstrasse 4, D-81545 München, Germany; ☎089-648185; fax 089-644428; e-mail church@ascension-munich.com; website www.ascension-munich.com. An Anglican/Episcopal church serving the English-speaking community. Sunday services are held at the Emmauskirche, Seybothstrasse 4, D-81545 München, Germany. Eucharist is celebrated at 9 am in the chapel and at 11.45 am in the Emmauskirche, with Family Eucharist every third Sunday. Sung Evening prayer is held on the first Wednesday of the month at *Skt. Willibrord*, Old-Catholic church, Blumenstrasse 36, München, Germany. Morning Prayers and Bible Study take place on Wednesday mornings in the chapel.

Nürnberg

St Johannniskirche: English language worship every 2nd Sunday in the month at 11am at the St. Joahanniskirche in the Johannis Cemetery, Johannisstrasse 53-57, Nürnberg, Germany. Information on services can be obtained by phone (0911-671813 or 957 8121).

Oberursel

International Christian Fellowship of the Taunus: Pastor Martin Levey, Hohemarkstr. 75 D-61440 Oberursel, Germany; ☎06171-923143; e-mail icfsec@debitel.net.

Stuttgart

For Anglican services in Stuttgart contact Mr Eric Jarman, Churchwarden; tel/fax 07151-68973; e-mail eric.renate@t-online.de. Services are divided between two churches in Stuttgart:

St Catherine's Church: Katharinenplatz 5, D-70182 Stuttgart, Germany, at 11 am on the first and third Sundays. *Evangelisches Gemeindezentrum:* Oberlinhaus, Margueritenweg, D-70569 Stuttgart, Germany, at 11.15am on the second, fourth and fifth Sundays. Services are Holy Comunion or Morning Prayer. *International Baptist Church:* Untere Waldplätze 38, D-70569 Stuttgart, Germany; ☎0711-687 4365; fax 0711-678 8026; e-mail email@ibcstuttgart.de; website www.ibcstuttgart.de. Morning Service 9.30am, Evening Service 6pm Wednesdays.

Wiesbaden

Church of St Augustine of Canterbury: Frankfurter Strasse 3, D-65189 Wiesbaden, Germany; ☎0611-306674; fax 0611-372270; website www.staugustines-wiesbaden.de. Anglican services are held at 10 am, with Sunday school. On the first Sunday a Family Service is held with the emphasis on children, so there is no Sunday School.

SOCIAL LIFE

THE GERMANS

The stereotypical image that all Germans are humourless and boring is not borne out by acquaintance. It is true that humour has its time and place, and joking in a formal situation can make a German very uncomfortable.

Nevertheless, Germans possess both wit and cheerfulness in abundance. The main difference between British and German humour is the use of sarcasm. In anglophone nations sarcasm is socially acceptable and indeed sarcastic banter makes up a great deal of daily social interaction. Friends think nothing of being each other's targets for mild abuse or of exchanging sarcastic remarks about a third party not present. In Germany, sarcasm is not usually socially acceptable and indeed is liable to cause great offence which is probably why people often think that the Germans humourless. Although Germans rarely make jokes about other people (except in the form of regional groups, eg Bavarians tell 'Prussian' jokes etc) money or business are two examples of subjects regarded as legitimate targets for jokes. In the same way that jokes about other people are not appreciated, jokes about oneself, particularly of the self-denigrating kind are also puzzling to Germans.

From the ruins of war, the German people have built one of the strongest economies in the world. In general they are very proud of their achievements and as far as they are concerned their way of doing things is best. Germans are competitive, ambitious and do not identify or sympathise with failure. A job well done is something to be proud of. Great store is set on the outward trappings of success, such as the car you drive, the size of your office, and where you take your holidays. They are efficient and conscientious, however, and can sometimes be slow to react to change and appear to be happy to stay set in the old ways. Careful thought and planning pervade almost every aspect of life, from decorating the house to business deals. There is a definite antipathy towards stepping out of line and eccentricity of even the mildest kind will attract open criticism. Policing each other's behaviour is not seen as offensive but as a social duty. There is still a desire to belong and a dislike of non-conformism, but in response to recent history, and the taunts of others (Britain's newspapers for example still wallows in '40s jingoism at times) the Germans are becoming more relaxed about life. For instance, the passers-by that would be prone to comment if a motorist parked untidily or a pedestrian crossed a road other than at a crossing point, are more likely to keep the comment to themselves, maybe discussing these bad habits amongst their friends later.

Manners and Customs

The golden rule to remember when dealing with Germans is that their behaviour in public is often in sharp contrast with the informality and warmth of their private life. An individual may initially strike you as cold, extremely formal and even mistrusting. When addressing a German it is customary to use Frau, Herr or the highest title the person possesses. The attention to manners can seem pedantic in the extreme but this is a sign of respect rather than an avoidance of you.

Another major difference is the wearing of Engagement and Wedding rings. These are worn on the third finger of the left hand to denote engagement, and at marriage the ring is moved to the right hand. Other points to bear in mind are that on your birthday you will be expected to provide drink and cakes for your work-mates, or to invite your close friends in for something similar. The 6th of December (*St Nikolaus*) is another such situation, children are traditionally given bags of sweets or small gifts, and bosses are expected to do likewise for their employees. It is also wise to have something for your closest colleagues.

While you may find yourself up against a reserve which can seem almost cool, around Christmas and New Year this all breaks down. Shoppers and staff will merrily wish each other *Frohe Weihnachten* (Merry Christmas), as will anyone you meet on the street, not to reply in kind would be considered as rude as shouting 'Bah ! Humbug !'. As Christmas passes this will change to *Guten Rutsch ins Neue Jahr* ('Good slide into the New Year').

MAKING FRIENDS

One of the most rewarding aspects of living in a foreign country is breaking down the barriers and forming lasting friendships. Perseverance is certainly required as making a friend of a German is easier said than done. There is a clear distinction made between an acquaintance (*ein Bekannter*) and a friend (*ein Freund*). This is most apparent when speaking German as the polite plural *Sie* is almost always used in formal and business situations (as discussed earlier in the section on language). In the same way as the French use 'vous' and 'tu', *du* is used only between friends and the transition from one to another is a significant event. Using *du* marks the entry into each other's private life and should never be taken lightly. The difference is most marked among the older generations and young people commonly use *du* even to relative strangers. A real friendship requires a lot of work and attention, and is effectively a lifetime commitment – one reason why it is such a lengthy process. However, Germans set great store by *Gemütlichkeit*, a combination of camaraderie and having a good time.

For those of you who need a rest from promoting cross-cultural links, the expatriate population in Germany has established a large number of English-speaking clubs and societies in most major towns. They can often provide a friendly face and guidance on how to settle into your new way of life.

ENGLISH SPEAKING CLUBS & SOCIETIES

There is much to be said for forging German friendships and creating an authentic German social life. However, being resident in a country where the language is unfamiliar can make the company of fellow expatriates a welcome relief, especially as they can help you settle in, and get by when culture shock strikes.

Many clubs are run by Germans as a way of expanding their English vocabulary and this can allow you to rest your vocal cords and mind for a while. Germany has many English-speaking, expatriate social and recreational clubs, so whether you want to indulge a hobby, cultivate a new skill or simply share a drink and a chat your with fellow expatriates there is a range of options. You can even make new friends from your German neighbours. Below is a list of social clubs which should provide a good starting point for any English speaking visitors, fuller lists are available from regional consular offices (note all British consulates keep lists online as pdf files, whereas of the US consulates only Frankfurt, Leipzig and Munich seem to have lists online). **Please bear in mind that the names and addresses of local contacts may change over time.**

Baden-Württemburg

Anglo-German Club, Pforzheim: Maurice Claypole, Industriestr. 12, D-75217 Birkenfeld; ☎07231-472155; fax 07231-472156; e-mail anglo-german@web.de.

Bayern

Deutsche-Britische Gesellschaft: Würzburg: Frau Elke Wagner, Madrider Ring 59, D-97084 Würzburg, Germany; ☎0931-67413.

Deutsche-Englischer Club Bamberg e.V.: Herr Werner Oppelt, Mainstr. 56a, D-96103 Bamberg, Germany.

Deutsche-Englische Gesellschaft: Herr Metzner, Frankenwaldstr. 104, D-95448 Bayreuth, Germany; website www.bnbt.de/~tr1605/.

English Speaking Union: website www.esu-bavaria.de.

Englisch Club Lindau: David Huckle, Alte Landstr. 32, D-88138 Sigmarszell, Germany; ☎08389-256; fax 08389-1649; e-mail englishclub @allgaeu.org.

Federation of German-American Clubs e.V.: Hochstr. 13, D-67657 Kaiserslautern, Germany; ☎0631-76679; fax 0631-370 5775; website www.verband-dt-am-clubs.de.

German-English Association: website www.gea-muc.de.

Verein zur Förderung von Wilton Park: Dr Paul Fischer, Ampostrasse 5, D-86179 Augsburg, Germany.

Berlin

American Women's Club, Berlin: Postfach 410951, D-11219 Berlin, Germany; ☎030-7970 6523; fax 030-7974 1865; website www.awc-of-berlin.de.

Berlin German-American Club: Klopstockstr. 14, D-10557 Berlin, Germany; ☎030-917214.

Berlin International Women's Club e. V.: BIWC Office, Wolfensteindamm 9, D-12165 Berlin; ☎030-8449 0650; fax 030-8449 0651; e-mail info@biwc.de; website www.biwc.de.

Bonn

American German Business Club: Beethovenallee 85, D-53173 Bonn, Germany; ☎0228-351 1474; fax 0228-36562; e-mail national@agbc.de; website www.agbc.de.

Bonn-Oxford Club: Adenauerallee 7, D-53111 Bonn. Contact Karin Watson (0228-621940) for details.

The Bonn Caledonian Society: John Walker, ☎0211-712 5043 is the chairman. Main activity: Scottish country dancing. Sept. to June, every Tuesday from 7.30 to 9.30 p.m.

Bremen

British-German Association Bremen e.V.: c/o Michael Shelton, Graf-Sponeck-Str. 16, D-28327 Bremen; ☎0421-239993; e-mail Mike@MShelton.de

Bremerhaven German-American Club: Postfach 120415, D-27518 Bremerhaven, Germany; ☎0471-44204.

Düsseldorf

American Women's Club, Düsseldorf: Postfach 310225, D-40481 Düsseldorf, Germany; ☎0211-408 0644; e-mail awcdinfo@fawco.org.

The British Women's Club: PO Box 1106, D-40636 Meersbuch, Germany. Open to UK and Commonwealth citizens.

Die Brücke: International Cultural Center of the Volkhochshule Düsseldorf, Kasernenstr. 6, D-40213 Düsseldorf, Germany; ☎0211-899 4996. Books, newspapers, videos and audio cassettes in English ☎0211-899 3448).

English Speakers' Circle: Susan Jones, Karolingerstrasse 7, D-40223 Düsseldorf, Germany; ☎0211-317 9322.

Frankfurt am Main

American Ladies Club: Trier Im Breul 17, D-54317 Gutweiler Germany; ☎06588-7178.

American Legion: Schwalbenstr. 19, D-64613 Öhringen Germany; ☎07941-61260; fax 07941-61260.

American Women's Club of the Taunus: Hollerberg 1 Postfach 1931, D-61409 Oberursel/Taunus, Germany; ☎06171-580835; fax 06171-715 7371; website www.awctaunus.org.

IAF-Verband Binationaler Familien und Partnerschaften: Ludolfusstr. 2-4, D-60487 Frankfurt am Main. A support group for multi-cultural marriages.

Hamburg

American Women's Club, Hamburg: Postfach 551066, D-22570 Hamburg, Germany; ☎040-8998 2707; fax 040-559 4860; website www.awchamburg.org.

Der Übersee-Club e.V.: Neuer Jungfernstieg 19, D-20354 Hamburg, Germany; ☎040-3552 9011; fax 040-3552 9010; e-mail ueberseeclub@t-online.de; website www.der-uebersee-club.de.

Hamburg English Language Teaching Association e.V.: Oktaviostr. 15, D-22043 Hamburg, Germany; fax 040-65 63 980.

Hamburger Cricket-Sportverband e. V. (HCSV): c/o Jamal A. Mirza, Hallerstrasse 1, D-20146 Hamburg, Germany; tel/fax 040-422 1917. The HCSV as a head organization represents various Cricket Clubs in Hamburg.

Harvard Club of Hamburg: President Wilfrid Boysan, c/o Reemtsma Cigarettenfabriken GmbH, Parkstrasse 51, D-22605 Hamburg, Germany.

Leyton-Wandsbek Freundschaftsbund: Rolf Mäkel, Grasnelkenweg 21, D-22391 Hamburg; 040-536 2787. Oldest town twinning scheme in Hamburg.

New Zealand Group: John Piggin, Kiwittsmoor 64, D-22417 Hamburg; ☎040-270 0662.

Professional Women's Forum e.V.: Pat Pledger MIPD, Görresring 1, D-22609 Hamburg; ☎040-821858; fax 040-820676; e-mail patpledger.b et@t-online.de. A networking group for career-minded women.

The Royal British Legion: Mr P. Bigglestone MBE, Jahnstrasse 9, D-21435 Stelle, Germany; tel/fa 04174-650153.

Royal OverSeas League: Mr Mahmood Sairally, Dipl Arch BDB RIBA HMRIAI, Honorary Correponding Secretary, Eichelhaeherkamp 62, D-22397 Hamburg, Germany; ☎040-608 38 61; fax 040-608 25 62; e-mail mahmood.sairally@t-on line.de.

Scottish Country Dancers of Hamburg: Mrs Valerie Puschmann, Freesienweg 40, D-22395 Hamburg; ☎040-600 7710.

Young Mother's Club: c/o Hans-Salb-Str. 24, D-22851 Norderstedt, Germany; ☎040-524 1796. An informal gathering of mothers and children of all ages on Friday afternoons in Hamburg-Nierdorf.

Hessen

Interessengemeinschaft mehrsrachiger Familien e.V. (Interest Group for Multilingual Families): J. Hagen, Benzstr. 17, D-64546 Mörfelden, Germany, fax 06105-921361; e-mail ImF-e.V.@gmx.de; website www.bklein.de/imf/index.html

Köln

American Women's Club, Cologne: c/o Amerika Haus, Apostelnkloster 13-15, D-50672 Cologne, Germany; e-mail info@awccologne.org; website www.awccologne.org.

Overseas Club (Anglo-German Social Club) Köln: Anthony Gray, Weyerstrasse 84, D-50676 Köln, Germany; ☎0221-923 0296; website www.overseasclub.de.

Leipzig

Club International e.V.: c/o Radisson Hotel SAS, Oberaltenburg 4, D-06217 Merseburg, Germany; ☎03461-452-528; fax 03461-452-300; e-mail geschaeftsste lle@club-international.de.

Cosmopolitan Women's Club of Leipzig e.V. (An English-speaking women's support club): Postfach 100401, 04004 Leipzig, Germany; ☎0341-550 3133; fax 0341-300342.

Freundeskreis Leipzig-Houston e.V. Förderverein für Deutsch-Amerikanische Begegnung (Leipzig-Houston Friends, Support Club for German-American Contacts): c/o Norbert Kühn, TriFugium, Barfussgässchen 11, D-04109 Leipzig, Germany; ☎0341-140 9460; fax 0341-140 9470; website www.leipzig-houston.com.

International Women's Club Leipzig: Beethovenstr. 35, D-04107 Leipzig, Germany; ☎0341-5649-662.

Leipzig Lions e.V.: Endersstr. 22, D-04177 Leipzig Stadion in der Ratzelstrasse, Grünau, Germany; ☎0341-48405-11; fax 0341-48405-20; website www.leipzig-lions.de.

Rotary Club Leipzig: website www.rc-leipzig.de/club.html.

München

American German Business Club (AGBC): Karolinenplatz 3, D-80333 München; ☎089-5502 8129; fax 089-5502 8149; e-mail agbc@trans.net.

Anglo-Bavarian Club, Munich e.V.: David Halliday, Kirchenweg 3, D-85598 Baldham, Germany; ☎08106-36982.

Columbus Society, Columbus Gesellschaft e.V.: Karolinenplatz 3, D-80333 München; ☎089-499 1499; fax 089-4900 2099; e-mail Colum-

bus-Society@t-online.de.

Deutsch-Amerikanischer Frauenclub München (German-American Women's Club): Amerika Haus, Karolinenplatz 3, D-80333 München, Germany.

Deutsch-Amerikanischer Gesangsverein München, German-American Choral Society: Scharnitzer Str. 29, D-82166 Gräfelfing, Germany; ☎089-852865.

Deutsch mit Freunden: c/o Micheal Koch, Tengstrasse 21, D-80798 München, Germany.

German-American Men's Club Munich: Elektrastr. 11, D-81925 München, Germany; ☎089-911463.

Gesellschaft für Auslandskunde e.V.: Karolinenplatz 3, , D-80333 München, Germany; ☎089-295497; fax 089-291 3186; e-mail info@auslandskunde.de.

Munich Caledonians: Christine Vavra, Greinerberg 14, D-81371 München, Germany; ☎089-723 7266.

Munich Scottish Association: c/o Sue Bollans, Keferstrasse 24b, D-80802 München, Germany.

Niedersachsen

Anglo-German Club: Bryan Ledger, Summerland 12, D-49090 Osnabrück, Germany; ☎0541-682065 (eves).

Deutsch Englische Gessellschaft Braunschweig: Mrs Treve Erdmenger, Steinhorstweise 20a, D-38108 Braunschweig, Germany; tel/fax 0531-352160; e-mail erdmenger@bs.gmx.de.

International Women's Association: Susan Aurich, Susseroder Str. 26, D-30559 Hannover, Germany; ☎0511-526306.

Kulturzentrum PFL (was Brücke der Nationen Oldenburg): c/o Herrn Hans-Dieter Remmers, Peterstrasse 3, D-26122 Oldenburg, Germany.

The Lion Drama Company: Contact Irma Ackermann, ☎05307-5424; fax 05307-930336; e-mail

I.ackermann@gmx.de; website
www.lion-drama-company.de/
deg.html.
English-speaking Ladies Group:
Contact Katherine Küppers;
tel/fax 0531-872685; e-mail
kathykueppers@gmx.de.

Nord-Rhein-Westfalen

Anglo-German Club Gütersloh: Herr
Frank Mertens, Alexanderweg 40,
D-33335 Gütersloh, Germany;
☎05241-76226.

Nürnberg

*Deutsch-Amerikanisches Institut
(DAI) Nürnberg:* Gleisbühlstr. 13,
D-90402 Nürnberg, Germany;
☎0911-230690; fax 0911-2306923.
Deutsch-Britische Gesellschaft Nürnberg:
c/o Herr Martin, Deutsche Bank
AG, Karolinenstrasse 30, D-90402
Nürnberg; fax 0911-201 4100; web-
site www.herzomedia.net/cs.

Rheinland-Pfalz

*Deutsch-Amerikanische Freundschaftsgruppe
Siegelbach e.V.:* Am Wäldchen 3,
D-67661 Kaiserlautern, Germany;
☎06301-8327; fax 06301-794714;
website www.gafriendship.com.
Provides German classes for English
speakers, as well as social activities
and trips for American and British
and local club members.

Schleswig-Holstein

Arbeitskreis Niebüll-Malmesbury:
Frau Diana Kluger, Klockries
48, D-25920 Risum-Lindholm,
Germany; ☎04661-2193; fax
04661-675222. Town-twinning asso-
ciation since 1976.
*Deutsche-Englische Gesellschaft e.V.,
Landesgruppe Schleswig-Holstein:* Dr L.
Homrich, Barstenkamp 35, D-24113
Molfsee; ☎0431-650790.

Stuttgart

Anglo-Stuttgart Society e.V.: Nicole Issler,
Klingenstrasse 89, D-70186 Stutt-
gart, Germany; ☎0711-480 0469.
British Club Stuttgart: Mrs A. Seyerle,
Hagebuttenweg 4a, D-70599 Stutt-
gart; ☎0711-455464.
*Deutsche-Englische Gesellschaft
Arbeitskreis Württemburg:* Manfred ten
Brink, Postfach 10 60 13, D-70049
Stuttgart; ☎0711-125 3952717.

Thüringen

*Deutsche-Englische Gesellschaft e.V. Landes-
gruppe Thüringen (Jena & Erfurt):*
Jens Mittelbach (Hon. Secretary),
Friedrich-Schiller-Universität Jena,
Institut für Anglistik/Amerikanistik,
Ernst-Abbe-Platz 8, Jena, Germany;
☎03641-944514; fax 03641-944512;
e-mail jens.mittelbach@rz.uni-je
na.de; website www.uni-jena.de/
x7muwo.

ENTERTAINMENT AND CULTURE

German culture has a rich history that has reached far beyond its geographical
boundaries and graced virtually every artistic stage. No classical music
discussion is complete without mentioning the names of Bach, Beethoven, and
Handel while Nietzsche and Hegel opened new areas of philosophical thought
and in literary circles Schiller, Goethe, and Brecht have broadened the reach of
the written word. Fine arts, music and theatre have always played an important
role in Germany and the state considers it as essential to promote cultural heritage.
Among current state-funded restoration projects are those at the cathedrals of
Cologne and Aachen, and at Hambach Castle, near Worms. The government

also funds the *Deutsche Akademie für Sprache und Dichtung* (German Academy for Language and Poetry), the *Germanische Nationalmuseum* in Nürnberg, and the Goethe Institute, which promotes German language and culture worldwide.

A comprehensive calendar of cultural events and entertainment in Germany is available from The German National Tourist Offices.

Nightlife

There is no German equivalent to the British pub, although there are a few of these in Germany. Bars are often known as a *Kneipe, Bierlokal,* or *Kölschlokale* (in Cologne), beerhalls are known as *Brauereikeller, Brauerei* or *Bierkeller* (in Bavaria). In wine growing areas wine bars are called *Weinstuben* and around Frankfurt cider is drunk in an *Apfelweinwirtschaft*. One of the best forms of evening entertainment are beer halls, the majority of which are owned by the major breweries. They are huge and relatively inexpensive. Drinking is often accompanied by bands and food. Most establishments open about 11.30am, and are required to close by 2am, unless a special licence has been granted. The exception to this rule are *Kneipen* in Berlin which only have to close for one hour in every 24 for cleaning. (Some even bypass this rule by cleaning one half of the bar at a time and leaving the other side open.) Drinking toasts are commonly *Zum Wohl, Prost* and *Prosit* which all mean 'Cheers!'.

Germany's hottest night life can be found in the St Pauli, St Georg and Reeperbahn areas of Hamburg. It has been dubbed the world's wickedest mile and lives up to its name. Things start at 10pm and carry on until dawn. Berlin too, has a notorious nightlife and at the last count had 6,000 or so bars, some most definitely of ill-repute. A peculiarity to Stuttgart are Broom Taverns (*Besenwirtschaften*). These literally have a broom hanging over the door and serve up the new wines during winter and early spring. The Altstadt, the heart of Düsseldorf's nightlife, boasts more than 200 bars, discos and nightclubs in one sq km. Frankfurt is not Germany's top night spot and when the wheels of business stop turning it sleeps. But it does have one of the finest selections of wine and beer restaurants in an area that has been dubbed Main-hatten.

The easiest way to find a decent place to drink, dance or just hang-out, according to your tastes is to make friends quickly, either with your co-workers or members of the local expatriate community.

Music

It has been said that there is no such thing as an unmusical German. This is a pleasant conceit but does possess a grain of truth. Between the 16th and 19th centuries German musical achievements were almost unrivalled. The Germans love their music, and opera is as much a national pastime as it is in Italy. It receives generous government subsidies and every major city has its own operatic company. Most foreign operas are sung in their original language. Every major city has its own philharmonic orchestra; Munich has four orchestras and Stuttgart five. Several states have their own Academies of Music. Singing is also a popular pastime and there are many choral societies across Germany for those of all ages and abilities. Jazz and Blues are also very popular and dozens of clubs host live music most evenings, there are a few Blues Festivals in Germany and bands like The Hamsters tour there regularly. Frankfurt is the jazz capital of the country with hundreds of clubs and the German Jazz festival in the spring. Rock and pop are of course popular, and rap has a definite following. While Britain and America may have musical influences on German pop-culture there is a fine if under publicised (across the world) reservoir of domestic talent. Certainly several major names in rock music like U2 and Julian Cope cite 'krautrock' and bands like Can as influential. While the synth band Kraftwerk have recently reformed to play dance festivals in response to the number of dance and techno outfits who regard their work as ground-breaking.

Cinema

As in almost every country across the globe Amercian-made films dominate the cinema scene, practically all films are dubbed into German, except in the larger towns, where you may find occasional original language screenings. There are also the 'art-house' cinemas which specialise in original language screenings, but these are rare. The current German film industry is very well established and on the increase; German directors such as Wim Wenders and Werner Herzog have an international reputation for high quality films. There are also several film festivals across Germany the main one being in Berlin where films from around the world compete for the coveted Golden and Silver Bear awards. Several other film festivals are held in Germany, including Würzburg's short film festival in February and Mannheim's international Film Week for young and progressive film-makers in the autumn.

Theatre

The fact that more than 200 theatres have been built since the war is ample testimony to the popularity of the stage. Germany had 190 theatre companies at the last count and at any one time you will be able to watch almost anything that takes your fancy. Especially popular at the moment are German works which are undergoing something of a revival. Mannheim is home to the 200-year-old Nationaltheater, the oldest municipal theatre in the country. Munich is regarded as one of Germany's main cultural centres, running a close second to the undisputed cultural capital Berlin, which has 18 theatres devoted solely to German works. Stuttgart has a rich year-round theatrical programme and Hamburg has become the ballet centre, holding its Ballet Festival in July. Bonn holds the distinction of having the greatest number of theatres, in proportion to its population, of any German city.

Festivals and Carnivals

Germans love festivals, and innumerable pageants and carnivals make the social calendar a colourful and eventful one. Almost every small town or village has its own summer fair, *Bierfest* or *Weinfest*. One of the most famous is Munich's *Oktoberfest*, starting in late September, which dates from 1810. Four and a half million litres of beer are drunk by six million visitors during the 16-day extravaganza; held every year in a tented village on the Theresien meadow. The next occurrence of festivities is technically part of the *Carneval* season, as while it is removed from the pre-Lentan festivals it is a forerunner to them. This event is the *Rheinische Karneval* and occurs in the Rhineland towns between Mainz and the Dutch border, and celebrates *Hoppeditz Erwachen* the awakening of Hoppeditz, spirit of Carnival.

The next major feature to appear in the calendar is Christmas, if you are lucky enough to be in the right town then you'll know that December has begun by the appearance of Christmas Market (*Weihnachtsmarkt* or *Christkindelmarkt*) booths in the main market square. The oldest and most famous of which is that of Nürnberg, photographs of which regularly appear in articles about German Christmas celebrations. These markets are usually open from the 1st to 24th of December, and sell a wide range of Christmas gifts, novelties, sweets and of course food and drink for the hungry shopper; including *Gluhwein* a spicy sweet mulled wine, excellent for warding of the chill. Many of the items on sale at these markets are hand-made.

German Christmas festivities take place on the 24th of December (*Heiligabend*) rather than the 25th, with presents being given in the evening after or before going to church, as there are three services. Christmas Day is called *Erste Weihnachtsfeiertag* and Boxing Day is the *Zweite Weihnachtsfeiertag*. Christmas trees are almost a religion in themselves as the Germans decorate not only their own indoor one, but also any handy tree in their garden, in addition to the efforts of the municipal lighting specialists.

Germany has not had such colourful characters as Guy Fawkes in its political history to give them an excuse for letting off fireworks so they make up for it by driving out evil spirits at the turn of the year. As fireworks are only available to buy just before New Years Day, and their use is limited to New Year's Eve a lot of money and explosives change hands in a very short time, in order to see the New Year in with a bang.

When the Christmas decorations come down on twelfth night the country begins preparations for Carnival. The *Fastnacht* or *Fasching* season peaks around the weekend before Lent. Starting with Women's Day (the Thursday before Shrove Tuesday) when women often cut off men's ties in symbolic revenge for the discrimination they suffer the rest of the year. This is associated mainly with Catholic areas of Germany, but is celebrated to some degree in most regions. People dress up, crack rude jokes, drink and generally buffoon around all day. Munich hosts 200 costume balls and in Düsseldorf the highlight is the 3km long *Rosenmontag* (Rose Monday, the day before Shrove Tuesday) parade of floats through the city streets. The biggest carnival is in Köln where its known as *Karneval*, organisers claim to be able to get every bar and restaurant in the city involved in the celebrations. Everything returns to normal on Ash Wednesday.

SPORT

Sports are a major leisure pursuit in Germany, with 87,000 clubs affiliated to the German Sports Federation (*Deutscher Sportbund*, www.dsb.de), these clubs have a membership of around 27 million, while another 12 million Germans enjoy activities outside of formal associations. Western Germany has a large network of sports facilities, in the eastern Länder facilities are rarer and less well equipped for mass sports. Football, gymnastics, tennis and shooting are by far the most popular activities to take part in; more static games like cricket, darts, and snooker do not seem to interest Germans as much. Football is the number one participation sport, with the national federation (*Deutscher Fussball-Bund*) having twice the membership of the tennis federation (*Deutscher Tennisbund*); which loses out to gymnastics (*Deutscher Turnerbund*) in the membership table (see below). Traditional associations (*Vereine*) play an important role in social life and there are clubs for every kind of hobby. Rifle clubs (*Schützenvereine*), each with its own ceremonies and uniforms, are among the most popular. However, the social nature of the activity is borne out by the fact that members seem to spend more time in the bar than on the range. In addition, adult evening schools (*Volkshochschule*), companies, churches, trade unions, universities and welfare organizations also provide ample opportunity for sports participation.

TABLE 6	MEMBERSHIP OF THE TOP TEN SPORTS ASSOCIATIONS
Association	**Membership**
German Football Federation	6,263,252
German Gymnastics Federation	4,604,485
German Tennis Federation	2,333,326
German Shooting Federation	1,540,929
German Athletics Association	831,618
German Handball Federation	838,409
German Table-Tennis Federation	750,049
German Equestrian Association	680,960
German Ski Federation	680,782
German Swimming Federation	631,744
German Basketball Federation	193,788

Sports Facilities

Today nearly every small town has its own swimming pool, athletics track and leisure complex. Responsibility for sport is shared between the Federal authorities, the Länder and the municipalities. The latter are responsible for the construction of sports facilities and promoting local clubs. The Länder support sports associations, which in turn promote sports for the broad masses of the German people. The Federation oversees top international and competitive sports at championship levels. State support is also given to disabled sports, games and activities for older people and the promotion of relations in sport with third world countries

Football

Football in Germany is not just a game, it is an obsession. The national league (*Bundesliga*) comprises 18 teams. In general, German club sides have not distinguished themselves in Europe in recent years. One of the reasons for this is that many of the leading players have been lured by excessive salaries abroad. However, flying the German football flag has been left in very capable hands. The national team was widely acclaimed as the best in the world during the 80s and since they're often successful at International level they are usually widely tipped as favourites in the World Cup.

Tennis

A 17-year-old by the name of Boris Becker changed tennis in Germany from the preserve of the upper classes to the game the whole nation wants to play. In 1985 he succeeded in becoming the youngest player, and first unseeded competitor, to win the men's singles championship at Wimbledon. Becker, and subsequently Steffi Graff and Michael Stich, have won glory to which all young Germans currently appear to be aspiring. The number of tennis facilities has expanded accordingly and every town now seems to have dozens of courts open to the public. A recent survey of German 14 year olds put tennis just behind football and ahead of Formula One in popularity.

Winter Sports

The German winter sports teams always do very well at international competitions and the public are provided with a host of winter sport facilities to emulate their idols. The German Alps are often overlooked, but together with the Harz, Sauerland, Rhön, Fichtel Mountains, Bavarian Forest and the Black Forest offer some fine skiing. Long-distance, cross-country and downhill skiing at medium- or high-altitude are all catered for.

Athletics

Athletics is very popular and excellent facilities exist from school levels upwards. At international level the combination of the east and west German athletics teams has created one of the most potent forces in the world. Recent allegations of drug using, however, have tarnished the image of the German Athletics Association.

Other

Swimming facilities are excellent and an estimated two-thirds of the German population swim regularly. Table tennis is also very popular, as are volleyball and handball. Motor sports are undergoing a revival and the main international venues include Hockenheim (which holds a Formula One Grand Prix every July) and the Nürburgring. For followers of the sport of kings, the horse racing calendar is dominated by Hamburg's Derby week in late June, and the spring and autumn seasons at Iffezheim, near Baden-Baden.

Health and Recreation

The Germans are the world's leading spa-goers, and the country has more than 350 registered spa and health resorts. The majority have ultra-modern amenities to pamper and relax guests. These include treatment centres, sanatoria, sports facilities, hotels, casinos, restaurants and bars. An estimated six million people attend a spa every year, nearly all of them reimbursed by health insurance. As spouses do not usually accompany each other on a spa *Kur* this can lead to problems and the 'spa romance' (*Kurschatten*) is a common occurrence.

Activity holidays are very popular. The North Sea, Baltic coasts and inland lakes, offer a variety of water sports, including 180 sailing schools. The number of golf courses is rising and horseriding is coming back into fashion.

Useful Addresses

Deutscher Sportbund (DSB) (The German Sports Federation): Otto-Fleck-Schneise 12, D-60528 Frankfurt, Germany; ☎069-67000; fax 069-674906; website www.dsb.de. The central sports organization, embracing 19 regional federations, more than 75 000 clubs are affiliated to it.

Der Deutsche Alpenverein e.V. (*German Alpine Club*): Von-Kahr-Str. 2-4, D-80997 München, Germany; ☎089-140030; fax 089-140 0311; website www.alpenverein.de.

Deutscher Basketball Bund e.V: Scwanenstr. 6-10, D-58089 Hagen, Germany; website www.basketball-bund.de.

Deutscher Fechter-Bund e.V. (*Fencing*): Am Neuen Lindenhof 2, D-53117 Bonn, Germany; ☎0228-989050; fax 0228-679430; website www.fechten.org.

Deutsche Fussball-Bund (*German Football Federation*): Otto-Fleck-Schneise 6, D-60528 Frankfurt am Main, Germany; ☎069-67880; fax 069-678 8266; website www.dfb.de.

Deutscher Golfverband (*Golf*): Viktoriastrasse 16, D-65185 Wiesbaden, Germany.

Deutscher Handball-Bund: Stobelallee 56, D-44139 Dortmund, Germany; ☎0231-911910; fax 0231-124061; e-mail presse@dhb.de; website www.dhb.de.

Deutscher Rugby-Verband: Ferdinand-Wilhelm-Fricke-Weg 2a, D-30169 Hannover, Germany; ☎0511-14763; fax 0511-161 0206; e-mail deutscher-rugby-verband@t-online.de; website www.rugby.de.

Deutscher Schwimm-Verband e.V: Korbacher Str. 93, D-Kassel, Germany; ☎0561-940830; fax 0561-940 8315; e-mail info@dsv.de; website www.dsv.de.

Deutscher Squash Rackets Verband e.V: Weidenweg 10, D-47059 Duisburg, Germany; ☎0203-315075; fax 0203-314813; e-mail squash.dsrv@t-online.de; website www.squashnet.de.

Deutscher Tischtennis-Bund (*Table Tennis*): Otto-Fleck-Schneise 12, D-60528 Frankfurt, Germany; ☎069-605 0190; fax 069-6950 1913; e-mail DTTB@tischtennis.de; website http://db.tischtennis.de.

SHOPPING

In the 1980s west German households headed the European league table when it came to possessing consumer durables. There was a consistently high level of consumer spending and most households were equipped with tv's, fridges, dish-washers, video recorders etc. Eighteen per cent of families had two cars and three-car households were not uncommon. The Germans appeared to know exactly what they liked, and promptly went out to buy it. Attention was paid more to quality than price, and in fact they preferred more expensive goods. These days price is now the main factor. Trends also showed that healthier and more environmentally friendly goods are becoming more popular. Many of these attitudes still persist but the money does not, due to the current unemployment situation, hence the popularity of 'preiswort' shops such as *Aldi*, and *Lidl*. Reently shop laws dating from the '30 have been repealed, which means that prices are no longer fixed across the market (the laws had been set up to allow small shops to remain in competition with department stores and big chains). Pundits are hoping that this will mean that soon there will be discounts, bargains and maybe even loyalty bonuses for customers. The British or American shopper should also be aware that all goods sold in Germany are in metric sizes and weights, including shoe and clothing sizes (see conversion table) which will differ from what they are used to.

The opening hours of shops can vary considerably, official opening hours tend to apply to large shops, department stores and supermarkets. The aim of the restrictions on opening hours is to ensure that staff are treated fairly, so don't begrudge them. These hours tend to be 9am to 6.30pm, Monday to Friday, although many larger stores stay open until 8pm on weekdays. On Saturdays shop generally close at 2pm, though city centres generally stay open up to around 4pm, except for the four Saturdays during Advent when many shops stay open until 6pm. Unlike Britain or America there is practically no Sunday trading, although flea markets (*flohmarkt*) are proving popular. Shops have a very urban existence, on the pedestrianised central streets of towns and cities, with access to trams and u-bahnen. Malls in the American sense do exist but on a much smaller scale, in other words they are more akin to English shopping centres; but with better parking and public transport connections.

Value Added Tax (*Mehrwertsteuer*) is charged on most goods and services, at the time of writing the rate was 16%. Some essential items, such as foodstuffs, are charged at the lower rate of 7%. Düsseldorf is Germany's shopping mecca, thanks to the exclusive and large Königsallee complex, known locally simply as the Kö. Berlin's KaDeWe is the largest department store in Europe. The food department, which alone occupies the entire sixth floor, displays some 25,000 different food products and has 22 lunch bars. Frankfurt's pedestrianised Zeil has the highest turnover of any shopping centre in Germany and Stuttgart's claim to fame is Breuninger, the Harrods of Germany. Almost all cities have a pedestrianised shopping area (*Fussgängerzone*) or at least such an area is traffic calmed (*verkehrsberuhigt*).

Treats from Home. For the homesick expat there are various stores across Germany run by expats with the needs of their fellows in mind. You may also find a few Germans shopping in there two, English tea is a prized luxury to some Germans, and more than a few remember Cadbury's chocolate form the parcels sent in amongst the Berlin airlift. There are also a few English-language bookshops across Germany, for the homesick, and you'll find that many larger stores will carry original language texts of the bestsellers and classics. Even toystores will carry English-language editions of some collectable card games such as *Magic* or *Lord of the Rings*. Useful shops for the expat include the following.

The Anglia English Bookshop: Schellingstrasse 3, D-80799 München, Germany.

Australia Shop: Marktplatz 13, D- 65183 Wiesbaden, Germany; ☎0611-308 2845.

The Body Shop: Luginsland 1, D-60313 Frankfurt, Germany; ☎069-291939; e-mail Info@the-body-shop.de; website www.the-body-shop.de.

Books Around...: Hohenstaufenring 43-45, D- 50674 Köln, Germany; ☎0221-240 8105.

British Bookshop, Berlin: Mauerstr. 83-84, D-10117 Berlin, Germany; ☎030-238 4680.

The British Bookshop: Borsenstrasse 17, D-60313 Frankfurt am

Main, Germany; ☎069-280492; fax 069-287701; e-mail British-Bookshop@t-online.de; website www.british-bookshop.de.
Broken English: Grimmstr. 19, D-10967 Berlin, Germany; ☎030-691 1227.
Duckbill & Gooseberry's British Shop: Alexanderstr. 26, D-64283 Darmstadt, Germany; ☎06151-75380; fax 06151-788033; website www.britishshop.de.
English Food Shop: Seeburgerstr. 3, D-13581 Berlin, Germany; ☎030-332 8420.
English Shop: Niddastr. 104, D-60329 Frankfurt am Main, Germany; ☎069-235755; fax 069-23460.
The English Shop: Schellingstr. 11, D-70174 Stuttgart, Germany; ☎0711-226 0902; fax 0711-226 1242; e-mail EnglishShopStuttgart@t-online.de. Thi shop sells everything from beans to boxer shorts, videos, pork scratchings, crisps and tea. There is also a bulletin board and the staff are always willing to help new expats. A website is to be set up soon.
Highlands Scottish Shop: Sandweg 6, D-60316 Frankfurt am Main, Germany; ☎069-490203.
Old London: Schmidstr. 2, D-80331 Munich, Germany; ☎089-2602 2952; fax 089-2602 2953.
Piccadilly English Shop: Gerauer Str. 11A, D-64546 Mörfelden-Walldorf, Germany; ☎06105-923267; fax 06105-923267; e-mail info@piccadillyshop.de; website www.piccadillyshop.de.
Pomeroy & Winterbottom: Reichenbachstr. 38, D-80469 München, Germany; ☎089-201 6901; fax 089-201 6938.
Words'Worth Booksellers: Schellingstrasse 21a, D-80799 München, Germany; ☎089-280 9141.
Warenhaus Hertie: Prager Str. 17, D-01069 Dresden, Germany; ☎0351-8610. Sells Englsh and American foodstuffs.

Food shopping: Germans prefer to shop at small specialised shops and boutiques (of which there has been a recent resurgence in the face of the supermarket construction boom of the 70s) but there are also many supermarkets, most notable of which are shops like *Aldi* or *Norma*. The goods on sale here being *preiswert* (inexpensive) due to the high volume sales their outlets can generate, which keeps prices down. They tend to have bulk quantities of goods but with a limited choice of brands. Their popularity with shoppers can be seen in the size of the checkout queues, although their till staff are amazingly quick at processing a large number of customers. Outdoor markets are also very popular. Farmers very often bring produce direct, so goods are both fresh and relatively inexpensive. It is important to note however that owing to strict health regulations the touching of fruits and vegetables before purchase is technically prohibited, but that doesn't stop shoppers from assessing quality for themselves. Queueing, in the British sense is not a common practice, German queues tend to be more spread out, and it is up to you to speak up and keep your place.

GERMAN FOOD

Germans have a reputation for liking *gutbürgerlich* food: solid, homely and well-cooked, one example is pork, potatoes, peas, dumplings and gravy. Vegetarians will have a hard time in the face of the amazing range of meat dishes especially the German sausage (*Wurst*). There are hundreds of varieties eaten the world over including Wienerwurst, Milzwurst, Bratwurst, Gelbwurst, Wollwurst, Leberwurst and Weisswurst. The list is seemingly endless in this German *Wurstkultur.* There are even specialised sausage kitchens (*Wurstküchen*). Bread is also something of a speciality. There are still more than 200 types of bread in production, including the famous *Pumpernickel,* a rich black rye bread.

The pig provides the staple element of most German menus, and virtually every part is eaten in a variety of ways: boiled with Sauerkraut in Frankfurt, roasted with dumplings in Munich and eaten as ham in Westphalia.

Traditionally lunch (*Mittagessen*) is the main meal of the day, when a cooked meal is prepared, the evening meal (*Abendbrot*) is usually made up of bread, sausage, cheese and pickles. Foreign cooking is growing in popularity, which often benefits the Turkish, Greek and other ethnic shopkeepers. Although, old German peasant recipes are also seeing something of a revival. With regard to eating out this means that foreign restaurants are now vying with the more traditional cuisine. Restaurants are clean and efficient, and they are required to display a printed menu, and show that tax and service (*Mehrwertsteuer und Bedienung*) are included, tipping is customary as a thank-you for good service.

DRINK

Health concerns and strict drink-driving laws have had a severe effect on the drinking habits of Germans. Contrary to popular belief Germans are not the world's greatest beer drinkers (that distinction goes to the Belgians) and they drink more coffee than beer. The consumption of soft drinks has risen, especially among the young, and mineral water sales have more than trebled since the early 1970s. Spirits are drunk in moderation and by far the most popular is *Schnaps* (which is also deemed to be the principal cause of alcoholism). The regions each have their own brews. These are too numerous to mention individually but include Cologne's *Kölsch*, *Apfelwein* in Frankfurt and Munich's *Weissbier,* brewed from wheat. There are also a few English and Irish style pubs across Germany, mind you there are also a few bars in Berlin which are so full of Irish staff that they may as well be pubs. But the wise expatriate will only repair to the just-like-home when feeling homesick, you can get a lot more from Germany if you mingle.

Beer

Beer lovers will love Germany, and those with an internet connection can find out about it all in advance at www.bier.de. Drinking litre mugs full of frothy beer is more than a pastime for Germans, it's an institution. They consume more than 145 litres per head per annum. The country has more than one-third of the world's breweries, with more than half (800) in Bavaria alone. It also has the second and third ranked beer producing cities in the world – namely Dortmund and Munich. Freising boasts the oldest brewery in the world, dating back to the early thirteenth century. Doctors have been known to prescribe it for patients and Augustine monks are reputed to supplement their Lenten diet with Munich's *Augustiner* beer. Bavarian brewers recently gave a nun their highest award for a beer she brews at her convent. Fortunately, the Germans do not keep it all to themselves and brand names such as Hofmeister and Becks are well-known throughout the world.

German beer's good taste and reputation is due in part to a strict purity code laid down five centuries ago by Duke William IV. This code is under threat, however, from EU officials who are trying to standardise beer throughout the Community (very few foreign beers meet the standards, and therefore cannot be imported). The reaction to this has been strong, but the rot appears to have already set in with traditional wooden barrels being replaced by pressurised metal ones.

Alt beers are not old or to be confused with English ale, the term 'alt' means old, as they are brewed to traditional top-fermented methods. *Bock* on the other hand is a bottom fermented brew, bocks come as dark or pale and proliferate around München. *Kölsch* is the local beer of Köln, and is served in tall slim glasses, usually holding 200ml. Another regional speciality is the *Berliner Weisse* a slightly sour tasting cloudy beer, it is often drunk with a shot (*Schuss*) of raspberry syrup or caraway schnapps. In German bars it is not customary to wait at the bar to be served, the standard bar uses a waiter service, so if you want a drink find a free table and wait.

Wine

Germans now annually drink about 26 litres of wine per head – an amount that has more than trebled in the last thirty years. Germany produces seven times less wine than France, but some of what it does produce, usually white, is among the finest in the world. Contrary to what wine merchants in Britain would have us believe, production is not confined to Liebfraumilch; the white wine most drunk in the UK. There are 11 official wine producing regions, all of which are located along rivers or around lakes. The two principal areas are the Rhine (sold in tall brown bottles) and Moselle (in tall green bottles). Throughout the summer and autumn a number of wine festivals (*Weinfeste*) are held. In August the Stuttgart Wine Village has on show more than 350 Baden-Württemberg wines. German wine is divided into two categories: *Tafelwein* (cheap table wine) and *Qualitätswein* (quality wine). The latter is the equivalent to the French *Apellation Controllée*. All *Tafelwein* is either dry (*trocken*) or medium dry (*halb trocken*). *Qualitätswein* can be sub-divided into the better quality *Qualitätswein mit Prädikat*, of which there are six grades, and *Qualitätswein eines bestimmten Anbaugebietes* (usually abbreviated to *Qualitätswein b.A.*). German Champagne-type wines are also available. The two leading brands are Deinhard, from Koblenz, and Henkell, from Wiesbaden.

RECYCLING

In a country which has had a 'Green' party since the early 1970s, it is hardly surprising that the Germans practise recycling packaging and other materials more than Britain or America. Paper, bottles, cans, plastic wrappings are all recyclable in Germany. In part this has come about from the worrying prospect of running out of places to dump rubbish, but the practical Germans have found a way to make it a sound economic and environmental proposition (see Chapter Six). Apart from the can and bottle banks on street corners or other convenient locations to housing areas, the local rubbish collections usually segregate rubbish by using different coloured or marked bags for each type of waste collected. Part of the cost of all this comes from the householder's nebenkosten, but the bulk of it is paid for by the packaging manufacturers, as they pay licence fees to display the various trademarks on their packaging which indicate that their product can be recycled. It is a legal obligation on the manufacturers and distributors of packaging that they take back anything they put into circulation and forward it for recycling.

Older readers may fondly remember being able to augment their pocket money by taking back bottles for the deposit on them, a practise discontinued in Britain. In Germany, however, it is still the case that you can get money back on your empties. The deposit is part of the sale price of the drink to encourage recycling and generally is between 20 and 25 cents.

CONVERSION CHART

LENGTH (NB 12inches 1 foot, 10 mm 1 cm, 100 cm 1 metre)

inches	1	2	3	4	5	6	9	12
cm	2.5	5	7.5	10	12.5	15.2	23	30

cm	1	2	3	5	10	20	25	50	75	100
inches	0.4	0.8	1.2	2	4	8	10	20	30	39

WEIGHT (NB 14lb = 1 stone, 2240 lb = 1 ton, 1,000 kg = 1 metric tonne)

lb	1	2	3	5	10	14	44	100	2246
kg	0.45	0.9	1.4	2.3	4.5	6.4	20	45	1016

kg	1	2	3	5	10	25	50	100	1000
lb	2.2	4.4	6.6	11	22	55	110	220	2204

DISTANCE

mile	1	5	10	20	30	40	50	75	100	150
km	1.6	8	16	32	48	64	80	120	161	241

km	1	5	10	20	30	40	50	100	150	200
mile	0.6	3.1	6.2	12	19	25	31	62	93	124

VOLUME

1 litre =	0.2 UK gallons	1 UK gallon = 4.5 litres
1 litre =	0.26 US gallons	1 US gallon = 3.8 litres

CLOTHES

UK	8	10	12	14	16	18	20
Europe	36	38	40	42	44	46	48
USA	6	8	10	12	14	18	

SHOES

UK	3	4	5	6	7	8	9	10	11
Europe	36	37	38	39	40	41/42	43	44	45
USA	2.5	3.3	4.5	5.5	6.5	7.5	8.5	9.5	10.5

METRICATION

Germany uses the metric system in all respects. In the long run it is much easier to learn and think in metric rather than to always try to convert from metric to imperial. In all cases measurements are quoted as a decimal and not a fraction.

PUBLIC HOLIDAYS

Germany, like Britain and America has a certain number of days per year which are Public Holidays, these can vary between 12 and 15 per year depending upon where you live. Most are religious in origin but some are wholly secular, especially the third of October which commemorates German Re-Unification. As in Britain expect most shops and travel services to be closed or operating reduced services. Likewise while many of them occur on specific dates Easter and Whitsun are moveable feasts, and others are specific only to certain länder, so it is best to contact the German Tourist Authority for details prior to departure.

PUBLIC HOLIDAYS ACROSS GERMANY

1 January New Year's Day (*Neujahrstag*)
March/April Good Friday (*Karfreitag*)
March/April Easter Monday (*Ostermontag*)
1 May Labour Day (*Tag der Arbeit*)
May Ascension Day (*Christi Himmelfahrt*)
May Whitsun/Pentecost (*Pfingstsonntag/montag*)
3 October German Unity Day (*Tag der Deutschen Einheit*)
25 December Christmas Day (*Erster Weihnachtstag*)
26 December Boxing Day (*der zweite Weihnachtstag*)

Public Holidays Limited by Region

6 January Epiphany (*Epiphaniasfest/Erscheinungsfest*) [1]
May/June Corpus Christi (*Fronleichnam*) [2]
15 August Feast of Assumption (*Mariä Himmelfahrt*) [3]
31 October Reformation Day (*Reformationstag*) [4]
1 November All Saints (*Alle Heiligen*) [5]
18 November Repentance Day (*Buss und Betthetag*) [6]

(1) This holiday only applies to Baden-Württemburg, Bayern, and Sachsen-Anhalt.
(2) Corpus Christi is celebrated in Baden-Württemburg, Bayern, Hessen, Nord-Rhein-Westfalen, Rheinland-Pfalz and Saarland, but also in the catholic areas of Sachsen and Thüringen.
(3) Only the Saarland and catholic areas of Bayern.
(4) Only the five new Länder (Brandenburg, Mecklenburg-Vorpommern, Sachsen, Sachsen-Anhalt and Thüringen) celebrate this day to mark Luther's Reformation.
(5) All Saints is celebrated with a public holiday by Baden-Württemburg, Bayern, Nord-Rhein-Westfalen, Rheinland-Pfalz and Saarland.
(6) Saxony is the only land to have this day as a holiday.

RETIREMENT

CHAPTER SUMMARY

○ Pensioner numbers in Germany have increased, and the retired will soon outnumber the working population.

○ The cost of many goods and services is cheaper in Germany than in the UK.

○ The German climate compares favourably with that in the UK.

○ The quality of life is often calmer and of a higher quality than in the UK.

○ **Finance:** You can have your UK or US pension paid in Germany.

○ **Socialising & Hobbies:** Most sizeable towns have an Anglo-German or expat group where you can meet people and take it turns to talk each other's language.

○ The Germans love gardening and tending small vegetable allotments

On average 10,000 British citizens retire from work every week. Many may dream of a cottage by the sea or a villa in Spain, but unless they have some prior link few will contemplate moving to Germany. However, there is no reason why retiring to Germany need be anything but a happy and rewarding experience. Provided you take all the necessary precautions before leaving and carry out sufficient background research as to where, when and how you intend to live, there are some real advantages to living in Germany. The climate in the south, and the scenery, compare favourably with anything the UK can offer. The Germans pride themselves on their efficiency and this is apparent in the excellent public services available. They are also a law-abiding and normally polite people. This chapter endeavours to deal with some of the bridges that will have to be crossed to facilitate a successful transition between the two countries.

THE DECISION TO LEAVE

Germany will never quite be like the UK and anyone contemplating a move must have a clear idea of what they are letting themselves in for. A successful relocation will require not just enthusiasm but a certain degree of adaptability. In addition, the cost of the move could be high. It is unlikely that anyone would decide to uproot themselves and move to a country without having been there before. The majority of individuals settling in Germany are more than likely to have experienced German life while working there. However, living permanently in country, especially on a pension, is not the same as working there on temporary secondment or taking one's holidays there. Before making a commitment to move it is advisable to consider living for a trial period, including the winter, in the area you wish to settle. Alternatively, if you have sufficient funds, you could buy a second home in Germany and should it be a success, sell your UK residence and move permanently.

ENTERING WITH RETIREMENT STATUS

Since 1 January 1992 pensioners from EU Member States have been able to live wherever they choose in the boundary-less European Union. As stated in the chapter on *Residence and Entry Regulations* people intending to retire to Germany require a residence permit (*Anmeldebescheinigung*), in compliance with the Foreign Nationals Act (*Ausländergesetz*). They will have to include pension details, proof of adequate medical insurance cover and supply evidence that individuals have 'sufficient' funds to support themselves without working. Under European Union regulations if you work in two or more EU states you will be able to combine state pension contributions paid in each country, for up to date information on this contact the Department of Social Security. UK and US pensions can be paid directly to individuals resident in Germany, and if your retirement scheme includes health insurance you should have the right to have the same cover as a retired German. To obtain these benefits you should inform your pension authorities of your planned move and Britons should obtain a form E121 from your health authority, this should be handed to the relevant authorities in your new homeland.

CHOOSING AND BUYING A RETIREMENT HOME

The main and obvious point to make regarding buying a retirement home is to choose something which is both within one's scope financially and in an area suitable for year-round living. Large numbers of expatriates live in the major cities (e.g. Berlin, Hamburg, Munich) and industrial areas. These are not normally the most picturesque regions and the choice of location is often due to work commitments. In general retired people are free to locate wherever they choose. Areas to consider in Germany include the southern sun belt, especially around Lake Constance or in Bavaria, and the north the coast and the Frisian Islands. However, it must be borne in mind that these areas are also amongst the most popular tourist spots in the summer months, and are prone to snow. Proximity to health services and other facilities is also an important consideration for anyone reliant on public transport. Once you have decided on your new home you will need to follow all the procedures regarding property purchase which are explained in Chapter Three, *Setting Up Home.*

HOBBIES AND INTERESTS

Once you have unpacked and settled into your new home, your thoughts will undoubtedly turn to socializing and the pursuit of interests for which you never quite had the time for in the past. In this department Germany boasts many opportunities. The Germans are keen on sports and recreation and for those looking for an active retirement there are some excellent facilities. Walking and cycling through southern Germany's stunning countryside are especially popular. Virtually every town has a leisure centre, swimming pool and tennis courts. There are also plenty of spectator events on offer, from football to motor racing.

Gardening is a very popular pastime and even inner city inhabitants can lease garden plots or allotments for planting flowers or growing vegetables. The Germans have spent a lot of time saving and displaying their rich heritage and there are many museums and restored buildings to be explored. Unemployment is rising along with social problems and there is some scope for doing voluntary work, for which both expatriate clubs and consulates can be useful sources of information.

PENSIONS

If you became entitled to a UK state pension before moving to Germany there is no reason why it cannot be paid to you in Germany. The one important point to note is that a UK pension is paid in sterling and therefore index linked with UK levels. This did at one time pose a problem due to the strength of the German mark against sterling. How it will fare against the Euro is harder to fathom, and the best advice given recent events is to wait and see.

People who move to Germany and work for an EU Employer before reaching pension age are usually insured under the social security laws of Germany. You will not usually have to pay UK National Insurance contributions but paragraphs 2-11 in the leaflet SA29 *Your Social Security, Health Care and Pension Rights*, explain when you have to or decide to, pay UK National Insurance Contributions.

Each EU country where you have paid insurance towards a pension will look at your insurance under its own scheme and work out how much pension you can have. Each EU country will also take into account any insurance you have paid in any other EU State to make sure you are paid the highest possible pension entitlement. Paragraph 20 of the leaflet SA29 explains how these calculations are made.

You can claim any of your pensions direct from any EU country that you have been insured in. If you have been insured in the UK and providing you have kept the DSS informed (address below) of any change in your address, you will usually be sent a claim form 4 months before you reach pension age in the UK.

State/Government Pensions

The German state pension plans are administered by the Land Insurance Agencies (*Landesversicherungsanstalten*) and the Federal Insurance Agency (*Bundesversicherungsanstalt für Angestellte*). To be eligible to receive a German state pension an individual must have paid a minimum of 60 months German insurance contributions. German pensions are only awarded if applied for, by the individual, to the German pensions authorities.

As an employee, you become a mandatory member of the national German pensions scheme (*Rentenversicherung*). An automatic deduction of approximately 19% of your gross annual salary (maximum €54,000), is made in monthly instalments. However, this cost is split equally between you and your employer. In real terms, you would contribute a maximum of approximately €430 per month and your employer pays the same (as of 2002).

If you are self-employed, and not just a sub-contractor, you will not be a mandatory member of German national pension scheme (see section on *Private Pensions*). Please note that recent changes in the law have become stricter regarding the definition of self-employed persons. Briefly, to qualify as self-employed you must have contracts with at least three different clients and each project should have an individual contract. Working for one client may mean that you are classed as 'employed'. As this is a new 'gray' area, it is recommended that you check your circumstances with a German tax advisor as a priority.

To clarify details about the German Pension system, before moving to Germany, you can visit the Bundesversicherungsanstalt website (www.bfa.de), where you can read or download specific information in English. The website includes information about the employment system, pension details – including tax treaties – and much more.

Company Pensions

Company pensions are rarely offered in Germany, but due to changes in German laws the number of them will probably increase dramatically over the next few years. One recent change now allows you to use deferred compensation and/or be part of a pension fund scheme funded fully or partially by your employer. However, you generally have a ten-year waiting period until you are vested.

Private Pensions

Many people now believe that European state pensions will not be able to provide sufficient provisions for their retirement and the necessity of investing in private pensions is becoming apparent. Traditionally, people moving to Germany have felt that the only real choice was between:

- Being tied down to a long-term German endowment policy (*Lebensversicherung*).
- An off-shore account that appears attractive for its 'international' feel, but does not enjoy tax breaks under German law.

The long-term German endowment has the advantage of enjoying tax breaks, but tends to have high upfront costs and very low surrender values in the first 5-10 years. This is not financially attractive if you plan to move on again or do not know your 'planned' length of stay in Germany.

Whilst offshore accounts offer geographic flexibility, they miss out on the opportunity to benefit on tax breaks.

However, there are some international products to legally take advantage of subsidies and tax breaks offered under German law. You can contact an independent investment advisor to obtain more information on this subject; one such is *Cathy J. Matz* (Hainstrasse 2, D-61476 Kronberg, Germany; ☎0700 INSURE ME or 0700-4678 7363; Fax 06173-4497; e-mail matz@insure-invest.de; website www.insure-invest.de), an independent, international insurance and investment advisor who's offices are based near Frankfurt am Main. Full service in both English and German. Offering a wide range of high quality German and international pensions plans.

Useful Addresses

The Pensions and Overseas Benefits Directorate: Tyneview Park, Newcastle upon Tyne, NE98 1BA; ☎0191-218 7777.

Inland Revenue: National Insurance Contributions Office, nternational Services, Longbenton, Newcastle Upon Tyne, NE98 1ZZ; ☎0845-915 4811.

Landesversicherungsanstalt Freie und Hansesstadt Hamburg: Abt. V, Grundsatzreferat, Sachgebiet Vertrag und Ausland, Postfach 60 15 60, D-22215 Hamburg.

Bundesversicherungsanstalt für Angestellte: Berlin, Germany; ☎030-8651; fax 030-8652 7240; website www.bfa.de.

FINANCE

Anyone considering retiring abroad should take specialist advice regarding their financial situation. The majority of people coming to retirement age have some capital to invest, or will have after selling their UK property. It is worth remembering that any nest egg must last you the rest of your life so resist the temptation to splash out on the first opportunity that comes your way. Those intending to maintain connections with both the UK and Germany will need advice on how their taxation affairs can best be arranged.

Taxation

The Department of Work and Pensions will not deduct tax from your UK state pension providing you can prove that you are resident in Germany. In this case payments must be transferred into a German bank account and will subsequently be liable for German income tax. A more complex situation arises if one spends time in both Germany and the UK and for this it is essential to get professional advice.

Offshore Banking

For a retired British citizen not resident in the UK, a number of high street banks, building societies and merchant banks offer attractive, long-term accounts through offices in Gibraltar, the Channel Islands and the Isle of Man. The minimum amount of money required to open a deposit account ranges from £500 to £10,000.

Section II

WORKING IN GERMANY

EMPLOYMENT

PERMANENT WORK

TEMPORARY WORK

BUSINESS AND INDUSTRY REPORT

STARTING A BUSINESS

EMPLOYMENT

CHAPTER SUMMARY

O EU nationals have the right to live and work in any other EU state.

O The qualifications issued in one EU state should be recognised in another – these issues are dealt with by a series of EU directives.

O **Unemployment:** In 1998 unemployment was 12% with the highest rates in the new Länder; it has dropped and risen since and is now about 10%.

   O German unemployment, sickness and industrial injury benefits are extremely generous.

O **Industry:** High-tech industries are at the forefront of their field and offer higher than average pay.

   O All jobs have to be registered with the national employment service.

   O German employers demand high standards of competence from their staff but reward them well.

O **Women at Work:** German companies are very progressive in providing maternity and paternity leave.

THE EMPLOYMENT SCENE

The employment scene in Germany has been complicated by the unification and redevelopment of the former East Germany. Over the last five years unemployment statistics leaped to record levels with 4.6 million workers out of employment, to subside to under 3.8 million only to rise again to 4.3 million. In part some of these troubles are due to the knock on effects of the terrorist attacks in New York. There are also deeper causes as the unification of Germany is an ongoing process and the economy is moving away from manufacturing. However, given German ingenuity, the work ethic and the shortage of ICT skilled workers, Germany is still a country to look at when seeking work in another country; either in the 'new' e-economy or within the financial services sector. These areas are set to see marked growth in employment. The European Central Bank now resides in Frankfurt and so there is a strong focus for the development of the city as an even larger financial hub than it was only a few years ago.

The climate may not have the allure of Italy or Spain, but with the right skills and some careful planning you can find a very rewarding position, especially as at present the opportunities and concomitant benefits of working in another country are not being exploited by many Europeans. In a country with one of the best-trained workforces in Europe, if not the world, competition for jobs is understandably high. Foreigners therefore have to offer skills (e.g. IT) or services which are in demand and which cannot be provided, or which have not yet been exploited by Germans themselves. The Common Market has created a demand for top flight executives with a knowledge of foreign markets and experts in fields like taxation and business law and for services which will facilitate commercial dealings between different Member States, all of which are expanding areas for investment. In theory, the principle of free movement of labour within the EU gives nationals of all EU countries the right to work in the Member State of their choice and to move around freely in search of work.

Foreigners who do get jobs, particularly those at management level or in high demand areas like Information Technology, will find their salaries are higher than in the UK, but this may be offset by more expensive living costs and higher taxes and health and social security contributions. On the plus side, greater employee benefits, better healthcare and one of the the shortest working weeks in Europe are amongst the attractions of working in Germany, and it is possible to 'shop around' to get yourself the best deal on accommodation.

RESIDENCE AND WORK REGULATIONS

Foreigners coming from another EU Member State to live and work in Germany will have the minimum of residence formalities and work permits are not required at all. EU nationals are required only to register with the *Einwohnermeldeamt* (local registration office), the *Stadtverwaltung* (City Council) or *Gemeindeverwaltung* (Community Council) – depending on whether they live in a city or in one of the rural communes – to gain their *Aufenthaltserlaubnis* (residence permit). This should be obtained within three months of arrival or as soon as you obtain a job, whichever is earlier.

Non-EU nationals will have to obtain a visa and residence permit before entering Germany. The exceptions to this are Americans and nationals of the European Free Trade Area (EFTA) non-EU states, i.e. Iceland, Liechtenstein, Norway and Switzerland.

Anyone applying for employment which involves the handling or serving of food is obliged to obtain a health certificate (*Gesundheitszeugnis*) from the local health department (*Gesundheitsamt*). A fee is charged for the compulsory medical examination involved.

Fuller details on residence and entry regulations can be found in Chapter Two, *Residence and Entry.*

EU PROFESSIONAL QUALIFICATIONS DIREC-TIVES

Each country in the EU has its own educational system and standards, which means that in spite of the single European market, professional and vocational qualifications are gained in different fashions. However, in order that qualified workers in one state can work freely in another state various commissions and professional bodies have worked to ensure that qualifications gained in one country are recognised by the competent authorities for that trade or profession in all countries of the EU. The work of these bodies is covered by the EC directives 89/48EEC and 92/51 EEC; the former concerns qualifications gained through higher education while the latter covers vocational qualifications. If you gained your qualification by a route other than university, but it confers the same right to practise as that of a university qualification, then your qualification is of equal validity under the directive. The directives also mean that National and Scottish Vocational Qualifications (NVQs/SVQs) are recognised by the EU states.

However, where there are significant differences in the training for a qualification, the EU directives do allow for the authorities of your new location to ask you to pass an aptitude test or undertake a period of supervised practice.

In the UK the organisation responsible for providing information on the comparability of qualifications is the *National Academic Recognition Information Centre* (UK NARIC, ECCTIS Ltd, Oriel House, Oriel Road, Cheltenham, GL50 1XP; ☎01242-260010; fax 01242-258611; e-mail naric@ecctis.co.uk; www.naric.org.uk). You should first ask the Jobcentre in the UK, or in Germany, if you are already there, to approach NARIC on your behalf. You can also approach NARIC directly, but there will be a charge of £25 for a statement of comparability of qualifications. For the recognition of vocational qualifications in Germany contact the *Zentralstelle für Ausländisches Bildungwesen* (Nassestr. 8, D-53113 Bonn, Germany; ☎0228-5010; fax 0228-501486). If your qualifications are vocational or in hotel and catering, the motor trade, travel and tourism or office work and you want to know how your qualifications stand up against the German equivalent, you can consult the Comparability Co-ordinator through your local Jobcentre or direct: Comparability Coordinator, Employment Dept., Qualifications and Standards Branch (QSI), Room E454, Moorfoot, Sheffield SP1 4PQ; ☎0114-259 4144.

Certificates of Experience

EU member states, other than the one in which qualifications were attained, may require evidence of one or more years of professional experience. In order to do this the home state can issue a Certificate of Experience. In Britain, those craftsmen wishing to practise their trade or profession in another EU state can obtain a *European Community Certificate of Experience*. These can be obtained from the *Department of Trade and Industry* (Certificates of Experience Unit, Department of Trade and Industry, Kingsgate House, 66-74 Victoria Street, London SW1E 6SW; ☎020-7215 4004; fax 020-7215 4489) requesting an application form for a European Community Certificate of Experience (form EC2/GN). The form will be accompanied by a copy of the Directive (see above) applicable to the job. The applicant should check whether he or she meets the terms of the Directive before completing the application form. To be eligible for a certificate you must normally (but not exclusively) have had managerial or self-employed experience for a number of years in the job concerned. The DTI charges £80 for a certificate and a smaller fee for an update/revision. The charge is to cover the costs of checking and authenticating the information submitted by the applicant.

The DTI also produces a booklet *Europe Open for Professionals* which is regularly updated.

SOURCES OF JOBS

EURES AND THE UK EMPLOYMENT SERVICE

EURES (European Employment Service) is a computerised network which exchanges information about living and working conditions and job vacancies between the employment services of the EU/EEA countries. In the UK, Ireland and other European countries, you can access the EURES network from national job centres. Job seekers can use EURES to find out about job vacancies in any member state plus some national background information including living and working conditions and taxation and social security. Advertising vacancies on the EURES network is free for employers, and all types of jobs from unskilled to executive and professional posts appear on the network (a total of about 5,000 vacancies are listed at any one time). It may soon be possible for job seekers as well as employers to advertise themselves on EURES.

The central point of contact in the UK for EURES is the Overseas Placing Unit (OPU) of the Employment Service (*Overseas Placing Unit:* Employment Service, Level 1, Rockingham House, 123 West Street, Sheffield S1 4ER; ☎0114-259 6000; www.employmentservice.gov.uk). However there are Euroadvisers across the UK; contact your local Jobcentre for more information. All local Employment Service Jobcentres have computer access to the vacancy details held by the OPU and can supply clients with a print-out and application form for such posts. The spectrum of jobs available varies from those for highly skilled craftsmen and women to seasonal work. EURES also has its own website (www.europa.eu.int/jobs/eures) with links to the government employment agency sites of eleven EU countries. Not all of them have databases that can be 'surfed', however, Germany is one of the ones which you can search online.

The Employment Service together with Careers Europe (www.careerseurope.co.uk) also publishes Eurofact sheets entitled 'Working in...', available from Jobcentres and Employment Service offices. These cover specific topics in all the EU/EEA states and give basic information on issues such as Accommodation, Education, Health Issues with contact names and addresses for more detailed help.

THE GERMAN NATIONAL EMPLOYMENT SERVICE

The Federal Employment Institute or *Bundesanstalt für Arbeit* (Regenburgerstr. 104, D-90237, Nürnberg) has a nationwide network of 181 offices, *Arbeitsamter* (Employment Offices) which are very important for job-finding. It is possible to use the Bundesanstalt's services from outside the country as they have a Central Placement Office (*Zentralstelle für Arbeitsvermittlung:* Villemombler Str. 76, D-53123 Bonn, Germany; ☎0228-7130; fax 0228-713 1111; website www.arbeitsamt.de). All applications addressed to the National Employment Service from abroad are processed centrally at this address; even if they are sent to the regional Arbeitsamter they will automatically be forwarded to the Zentralstelle. Although nationals of any country can apply through the Zentralstelle, only EU nationals can expect the same treatment as German nationals. Other nationalities will generally need some trade in demand in order to be considered. There is no obligation to use the National Employment Service; many people bypass it by writing to employers direct (see *Temporary Employment* below).

Anyone who goes to Germany to look for work can find the address of the nearest Arbeitsamt (employment office) by consulting the local German telephone book.

The one exception to the rule of preferential treatment for EU and German nationals is the Zentralstelle's Student Employment Department which will accept German-speaking students of any nationality (aged 18-30 and with proof of university enrolment) for summer work lasting 2-3 months.

There are also the *Raphaels-Werk* (*Raphaels-Werk e.V.:* Vilbeler Str. 36, D-60313 Frankfurt am Main, Germany; website www.raphaels-werk.de) employment advice agencies across Germany, which deal with employment issues and often have a EURES adviser on the staff, although they were set up to advise people rather than find them jobs. They also specialise in advising Germans returning to home to Germany after long periods overseas.

Other Employment Agencies

The Federal Employment Institute is at present reviewing its policy of discouraging the setting up of private employment agencies (*Zeitarbeitsbüros, Stelle nvermittlungsbüros*) in Germany and the number of these is likely to increase in the future. The international chains dealing in temporary work including Manpower (with 75 offices), Adecco, and Randstad (with around 630 offices), have had branches in large cities for some years.

Elan Computing GmbH: Gruneburgweg 9, D-60322 Frankfurt, Germany; ☎069-915 0960; fax 069-9150 9666; website www.elanit.dk.

Euro-London Appointments: Goethestrasse 23, D-60313 Frankfurt, Germany; ☎069-219320; fax 069-2193 2111; e-mail frankfurt@eurolondon.com; website www.eurolondon.com.

Job Partners GmbH: Business Service Park, Janderstrasse 8, D-68199 Mannheim, Germany; ☎0621-845 5150; fax 0621-845 5100; website www.jobpartners.com. Specialist in online recruitment.

THE INTERNET

In addition to the vast store of knowledge accessible from your computer the internet has recently started to make life easier for the prospective expatriate worker. Not only can you uncover a wealth of information about your intended location and companies operating there, but you can also look for jobs. More than a few employment agencies now have websites through which you can not only read about vacancies, but often apply for them too. If the agency sites do not have the type of job or country that you are looking for then there are also websites of international newspapers, such as the *International Herald Tribune* (see below) which have classified sections on-line including situations vacant. Below is a list of useful websites including that of the German Employment Agency, however, due to the nature of the internet some of these addresses may change over time and there is no guarantee that there will be jobs in Germany listed every day. We should also point out that most German based websites (.de) do not have an English version, and in some cases you will need a web-browser which can read 'frames'.

USEFUL WEBSITES

Arbeit-Online: www.arbeit-online.de.
Arbeitsmarkt Online: www.mamas.de.
IT-Arbeitsmarkt: www.it-arbeitsmarkt.de
Job Office: www.job-office.com.
Jobsite: www.jobsite.co.uk (IT, accounting, sales, & management recruitment).
Karrierfuehrer: www.karrierefuehrer.de.
Netjobs: www.netjobs.com (Canadian website with 500 opportunites per week).
Overseas Jobs: www.overseasjobs.com.
Stepstone: www.stepstone.de (career portal).
Track International: www.trackint.com (IT specialists).
Job Ware: www.jobware.net
Monster.Com: www.monster.com the biggest online jobs and expat work website.
PayAway: www.payaway.co.uk.

NEWSPAPERS

The combined effects of the Single Market and the implementation of the EU Professional Qualifications Directives (see above) are likely to trigger a spate of trans-continental job advertising and it is probable that UK newspapers will run an increasing number of recruitment advertisements from other member states including Germany. Most British newspapers including, *The Times, Financial Times* and *The Guardian* carry regular job adverts from European countries. The *Times Educational Supplement* (published Fridays) and the Education pages of the Tuesday edition of the *Guardian,* carry advertisements for teaching English abroad. The *Guardian* also has a Europe supplement on Fridays, which includes a job section.

A selection of vacancies is published in the fortnightly subscription newspaper *Overseas Jobs Express* (Ambachtsmark 1, 1355 EA Almere, The Netherlands, or 20 New Road, Brighton, BN1 1UF; ☎01273-699611; fax 01273-699778; website www.overseasjobsexpress.co.uk). In addition to articles from a range of working travellers, it includes vacancy listings organised under the following jobs headings: Education/TEFL, Hotel and Catering, Information Technology and Trade, among others. Recent issues offered the following jobs in Germany: bilingual secretary, hotel staff, computer technicians and au pair/nanny.

Alternatively, a wide range of casual jobs, including secretarial, agricultural, tourism and domestic work, is advertised in the directory *Summer Jobs Abroad* while *Teaching English Abroad* lists schools worldwide which employ English language teachers each year with details of the qualifications accepted and how to get jobs in them. These publications are available from Vacation Work, (9 Park End Street, Oxford OX1 1HJ; ☎01865-241978; fax 01865-790885; www.vacatio nwork.co.uk).

International newspapers circulate editions across several national boundaries and usually carry a modest amount of job advertising. Presently, the newspapers to consult include the *Wall Street Journal Europe, Financial Times* and the *International Herald Tribune*. As well as employers advertising in these papers, individuals can place their own adverts for any kind of job, although bilingual secretaries and assistants, marketing managers and other professionally qualified people seeking to relocate abroad are in the greatest demand. Obviously advertising rates vary, but anyone interested should contact the advertising department at the addresses listed below.

Useful Addresses

Financial Times: 1 Southwark Bridge, London SE1 9HL; ☎020-7873-3000; www.ft.com The FT is printed in English in the UK, Germany, France, the USA and Japan and is distributed worldwide. International appointments appear on Thursdays in all editions.

International Herald Tribune: 40 Marsh Wall, London; ☎020-751 0570 (subscriptions UK 0800-895965, Europe 00800-44 487 827); e-mail (subscriptions) subs@iht.com; website www.iht.com.

Wall Street Journal: Dow Jones International, First Floor, 90 Long Acre, London WC2E 9PR; ☎020-7334 0008; www.dowjones.com. European edition published in Brussels: *Wall Street Journal Europe,* Blvd. Brand Whitlock 87, 1200 Brussels; ☎+32 27 41 12 11. The recruitment section which covers appointments and business opportunities worldwide appears on Tuesdays.

Advertising in Newspapers

The agents *International Graphic Press Ltd* (4 Wimpole Street, London, W1M 7AB; ☎020-7436 1199; fax 020-7436 9900; website www.igpmedia.com) represent *Der Spiegel, Manager Magazin, TetilWirtschaft,* and *Harvard Business Magazine.*

Anyone wishing to advertise in the widely read *Frankfurter Allgemeine Zeitung* should contact their London office (2nd Floor, West, Bedford Chambers, Covent Garden Piazza, London, WC2E 8HA; ☎020-7836 5540; website www.faz.de). Situations wanted usually appear in the Wednesday edition.

It is also possible to advertise in the British Chamber of Commerce journal, further details can be obtained from the Secretary, BCCG, Severinstrasse 60, D-50678 Köln, Germany.

PROFESSIONAL AND TRADE PUBLICATIONS

Professional journals and magazines are another possible source of job vacancies abroad, from companies wishing to set up offices elsewhere in Europe and foreign firms advertising for staff e.g. *The Architects' Journal, The Architectural Review, Accountancy, Administrator, Brewing & Distilling International* and *The Bookseller* to name but a few. Anyone in the air transport industry should consult *Flight International* while those employed in the catering trade could try *Caterer and Hotel Keeper* and agricultural workers *Farmers Weekly.* Although published in the UK, some of these magazines are considered world authorities in their field and have a correspondingly wide international readership.

An exhaustive list of trade magazines can be found in media directories, for example *Benn's Media* and *Writers' and Artists' Yearbook* both of which are available in reference libraries.

PROFESSIONAL ASSOCIATIONS

Those readers who hold professional qualifications are probably already aware of the benefits of membership in a professional association. They may not know though, that during the negotiations involved in the mutual recognition of qualifications, many professional associations negotiated with their counterparts in other member states and can therefore be helpful in providing contacts.

For British readers details of all professional associations may be found in the directory *Trade Associations and Professional Bodies of the UK*, available at most UK reference libraries.

It is also worth trying to contact the German equivalent of your professional association, who will often be able to provide the address of their counterpart. If not, try contacting them through the Chamber of Commerce, or the information department of the German Embassy. Alternatively you can consult your trade union for information, as they may have links with their counterpart organisation in Germany. Below is a list of addresses of the main British professional organisations; unfortunately pressures of space mean that the list is not as comprehensive as it could be.

Useful Addresses

Architecture & Surveying Institute: St Mary House, 15 St Mary Street, Chippenham, Wiltshire; ☎01249-444505; fax 01249-443602; asi@asi.org.uk .

Architects Registration Board for the United Kingdom: 8 Weymouth Street, London W1W 5BU; ☎020-7580 5861; fax 020-7436 5269; www.arb.org.uk.

Association of Professional Music Therapists: Mrs Diana Asbridge, 26 Hamlyn Road, Glastonbury, Somerset, BA6 8HT; tel/fax 01458-834919; A P M T o f f i c e @ a o l . c o m ; www.apmt.org.uk.

Biochemical Society: Biochemical Society Membership Office, Commerce Way, Whitehall Industrial Estate, Colchester, Essex CO2 8HP; tel: 01206-796351; fax: 01206-799331; www.biochemsoc.org.uk.

British Computer Society: 1 Sandford Street, Swindon SN1 1HJ; ☎01793-417424; fax 01793-480270; www.bcs.org.uk.

British Dietetic Association: 5th Floor, Charles House, 148/9 Great Charles Street, Queensway, Birmingham; B3 3HT; ☎0121-200 8080; fax 0121-200 8081; www.bda.uk.com.

British Medical Association: BMA House, Tavistock Square, London WC1H 9JP; ☎020-7387 4499; fax: 020-7383 6400. The BMA's International Department gives extensive help and advice to its members wishing to work elsewhere in Europe, and to incoming doctors from other countries.

Chartered Institute of Bankers: See Institute of Finacial Services below.

Chartered Institute of Building: Englemere Kings Ride, Ascot, Berks SL5 7TB; ☎01344-630700; fax 01344-630777; www.ciob.org.uk.

Chartered Institute of Building Services Engineers: 222 Balham High Road, Balham, London SW12 9BS; ☎020-8675 5211; fax 020-8675 5449; www.cibse.org.

Chartered Institute of Housing: Octavia House, Westwood Way, Coventry, CV4 8JP; ☎024-7685 1788; fa 024-7642 1756; website www.cih.org.

Chartered Institute of Marketing (CIM): Moor Hall, Cookham, Maidenhead, Berks SL6 9QH; ☎01628-427500; fax 01628-427499; m a r k e t i n g @ c i m . c o . u k ; www.cim.co.uk).

Faculty of Advocates: Parliament House, 11 Parliament Square, Edinburgh EH1 1RF; ☎0131-226 5071; www.advocates.org.uk.

General Council of the Bar (The Bar Council): 3 Bedford Row, London WC1R 4DB Tel: 020-7242 0082; www.barcouncil.org.uk.

General Dental Council: 37 Wimpole Street, London W1G 8DQ; ☎020-7887 3800; fax 020-7224 3294; www.gdc-uk.org.

General Optical Council: 41 Harley Street, London W1N 2DJ; ☎020-7580 3898; fax 020-7436 3525; www.optical.org.

Institute of Actuaries: Napier House, 4 Worcester Street, Gloucester Green, Oxford OX1 2AW; 01865-268200; fax 01865-268211; www.actuaries.org.uk.

Institute of Biology: 20-22 Queensberry Place, London SW7 2DZ; ☎020-7581 8333; fax 020-7823 9409; www.iob.org.

Institute of Cast Metals Engineers: Bordersley Hall, Alvchurch, Birmingham B48 7QA; ☎01527-596100; fax 01527-596102; www.ibf.org.uk.

Institute of Chartered Accountants in England & Wales: Chartered Accounts' Hall, P O Box 433, Moorgate Place, London EC2P 2BJ; ☎020-7920 8100; fax 020-7920 8547; www.icaew.co.uk. Is able to offer members advice on working within the EU.

Institute of Chartered Foresters: 7A Colme Street, Edinburgh EH3 6AA;

☎0131-225 2705; www.charteredfo resters.org

Institute of Chartered Secretaries and Administrators: 16 Park Crescent, London W1N 4AH; ☎020- 7580 4741; fax 020-7323 1132; www.icsa.co.uk.

Institute of Chartered Shipbrokers: London Branch, 3 St Helen's Place, London EC3A 6EJ; ☎020-7628 5559; fax 020-7628 5445; www.ics.org.uk.

The Institution of Chemical Engineers: 165-189 Railway Terrace, Rugby CV21 3HQ; ☎01788-578214; fax 01788-560833; www.icheme.org.

Institute of Civil Engineers: 1 Great George Street, Westminster, London SW1P 3AA; ☎020-7222 7722; fax 020-7222 7500; www.ice.org.uk. Also has an international recruitment agency: Thomas Telford Recruitment Consultancy, Thomas Telford House, 1 Heron Quay, London E14 4JD; Customer Services ☎020-7665 2464; www.t-telford.co.uk.

Institute of Linguists: Saxon House, 48 Southwark Street, London, SE21 1UN; ☎020-7940 3100; fax 020-7940 3101; website www.iol.org.uk.

The Institution of Electrical Engineers: Savoy Place, London, WC2R 0BL; ☎020-7240 1871; fax 020-7240 7735; www.iee.org.uk.

Institute of Financial Services: Administration Centre, IFS House, 4-9 Burgate Lane, Canterbury, Kent CT1 2XJ; ☎01227-762600; fax 01227-763788; www.cib.org.uk.

Institution of Gas Engineers: 21 Portland Place, London W1B 1PY; ☎020-7636 6603; fax 020-7636 6602; www.igaseng.com.

Institute of Marine Engineers: 80 Coleman Street, London EC2R 5BJ; ☎020-7382 2600; fax 020-7382 2670; www.imare.org.uk.

The Institution of Mechanical Engineers, 1 Birdcage Walk, London SW1H 9JJ; ☎020-7222 7899; fax: 020-7222 4557; www.imeche.org.uk.

Institute of Mining and Metallurgy: Danum House, South Parade, Doncaster DN1 2DY; ☎01302-320486; fax 01302-380900; www.imm.org.uk.

Library Association: 7 Ridgmount Street, London WC1E 7AE; ☎020-7255 0500; fax 020-7255 0501; www.la-hq.org.uk.

The Registrar and Chief Executive, United Kingdom Central Council for Nursing, Midwifery and Health Visiting: 23 Portland Place, London W1B 1PZ; ☎020-7637 7181; fax 020-7436 2924; www.ukcc.org.uk.

Royal Aeronautical Society: 4 Hamilton Place, London W1V OBQ; ☎020-7670 4300; fax 020-7670 4309; www.raes.org.uk.

Royal College of Speech and Language Therapists: 2 White Hart Yard, London SE1 1NX; ☎020-7378 1200; fax 020-7403 7254; www.rcslt.org.uk.

Royal Pharmaceutical Society of Great Britain: 1 Lambeth High Street, London SE1 7JN; ☎020-7735 9141; fax 020-7735 7629; www.rpsgb.org.uk.

Royal Town Planning Institute: 41 Botolph Lane, London, EC3R 8DL; ☎020-7929 9494; fax 020-7929 9490; www.rtpi.org.uk.

Royal College of Veterinary Surgeons: Belgravia House, 62-64 Horseferry Road, London SW1P 2AF; ☎020-7222 2001; fax 020-7222 2004; www.rcvs.org.uk.

Society and College of Radiographers: 207 Providence Square, Mill Street, London SE1 2EW; ☎020-7740 7200; fax 020-7740 7204; www.sor.org.

GERMAN CHAMBERS OF COMMERCE (*INDUS-TRIE-UND HANDELSKAMMER*)

The main function of the German chambers of commerce is not to provide assistance with finding jobs, but rather to promote the business interests of their members. However, they are an important source of potentially useful information and can provide lists of their member companies, both British and German, which could be utilised for speculative job applications. In some cases, chambers of commerce may also be useful sources of job demands in their area. A list of chambers of commerce can be found in Chapter Seven, *Setting up a Business*.

THE SPECULATIVE APPLICATION

If you are not using one of the professional recruiting agencies but intend to apply speculatively, direct to potential employers, it is as well to accept that you may have to fire off a good many letters of application before even one positive response is received. It is therefore advisable to target applications where they have the best chance of falling on fertile ground. This means that your preparations should include thorough research into the types of companies likely to have positions for which you are qualified. Such research can often be carried out at Trade Fairs.

The most important constituents of the speculative application after research, are the CV and the letter of application. The CV should contain concise information and should if possible be no more than one page (two pages maximum), and the information should create the best possible impression. For this reason, many people entrust the preparation and presentation of their CV to a company that specialises in this type of service.

The covering letter with a CV should be tailored to the company/type of job for which you are applying and if possible should appear as if individually prepared. The temptation to pour out reams of personal history should be resisted as the full dynamism and drive of your personality should be unfolded at an interview and not at the application stage. Make sure that you indicate clearly the job(s) in which you are interested. If possible, you should find out the name of the person to whom the letter should be addressed. One telephone call is usually sufficient to obtain this information. If you feel that the letter would be more effective in German (i.e. understood) then the *Institute of Translation and Interpreting* (Exchange House, 494 Midsummer Blvd., Milton Keynes, MK9 2EA; ☎01908-255905; fax 01908-255700; e-mail info@iti.org.uk; website www.iti.org.uk.) provides a good service, putting callers in touch with translators who will provide a fluent translation.

Note that speculative applications need not be confined to employers; they can also be sent to recruitment agencies and search consultants.

If you are offered an interview, remember that first impressions and appearances are very important, and this is especially so in Germany. Dress smartly, but conservatively for interviews (a tie is a must for men), and address all adult women as Frau whether they are married or not, and adult men as Herr. If you do not know someone's name it is correct to address her or him by their title: Frau Doktor, Herr

Direktor, etc. Handshaking both on arrival and departure is customary. Reserve, formality and strict punctuality are still key factors in business relationships, far more so than in the UK or America. As with a job interview in any country, it is recommended that you find out as much background information as possible about the company in advance of the interview. An interest based on a thorough knowledge and hard facts is bound to impress a potential employer.

TEMPORARY WORK

TEACHING ENGLISH

It seems that in whichever foreign country you are thinking of living and working, teaching English is one of the main employment possibilities. However, it is true to say that in some countries, notably Spain and Italy, the demand is considerably greater than in others. Germany has an excellent state education system which ensures that a very high proportion of Germans have a good grounding in English. The result is that there is less demand for beginners' courses at language schools and evening classes. The greatest demand is from business people taking courses in their own time or ones organised by their firms. Even so, many German business people tend to prefer a summer language course in Britain to one taken at home.

Unification has thrown up increased opportunities for English teachers in that eastern Germans, many of whom never had the chance to learn English under the communists, want to learn commercial English at *Volkshochschulen* (People's High School), where various adult education courses are run free of charge. An additional possibility for teaching English is in secondary schools throughout Germany which often employ native English-speakers as assistant English teachers (*Helferen*). Such posts are normally reserved for students of German and can be arranged through the *The Education and Training Group* of the *British Council*.

Prospects for Teachers

The best prospects for teachers are still to be found teaching the business and professional community even though the market has been declining. Training budgets have been reduced and more companies have been exploring the possibilities of online courses which are much cheaper than face-to-face tuition. However government incentives are still available for companies to provide training to their employees and one of the most popular options is the in-company language course. From the teacher's point of view this means plenty of highly paid positions for EFL teachers, as well as a number of agencies and consultancies which supply teachers to their clients. One advantage of working for a language school is that initially it may be a useful source of contacts for more lucrative company English teaching, translation and private tuition jobs. The worldwide chain of language schools *inlingua* has schools in Germany which can be approached individually or through theirUK head office (see below). Some language schools pay newly arrived teachers less than €20 an hour though company courses often pay considerably more. Freelancers should bear in mind that contributions will reduce gross earnings by up to half. Compulsory payments of 19.1% of total pay must be made to the national German pension agency, the BfA plus another huge percentage must be paid for medical insurance.

Qualifications

Perhaps not surprisingly, a business or economics background is extremely useful and sometimes essential when chasing one of the company jobs above. This is often more important than the type of degree held, or previous teaching experience gained. For instance it is much less important to know what a participle is than to have an in-depth knowledge of international banking. Many schools offer *Oberstufe*, advanced or specialist courses dealing with a particular sector of business or banking, or for bilingual secretaries etc., where even a Cambridge Diploma in English Language Teaching to Adults (DELTA) would not be of much relevance.

Another key qualification is a reasonable knowledge of German because very few schools would be willing to consider you without this. Even though the most utilised teaching method is the total immersion system, teachers are still expected to offer explanations in German. If the school prepares its clients for the London Chamber of Commerce Exams (called LCCI), the teacher will be expected not only to understand the syllabus but to interpret and teach it with confidence. One other qualification usually required is a driving licence so that teachers can hurtle from one assignment to another. Anyone with the above accomplishments should have little difficulty finding a job in a German city.

Training:

Despite not being the most important qualification for teaching English in Germany, English as a Foreign Language (EFL) qualifications can be useful in building up confidence. There is a bewildering array of courses available, the best known of which are probably the Cambridge courses. A comprehensive guide to all the courses on offer in Britain and abroad can be found in *Teaching English Abroad* from Vacation-Work Publications and the *ELT Guide* available in bookshops. The British Council website (www.britishcouncil.org/english) includes information and advice useful to someone considering EFL teaching as well as downloadable materials and teaching resources.

Sources of Teaching Jobs

Some jobs are advertised in the British press, although there are currently more advertisements for TEFL courses than vacancies. The best if not the only places to look, are the *Education* section of the *Guardian* printed on Tuesdays and the *Times Educational Supplement* which comes out on Fridays. The monthly trade paper *EL Gazette* is an excellent source of news and developments in the TEFL industry, while the recruitment section *EL Prospects* carries adverts for posts worldwide, many for senior positions. Nevertheless it is worth consulting regularly, and has been updated with the introduction of a job grid, which carries more than 100 jobs each month. Single issues cost £3, £20 for 6 months or £32 for a year's UK subscription (£44 worldwide). The UK subscription agent TG Scott can be contacted on 01732-884023 while the editorial office is at Dilke House, 1 Malet Street, London, WC1E 7JA; ☎020-7255 1969. A useful resource for ELT professionals is the website of the Munich English Language Teachers' Association or MELTA (www.melta.de) which includes an up-to-date listing of teaching vacancies in and around Munich. It also lists about 30 companies with ongoing trainer requirements. A bulletin board for English teachers in Germany can be seen at http://pub95.ezboard.com/belt.

The best source of job ads for American TEFL teachers is the *TESOL Placement Bulletin* (TESOL Inc., 700 S Washington Street, Suite 200, Alexandria, VA 22314, USA; ☎703-836 0774; fax 703-836 6447; website www.tesol.org). Note however that it lists very few vacancies in Europe because of visa difficulties for non-European nationals. American teachers might prefer to contact one of the German-American Institutes in Heidelberg, Nürnberg Regensburg or Tübingen.

The Education and Training Group of the *British Council* (10 Spring Gardens, London, SW1A 2BN; ☎020-7389 4596; website www.britishcouncil.org/ languageassistants) can direct you to short and mid term placements in Germany. For more details of these see their entry in the section on *Permanent Work*.

Another option is to contact the individual *Volkshochschulen* directly. The relevant ones of the 1,400 VHHs across Germany can be obtained from the *Deutscher Volkhochschul-Verband e.V.* (Obere Wilhelmstrasse 32, D-53225 Bonn; ☎0228-975690; fax 0228-9756930; website www.dvv-vhs.de or www.vhs.de).

TEFL Language Schools in Germany:

American Language Academy: Charlottenstr. 65, 10117 Berlin; ☎030-2039 7811; fax 030-2039 7813; e-mail info@ala-germany.de; website www.ala-germany.com. Business English is required by client companies.

Cambridge Institut, Hildegardstrasse 8, 80539 München; ☎089-221114; www.cambridgeinstitut.de.

Die Neue Schule: Gieselerstrasse 30a, D-10713 Berlin, Germany; ☎030-873 0373; e-mail info@neueschule.de; website www.neueschule.de.

Englisches Institut Köln: Gertrudenstr. 24-28 D-50667 Köln; ☎0221-257 8274/5; e-mail info@englisches-institut-koeln.de; website www.englisches-institut-koeln.de.

Euro Fremdsprachenschule Ingolstadt e.V.: Esplanade 36, D-85049 Ingolstadt, Germany; ☎0841-17001; e-mail sw@euro-ingolstadt.de. Vocational language college which employs 25 language teachers.

inlingua Teacher Training & Recruitment, Rodney Lodge, Rodney Road, Cheltenham, Glos. GL50 1JF; ☎01242-253171; fax 01242-253181; e-mail recruitment@inlingua-cheltenham.co.uk; website www.inlingua.de. Many vacancies for qualified TEFL teachers at schools throughout Germany.

Linguarama Sprachinstitut GmbH: Lipsia-Haus, Barfussgässchen 12, D-04109 Leipzig, Germany; ☎0341-213 1464; fax 0341-213 1482; e-mail leipzig@linguarama.com. Linguarama has other schools in Germany (see www.lingarama.com for contact details).

Sprachschule-Centrum Dreieich: Frankfurterstr. 114, D-63268 Dreieich, Germany; ☎06103-373931; fax 06103-34783.

English Language Teachers' Associations (ELTAs) in Germany

The following list is provided as a public service to teachers of English looking for contact to professional organisations. Generally, the listed associations are officially registered, non-profit organisations which present professional development workshops and seminars on a regular basis and publish newsletters for their members, who are native and non-native speakers of English from a wide variety of teaching and training fields. For more detailed information about an individual association's activities and membership details, get in touch with the local contact person listed below.

ELTAB-B – Berlin-Brandenburg: Steffen Skowronek, Johanna-Just-Str. 6, 14480 Potsdam, Germany; ☎0331-623812; fax 030-76677241; e-mail skowron@rz.uni-potsdam.de; website www.eltabb.com.

ELTAF e.V. – Frankfurt/Rhine-Main-Neckar: Libby Simms, Matthias-Claudius-Str. 13, 65185 Wiesbaden, Germany; ☎0611-303113; fax 0611-303143; e-mail ELTAF@gmx.de.

ELTA-Rhine e.V. – Bonn-Cologne-Düsseldorf: Graham Sutherland, Aquinostr. 5, 50670 Köln, Germany; ☎: 0221-7201544; fax 0221-7392865; e-mail GrahamSutherland@compuserve.com; website www.elta-rhine.de.

ELTAS e.V. – Stuttgart: Cornelia Kreis-Meyer, Dornbuschweg 3, 71229 Leonberg, Germany; ☎07152-27391; fax 07152-27317; e-mail cktrans@t-online.de; website www.eltas.de.

HELTA e.V. – Hamburg: Oktaviostr. 15, 22043 Hamburg, Germany; fax 040-6563980; website http://helta.englishteachers.com/.

MELTA – Munich: Munich English Language Teachers' Association e.V. Leopoldstr. 108a, 80802 Munich; website www.melta.de.

RELTA e.V. – Lake Constance Areas, Allgau & Bavaria: Avril Soecknick, Uhlandweg 37,, D-88239 Wangen, Germany; ☎07522-22109; fax 07544-912852; e-mail Frank.Avril.Soecknick@t-online.de.

AU PAIR AND DOMESTIC WORK

If you want to try out life in a specific city in Germany, au pairing can be a useful way to do this. It can also be a stepping-stone, which gives you time to learn or improve your German while gradually acclimatising to the country and providing an opportunity to build up potentially useful contacts. In Germany, as anywhere, au-pairing is a case of free board and some pocket money (from about €210 per month) in return for about 25 hours of childcare and domestic duties per week. Au-pairing has the advantage of being open to both young men and women and providing them with an initially secure base in a strange country. Be warned that standards of cleanliness are high in Germany and idleness is not appreciated, so the workload of household chores can be rather demanding, and may turn out to be more than you were told to expect. Au pairs have the opportunity to attend free evening classes in German at the local *Volkshochschulen* which in some cities can resemble a meeting of the United Nations. Alternatively, advanced and serious students can enrol for German courses at most German universities. The cost of everyday travel is usually provided by the family, in the form of an integrated season ticket, valid on most forms of local transport.

Sources of Jobs:

Among the longest established agencies is the non-profit Roman Catholic agency IN VIA whose full title is *Katholische Mädchensozialarbeit, Deutscher Verband e.V.* with branches throughout Germany and one in England. Its Protestant counterpart is affiliated to the YWCA: *Verein für Internationale Jugendarbeit.* VIJ has 23 offices in Germany and places both male and female au pairs for a preferred minimum stay of one year.

Dozens of secular agents have recently popped up all over Germany, many of them members of the *Au-pair Society e.V.*, Erlenweg 4, 53881 Euskirchen, Germany (02255-959804/fax 02255-959805; e-mail info@au-pair-society.org). The Society's website www.au-pair-society.org carries contact details for its nearly 50 members with links to agency websites if available. Commercial au pair agencies do not charge a placement fee to incoming au pairs.

Au Pair in Germany, Baunscheidtstr. 11, 53113 Bonn; ☎0228-95 73 00; fax 0228-95 73 010; e-mail gijk@gijk.de; website www.gijk.de. Part of GIJK (Gesellschaft für Internationale Jugendkontakte), an exchange organisation for German and other European young people.

Au-Pair Interconnection, Staufenstrasse 17, 86899 Landsberg am Lech; ☎08191-941 378; e-mail aupairscp@t-online.de; website www.aupair-interconnection.de.

Au Pair Network International, Beethovenallee 21, 53173 Bonn; ☎0228-956950; website www.step-in.de.

IN VIA, Ludwigstr. 36, 79104 Freiburg; ☎0761-200206/7/8; fax 0761-200638; e-mail Marianne.Schmidle@carita s.de; website www.invia.caritas.de. Branches in most German cities. Affiliated to international Catholic organisation ACISJF.

Munichaupair, Daiserstr. 56, 81371 Munich; ☎089-7672 9510; website www.munichaupair.com.

Only 4 Me Au Pair Agency, Mainzer Landstrasse 47, D-69329 Frankfurt (Postal address: Postfach 900259, D-60442 Frankfurt); ☎069-2470 5816; e-mail aupaironly@aol.com; website www.aupaironly.de.

Verein für Internationale Jugendarbeit,

Goetheallee 10, 53225 Bonn; ☎0228-698952; fax 0228-694166; e-mail au-pair.vij@netcologne.de; website www.vij-Deutschland.de.

Many UK-based au pair and domestic agencies can find placements in Germany. A useful source of agency addresses is *The Au Pair and Nanny's Guide to Working Abroad*; the 2002 edition is available in bookshops or from Vacation Work Publications (9 Park End Street, Oxford OX1 1HJ; ☎01865-241978; fax 01865-790885; e-mail info@vacationwork.co.uk; www.vacationwork.co.uk).

Agencies for au pair work in Germany:

Au Pair International, 115 High Street, Uckfield, East Sussex TN22 1RN; ☎01825-761420; fax 01825-769050; e-mail aupairinternat@onetel.net.u k; website www.aupairinternationa l.co.uk.

Au Pair Network International, 118 Cromwell Road, London SW7 4ET; ☎020-7370 3798; fax 020-7370 4718; website www.apni.org.uk.

Bloomsbury Bureau, PO Box 12749, 37 Store St, London WC1E 7BH; ☎020-7813 4061; fax 020-7813 4038; e-mail bloomsburo@aol.com.

German Catholic Social Centre, Lioba House, 40 Exeter Road, London NW2 4SB; ☎020-8452 8566; fax 020-8452 4114; e-mail germancentre@germancentre.free-online.co.uk. UK branch of IN VIA.

Solihull Au Pair & Nanny Agency, 1565 Stratford Road, Hall Green, Birmingham B28 9JA; ☎0121-733 6444; fax 0121-733 6555; e-mail solihull@100s-aupairs.co.uk; website www.100s-aupairs.co.uk.

All salaries/pocket money will be paid in Euros. Au Pairs receive the equivalent of £45-£50 per week while mother's helps are paid the equivalent of £125-£150 per week and nannies £175 per week upwards depending on experience and working hours. Duration of stay should be a minimum of 6-12 months.

If you are already in Germany, you can consult an agency in the region where you wish to work or find a job by advertising in the jobs wanted section of regional newspapers. Another possibility is to use one's contacts to put up notices on school and hospital notice boards.

Domestic Work

For those who are not daunted by German standards of hygiene there is plenty of cleaning work available. Use the Yellow Pages for the names and addresses of cleaning firms to ask for work or put up notices on supermarket notice boards where they are likely to catch the eye of German housewives. Cleaning and other casual jobs such as working on supermarket checkouts, on factory lines, gardening etc. can be obtained through the student employment departments at Universities.

AGRICULTURAL WORK

Unlike France and other European countries, farming in Germany accounts for a very small part of German GNP and only about 3.2 of the working population are engaged on the land. Farming is a declining business in Germany. Some farms are highly mechanised, but the majority are smallholdings (the average size is 42 acres). Either way, they do not normally require a large number of itinerant workers, except possibly during harvest time at fruit-growing farms. In such cases, the work is often done by the same local people every year, but farmers do take on occasional foreigners as well.

The most important area for fruit picking is the Altes Land, which lies between Stade and Hamburg to the south of the Elbe and includes the towns of Steinkirchen, Jork and Horneburg. The main crops are cherries, which are picked in July and August, and apples in September and October. Apples and other fruit are grown in an area between Heidelberg and Darmstadt called the Bergstrasse, and also in the far south, around Friedrichshafen and Ravensburg near Lake Konstanz. The Bodensee area is also recommended for apple picking. The other work for which casual labour is traditionally used, is the grape gathering which takes place in autumn along the banks of the Rhine and Mosel rivers. There are reports however that over recent years, hordes of hard drinking, hard working Poles have monopolised such vacancies, particularly along the Mosel valley.

This has made it virtually impossible for other foreigners to get a look in. If you are willing to have a try, such work is best obtained on the spot. Although the harvest does not begin until October, farmers have often recruited their workers by August.

The *Happy Hands* working holiday scheme places young people from the UK and other students from Europe who know some German in the field of rural tourism. Participants are given monthly pocket money and full board and lodging with families on farms or in country hotels. In return they look after children and/or horses and farm animals. The preferred stay is three to six months though a six-week commitment is also allowed; details available from Happy Hands, Roemerberg 8, 60311 Frankfurt; 069-293733; Anne.Gleichen@t-online.de/ www.workingholidays.de. The registration fee is a steep DM450. Note that the scheme is also open to unemployed people on benefit though is best suited to students who want to improve their German and agriculture students interested in organic farming.

Those who wish to volunteer to work on organic farms should contact the German branch of *WWOOF* (Willing Workers on Organic Farms), Postfach 210 259, 01263 Dresden (info@wwoof.de). Membership gives access to about 160 farm addresses.

TOURISM AND CATERING

The German hotel industry relies heavily on immigrants and students during the summer months, and has the advantage of not necessarily requiring a knowledge of German as a condition of acceptance (e.g. for washing up or kitchen portering). Pubs and restaurants (including MacDonalds) are a fruitful source of casual jobs. Owing to a series of punitive regulations, the hygiene standard required of German catering establishments has health department inspectors making routine monthly visits to catering premises. Jobs in catering establishments are advertised in local newspapers and through notices pinned on the doors of the establishments themselves, e.g. for: *Küchenhilfe* (kitchen assistant), *Spüler* (dishwasher), *Kellner/Bedienung* (bar/waiting staff), *Büfettier* (bartender), *Büfettkräfte* (fast-food server). Jobs of this kind are likely to be easily available in all large cities, university towns and tourist areas. For hotel jobs, the best prospects are likely to be in the Bavarian Alps (along the border with Austria), the Böhmerwald (along the southeast border), the Schwarzwald (in the south-west), the Rhine and Mosel tourist routes, and the seaside resorts along the Baltic and North Seas.

The wages for hotel work are usually reasonable, around £400 per month net including board and lodging. Other possibilities for catering and hotel work for those who do not have a command of German exist on the American and, to a much lesser extent, British army bases. However, since the end of the Cold War these have been reduced drastically and casual jobs have likewise decreased. Recruitment for American bases takes place through Civilian Personnel Offices (CPO's). Applicants' details are computerised and fed into the Civilian Automated Referral System (CARS) which is a centralised clearinghouse for vacancies on American bases in Germany. For some bases a base pass is needed to gain entry to the on-site CPO and this is best obtained through local contacts with G.I.'s. In some areas the local Arbeitsamt will carry vacancies on both American and British bases. The American army also has several recreation centres for army personnel of which the ones at Chiemsee (near Munich) and Garmisch-Partenkirchen (near the Austrian border) are two of the best known, and these are also worth trying for catering jobs.

In addition to hotel work, jobs connected with tourism can include working for coastal campsite/caravan park operators, either British or German. The hours are long and spoken German is essential. The German operators pay better than the British ones. Applications should be submitted in the spring.

Useful Addresses and Publications

Alpotels (Employment Agency): 17 High Street, Gretton, Northamptonshire NN17 3DE; ☎01536-771150; e-mail jobs@jobs-in-the-alps.com. Recruits and carries out interviews for employers looking for seasonal hotel staff.

Armed Forces Recreation Centers (AFRCs), Civilian Personnel Office (CPO), Lazarettstr. 7, 82467 Garmisch-Partenkirchen; ☎08821-729112; fax 08821-729213; website www.afrceurope.com/cpo/empl.htm.

Camping-und Ferienpark Wulfener Hals: D-23769 Wulfen auf Fehmarn, Germany; ☎04371-8628150. Employs general assistants, catering and kitchen staff and children's entertainers.

Canvas Holidays: East Port House, 12 East Port, Dunfermline, Fife KY12 7JG; ☎01383-629018; fax 01383-629071; website www.canvasholidays.com. Always looking for enthusiastic campsite couriers.

Directory of Summer Jobs Abroad: Annual publication containing list of German hotels requiring seasonal staff. Available from bookshops and Vacation Work; see book list at end of book.

Zentral und Internationale Management – und Fachvermittlung für Hotel und Gaststätpersonal (ZIHOGA): (Central and International Recruitment Service for Hotel and Catering Staff), Villemombler Str. 76, D-53123 Bonn, Germany; ☎0228-7130; fax 0228-713 1122; website http://195.185.214.164/zihoga/. This office mostly deals in training placements of a minimum of 12 months, although it can place seasonal workers in posts lasting 3 months.

VOLUNTARY WORK

For those considering a short stay in Germany there are a number of organisations which arrange a variety of unpaid work schemes including helping disabled children and adults, ecological surveying, archaeology and environmental conservation work. Volunteers are required to pay their own travel costs and a registration fee, but in return for the 30-35 hours work a week receive free board and lodging. The bonus of such work is that you get to see Germany, practise your German and make contacts, all of which may prove useful should you wish to work or study in Germany later. Volunteers are usually accepted between the ages of 18 and 30. For further details contact:

International Begegnung in Gemeinschaftsdiensten e.V.: Schlosserstrasse 28, D-70180 Stuttgart, Germany; ☎0711-649 1128; fax 0711-640 9867; e-mail IBG-workca mps@t-online.de website www.workcamps.com.

IJGD – International Jugendgemeinschaftsdienste e.V.: Kaiserstrasse 43, D-53113 Bonn, Germany; ☎0228-228 0011; fax 0228-228 0024; e-mail ijgdbonn@ijgd.de; website www.ijgd.de.

Vereinigung Junger Freiwilliger: Hans-Otto-strasse 7, D-10407 Berlin, Germany; ☎030-4285 0603; fax 030-4285 0604; e-mail office@vjf.de; website www.vjf.de.

WORK EXPERIENCE FOR AMERICANS

Council Exchanges in New York administers two programmes in Germany. American students who have studied some German at college can work for up to three months between mid-May and mid-October or students who can fix up a career-related internship can work for up to six months at any time of year. Similarly InterExchange can place full-time students in German resorts during the summer provided they have intermediate German. Applications must be in by the middle of February.

Similar six-month internships for American students or recent graduates in business, finance, marketing, engineering, journalism, IT or technical fields are available through CDS International. If needed, the first month can be spent at an intensive language course, after which participants undertake a paid internship which they have secured previously with the help of the Carl Duisberg Gesellschaft e.V. (CDG), the partner organisations of CDS International. Longer placements of 12-18 months are also available. CDS also run the one-year study-internship programme, Congress-Bundestag Youth Exchange Program, specifically for younger candidates who have left high school but who know what field they intend to pursue.

Alliances Abroad places interns in unpaid company positions in their field of interest in or near major German cities. Internships can be fixed up for one to three months for a substantial fee.

The AGABUR Foundation Inc runs a professional programme which includes language training, university study and optional paid internships in Germany. The summer programme costs $2,900 plus $500 for an internship on a German farm.

AGABUR Foundation Inc., 9 Eastwood Road, Storrs, CT 06268; ☎860-429-1279; website www.mannheim-program@necaweb.com.

Alliances Abroad, 702 West Ave, Austin, TX 78701; ☎1-888-622-7623; e-mail info@alliancesabroad.com; website www.alliancesabroad.com.

CDS International Inc., 871 United Nations Plaza, 15th Floor, New York, NY 10017-1814; ☎212-497-3500; website www.cdsintl.org.

Council Exchanges, 205 East 42nd St, New York, NY 10017; ☎212-226-8624; website www.councilexchanges.org.

InterExchange Inc, 161 Sixth Avenue, New York, NY 10013; ☎212-924-0446; e-mail info@interexchange.org; website www.interexchange.org.

PERMANENT WORK

BUILDING AND CONSTRUCTION WORK

The unification of 1990 set off a long-term construction boom in Germany, although the bulk of the work lay in Berlin and the eastern Länder where multifarious construction projects were undertaken. However, with the economic downturn suffered by Germany recently, the construction industry has entered a slump, although this is only a relative term given the number of construction projects underway. These range from new office buildings and accommodation in Berlin and the rebuilding of Dresden's Frauenkirche to the upgrading of several autobahns.

British companies already involved in building projects in Germany include Balfour Beatty, The Carroll Group, Ove Arup, Nicholas Grimshaw and Partners, and Sir Norman Foster's architecural practice. The construction industry should pick up even with construction giant Holzmann having gone bust recently. Financial problems effect the whole of the German building industry but are more noticeable in the new länder, where there are less reserves to keep building projects going during hard times.

One of the unpleasant side effects of the slump in the building industry and the general downward trend of the German economy was that the inferiority the easterners feel towards the west was exacerbated thus increasing xenophobia. In many cases, this is brought on by the perception that foreigners are taking their jobs, which is in many cases true, as it is easier to pay someone cash in hand at half the official rate than to pay the official rate and the employer's share of benefits contributions. The problem for British building workers is that very often they are being employed legitimately, but German workers consider them to be on the same level as the various Poles, Turks and other Eastern Europeans, who are effectively cheating them out of jobs. The German Building, Agricultural and Environmental union (*Industriegewerkschaft Bauen-Agrar-Umwelt*) has, together with the GMB in Britain, put together an explanatory bilingual booklet on the terms and conditions which apply to building and construction workers, including details of the minimum wages due to building site workers. The booklet *Fellow Worker, Do You Know Your Rights?* is available from the GMB (St Georges Lodge, 79 The Burrows, Hendon, London, NW4 4AY; website www.gmb.org.uk), and can be ordered by calling freephone 0800-834690.

However, while the danger to foreigners from right-wing extremists is very real, it is not endemic to the whole of Germany and should not deter anyone who takes reasonable precautions to avoid the trouble. If possible, talk to people who have already been to Germany and can recommend both an agency and an area. If possible try to find out who the middlemen are contracting for in Germany and contact the Germans direct. Failing this, it is worth going out to Germany to try to find work on the spot. The main cities are likely to prove fruitful and some useful research can be carried out in the favoured watering holes of the of expat construction workers. It won't be worth it, even with the EU's generous labour regulations if you don't know some German before you go and continue to brush it up at the evening classes available at the local *Volkshochschule* when you are in Germany.

SECRETARIAL AND ADMINISTRATIVE WORK

Opportunities are both widely available and lucrative for bilingual secretaries and administrators in Germany. For anyone thinking of doing this kind of work there are a number of UK-based agencies that specialise in placing polyglots with secretarial and office management skills. Such agencies only handle applicants who are genuinely bilingual, have recognised secretarial qualifications/administrative experience, and are interested in permanent positions lasting for a minimum of one year, but preferably longer. Salaries vary according to age, experience and area.

Useful Addresses

Bilingual People Ltd: 38 Dover Street, London, W1X 3RB; ☎020-7491 2400; fax 020-7491 1900; e-mail admin@bilingualpeople.com. Providers of permanent, contract and temporary staff in all fields such as Secretarial, PA, Translation, Interpretation, Sales & Marketing, Banking, Legal, Customer Services & Administration. They have many years experience of providing staff, both in the UK and abroad who are fluent in two or more languages.

Institute of Linguists: Saxon House, 48 Southwark Street, London, SE21 1UN; ☎020-7940 3100; fax 020-7940 3101; website www.iol.org.uk. The Institute cannot find employment but does offer general advice on careers with languages, how to make use of qualifications already held, and details of qualifications required for specific jobs connected with languages.

Institute of Translating and Interpreting (ITI): 494 Midsummer Blvd., Milton Keynes, MK9 2EA; ☎01908-255905; fax 01908-255700; e-mail info@iti.org.uk; website www.iti.org.uk. ITI is a professional association of translators and interpreters aiming to promote the highest standards in translating and interpreting. It has strong corporate membership and runs professional development courses and conferences. Membership is open to those with a proven involvement in translation and interpreting (including students). ITI's Directory of Members, its bi-monthly bulletin and other publications are available from the Secretariat. The Secretariat also offers a referral service whereby enquirers can be given, free of charge, the names of suitable members for any interpreting/translating assignment.

TheBigword Recruitment: 59 Charlotte Street, London, W1T 4PE; ☎020-7307 8870; fax 020-7839 6756; e-mail recruitment@thebigword.com; website www.thebigword.com. Specialises in bilingual secretaries and personal assistants, occasional posts in Germany for administrators and secretarial staff.

TEACHING

Teaching in German State Schools

About twenty-five years ago, the Germans had a big recruitment drive for English teachers to teach in German state schools, but over the years the shortage eased as German teachers became increasingly proficient at teaching English. Following the implementation in Germany of 1992 EU directives on the mutual acceptance of qualifications within the EU (including teaching qualifications), British teachers can compete freely for positions in German schools and should reasonably expect that their applications will be favourably scrutinised. As educational policy is organised on a Länder basis, any teacher interested in working in the state system should contact the *Kultursministerium* (Education Ministry) of whichever of the sixteen Länder they wish to work in. However one crucial difference will remain between the status of German nationals and foreigners employed as teachers in state schools. Teachers who are German nationals are *Beamte* (civil servants) and as such are entitled to job security for life and perks such as reduced national insurance contributions. This status difference between German and non-German nationals will remain, even under the EU Directives.

As well as trying to find positions in Germany through agencies, one can always scan the recruitment sections of publications such as *The Guardian's'* Education Supplement, *The Times Educational Supplement*, and the *EL Gazette* (see page 194 in the section on *Temporary Work*). Suitably qualified Americans can browse the *TESOL Placement Bulletin*, while most of the jobs advertised in these publications are likely to be for short-term work, some may be of a more permanent nature.

As an alternative to applying direct to Germany, or shuffling through piles of newspapers, teachers can apply to *The Education and Training Group* of the *British Council* (10 Spring Gardens, London, SW1A 2BN; ☎020-7389 4596; website www.britishcouncil.org/languageassistants) which arranges placements in German schools. Placements can be for a few weeks, a term, a year or longer depending on the scheme involved:

Helpers (*Helfer*). These positions can be arranged in Germany for 18-20 year olds with A level German. Posts are for a half or full academic year. Helpers receive free board and lodging, normally within the school and a monthly allowance. However travel arrangements to Germany are at the helper's expense. Most schools are located in small towns or isolated districts and applicants will be appointed according to suitability for the post rather than area of preference. Helpers teach English under the guidance of the permanent staff for 12-14 hours per week. It should be possible to attend other classes at the school which are of personal interest. It is essential to apply early. The closing date for applications is 31st March.

English Language Assistants. A senior version of the above. Applicants should normally be aged 20-30 years (up to 40 is possible), and have completed at least two years of a degree or diploma course. For positions in the new Länder where conditions are difficult, graduates with previous experience of the assistant scheme, or with some teaching experience are preferred. Posts are for a minimum of one academic year and a monthly allowance is paid. Applicants have to pay their own travel expenses and for board and lodging. As the scheme is expensive for the participant it is advisable to obtain sponsorship e.g. from their institute of higher education.

Post to Post Teacher Exchange Programmes. For qualified teachers of modern languages or related subjects with more than two years' experience. Exchanges are for four weeks, one term or one year.

In America budding teachers of German can obtain help from the *German*

American Fulbright Commision (United States Department of State (E/ASX), Office of Global Educational Programs, 301 Fourth Street SW, Room 349, Washington DC 20547, USA; ☎202-619 4556; fax 202-401 1433. Or *IEE Fulbright Program:* 809 UN Plaza, New York, NY 10017-3580; ☎212-984 5330; fax 212-984 5325; website http://www.iee.org/fulbright) which places teaching assistants (*Pedagogischer Austauschdienst*) in German schools. Candidates are paid a monthly stipend in addition to free flights and insurance.

Teaching in International Schools

The definition of an international school covers primary and secondary schools which either follow the British curriculum or a US-style curriculum or a combination of the two, plus elements from other sources. An increasing number of schools are also offering the International Baccalaureate which is recognised worldwide as a university entrance qualification. The main language of instruction is usually English and the clientele is largely the offspring of the expatriate population. There are international schools in most of the large cities in Germany i.e. where there are expatriate communities (see *Daily Life* for details). Most of the schools are members of the European Council of International Schools which handles staff applications for their member schools in Germany. Vacancies are advertised on the ECIS website (www.ecis.org) which also hosts their On-line Directory of International Schools. This allows the interested surfer to browse information about 800 international schools; a newsletter and the International Schools Journal, an academic journal concerned with international education issues. Applications are welcome from teachers who are suitably qualified and who have a minimum of two year's recent full-time experience within the age range 3-18. Registered candidates' applications are matched to current vacancies and they may be invited to the twice yearly London Recruitment Centres which are attended by school representatives from all over the world. As well as the UK office there are offices in the US, Australia and Spain.

In addition to the publications mentioned above American teachers can consult *The International Educator* a quarterly publication, also available in Britain, which focuses on jobs in international English-medium schools, such as the International or European Schools found in Germany, and thus follow either American curriculum or International Baccalaureate. The schools which advertise in *TIE* are looking for state-certified teachers in all subjects including ESL/EFL, although they are normally for educators used to dealing with children not adults. The journal comes out in January, April, September and November, with an additional Jobs Only Supplement in May/June. A one year subscription to the journal costs £28 ($45 for the US & Canada), while membership costs £40/$65.

Teaching in the European Schools

The other possibilities for teaching jobs are the European Schools, which in Germany are in Karlsruhe, Munich and Frankfurt. There are twelve European schools in the European Community, which cater primarily for the children of officials employed in EU institutions. The schools are divided up into mother tongue language groups and the UK and Irish governments recruit staff for the English language sections. The Department for Education and Employment directly recruits and employs some 200 UK teachers for these schools. The

Department's main recruitment for vacancies arising in September usually takes place in the preceding January or February. Posts are advertised in the national press at this time and, less frequently at other times throughout the year as and when occasional vacancies arise. Applications are only accepted in response to these advertisements.

Useful Addresses

Deutscher Volkhochschule-Verband e.V.: Obere Wilhelmstrasse 32, D-53225 Bonn, Germany; ☎0228-975 6920; fax 0228-975 6930; e-mail buero@dvv-vhs.de; website www.dvv-vhs.de. There is an overall list of vacancies in the 1000 Volkshochschulen across Germany, which cn be found online at www.vhs.de.

The Department for Education and Skills: European Schools Team, Department for Education and Skills, Caxton House, Tothill Street, London, SW1H 9NF; ☎020-7340 4384; fax 020-7340 4121.

European Council of International Schools: 21 Lavant Street, Petersfield, Hampshire GU32 3EL; ☎01730-268244; fax 01730-267914; e-mail staffingserv ices@ecis.org; website www.ecis.org. ECIS has an office in America but this is not concerned with recruitment (*ECIS Office of the Americas:* 105 Tuxford Terrace, Basking Ridge, New Jersey 07920, USA).

IATEFL – International Association of Teachers of English as a Foreign Language: 3 Kingsdown Chambers, Whitstable, Kent, CT5 2FL; ☎01227-276528; fax 01227-274415; website www.iatefl.org.

The International Educator: PO Box 513, Cummaquid, MA 02637 USA and 102a Pope's Lane, London, W5 4NS; ☎020-8840 2587; e-mail ksenior@tieonline.com; website www.tieonline.com.

International Schools Recruitment Centres in the US

International Schools Services (ISS): 15 Roszel Road, PO Box 5910, Princeton, NJ 08543, USA; ☎609-452-0990; fax 609-452-2690; e-mail edustaffing@iss.edu; website www.iss.edu.

University of Northern Iowa, Overseas Placement Service for Educators: University of Northern Iowa Career Center, SSC 19, Cedar Falls, Iowa 50614-0390, USA; ☎319-273-2083; fax 319-273-6998; e-mail overseas. placement@uni.edu; website www.uni.edu/placement/overseas.

Service Children's Education

As mentioned earlier in *Daily Life* an independent agency, The *Service Children's Education Service* operates schools on the remaining military bases in Germany. These primary, middle and secondary level schools are primarily for the children of service personnel and other entitled personnel serving abroad. Occasionally vacancies for teachers occur. To apply for a teaching post with the SCE you must respond to an advertisement placed in the *Times Educational Supplement* (Overseas Appointment section). Unfortunately speculative letters of application and CVs cannot be kept on file.

INFORMATION TECHNOLOGY

In recent years the demand for IT professionals has increased enormously, with employers crying out for skilled staff. Hence the recently introduced programmes to retrain non-IT staff and to make immigration easy for IT professionals. At present it is an employee's market, with staff commanding very high salaries. Although the jobs on offer vary, if you are looking for a permanent post you will be asked to show certificates for any qualifications which you have. On the other hand contracted staff are taken on trust and so will be expected to do what they claim and if they don't have the skills to back up their claims, then they will be back out on the street in a few hours.

Useful Addresses

Computer Futures Group: 2 Foubert's Place, Regent Street, London, W1V 2AD; CONTRACT: ☎0207-446 6666; fax 0207 446 0095; e-mail co ntract@compfutures.com. PERMA-NENT: ☎0207-446 6644; fax 0207 446 0099; e-mail permanent@compf utures.com. Germany: Schillerstrasse 10, D-60313 Frankfurt, Germany; ☎069-1338 5151; fax 069-1338 5152; e-mail jobs@compfutures.de. www.compfutures.co.uk. The UK's largest independent international recruitment consultancy offering both permanent and contract Information Technology recruitment services for clients and candidates.

Easysoft Applications Ltd: The Old Forge, St. Nicholas, South Elmham, Harleston, Norfolk IP20 OPS; ☎01986-782231; fax 07092-017033; e-mail jobs@easysoft.uk.com; website www.easysoft.uk.com. In business for 20 years with offices in Cologne, they place consultants with B2B, ERP, SAP and Oracle experience.

Track International Ltd: ☎01872-573937; fax 01872-571282; e-mail gt@trackint.com website www.trackint.com. Track International Ltd is an employment agency specialising in the placement of IT Professionals in Permanent or Contract positions throughout Europe. Their website has regularly updated listings of places available, and they can advise on the life in Germany.

MEDICINE & NURSING

There are regular vacancies for British qualified nurses in Germany, as well as vacancies for laboratory technicians and MLSOs. Attractive packages are usually offered including subsidised accommodation, free flights, 38 hour week, free language tuition and an average nurse to patient ratio of 1:3. More information for health professionals seeking work abroad can be found in Vacation Work's book Health Professionals Abroad.

Medacs Healthcare Services plc: FREEPOST BD2364, The Old Surgery, 49 Otley Street, Skipton, North Yorkshire BD23 1BR; Freephone 0800 442200; Freefax 0800 442220; website www.medacs.com/intromainfr.htm.

Bundesministerium für Gesundheit (German Health Ministry): Am Propsthof 78a, D-53121 Bonn, Germany; ☎01888-4410; fax 01888-441 4900; website www.bmgesundheit.de.

Bundesärztekammer Arbeitsgemeinschaft der deutschen Ärztekammern (German Medical Association): Herbert-Lewin-Str. 1, D-50931 Köln, Germany; ☎0221-40040; e-mail baek@dgn.de; website www.bundesaerztekammer.de.

German Nursing Association (Deutscher Berufsverband für Pflegeberufe e.V.): Geisbergstrasse 39, D-10777 Berlin, Germany; ☎030-219 1570; fax 030-2191 5777; e-mail dbfk@dbfk.de; website www.dbfk.de.

MANAGERS AND EXECUTIVES

There is always a demand amongst international companies in Germany for British and American managers and other top-level executives. The typical sought-after candidate is someone who has a background in the industrial or financial sectors, or perhaps less obviously, skills acquired in the armed services, accountancy or the law which can be utilised by international companies. Other vital requirements are that candidates should speak fluent German and have a knowledge of foreign markets and mentalities. Of particular interest to many German companies are those with experience in dealing with the Japanese. Also in demand are export managers which Germany needs to combat the increasing threat from far eastern markets.

Those who have the requisite background and skills for executive jobs can contact multinationals and German international firms directly. Alternatively speculative letters to agencies that specialise in executive search and selection in Germany and the UK will almost certainly not be wasted.

Fischer & Partner GmbH: Altheimer Eck 3, D-80331 München, Germany; ☎089-2323890; fax 089-260 7314; e-mail info@fischerpartner.de; website www.eurorecruit.com. German partner firm of the Eurorecruit Group which includes *Miller, Brand Ltd.*

Miller, Brand Ltd: 16 Hatton Wall, London, EC1N 8JH; ☎020-7404 7608; fax 020-7831 0678; e-mail g3@g3solutions.net or millerbrand@eurorecruit.com. Recruit middle and senior managers and other professionals for posts across the EU, Eastern Europe and Hong Kong. They have associated offices in Belgium, Denmark, France, Finland, Germany, the Netherlands, Italy, Norway, Spain and Sweden.

Opta Resources: 7-11 Station Road, Reading, RG1 1LG; ☎0118-902 2990; fax 0118-902 2999. Is primarily a management consultancy specialising in the telecommunications industry. Experienced personnel with technical or business backgrounds in this area are required for work on a sub-contractor basis.

ASPECTS OF EMPLOYMENT

SALARIES

German salaries are amongst the highest in the world averaging the equivalent of over £20 per hour. However, after taxes and social security deductions, a salary will be reduced by around half to produce the net pay. On top of their standard salary most German workers receive Christmas bonuses and extra pay towards their holidays. While there are no official minimum wages set by the German government, strong unions and the activities of workers councils have ensured that there are widely perceived minimum figures for most types of employment, even if wage negotiations tend to occur on a case by case basis. The exception to this is the construction industry which has negotiated a minimum wage for building site workers, although there is a lower rate for eastern Germany.

INCOME TAX

Income tax (*Lohnsteuer*) in Germany is graduated, according to how much you earn; for married people the income liable for taxation is the whole income of the couple, although the income limits appear to be simply duplicated. When you begin working for a German employer you should give them the tax card (*Lohnsteuerkarte*) that you obtained when registering at the Einwohnermeldeamt. The German tax-year is the calendar year, and if you earn more than a certain amount you will be required to complete an income tax declaration (*Einkommenste uer-Erklärung*), these are available at local tax offices (*Finanzbehörde/Finanzamt*) and should be completed by May of the year following the tax year declared (ie the tax year 2004 should be declared by May 2005). If you are expecting a tax rebate then it is wise to complete your declaration as soon as possible, conversely if you submit your declaration late then you may be fined. Details of the tax rates levied can be obtained from the Finanzamt. Although German income tax is not the highest in the EU, social security deductions are amongst the steepest (see below). There is more information on taxation in the chapter *Daily Life*.

The following is only a simplified explanation of the UK tax system as it affects expatriate workers, and we recommend that you confirm your tax situation prior to arranging any work abroad. Simply put if you are working on a long term basis abroad your UK tax liability depends on several factors, the principal one being whether, or not, you are classed as resident in the UK for that tax year. If you are in the UK for more than 183 days then you are classed as 'Resident'

In the simplest case, a UK citizen who works abroad for an entire tax year is not normally liable for UK tax on income earned overseas, there will though be a UK tax liability on any UK sources of income. The tax year in the UK runs from 6th April to 5th April the following year, so if at all possible it is always best to move at the end of a tax year.

At present if you are non-resident for a tax year you are not liable for tax on any savings or investments in the UK, and will in effect be treated as a new taxpayer on your return to work in Britain. Being non-resident allows you to return to the UK for a maximum of 91 days in that tax year without forfeiting your status. So be careful to keep track of your trips home and that you return to the UK to work at the right time of year.

Should the expatriate for whatever reason return to work in Britain part way through a tax year or stay longer than the allowed 91 days they will be taxed on all forms of income, both wages and investments. However the taxes paid on the wages earned abroad (ie German wages and subsequent tax) will be taken into account, in calculating their UK tax bill. So its not as bad as it first seems, so long as you keep your wage slips and tax documentation from Germany.

In order to help people understand the situation the Inland Revenue produces some leaflets: IR20 *Resident and Non-Residents: Liability to Tax in the UK*, IR139 *Income from Abroad ? A Guide to UK Tax on Overseas Income*. Enquiries regarding residence status may be addressed to the Inland Revenue Centre for non-Residents (St. John's House, Merton Road, Bootle, Merseyside L69 9BB; 0845-070 0040).

Always consult your tax authorities for clarification and up to date information.

WORKING CONDITIONS

German blue collar workers work fewer hours than their British, French or American counterparts, but as their productivity statistics show, they work more productively and more efficiently. Only 14% of the German workforce works a 40 hour week, compared to 47% in Britain; at present the weekly average is 35 hours (in some cases this is shift work) but in some industries unions have negotiated a 29 hour week in a bid to stave off redundancies. In order to be off sick from work, a doctor's note is required only after three days illness and employees receive full pay for the first six weeks of their illness after which sickness benefit is paid. Employees in Germany are entitled to an average of 41 days holiday a year (including public holidays) compared with 47 days in France and 25 days in Japan. Although Germans once had the reputation of taking work too seriously, it seems that now they have achieved the standard of living to which most aspire, the famous work ethic is in decline. However, although the signs of this are evident in the office workers who stream home at 3pm on Fridays for the weekend, it should not tempt the unwary into considering Germany a soft billet. When they are working, Germans are still perfectionists.

HEALTH AND SOCIAL SECURITY DEDUCTIONS

In both France and Germany, unemployment benefits and pensions are directly related to the amount of money being paid into the system by those in work. It can be said however, that workers in Germany get better value for money from their taxes and deductions than some of their EU neighbours, through the generous social security system (see below). As a worker in Germany, unless registered as self-employed and retained in the UK tax scheme, you will have to pay contributions for sickness (and maternity), unemployment, invalidity, old age and survivor's insurance. The amount of your contributions is determined as a percentage of your wages in each tax/calendar year, which will be deducted by your employer for forwarding to the relevant authorities, as a rule the contributions are borne half and half by employer and employee. Contributions for insurance against accidents at work are paid for solely by the employer.

The contribution for sickness insurance is currently around 12-14%, with an added 1.7% for long-term care. Pension contributions amount to 19.1% and unemployment insurance is another 6.5%.

BENEFITS

The following is a brief introduction and breakdown of the main benefits available to those living and working in Germany. Further details with explanatory notes can be obtained from the Federal Ministry for Labour and Social Affairs (*Bundesministerium für Arbeit und Sozialordnung:* Postfach 14 02 80, D-53107 Bonn) which also publishes an English-language version of these benefits in a booklet entitled *Social Security At The Glance.*

Unemployment Benefit (Arbeitslosengeld)

In order to qualify for unemployment benefit, a person must have worked more than 18 hours a week for not less than 360 days in the previous three years. Those working for fewer than 18 hours a week can also claim unemployment benefit in certain circumstances. Trainees, who have become unemployed on finishing their training are also eligible for unemployment benefit. The level of unemployment benefit is 67% of previous net wages if you have at least one child and 60% if not. Generally, anyone unemployed will also have their accommodation paid for and in addition the State will also provide for continuing health and pension contributions. To claim benefit you must register as unemployed with the local Arbeitsamt, be available for work and willing to accept any suitable employment offered to you. The length of time over which benefits will be paid to you depends upon the length of time that you were in work. It begins at 156 days for workers under 42 who have worked the minimum of 360 days in the last three years and rises to a maximum of 832 days for those over 54 who have worked for 1,920 days in the last seven years.

Benefit will not be awarded for a period of 12 weeks (*Sperrzeit*) if you terminated your employment, you refuse work offered by the Arbeitsamt, or you refuse to take part in reasonable activities aimed at providing you with a vocational reward.

Unemployment Assistance (Arbeitslosenhilfe)

Is paid to those who are still unemployed at the end of their entitlement to unemployment benefit, but is means tested. Assistance is paid out at 67% and 60% of previous earnings according to whether or not you have children. Also eligible are general school and university graduates and those who have completed vocational training provided they have been employed for at least 26 weeks before taking up schooling.

If you become unemployed in Germany, you should register with the local Arbeitsamt and ask for information on benefits. Unemployment benefit or assistance will be paid into your bank account fortnightly so it is advisable to open a German account in advance of claiming.

Claiming UK Benefit in Germany

UK citizens who are unemployed in the UK can go to Germany to look for work and claim UK unemployment benefit for up to three months, provided they have been available for work and claiming benefits for four weeks before leaving the UK. In order to claim UK benefit in Germany a certificate of authorisation from the UK Department of Employment must be presented to the Arbeitsamt on arrival in Germany. The procedure is to inform the office where you are claiming unemployment benefit in the UK of your intention to seek work in Germany and request form E303. You can only obtain benefits in Germany if you register with an Arbeitsamt within seven days of leaving the UK, and as there may be a delay in your receiving the money, you should take sufficient funds with you to survive on.

Other Benefits

Shortened Working-Week Allowance (*Kurzarbeitergeld*). If a company is forced to put its workforce on reduced working week for justifiable economic reasons, an allowance covering 60% (67% if you have children) of the net wages lost will be paid for six months. This allowance is applied for at the Arbeitsamt, by the company or works council.

Winter Allowance. To promote year-round employment in the building trade, building workers receive a winter allowance, for hours worked between the 1st of December and the 31st of March, excluding the period of 25th December-1st January.

Children's Allowances (*Bundeskindergeldgesetz*). Children's allowances are granted to those whose permanent or ordinary residence is in Germany. The rates are graduated according to the number of children: €140 (per month) for the first and second child; €155 for the third and €180 for each additional child. These benefits are reduced for those earning more than a government set limit. All dependent children are covered including step, illegitimate and children by a previous relationship and grandchildren if they live in the same household or are primarily maintained by the claimant. The same is also true for foster children where a care and custody relationship no longer exists with their natural parents. Generally the allowance is paid for children up to the age of 16.

However, if a child remains in the education system or takes up vocational training they are eligible up to the age of 27. Those in vocational training are only eligible if they earn less than a set rateper month or are entitled to wage replacement benefits (under a set limit per month). Benefits also remain payable to over 16s who: are disabled, undertake a year of voluntary work, or who interrupt their training to look after a child of their own. There is, in addition to the Child Benefit, an income tax allowance for those with children.

SAVINGS BENEFITS

The German government promotes the creation of capital by employees by offering savings allowances or tax concessions for equity participation in a company. All employees in Germany including foreigners may invest in a government savings scheme under the *Vermögensbildungsgesetz* (Asset Accumulation Acts), provided their taxable income is below annaul thresholds. At the employee's request, if they are eligible for capital forming payments in addition to their wages, or if they ask for a portion of their wages to be deposited instead, the employer is obliged to deposit payments into one of the state-promoted investment schemes.

The government will then top up the savings with a tax-free savings benefit which the employer pays out together with the employee's wages. The savings allowance is 10% of the payments deposited up to a government set limit per year. For those taking part in investment in their employer's company the tax concession allows your employer to offer you a discount on the amount to be invested. This benefits the saver as they are exempt from taxes on the saving, if the discount is below a certain figure. In order that capital is built up there are 'blocking periods' so that capital can only be disposed of after 6 or 7 years.

It is quite common in Germany for collective agreements between unions and employers to contain provisions for additional assets accumulation benefits which can be used to take out a life assurance policy. There is a similar scheme for those who are not employed, Home Savings Benefits, whereby annual savings up to certain ceilings receive government assistance.

PENSIONS

The State Pension Scheme

As stated earlier in Chapter Five *Retirement,* people who move to Germany and work for an EU Employer before reaching pension age are usually insured under the social security laws of Germany, due to the contributions paid from their wages. If you have worked in other EU states prior to working and retiring in Germany, then under EU law, any pension contributions already paid will also count towards a pension payable to you in Germany. Each EU country where you have paid insurance towards a pension, will look at your insurance under its own scheme and work out how much pension you can have. Each EU country will also take into account any insurance you have paid in any other EU State to make sure you are paid the highest possible pension entitlement.

You can claim any of your pensions direct from any EU country that you have been insured in. If you have been insured in the UK and providing you have kept the DSS informed of any change in your address, you will usually be sent a claim form 4 months before you reach pension age in the UK.

In order to receive any pension due to you in Germany, you must apply to either the *Land* Insurance Agencies (*Landesversicherungsanstalten*) or the Federal Insurance Agency (*Bundesversicherungsanstalt für Angestellte*). To be eligible to receive a German pension an individual must have paid a minimum of 60 months German insurance contributions.

Company Pension Funds

Company pension funds are popular and protected in Germany. The practice of self-investment (pension funds investing in their own companies) is perfectly acceptable in Germany and the pension fund is not kept separate from the company's assets. The balance sheet of a German company will show the pension funds and provision for future payments. If the company goes bankrupt, the pension fund is liable to disappear with it. However, pensioners in Germany are protected by the compulsory state insurance scheme, underpinned by a statutory levy imposed on the rest of industry. The levy ensures that a collapsed company's pension fund liabilities will be covered by industry as a whole. Together these measures make German pensioners some of the most secure in the EU.

WOMEN IN WORK

As in much of the western world German women achieved suffrage rather late in the political history of their nation, only gaining the right to vote in 1918. Having won the opportunity to attend university towards the end of the nineteenth century women finally began to make headway in the professions, this increased during the Weimar Republic of the 1920s. A reversal of fortune came under the Nazis when women were firmly relegated back to *Kinder, Kirche, Küche* (children, church and hearth). After the outbreak of the Second World War, as more and more men were called to fight, the Nazi regime was forced to allow women back into higher education to keep the country running and the schools functioning. After the war, women were able to continue developing their potential in the professions and the workplace. The Basic Law enshrined equality of the sexes in the constitution, however, for many years this was still more a wish than reality.

In spite of a high proportion of university-educated women (46% of all students) Germany still has a machismo problem when it comes to women at the top. While there are 2 million more women than men in Germany they only hold 31% of the seats in the Bundestag, although the President, and one of the Vice-Presidents, of the Bundestag are women. In 1991 the Federal Ministry for Family Affairs, Senior Citizens, Women and Youth was founded (initially as the Ministry for Women and Youth), now all state governments have ministers or commissions for women's affairs and equality. There is also a powerful 'women's lobby' the German Women's Council (*Deutscher Frauenrat:* Axel-Springer-Str. 54a, D-10117 Berlin, Germany; ☎030-204 5690; fax 030-2045 6944; website www.frauenrat.de), which represents 50 women's associations and has a membership of over 11 million.

Although Germany has women (Protestant) priests, and women in Germany frequently carve out names for themselves as freelances in the media, few are selected for executive positions. The same applies to senior positions in industry, banking and business where a minute 2% of women are to be found at the top. This has very little to do with talent and much to do with the fact that their way is barred by men determined to hang on to the senior positions. The one obvious course of action open to women and one which they are increasingly taking up, is to start their own businesses. In western Germany, over three-quarters of all new businesses are being founded by women, a handful of whom have been outstandingly successful. This is also a trend in Europe generally, where the number of female-owned companies has doubled in the past ten years.

Women wanting to further their careers in Germany will either have to enter a partnership with Germans or choose to start their own business in a sphere where they are most likely to succeed, e.g. legal and financial services, a language school, translating or relocation agency. A check of the relocation agency listings will show that this has been a very successful area for female entrepreneurs.

Legislation aimed at creating equal pay in Germany has been enacted but seems difficult to enforce as statistics show that in practice women earn less than men, mostly through the way that work is assigned. The differential is argued away by the claim that men do more overtime or night work and the heavier jobs. However, if a women is doing the same or substantially similar work as a man she can take her employer to court if she is paid less. As mentioned in Chapter Seven, *Starting a Business*, employment costs are high in Germany and one way of reducing them is to avoid the generous paid maternity leave (see below), by choosing men.

Maternity benefits

As soon as a working woman obtains a certificate of pregnancy from her doctor she will receive a maternity care certificate from her health insurance agency which entitles her to free maternity care before and after delivery. She is also entitled to fully paid maternity leave for a period of six weeks before delivery and eight weeks after (12 for multiple births). The expectant mother can work in the pre-natal six week rest period but only if she expressly wishes to, but all work is prohibited in the eight week rest period. The employee's health insurance agency makes tax free payments and employers are required to make up the balance if you were paid more than the health insurance pays. The employee is also allowed time off work for breast feeding.

Parental Leave

The parental leave system was introduced so that children will be in parental care up to the age of 3 years. The system allows the parents to decide who will look after their child, should both of them be in gainful employment, or if one is unemployed or in training the other can take parental leave. During child-raising leave the employee is protected against dismissal, although if you wish to take up this leave you should approach your employer at least 4 weeks in advance and state how long you intend to take off work. During the first six months of parental leave all parents are entitled to the same allowance of €300 per month. After this period the payment is dependent on income and benefit is reduced. Either parent is also entitled to take five days paid leave to care for a sick child under eight years old.

In the private sector parental leave arrangements may be more flexible depending on the needs of the employer. For instance, sometimes career breaks can be arranged where an employee, by arrangement with the employer, takes a period of full-time leave which is normally unpaid but with a job guarantee. There may also be scope for part-time and flexible working hours made by arrangement with individual employers.

Childcare Provision Relevant to Working Women

Women in most EC countries rightly complain that childcare provision is insufficient to allow them to continue working full-time following a period of maternity leave. Belgium and Denmark are the only two countries with an outstanding record in this respect and, surprisingly perhaps, Germany does not compete with them, especially in the realm of pre-kindergarten (ages 1-3) care.

Around 3% of children under three are cared for in publicly funded nurseries (*Krippen*), or mixed-age centres which take children from 0-6 years. Occasionally, children of two years are accepted in kindergartens but this is in defiance of official regulations. Also, in some instances child-minders' (*Tagesmutter*) fees may be subsidised from public funds.

For children from three to six years childcare is readily available in the form of kindergartens, the majority of which are provided by national private organizations with public funding. Around 70% of children in this age-band attend kindergarten. Only around 12% of kindergartens are open for eight hours. The usual pattern is for them to open for four hours in the morning with a two-hour break for lunch when children have to go home before returning for a two-hour session in the afternoon. Since January 1996, children have had a legal right to attend kindergarten, and by now enough kindergartens and child-care establishments should have been built to allow any parent in Germany to send their children to one. However, attendance is voluntary and these places are funded by parental contributions, graded according to income.

At primary school level, only a few schools are open all day. The majority operate for four or five hours in the morning and many have hours that vary from day to day; children cannot eat lunch at school. Such short and irregular school hours, plus the expectation that mothers will devote a considerable time to helping their children with homework, mean that it is unrealistic for the majority of women to work full-time.

TRADE UNIONS

The origin of German trade unionism goes back to the 1880's and Bismarck's precocious industrial reforms, which included the setting up of workers' councils in factories. Today, such councils constitute an integral part of German labour management. Up to the Nazi era, German trade unions had a membership of around 6.5 million and, in common with other European countries, this was splintered into hundreds of different bodies representing variants of different ideologies as well as religious differences. Once the Nazis seized power, trade unions were abolished and their leaders imprisoned. After the War the unions were reorganised under the guidance of British union leaders, who helped the Germans set up a rational grouping of seventeen trade unions that continues today. Around 9 million German workers are members of trade unions, at present, marking a drop of 17% in union membership since 1985.

In Germany, annual wage increases are decided by means of collective bargaining (agreement between the employers' associations with the appropriate trade unions). Once agreement has been reached, it is legally binding on both parties thus making strikes illegal except under certain conditions. A strike can only be called as a last resort and only if there is a 75% majority in favour of such action.

The German Federation of Trade Unions (*Deutscher Gewerkschaftsbund* (*DGB*): Burgstrasse 29-30, D- 10178 Berlin, Germany; ☎030-2406 0211; website www.dgb.de) is organised so that within one works, all employees belong to the same union, irrespective of their speciality. Trade unions are independent of government, political parties, religious interests, the works administration and employers.

The main unions belonging to the DGB are:
ver di: Vereinte Dienstleistungsgewerkschaft, Postdamer Platz 10, D-10785

Berlin, Germany; ☎030-69560; fax 030-6956 3956; website www.verdi.de. In March 2001 Germany's largest service sector union was formed, representing 2.83 million workers in the media, post, public services and banking sectors. It was formed by the merging of the *ÖTV* (public services, *HPV* (banking), *DPG* (post), *DAG* (salaried staff) and *IG Medien* (media workers) unions.

IG Metall: IG Metall Vorstand, D-60519 Frankfurt, Germany; ☎069-66930; fax 069-6693 2843; e-mail vorstand@igmetall.de; website www.igmetall.de. IG Metall is Germany's second largest union with 2.6 million members. Once it represented the steel and metal workers, but mergers mean that now it represents workers in tetiles, garments, wood and plastic production.

IG Bauen-Agrar-Umwelt: Olof-Palme-Strasse 19, D- 60439 Frankfurt am Main, Germany; website www.igbau.de. The union for construction workers with approximately 585,359 members.

Gewerkschaft der Polizei: Stromstrasse 4, D-10555 Berlin, Germany; website www.gdp.de/. The police union, with approximately 190,617 members.

Gewerkschaft der Eisenbahner Deutschlands Transnet: Weilburger Strasse 24, D- 60326 Frankfurt am Main, Germany; ☎030/424390-70; fax 7536-444; website www.gded.de. The German railwaymen's union, with approximately 338,106 members.

IG BCE – Industriegewerkschaft Bergbau, Chemie, Energie: Königsworther Platz 6, D-30167 Hannover, Germany; ☎0511-763 1453; fax 0511-763 1715; website www.igbce.de. Approximately 857,050 members in the chemical, energy, paper and ceramics industries.

Gewerkschaft Erziehung und Wissenschaft: Reifenberger Str. 21, D-60489 Frankfurt, Germany; ☎069-789730; fax 069/78973-202; e-mail Info@gew.de; website www.gew.de/ Education and science; approximately 273,787 members.

Gewerkschaft Nahrung-Genuss-Gaststätten: Haubachstr. 76, D-22765 Hamburg, Germany; ☎040-380130; fax 040-3801 3220; website www.gewerkschaft-ngg.de or www.ngg.net. Covering workers in food, beverages and catering, with approximately 270,016 members.

As stated, the unions protect their members' economic interests through the collective bargaining process. However, their role extends over a wider range of workers' affairs: in the social sphere it embraces social and cultural policy as well as working conditions. Union membership is not compulsory but if taken out, dues based on a percentage of gross earnings have to be paid annually by the employee. In the event of a strike, or other dispute with the company, such as litigation arising from a dispute in an employment relationship, the union will provide financial assistance. For example, for every day of a strike, workers' organisations in the public services pay three times the member's contributions.

ETIQUETTE AT WORK

The formality of German business etiquette can come as a surprise to those accustomed to the more informal working atmospheres found in other European countries or the USA. In German offices it is usual to shake hands with everyone on arrival at work and before leaving. Calling associates by their first names is uncommon; even people who have been working together for years still call each other Herr or Frau followed by the surname. Even more approachable employees such as secretaries and receptionists are traditionally accorded the same respectful form of address; in fact it would be considered patronising to call them by their first names. In Germany, if a man puts his arm round his secretary or calls her by her first name, it will be automatically assumed that they are romantically involved. The same formality surrounds the polite form of address *Sie* (you), which should always be used, unless one is invited to use the informal version, *du*. Amongst younger people, working relationships are much less formal, probably because in most schools, pupils invariably address their teachers by the familiar second person and this habit has now entered the workplace with them. However, it is always wisest to wait for your colleagues to initiate any changes in how you address each other.

Using professional titles is another point of etiquette. It is also indicative of the fact that in continental Europe generally, status tends to be linked to profession. On the whole, use of titles is however declining, so making a mistake in this respect is not considered unpardonable, especially on the part of a non-German. On the other hand, over use of titles can easily make you look ridiculous. The best policy, if you are unsure is simply to ask people how they wish to be addressed. As a foreigner, you can easily get away with this. Academic doctorates are not commonly used in Britain as part of forms of address, but in Germany both medical and academic doctors can be addressed as Herr or Frau Doktor. Other titles which may be used are *Herr/Frau Professor, Herr Pfarrer* (for a vicar), and occasionally, *Herr Ingenieur* (engineer). If the German concerned has more than one degree, e.g. *Professor Doktor,* both may be used in addressing him or her, however in such a case most people would consider *Herr/Frau Professor* sufficient.

REGIONAL BUSINESS AND INDUSTRY REPORT

The following breakdown of industry and business interests region by region indicates the types of skills likely to be in demand:

BADEN-WÜRTTEMBERG

With the third largest länder population and borders with Switzerland and France, Baden-Württemberg has access to a market of 200 million people. The capital, Stuttgart is highly industrial, largely as a result of being the home of Daimler-Benz, the car manufacturer. The state's GDP recently exceeded those of Belgium, Switzerland or Sweden. World famous names such as Mercedes-Benz, Bosch, Porsche, Dornier and Zeiss all have locations in the state. Half of Germany's net inward investment flows into Baden-Württemberg with companies such as Hewlett-Packard, IBM, Minolta, Sony, Nokia, Kodak and Michelin establishing presences in the region.

Germany leads the world in environmental technology and Baden-Württemberg produces a quarter of its environmental products and services. Technology is one of the keys to this prosperity, microelectronics, precision engineering, telecommunications and biotechnology all play major roles in the state's economic framework. 62 million DM were spent recently on a multi-media 'data-highway' project to link various firms, universities and research centres. This being constructed as a joint venture by Deutsche Telekom, IBM, Hewlett-Packard, Alcatel and Bosch-ANT.

Technological expertise is largely focused on Karlsruhe which is one of the leading *Technologieregionen* and is backed financially by the Fridericiana University, which has a renowned computer science faculty, and around 100 other scientific and technological institutes. In the Karlsruhe region, there is now a ratio of 32 scientists to 1,000 workers. Many companies are attracted to the area because of the availability of highly trained staff, the result of one of Europe's most highly-concentrated and mature Research and Development infrastructures. The state has 9 universities, 39 polytechnics, and 38 research institutes, the results of their labours are translated into practical applications by the 269 technology transfer centres.

BAYERN (BAVARIA)

Once Germany's largest agricultural economy, Bayern has swapped its ploughs for lathes. Agriculture now only accounts for less than 2% of the state's production figures, manufacturing and the engineering processes have taken over with an expanding IT market making Bayern Germany's 'Silicon Valley'. Over a third of companies in the region are involved in technology information and data processing. The automobile sector is also present in force not least because Bavaria is the birthplace of Bayerische Motoren-Werke (BMW), which has several plants in this, its home territory. Other sectors with a flourishing presence include electrical and mechanical engineering, railway vehicle construction, textiles, fashion, publishing and finance. The state capital München has become the focus of an expanding industrial area, with automotive, aerospace, electrical and electronics firms setting up there. Other centres are Nürnberg-Furth with companies like Siemens, Grundig and Playmobil having production sites there, Regensburg, with electrical engineering and a BMW factory, Schweinfurt is the hub of Europe's ballbearing manufacture, Würzburg is a major centre for printing machinery and Augsburg which has engineering and textiles firms. Bavaria's per capita income is the highest in Germany. Currently 700,000 enterprises are operating in the state, a potent supply of investment and partnership opportunities.

Bayern has two international airports at München and Nürnberg, and the Main-Danube Canal runs through the state linking the Black Sea with the North Sea via the Rhine. It is also at the intersection of rail lines stretching from Lisbon to Prague and Naples to Stockholm.

The area around Munich is home to a quarter of the state's population, amongst them many foreign residents. Munich is a technology centre with several universities and technical colleges specializing in scientific disciplines including bio-technology, experimental physics and engineering automation. With its various universities and scientific research institutes Bayern offers a wide intellectual base for businesses investing in applied technology. Fields of study cover microsystems, bio-sensors, bio-technology and medicines.

BERLIN

Berlin is a city state facing many changes, from the collapse of its infamous wall and the inherent problems of reintegrating two disparate halves of a city into one; to the need to prepare for its forthcoming role as the new Federal Capital. With unification Berlin has resumed its role as an industrial and commercial hub for Eastern and Central Europe. Great efforts are being made to modernise the city's infrastructure of roads, underground and regional railways, and its external links. The autobahn route to Nürnberg and Bavaria has been modernised by the Federal transport authority. In addition to these links Berlin has three airports.

Germany's largest industrial centre, concentrating on engineering, pharmaceuticals, electrical goods and textiles, Berlin was the birthplace of firms such as Siemens and AEG. It is likely to remain one of central Europe's largest industrial centres, as the Berlin Senate has plans for 21 contiguous industrial sites totalling 3,300 hectares of manufacturing area. However, there is also a large supply of business locations available throughout the city, and it is likely that while Berlin will become a focus for business activity, much of its economy will be determined by private services.

Berlin is an excellent location for innovative enterprises, with its highly qualified workforce, expanding service sector and improved transport links, at present it has the highest figures in Germany for newly created firms. In part this is due to the interplay between the three universities, 14 technical colleges and 250 research institutes, and the new business centres.

BRANDENBURG

Surrounding the city-state of Berlin means that the region sits astride the London-Moscow and Stockholm-Budapest axes, and can therefore take advantage of trade routes. Close co-operation with neighbouring Poland already offers opportunities from procuring raw materials to processing and sales activities. In addition to being close enough to make use of Berlin's universities, Brandenburg has three universities and five technical colleges of its own.

Manufacturing and development businesses in the region have expertise in traffic control, microsystems, energy and construction technology, electronics optics, synthetic chemistry and bio-technology. The länder investment council has developed a 'one-stop-shop' system to help investors with reduced red-tape and generous grants. Tax-deductions and deprecation allowances allow the retrieval of up to 50% of costs. These favourable conditions have already attracted firms such as BMW/Rolls-Royce (aero-engine development), Readymix (cement plant), BASF, Bosch-Siemens Appliances (synthetic chemicals) and MAN (heavy-duty machinery). In addition, opportunities in media related business are likely to grow as the German Film industry returns to its cradle at Potsdam-Babelsberg.

New transport links will have fringe benefits for the region; the new airport at Berlin-Schönefeld Brandenburg, and the magnetic rail system between Hamburg and Berlin are examples. The region's many canals and rail lines are being renewed or redeveloped with the Federal Government's commitment to upgrading the infrastructure of the eastern länder.

HANSESTADT BREMEN

Of the three German city-states, Bremen, with its satellite port Bremerhaven, is the smallest and also a two-city, city-state. Both ports are free ports, and have one of the world's largest covered container terminals. As well as freight handling the city can arrange Europe wide distribution, with its road/rail terminals and storage facilities. The city has autobahn and high speed rail links with all the main European towns and cities.

Not only a cargo port, Bremen has a history of food processing stemming from a productive fishing fleet; long established industries include fish processing, and the production of cigarettes, coffee, chocolate, and beer. Naturally the city has a shipbuilding industry, but apart from constructing and refitting cargo carriers the yards also produce luxury yachts, ferries, cruise liners and research vessels. Arising from this the city is a centre for the development and production of marine electronics including radars, sonars and other navigational aids. With an international airport nearby Bremen is also the headquarters of MBB/Erno, one of the powerhouses behind the European space rocket, Ariane and the highly successful Airbus project. Components for Ariane, the Eureca space research platform and the A320 Airbus are manufactured and assembled in Bremen.

The presence of the aerospace industries has attracted many research centres and institutions which are research leaders into physics, telecommunications, magnetic waves, superconductor research and software development. The city can also boast the 146m high drop tower of the Centre for Applied Aerospace Technology and Microgravitation, which is used by scientists across the globe to research gravity, anti-gravity and weightlessness. Other research institutes include the Max Planck Institute for Marine Microbiology, the Alfred Wegener Institute for Polar and Maritime Research and the Frauenhofer Institute for Applied Material Research. Bremen's Innovation and Technology Centre (BITZ) provides accommodation, know-how and contacts between researchers and technology minded businesses.

The automobile industry has been in Bremen since 1978 in the form of a Mercedes Benz plant manufacturing its latest models.

HANSESTADT HAMBURG

Germany's second largest city, Hamburg has a long tradition of being a great trading city dating from the 13th century when it was part of the Hanseatic League. These days modern Hamburg is working with its neighbours Lower Saxony and Schleswig-Holstein to outline a development plan for this area of Germany. Hamburg is Germany's largest seaport and Europe's second largest container port, with some 70 docks for inland canal and sea-going cargo vessels. The port's nucleus is the *Freihafen*, one of the world's largest freeports. Hamburg is an important distribution centre. Already the headquarters of several of the world's main shipping lines, Hamburg is also attracting an increasing number of industries from Asia, the United States and Europe. In addition to the 1,800 firms based here, which are engaged in foreign trade, there are now over 30 trade centres in Hamburg including the China United Trade Corporation whose headquarters in Hamburg is the commercial conduit for Chinese trade relations with the whole of Europe. Hamburg is also Germany's most Anglophile city and therefore very welcoming to British enterprises.

Hamburg is an important transport hub for northern Europe, as well as the sea trade, rail traffic and a large portion of the road traffic to and from Scandinavia, passes over the Elbe bridges or through tunnels. The city's airport (Germany's fourth largest) is linked to the network of regional airports across Germany, and has flights to the European capitals and the main American cities.

The reunificaton of Germany tripled its cargo traffic with the return of access to its traditional hinterland. The city's GNP has grown over the last decade as has its population, as new firms have set up in the area in addition to the traditional port industries, of shipbuilding, engineering and refining. Industries in Hamburg now include aviation, aerospace, precision and optical engineering and of the workforce of 780,000, 145,000 are employed in manufacturing. The port activity of refining and processing chemicals means a ready supply of raw materials for the Boots factory based near Hamburg.

For a long time Hamburg has had a large service sector to meet the needs of the city's merchants, since the war this has included the media as the main newspaper publishers set up home here. These have been followed by the leading German television and film companies. Within the service industry Hamburg is Germany's largest insurance centre, second largest banking centre and has one of the world's oldest stock exchanges.

HESSEN (HESSE)

Hessen is dominated by the world financial centre of Frankfurt am Main. Around 370 banks are based in Frankfurt and between them employ over 45,000 people. In addition to the banks, there are many insurance and advertising companies. Frankfurt is home to the European Central Bank, which oversees the economies of the Eurozon countries and its new currency.

The centre of Frankfurt, is dominated by a cluster of skyscrapers including the 55-floor Messe Turm which purports to be the highest office tower in Europe and is undoubtedly home to some of the larger and more important trade fairs, especially the famous Frankfurt Book Fair each year. The city's airport is the busiest in continental Europe with around 30 million passengers a year and Europe's largest air-freight facility. Hesse is also home to some of Germany's major industrial companies amongst them, Opel (part of General Motors), Hoechst (chemicals) and the international companies AEG, Metallgesellschaft and Degussa.

Apart from financial services, international trade is very important to Hessen, every third job depends on exports, and these account for 30% of annual turnover. Trade with Britain is healthy, especially from a British viewpoint.

As a place in which to live and work, Frankfurt may not be the most beautiful German city, but a recent survey put it into fifth place in a business magazines study of enterprise-friendly cities; a place which was won on so called 'soft-location factors' as well as those which suited good business.

MECKLENBURG-VORPOMMERN (MECKLENBURG-WEST POMERANIA)

Sparsely populated the region has plenty of room for agriculture and related processing industries. Its clean, almost unsullied environment makes it an ideal location for producing foodstuffs and one global manufacturer who has noticed this potential is Nestlé, which has a large baby-food production facility here. Youth is another point in the region's favour as 42% of the available workforce is under 35.

Geographically Mecklenburg-Vorpommern can be seen as Germany's northern gateway through its Baltic ports which give access to 25 million Scandinavian consumers. This also makes the region an excellent base for firms interested in importing goods and raw materials from Sweden and Finland. With the fall of communism the old Hanseatic trade routes to the Baltic states are being revived, which should help the port industries of Rostock.

The most up to date transport and logistics technologies facilitate short and efficient travel or shipment by road, rail, sea or air, which means that producers of perishable goods benefit accordingly, and thus are at the root of the state's economy. However, shipbuilding and marine technology continue to hold a large share, in the face of competition from new technologies such as micro-electronics and microsystems. These new industries are benefiting from the state having two of the oldest universities in Europe, and a network of technology transfer agencies, which arrange for good ideas to be converted into practical applications.

NIEDERSACHSEN (LOWER SAXONY)

Formerly dependent on heavy industry, agriculture and shipbuilding, Niedersachsen has been transformed by unification into a transport and communications nexus. Its dense network of canals and navigable waterways allow the easy transport of goods and materials from central and eastern Europe to the ports of Hamburg and Bremen for onward shipment worldwide. The state capital Hannover is a hub for the major trans-European motor routes (E3 Denmark-Portugal, E4 Helsinki-Lisbon, and E8 London-Moscow). The state has a co-ordinated network of ISDN and fibre-optic cables for high-speed data communications, and Hannover's trade fair often hosts CeBIT the world's largest information and communication technology exhibitions.

Industry still has a home here and the state's industrial workforce accounts for 9.5% of total German turnover. Business incentives in the region include remarkably low prices for property; developed property, undeveloped land, and development plots for industrial use are respectively 46%, 30% and 20% below the national average. Among the major foreign and domestic firms with their headquarters in Niedersachsen are companies like Volkswagen (automobiles), Bahlsen (foods), Siemens (electronics), Blaupunkt (electronics), BEB Erdgas (energy), Alcan and WABCO Westinghouse. Other firms with sites in the state are Dow Chemical, ICI, Matsushita, Konica, Minolta and Citibank. Siemens employ some 10,000 workers in the region and Daimler-Benz have recently set up a new vehicle test track.

Niedersachsen's economic policy is geared towards flexibility and support for investment and expansion, with institutes promoting technology transfer and energy conservation. Other service agencies have been created to advise businesses with scientific expertise, and provide assistance in setting up in the region.

NORD-RHEIN-WESTFALEN (NORTH-RHINE-WEST-PHALIA)

The most densely populated German state, with a population of 18 million, is also Germany's economic powerhouse; at times it has generated a quarter of Germany's GDP. The state capital, Düsseldorf is host to many foreign companies and several thousand foreign residents including Japanese, Americans, British and Scandinavians. Nord-Rhein-Westfalen (NRW) is the home of Germany's famous industrial heart the Ruhr, although the heavy industries which once dominated the area have declined in size. Where once the iron, steel and coal industry employed almost half of the state's workers this figure is now closer to one tenth. The main industrial strengths of the relgion are in the chemical, plant, and engineering sectors, with service oriented firms accounting for half of the state's turnover. More than a third of Germany's top 500 companies have their headquarters in NRW, including Bertelsmann, one of the world's largest media companies. Düsseldorf, the state capital, is one of Germany's largest banking and international finance centres, with its stock exchange being the fourth largest in Europe. After London Düsseldorf is the second largest Japanese business centre in Europe. Nearly half of Germany's trade fairs are held in the region attracting 5 million visitors from 150 nations.

NRW has six new freight centres for road/rail transport, and Aachen is Germany's leading border crossing for goods transport. Overall NRW is responsible for almost half of Germany's wholesale foreign trade turnover, and with a 23% share of total exports, its the largest exporter. Of the three international airports in the state, Düsseldorf is the second largest in Germany, handling over 7 million passengers a year. Added to these are the five regional airports and eight airfields used for chartered and private business flights. The main transport link however, is the Rhine, this connects Europe's largest port at Rotterdam with the Black Sea, via Duisburg and the Rhine-Main-Danube canal. Duisburg is not just a freeport on the Rhine but is the world's largest inland-waterway port.

Intellectually, the state is a leader in research and development for industry with the largest percentage of any workforce employed in this sector. Half a million students are enrolled at the 50 colleges and universities, six out of ten of Germany's largest institutions are in NRW. There are three national research centres and ten Max Planck Institutes here, not to mention several Frauenhofer Society facilities. The state has set up 48 technology centres to interface with industry, resulting in the setting up of 850 companies. the change from heavy industry to services has lead to a 'greening' of the region and a third of Germany's environmental technology research occurs here.

Other industrial companies located there include: Ford, Toyota, Mazda, Renault, Sony and Henkel. Although the state is dominated by industry, Düsseldorf and the other important city of Köln are also centres for the advertising and fashion industries. More than 800 foreign firms are located in Köln and the surrounding area. As a major German media centre, Köln has resident broadcasting companies, publishing houses, record companies, advertising agencies, film and video production companies and others dealing with telematic and computer technology. In addition, Köln is the site of Europe's first Media Park, a centre for information and technology companies, which will facilitate co-operation and developments in different media: information technology and audiovisual.

RHEINLAND-PFALZ (RHINELAND-PALATINATE)

Rheinland-Pfalz lies at the heart of a consumer market with a population of 40 million, and borders the economic centres of the Rhine-Ruhr, Rhine-Main, Belgium and the mega region Saar-Lor-Lux. Primarily known for its high quality wines, the region's vineyards produce two thirds of Germany's wine.

Apart from the wine trade, the region's forests and spas attract over seven million tourists a year, either to relax or to seek a cure. Rheinland-Pfalz is also the location of the 'German-Wine Route', a tourist trail around the various vineyards and historical towns of the area.

The state is also home to the headquarters of BASF, the giant chemical concern, at Ludwigshafen and millions of marks and euros have been invested in economic infrastructure over the last few years as the state develops its business base. At present the majority of firms in the region are small enterprises and only 2% of manufacturing firms here employ more than 500 staff.

SAARLAND

Saarland's historically close links with France have led in recent years to its participation in the Saar-Lor-Lux European Mega-region (a cross-border association of Saarland, Luxembourg and the Lorraine province of France). In this interface between regional markets, there is a great deal of cross border trade and employment, and as Britain's main trading partners are France and Germany, this is are is an excellent investment and expansion opportunity for British firms. In recent years five major US companies have invested in the Saarland as a business base for Germany and Europe.

The Saarland has recently-founded research centres for artificial intelligence, microsystems and medically-oriented technology, including the Max Planck Institute for Computer Science. Already, Siemens, Wang, IBM and over a dozen smaller computer software companies have set up operations there. The highly trained workforce with skills in CAD/CAM and CASE has attracted the American company Litton Industries, while the Ford plant at Saarlouis employs 7,000 staff and produces 1,400 cars a day. Plastics processing, electronics, computers and IT are all major employment areas, with companies like Bosch, ABB and SKF. According to the British-German Chamber of Commerce the region has lower than average labour costs and low prices for industrial or commercial property.

SACHSEN (SAXONY)

Once the industrial heartland of former East Germany, Saxony accounted for a third of the entire East German production and was home to the nationally celebrated Trabant motor car. Now with its borders with Poland and the Czech Republic it is an economic gateway to Central and South Eastern Europe. An industrial region before the birth of the Ruhr region, Saxony is building on its past. GDP Growth in recently stood at 7.4%, the highest of all the German states, with a predicted continuation at 7% until at least 2010. While mechanical engineering takes the lion's share of the states productivity; the electronics, electrical engineering, environmental technology, automotive, chemical, glass and ceramics industries, all play a noticeable part.

Since 1990 around 8,800 industrial projects have been subsidised by the federal and land government. This investment means the region is now home to a brand new Volkswagen factory, as well as inducing Siemens Advanced Micro Devices and Canon to set up production facilities in Saxony. Leipzig recently became home to Europe's biggest mail order warehouse with Quelle making Germany's largest logistics investment in German history. While in April 1996 part of the old airport was reopened as a new trade fair centre, with design work by a firm of British architects. Saxony currently has 400 industrial estates of which 288 are supported by the länder government.

Six out of ten Saxons have specialised skills training and one in five is a graduate. With its four universities, thirteen colleges or other higher education establishments and 40 research companies the state has an excellent Research and Development infrastructure.

In addition to this immense sums are being invested in upgrading the Elbe ports and the inter-connections between road, rail and canal. Dresden and Leipzig/Halle are to be connected to the high speed rail network (ICE) and their airports are being modernised. At present until the development of Berlin-Schönefeld Leipzig /Halle is eastern Germany's second largest airport. New motorway routes to Prague and Wroclaw are under construction, and Poland has plans in development for a motorway which will run between Görlitz in Saxony and the Ukraine.

SACHSEN-ANHALT (SAXONY-ANHALT)

The state's geographic location means that economically it benefits from its proximity to Berlin, and the Rhine-Ruhr. The state also straddles the routes between Hamburg, Bremen and south-east Europe, and by extension its links with the Ruhr also bring it into contact with the Rhine-Main area. Most of the top priority, post-reunification, transport projects directly affected the state and its economic/industrial potential. These include the high-speed Hannover-Berlin rail link, the six-lane trunk routes Berlin-Hannover and Berlin-Nürnberg, as well as the Halle-Magdeburg motorway. A motorway linking Halle and Göttingen is also being planned at present. Magdeburg's harbour on the Elbe has been improved and the telecommunications network of Sachsen-Anhalt extended, giving the region a sound modern infrastructure for businesses to grow in.

Government retraining means the workforce that ran East Germany's chemical industry is highly qualified and adaptable, coupled with EU and regional funding programmes this makes the state a good candidate for industrial investment. Since

1990 over 300 new industrial and commercial estates have been constructed, with lower than average prices for floorspace. The construction of new power plants and the upgrading of the chemical industry throughout the eastern länder will probably mean that the region will attract investment into the state's control instruments industry.

SCHLESWIG-HOLSTEIN

According to a recent report from the German Institute for Urban Studies, Schleswig-Holstein has the second-best economic climate in Germany. The state's GDP has grown consistently over the years improving by 21% over the period 1990-1995. As a small state with little in the way of raw materials or industrial heritage Schleswig-Holstein is reinventing itself as a home for modern technology. New investment in the region includes the founding of a microchip production site by a subsidiary of Daimler-Benz and the expansion of their facility at Flensburg by Motorola. The state is also home to a number of research institutes with links to industry, the most famous of which is the Frauenhofer Institute for Silicon Technology at Itzehoe.

Recent improvements in communications have been the construction of new motorways and a fourth tunnel under the Elbe as well as a new crossing west of Hamburg. While the state has a history of sea-borne links with Scandinavia, airports are an expanding line of communication as the airport at Hamburg-Fuhlsbüttel is just over the state border in addition to the number of regional airports with flights to Cologne/Bonn or Frankfurt.

Although micro-electronics are not likely to overtake sea trade as the region's main industry for a while yet, a more likely contender, given the shorter German working week, is the tourism and leisure industry. Given the picturesque and varied coast, its historic Hanseatic ports (Lübeck was recently made a World Heritage Site) and its many lakes and nature reserves (see Chapter One) the state is becoming a leading tourist destination.

THÜRINGEN (THÜRINGIA)

As part of the Federal drive to rebuild the transport system of the eastern länder, Thüringen will benefit from new motorway links with Berlin, Bayern, Leipzig and the Ruhr. The international airport at Leipzig is a short distance across the state border and Erfurt's own airport was expanded to form part of a chain of regional airports.

Thüringen's main industrial strengths are in the automotive, engineering, electronics and ceramics industries. The well known pre-war optical firm of Carl Zeiss is still going strong and with Jenoptik exports opto-electronic precision tools around the world. General Motors has a site at Eisenach employing 2,000 people in the production of 16,000 Opel cars annually, and ICL-Fujitsu has a computer production facility with an annual capacity to turn out 300,000 PCs. Other investors in the region are Coca-Cola (soft drinks), Cresson (foods), AMS (semi-conductors) and Langenscheidt (publishers). Tourism is also a major source of income as the state has 1,400 castles, one of which the Wartburg is the start of the 'Classical Route' a tour through Germany's cultural and intellectual history.

DIRECTORY OF MAJOR EMPLOYERS

The following lists have been compiled with the help of the British-German Chamber of Commerce and lists major British firms with offices, subsidiaries or partners in Germany, it includes some firms who have offices in Britain which may recruit for posts in Germany. Lists of foreign-owned firms doing business in Germany can be obtained from the relevant chambers of commerce listed below.

CHAMBERS OF COMMERCE

○ *American Chamber of Commerce in Germany:* Rossmarkt 12, D-60311 Frankfurt am Main, Germany; ☎ 069-929 1040; fax 069-9291 0411; www.amcham.de.

○ *Austrade* (Australia's Eport & Investment Agency): Grüneburgweg 58-62, D-60311 Frankfurt, Germany; ☎ 069-905580; fax 069-9055 8119.

○ *British Chamber of Commerce in Germany:* Severinstrasse 60, D-50678 Köln, Germany; ☎ 0221-314458; fax 0221-315335; www.bccg.de.

○ *Canadian Embassy – Commercial Division:* Friedrichstr. 95, D-10117 Berlin, Germany; ☎ 030-203120.

Australian Firms

ANZ Banking Group Ltd: Mainzer Landstr. 46, D-60325 Frankfurt, Germany; ☎069-710 0080; fax 7100 0821.

Macquarie Bank: Residenzstr. 17, D-80333 München, Germany; ☎089-291873.

Australian Wine Bureau: Grüneburgweg 58-62, D-60322 Frankfurt, Germany; ☎069-9055 8400; fax 069-9055 8409; e-mail WineBureau@aol.com; www.wineaustralia.com.au.

Meat and Livestock Australia: Grüneburgweg 58-62, D-60322 Frankfurt, Germany; ☎069-9055 8500; fax 9055 8519.

Australia Service; Friesenstr. 72, D-50670 Köln, Germany; ☎0221-121617.

Australia Shop: Marktplatz 13, D-65183 Wiesbaden, Germany; tel/fax 0611-3082545; www.australia-shop.com.

Australian Fashion House GmbH: Am Gebr. Hofmann Ring 1, D-97246 Eibelstadt, Germany; ☎09303-99737; fax 09303-99757; e-mail scippis@t-online.de.

Australian Food & Wine: Glaslstr. 2, D-83700 Rottach-Egern, Germany; ☎08022-704609; fax 08022-704614; www.australian-food-wine.com.

Outback Im- & Export Brandes & Neumann oHG: Am Wolfsberg 9, D-28865 Lilienthal, Germany; ☎04298-939025; fax 04298-939026; www.australiana.de.

Outback-Shop Never-Never- Land: Hertinger Str. 65, D-59423 Unna, Germany; ☎02303-9861620; fax 02303-9861629; www.outbackshop.de.

Aboriginal Art – Galerie Bähr: Eichendorffstr. 13, D-67346 Speyer, Germany; tel/fax 06232-78924; www.aboriginal-art.de.

Aboriginal Art Gallery Berlin: Rykestr. 37, D-10405 Berlin, Germany; ☎030-4412473; www.aboriginal-art-gallery.de.

Aboriginal Fine Art - Galerie für die

Kunst Australiens: Hauptstr. 15a,
D-46459 Rees-Millingen, Germany;
☎*02851-6066.*
Koogarah – Didgeridoos and Aboriginal
Products: August-Bebel-Str. 16-18,
D-33602 Bielefeld, Germany;
☎0521-895103; fax 0521-895109;
www.didgeridoo.net.

Renate Schenk Verlag: Heinkstr. 10,
D-04347 Leipzig, Germany;
☎0341-2300825; fax 0341-2300826;
www.schenk-verlag.de.
Wakefield Wines GmbH: Rungestr.
17, D-10179 Berlin, Germany;
☎030-2756 0100; fax 030-2756
0102; www.wakefield.de.

BRITISH FIRMS IN GERMANY

BUSINESS SECTOR CODES	
100	Mineral Products, Energy
105	Foodstuffs
110	Colours, Paints & Plastics
111	Pharmaceutcals
112	Cosmetics
113	Other Chemical Products
120	Textiles & Clothing
125	Building Materials
126	Air Conditioning
130	Metalwork
135	Machinery
136	Tools
137	Vehicles
145	Electrical Equipment
150	Data Procssing Equipment
152	Medical Equipment
160	Photographic
165	Communications Equipment
199	Other Products
200	Banking
201	Insurance
202	Tax Consultants, Legal Advisors
203	Consultants
204	Property Services
206	Auctioneers
210	Building & Construction
215	Hotels & Restaurants
220	Transport
225	Architects
226	Computer Software and Services
230	Telecommunications
231	Holding Companies
232	Information Services
233	Printing & Publishing
240	Tourism
250	Wholesale, Retail
299	Other Services

ALBRIGHT & WILSON Gmbh: Frankfurter str. 181, D-63263 Neu-Isenburg, Germany. **200**

ALCAN CHEMICALS EUROPE LTD: Gartenstr.6, D-53894 Mechernich, Germany. **100**

ALCAN DEUTSCHLAND Gmbh: Hannoverschestr. 2, D-37075 Gottingen, Germany. **130**

ALLOTT & LOMAX: Herweg 38 b, D-51429 Bergisch Gladbach, Germany. **225**

ALPHA TELECOM Gmbh: Eschersheimer Landstr.10, D-60322 Frankfurt, Germany. **230**

(The General Electric Co Plc) ALSTOM LHB Gmbh: Linke-Hofmann-Busch-Str.1, D-38239 SALZGITTER, Germany. **137**

ALTAI GERMANY: Planckstr. 15c, D-40699 Erkrath, Germany. **210**

AMEC Gmbh: Von-Miller-Str 13, D-67661 Kaiserlautern, Germany. **210**

AMERSHAM BUCHLER Gmbh & Co.KG: Gieswelweg 1, D-38110 Braunschweig, Germany. **111**

ANGLO SAXON MASCHINEN VERTRIEB Gmbh: Ziegelestr. 1, D-01844 Langburkersdorf, Germany. **135**

(Cadbury Schweppes Plc) APOLLINARIS & SCHWEPPES Gmbh & Co: Fischertwiete 1, Chile-haus B, D-20095 Hamburg, Germany. **105**

ARIES ETRANKEVERTRIEB Gmbh: Bahnstr 10, D-65205 Wiesbaden, Germany. **299**

AUTOHAUS FERNSTRABE Gmbh: Fernstrabe, D-66538 Neunkirchen, Germany. **250**

AUTOHAUS FEYOCK PIRMASENS Gmbh: Zweibrucker Str. 173, D-66954 Primasens, Germany. **250**

AVIS AUTOVERMIETUNG Gmbh & Co.KG: Zimmermuhlenweg 21, D-61437 Oberursel, Germany. **240**

AVON AUTOMOTIVE (Deutschland) Gmbh: Vahrenwalder Platz 3, D-30165 Hannover, Germany. **137**

BABCOCK MATERIALS (Handling Division) Gmbh: Schanzenstrabe, D-21614 Buxtehude, Germany. **233**

(Greenhill International Insurance Holdings Ltd) BAIA UNDERWRITING Gmbh: Kart-Rudolf-Str. 178, D-0215 Düsseldorf,, Germany. **201**

BARCLAYCARD: Albert-einstein-Ring 3, D-22751 Hamburg, Germany. **200**

BARCLAYS BANK PLC: Niederlassung Frankfurt, Bockenheimer Landstrasse 38-40, D-60323 Frankfurt am Main, Germany. **200**

BARCLAYS INDUSTRIE BANK Gmbh: Morfelder Landstr. 55, D-60598 Frankfurt am Main, Germany. **200**

BATIG GESELLSCHAFT FUR BETEILLGUNGEN Gmbh: Alsterufer 4, D-20354 Hamburg, Germany. **105**

BAU BORNA Gmbh: Abtsdorfer Str. 36, D-04552 Borna, Germany. **210**

BBC BURO: Platz vor dem Neuen Tor 4, D-10115 Berlin, Germany. **231**

(Boots Contract Manufacturing) BCM KOSMETIK Gmbh: Messenhauser Str. 22, D-63128 Dietzenbach, Germany. **112**

(The Shell Petroleum Co Plc) BEB ERDGAS UND ERDOL Gmbh: Riethorst 12, D-30659 Hanover, Germany. **100**

(Smiths Industries Aerospace Defence Systems Ltd) BENZING VENTILATOREN Gmbh: Werastr. 2, D-78056 Villingen-Schwenningen, Germany. **145**

(31 Group Plc) BERG MANTELPROFILWEK Gmbh: Ruschfeld 1, D-33397 Rietberg, Germany. **199**

BERLIN HILTON: Mohrenstr. 57, D-47495 Rhienberg, Germany. **215**

(Blackwell Science Ltd) BLACKWELL WISSENSCHFTSVERLAG Gmbh: Kurfurstendamm 57, D-11070 Berlin, Germany. **233**

BLUME Gmbh: (Member of the CORUS Group) Umschlag 10, D-45478 Mulheim an der Ruhr, Ger-

Germany. **230**
GILLETTE DEUTSCHLAND Gmbh & Co: Oberlandstr. 75-84, D-14052 Berlin, Germany. **199**
GKN AUTOMOTIVE GmbH: Hauptstrasse 150, D-53797 Lohmar, Germany. **137**
GLAXO VERWALTUNGS-Gmbh: Industriestrasse 32-36, D-23843 Oldesole, Germany. **232**
GLAXO WELLCOME Gmbh & Co: Am Trippelsberg 48, D-40589 Düsseldorf, Germany. **111**
(Smith-Kline Beecham Plc) GLAXO SMITH KLINE CONSUMER HEALTHCARE: Gmbh & Co KG,Busmatten 1, D-77815 Buhl, Germany. **111**
(The Morgan Crucible Company Plc) GOSSELER THERMAL CERAMICS Gmbh: Borsigsr. 4-6, D-21465 Reinbek, Germany. **135**
GUINNESS Gmbh: Limbecker Str.20-28, D-45127 Essen, Germany. **105**
(Allied Textile Companies Plc) HALMOND TEPPICHWERKE Gmbh: Carl-Wilhelm-Koch Str. 6,08606 Oelsnitz, Germany. **120**
(Royal Ordnance Plc) HECKLER & KOCK MASCHINEN-und-ANLAGENBAU: Seedorfer Str. 91, D-78713 Schramberg, Germany. **199**
(The Boots Company Ltd) HERMAL -KURT HERMANN Gmbh & Co: Scholzstr. 3, D-21465 Reinbeck, Germany. **111**
ICI PAINTS DECO Gmbh: Ittepartk 2-4, D-40724 Hilden, Germany. **250**
(ICL International Computer Ltd) IC RETAIL SYSTEMS Gmbh: Vgelsander Weg 91, D-40470 Düsseldorf, Germany. **145**
ILFORD IMAGING Gmbh: Heinrich-Hertz Str. 1, D-63303 Dreieich, Germany. **160**
INCHAPE Automobile GmbH: Nortkirchenstr. 111, D-44263 Dortmund,

Germany. **250**
JAGUAR DEUTSCHLAND Gmbh: Franfurter Str., D-61476 Kronberg, Germany. **137**
(Bicc Cables Projects Ltd) KAISER KWO KABEL ENGERGIE Gmbh & Co KG: Riedelstr. 1, D-12347 Berlin, Germany. **145**
KALAMAZOO COMPUTER GROUP Gmbh: Rendsburger Str. 34, D-30659 Hamburg, Germany. **226**
KLEINWORT BENSON DEUTSCHLAND Gmbh: Wilhelm-Leuschner Str 41, D-60329 Frankfurt am Main, Germany. **200**
(Sun Alliance & London Insurance Co) KONIG ELEKTRONIK Gmbh: Steinstr 1-5, D-64385 Reichelsheim, Germany. **145**
LUCAS AUTOMOTIVE GmbH: Carl-Spaeter-Str. 8, D-56070 Koblenz, Germany. **137**
MARLEY FLOORS Gmbh: Curslacker Neuer Deich 66, D-21029 Hamburg, Germany. **125**
OXFORD INSTRUMENTS Gmbh: Otton-Von Guericke Ring 10, D-65205 Wiesbaden, Germany. **250**
P & O NEDLLOYD LTD: Branch Germany, Am Sandtorkai 37, D-20457 Hamburg, Germany. **220**
P & O STENA LINE LTD: Graf Adolf Str 41, D-40210 Düsseldorf, Germany. **220**
P & O TRANS EUROPEAN MANAGEMENT Gmbh: Furstenberger strasse 3-9, D-60322 Frankfurt am Main, Germany. **220**
PENGUIN BOOKS DEUTSCHLAND Gmbh: Metzlerstr 26, D-60594 Frankfurt am Main, Germany. **233**
PILKINGTON DEUTSCHLAND Gmbh: Auf der Reihe 2, D-45884 Gelsenkirchen,Germany. **199**
(Kwik-Fit Holdings Plc) PIT-STOP AUTO SERVICE Gmbh: Seligenstadter Grund 11, D-63150 Heusenstamm, Germany. **137**
PORTAKABIN Gmbh: Siemensring 24,

STARTING A BUSINESS

CHAPTER SUMMARY

○ **Incentives:** The EU has a policy of encouraging the creation of small and medium-sized businesses.

- ○ Financial incentives for start-ups vary among the Länder.

- ○ Many Länder business information offices have websites with information in English and other languages.

○ Corporation taxes have been overhauled and the rates levied are dropping.

○ The adoption of the euro currency makes it easy to compare prices across Europe.

○ British-owned businesses in Germany include petro-chemicals, financial services, surveying and construction.

- ○ Buying an existing business is cheaper than starting from scratch.

- ○ Laws of partnership are complicated and there are many types.

○ **Employing staff:** Recruiting through the national employment service is free.

○ **The environment:** In Germany, waste disposal and reclamation is based on the principle that the 'polluter pays'.

- ○ Companies involve staff and unions in the business more than in the UK or USA; seeking consensus over wages, working hours and improving the company.

In Germany the effect of the Single Market is less of a novelty than in some other EU countries as Germany has for some decades imposed no extra restrictions on foreign investors other than those in force against German nationals themselves. Foreign enterprises have long been welcomed in Germany, particularly if they provide new employment opportunities. There are no regulations prohibiting foreign corporations from buying up the total capital stock of a German company, neither are there any restrictions on the transfer of profits to foreign investors or the repatriation of capital, all of which provide an encouraging climate for foreign entrepreneurs.

At the time of writing, Germany is facing immense economic, social and industrial challenges arising from the unification of 1990 and the following recession. The German economy, which until the early 1990s showed remarkable resilience, is now showing a slight decline. On the positive side, the German economy has built up a reputation for stability, especially in the corporate sector.

In eastern Germany, the inefficient pre-unification economy is in the throes of transition to a market economy. There are modest signs that the huge investment programme, which has led to half a million new firms being created in the east is beginning to show minor returns.

In order to set up a business in Germany, you would need to have experience of running a successful business and be looking to Germany for greater opportunities for business expansion, or self-employment as a career advancement. Opportunities for practising a profession, e.g. law, would be extremely limited without a thorough knowledge of German. Those most likely to succeed are entrepreneurs with a track record, who speak German and can integrate into German business life and those interested in partnerships with German individuals and firms. This chapter outlines the main ways of approaching these objectives.

THE GERMAN CONTEXT FOR SMALL BUSINESSES

Unlike other EU countries such as Spain and Portugal where the majority of businesses have always been on a small scale, Germany was dominated before the Second World War by mega-companies, the so-called cartels, with worldwide operations. The concept of small business promotion is entirely a post-war one designed as an antidote to the pre-war cartels. Despite the traditional dominance of large-scale industries, the German government has shown itself extremely keen to encourage the starting up of small businesses and offers a large amount of additional support in the form of various incentives including the provision of capital at below market rates. The development of small businesses in Germany has been phenomenally successful so that around 70% of exports are generated by companies employing fewer than 25 staff.

There is no single definition for a small business as it varies from country to country. A small business in Germany usually means one with up to nine employees and a turnover of around £500,000. The term SME (Small and Medium Enterprises) is currently used by the European Commission to refer to enterprises with fewer than 500 employees and with capital no more than one third owned by a larger concern. The German term, *Mittelstand* eludes precise translation but embraces independent professionals and small and medium sized enterprises.

SME policy has been an integral part of German economic policy since

1960 when the first small business legislation was passed. Anyone used to the UK attitude to small businesses in which their worth is evaluated almost solely on their financial contribution to the economy, should note that the German approach is philosophical as well as material. In Germany, as in the rest of continental Europe, small businesses are viewed as a social as well as an economic asset. The German credo is that the value of small businesses should not just be measured in terms of their contribution to the GNP, but also to their direct and indirect stimulation of the productive efficiency of larger companies through competition and sub-contracting which in turn contribute to the overall efficiency of the economy. The added social dimension is in the widely held belief that small businesses are needed to prevent an imbalance in the sources of power and wealth as happened between the wars. The other main difference between Britain and Germany is that unlike Britain where the promotion of SMEs has been vested in central agencies and voluntary bodies in the private sector, the Germans have evolved a more locally based system of implementation. The decentralised German system works through the Länder governments, a network of trade associations and the public law chambers of Trade Craft and Industry. Under the law in Germany all businesses must belong to and are monitored by their local chamber of commerce.

PROCEDURES INVOLVED IN STARTING A NEW BUSINESS

Licences and Certificates Of Experience

Under the Treaty of Rome, the national of any EU country is free to set up business in another EU member country on equal terms with nationals of that country. Despite EU measures towards harmonising laws and taxes across the EU, there remain some laws which differ from country to country. In Germany certain industries are subject to strict regulations in order to safeguard health and restrict unqualified persons. Enterprises that deal with food, pharmaceuticals, medicine, banking, insurance, hotels and restaurants, handicrafts and transport all require a special licence.

Proof of professional qualification and in some cases a Certificate of Experience are also needed by those wishing to open a business in Germany. In the UK, Certificates of Experience for Germany can be issued by the Department of Trade and Industry. For further details of the trades and professions covered by the EU directive on professional qualifications, see Chapter Six, *Employment*.

Government Incentives

The procedures for starting a business in Germany have become extremely well-organised since the introduction of small business legislation over thirty years ago. There are various government incentives aimed at both Germans and foreigners, for specific territories and industries. These include investment grants and subsidies, tax incentives and financial assistance through long-term soft loans. In addition some Municipal and Länder governments provide land at low prices or reduced rents, infrastructure improvements and low utility costs.

Grants are also provided to small firms to promote new businesses, research and development, vocational training, management consultancy and foreign trade.

In the new länder there are a number of financial incentives for the new business to encourage enterprises to set up there. These range from grants and loans, through capital equity loans to company reinforcement programmes to help finance expansion. Details of these can be obtained from the Foreign Investor Information Centre at the Federal Ministry of Economics (see below and *Useful Publications* on p.230)

As already mentioned implementation of incentives is dealt with at local level and applications and enquiries about incentives should therefore be addressed to the different agencies in the various Länder. The following is a list of some of these agencies:

Commisioner for Foreign Investment: Markgrafenstr.34, D-10117 Berlin, Germany; ☎030-206570; fax 030-2065 7111; e-mail office@fdin.de; www.business-in-germany.de.

Wirtschaftsförderung Berlin GmbH: Fasanenstrasse 85, D-10623 Berlin, Germany; ☎030-399800; fax 030-3998 0239; e-mail info@wf-berlin.de; www.berlin.de/bbdc.

Zukunfts Agentur Brandenburg GbH: Steinstrasse 104-106, D-14480 Potsdam, Germany; ☎0331-660 3000; e-mail investor@zab-brandenburg.de; www.zab-brandenburg.de.

Hamburgische Gesellschaft für Wirtschaftsförderung GmbH: Hamburger Strasse 11, D22083 Hamburg; ☎040-2270190; fax 040-2270 1929.

HLT Wirschaftförderung Hessen Investitionsbank AG: Postfach 170228, D-60076 Frankfurt, Germany; ☎069-133 8500; fax 069-1338 5055; e-mail info@ibh-hessen.de; www.ibh-hessen.de.

IPA Investment Promotion Agency Niedersachsen: Hamburger Allee 4, D-30161 Hannover, Germany; ☎0511-343466; fax 0511-31 5909; e-mail info@ipa-niedersachsen.de; www.ipa-niedersachsen.de.

Gesellschaft für Wirschaftförderung Nordrhein-Westfalen mbH (GfW): PO Box 200309, D-40101 Düsseldorf, Germany; ☎0211-130000; fax 0211-1300 0154; e-mail gfw@gfw-nrw.de; www.gfw-nrw.de.

Investitions und Strukturbank Rheinland-Pfalz (ISB) GmbH: Holzhofstr. 4, D-55116 Mainz, Germany; ☎06131-985200; fax 06131-985299.

Wirschaftförderungsgesesllschaft für das Land Sachsen-Anhalt mbH: Kantsstr. 5, D-39104 Magdeburg, Germany; ☎0391-568990; fax 0391-568 9950.

Wirschaftsförderung Schleswig-Holstein GmbH: Lorentzendamm 43, D-24103 Kiel, Germany; ☎0431-593390; fax 0431-5933930.

INFORMATION AND ADVICE IN GERMANY

Other information and advice in Germany is provided by chambers of commerce and professional trade associations. In Germany all such bodies are state subsidised and have public law status. The chambers of commerce can provide information on government regulations, market opportunities, exports and premises as well as accountancy and payroll management. Other sources of information for potential investors include their nearest consulate/Embassy, all of which have Commercial Sections and the German banks.

The British Chamber of Commerce in Germany

Formed in 1960 by British and German businessmen, the chamber provides a forum for the exchange of information and the sharing of experience to benefit the development of trade between Britain and Germany. The BCCG also arranges trade fairs and 'British Days' which help to raise the profile of British firms in Germany. At the time of writing the membership included around 800 businesses, including Thomas Cook, Siemens, & Deutsche Bank, which are engaged in a variety of activities servicing bi-directional trade and investment.

As well as providing its own services the BCCG also represents the Confederation of British Industry in Germany and has access to all the services provided by both the Council of British Chambers of Commerce in Continental Europe and the Association of British Chambers of Commerce. With its own regional groups ranging across Germany from Berlin to Munich (including one in London), it can provide up to date local and national help for the business seeking to establish a presence in Germany. In addition to a monthly bilingual newsletter, the BCCG produces an annual directory of members (including regional trade reports) which with a round of meetings and discussions creates a networking environment for the modern manager. Full membership details can be arranged by contacting the Chamber at the above address.

Useful Addresses

American Chamber of Commerce in Germany: Rossmarkt 12, D-60311 Frankfurt am Main; ☎069-929 1040.

British Chamber of Commerce in Germany: General Office, Severinstrasse 60, D-50678 Köln, ☎0221-314458; fax 0221-315335.

Triple D GmbH: Westendstrasse 135, D-80339 München, Germany; ☎089-5108 5780; fax 089-5108 5781; e-mail DDDowdy@TripleD.de; www.TripleD.de.

German-British Chamber of Industry & Commerce (Deutsche-Britische Industrie und Handelskammer): 16 Buckingham Gate, London SW1E 6LB; ☎020-7976 4100; fax 020-7976 4101; www.germanbritishchamber.co.uk.

Export Promotions (Germany): Mr J.L.Dumbrell, Riverholme, The Towpath, Shepperton, TW17 9LL; ☎01932-267272; fax 01932-267171; e-mail john@infogermany.co.uk. A Consultancy specialising in how to enter the German Market that provides advice on how to find an agent, set up a company in German and how to live and work in Germany. Cultural Briefings are a speciality.

Robert Hanslip: 19 Ashley Close, Earley, Reading, RG6 2QY; ☎0118-986 1496; e-mail hanslips@aol.com. International Business Consultant with many years experience with the Hamburg Business Development Corporation.

Think4You AG: Hanauer Landstr. 135-137, D-60314 Frankfurt, Germany; ☎069-2424 1817; fax 069-2424 1860; www.think4you.com. eBusiness consultants and specialists in business translations and presentation.

German Chambers of Commerce

Below are listed Chambers of Commerce (*Industrie und Handelskammern*) in Germany.

AACHEN: Theaterstrasse 6-10, D-52062 Aachen; ☎0241-44600; fax 0241-446 0259; e-mail info@aachen.ihk.de; www.aachen.ihk.de.

AUGSBURG: Stettenstrasse 1 u. 3,

D-86150 Augsburg; ☎0821-31620; fax 0821-3162323; e-mail info@augsburg.ihk.de; www .augsburg.ihk.de.

BERLIN: Hardenbergstrasse 16-18, D-10623 Berlin; ☎030-315100; fax 030-31510278; www.berlin.ihk.de.

BONN: Bonner Talweg 17, D-53113 Bonn; ☎0228-22840; fax 0228-228 4170; www.ihk-bonn.de.

BREMEN: Am Markt 13, Haus Schütting, D-28195 Bremen; ☎0421-36370; fax 0421-363 7299; www.bremen.de.

DORTMUND: Märkische Strasse 120, D-44141 Dortmund; ☎0231-54170; fax 0231-541 7109; www.ihk.de/dortmund.

DRESDEN: Niedersedlitzer Strasse 63, D-01257 Dresden; ☎0351-28020; fax 0351-280 2280; www.dresden.ihk.de.

DÜSSELDORF: Ernst-Schnei-der-Platz 1, D-40212 Düsseldorf; ☎0211-35570; fax 0211-355 7400; e-mail ihkdus@duesseldorf.ihk.de; www.duesseldorf.ihk.de.

ESSEN: Am Waldthausenpark 2, D-45127 Essen; ☎0201-18920; fax 0201-207866; www.ihk.de/essen.

FRANKFURT/MAIN: Börsenplatz, D-60313 Frankfurt am Main; ☎069-21970; fax 069-2197 1424; www.ihk.de.frankfurt-main/.

FRANKFURT/ODER: Humboldt-strasse 3, D-15230 Frankfurt/Oder; ☎0335-56210; fax 0335-325492; www.ihk.de.ffo.

HAMBURG: Adolphsplatz 1, D-20457 Hamburg; ☎040-361380; fax 040-361 38401; e-mail servic e@hamburg.handelskammer.de; www.handelskammer.de/hamburg.

HANNOVER: Sitz Hannover, Schiff-graben 49, D-30175 Hannover; ☎0511-31070; fax 0511-310 7333; www.hannover.ihk.de.

KIEL: Lorentzdamm 24, D-24103 Kiel; ☎0431-51940; fax 0431-519 4234; e-mail ihk@kiel.ihk.de; www.ihk.de/kiel.

KOBLENZ: Schlossstrasse 2, D-56068 Koblenz; ☎0261-1060; fax 0261-106234; e-mail service@koblenz.ihk.de; www.ihk-koblenz.de.

KÖLN: Unter Sachsenhausen 10-26, D-50667 Köln; ☎0221-16400; fax 0221-164 0123; www.ihk-koeln.de.

LEIPZIG: Goerdelerring 5, D-04109 Leipzig; tel0341-12670; fax 0341-126 7421.

MANNHEIM: Postfach 10 16 61, D-68016 Mannheim; ☎0621-17090; fax 0621-170 9100; www.mannheim.ihk.de.

MÜNCHEN: Max-Joseph-Strasse 2, D-80333 München; ☎089-51160; fax 089-511 6360; www.muenchen.ihk.de.

NÜRNBERG: Hauptmarkt 25-27, D-90403 Nürnberg; ☎0911-13350; fax 0911-133 5200; e-mail info@ihk-nuernberg.de; www.ihk-nuernberg.de.

OSNABRÜCK: Neuer Graben 38, D-49074 Osnabrück; ☎0541-3530; fax 0541-353171; e-mail ihk@osnabrueck.ihk.de.

POTSDAM: Grosse Weinmeister-strasse 59, D-14469 Potsdam; ☎0331-27860; fax 0331-278 6111; www.ihk.de/potsdam.

STUTTGART: Jägerstrasse 30, D-70174 Stuttgart; ☎0711-20050; fax 0711-200 5354; www.stuttgart.ihk.de.

TRIER: Kornmarkt 6, D-54290 Trier; ☎0651-97770; fax 0651-977 7153; e-mail info@trier.ihk.de.

ULM: Olgastrasse 101, D-89073 Ulm (Donau); ☎0731-1730; fax 0731-173173; www.ulm.ihk.de.

WIESBADEN: Wilhelmstrasse 24-26, D-65183 Wiesbaden; ☎0611-15000; fax 0611-377271.

WÜRZBURG: Mainaustrasse 33, D-97082 Würzburg; ☎0931-41940; fax 0931-419 4100; e-mail info@wuerzburg.ihk.de; www.wuerzburg.ihk.de.

SME POLICY AND EURO-INFO CENTRES

The main EU initiative on small and medium-sized businesses (SMEs) was outlined in the 1985 meeting of the European Council. The Commission adopted a policy that was aimed at creating a favourable climate for small businesses. The aims of the policy included provision of capital, promoting the spirit of enterprise through education and training and simplifying the administrative burden for SME's. The EU promotes cross-border co-operation between SMEs through a network of Euro-Info Centres (EICs). These provide SMEs at local level in the UK with a service to enable them to enter the markets of other EU member countries and also updated data on markets, standards, sources of finance from the EU etc. It is also important for SME's to be aware of their rights under EU law and of the means of ensuring their enforcement. Advice can be sought through the Euro-Info Centre network (see below).

Useful Addresses:

The European Commission: Jean Monnet House, 8 Storey's Gate, London SW1P 3AT; ☎020-7973 1992; fax 020-7973 1900. For further information visit the; www.europe.org.uk which gives contact details for regional EU information providers.

London Chamber of Commerce: 33 Queen Street, London EC4R 1AP; ☎020-7248 4444; fax 020-7489 0391; e-mail lc@londonchamber.co.uk; www.londonchamber.co.uk.

Euro-Information Centres in the UK

BELFAST: Euro Info Centre, Invest Northern Ireland, LEDU House, Upper Galwally, Belfast, BT8 4TB; 02890-491031; fax 02890-691432.

BIRMINGHAM: Euro Info Centre, Birmingham Chamber of Industry and Commerce,75 Harborne Road, Birmingham, B15 3DH; ☎0121-455 0268; 0121-455 8670; e-mail birmingham@euro-ingo.org.uk; www.birmingham-chamber.com.

BRADFORD: West Yorkshire Euro Info Centre, 4th Floor, Olican House, 35 Chapel St, Bradford, BD1 5RE; ☎01274-434262; e-mail eic@bradford.gov.uk; www.bradford.gov.uk/euroinfocentre.

BRISTOL: Euro Info Centre, Bristol Chamber of Commerce and Industry, 16 Clifton Park, Bristol, BS8 3BY; ☎0117-973 7373; fax 0117-923 8024; e-mail bristoleic@businesswest.co.uk.

CARDIFF: Wales Euro Info Centre, Guest Building, PO Box 430, Cardiff CF10 3XT; ☎0290-2022 9525; fax 0290-2022 9740; www.waleseic.org.uk.

EXETER: Euro Info Centre, Exeter Enterprises Ltd., The Innovation Centre, University of Exeter, Exeter EX4 4RN; ☎01392-214085; fax 01392-264375; e-mail europa@exeter.ac.uk; www.e.ac.uk/euroinfo.

GLASGOW: Euro Info Centre, Small Business Gateway, 150 Broomielaw, Atlantic Quay, Glasgow G2 8LU; ☎0141-228 2797; fax 0141-228 2327; e-mail euroinfocentre@scotnet.co.uk.

HULL: Euro Info Centre Humberside, The University of Hull, Cottingham Road, Hull, HU6 7RX;

☎01482-465940; fax 01482-466488; e-mail euro-info-centre@hull.ac.uk; www.hull.ac.uk/euroinfo.

INVERNESS: Euro Business Services, 20 Bridge Street, Inverness IV1 1QR; ☎01463-702560; fax 01463-715400; e-mail eic@euro-info.co.uk.

KENT: Euro Info Centre, 26 Kings Hill, West Malling, ME14 2LL; ☎0345-226655; fax 01732-841109; e-mail eic@kent.businesslink.co.uk.

LEICESTER: Euro Info Centre, 10 York Road, Leicester, LE1 5TS; 0116-255 9944; fax 0116-258 7333.

LIVERPOOL: Euro Info Centre 1 Old Hall Street, Liverpool, L3 9HG; ☎0151-298 1928; fax 0151-224 2401; e-mail info@eicnw.co.uk.

LONDON: London Chamber of Commerce and Industry, 33 Queen Street, London, EC4R 1AP; ☎020-7248 4444; fax 020-7489 0391; e-mail lc@londonchamber.co.uk; www.londonchamber.co.uk. website spectrum.tcns.co.uk/uk/kent-euro/welcome.ht

MANCHESTER: Greater Manchester Euro Info Centre, Chamber Business Enterprises, Churchgate House, 56 Oxford Street, Manchester, M60 7HJ; ☎0161-237 4020; fax 0161-236 1341; e-mail eic@c-b-e.co.uk; www.tvc.org.uk.

NEWCASTLE: North of England EIC, St Georges House, Team Valley, Gateshead, Tyne and Wear, NE11 0NA; 0191-497 7660; fax 0191-487 5690; e-mail eic@onenortheast.co.uk; www.eic-northofengland.com.

NORWICH: Euro Info Centre, East Anglia, Norfolk and Norwich Millenium Library, Millenium Plain, Norwich, NR2 1AW; ☎01603-774775; fax 01603-774779; www.euro-info.org.uk.

NOTTINGHAM: Euro Info Centre, The Nottingham Chamber of Commerce and Industry, 309 Haydn Road, Nottingham, NG5 1DG; ☎0115-962 9623; fax 0115-985 6612.

SLOUGH: Euro Info Centre, Thames Valley Chamber of Commerce and Industry, Commerce House, 2-6 Bath Road, Slough, SL1 3SB; ☎01753-870580; fax 01753-524644; e-mail enquiries@thamesvalleychamber.co.uk.

SOUTHAMPTON: Euro Info Centre, Northguild Civic Centre, Southampton S014 7LW; ☎02380-832866; fax 02380-231714; e-mail southarea.eic@southampton.gov.uk.

RELOCATION AGENCIES & CONSULTANTS

General relocation agencies that can help you relocate everything from your business to your family possessions to Germany are an expanding field of business, with some very experienced and helpful staff. In addition to those listed on p.59-61 the following organisations offer business advice and/or practical help with the procedures involved in setting up a business:

Another World Services Inc.: 31 Green Briar Road, Thorndale PA 19372, USA; ☎610-380-4590; www.awservice.net. Independent services company specialising in relocation and moving services for corporate clients.

UBI-Bischof: Franz-Georg Bischof, Aubinger Str 86, D-81243 München; ☎089-871 3624; fax 089-874083; e-mail fg@bischof-muc.de; www.bischof-muc.de. Enterprise consultant and press agency. Acts as a facilitator for those wishing to enter the German market. Has excellent connections with almost all industries, especially high tech. Can assist with all aspects of business including finding offices, preparing business foundations and handling advertising. Willing to act as partner, distributor, agency for UK companies or those interested in Global player strategies.

BUSINESS STRUCTURES

In order to operate commercially in Germany, an individual or company must choose one of the various legal business forms from sole proprietorship to corporation. The tax burden for companies has been cut in recent years making Germany a more advantageous location for setting up a company. However, you will still need to do your homework. The American Chamber of Commerce has produced a document *A Roadmap to Starting a Company in Germany* which covers all the main points.

The start up costs of establishing a business will include notary and lawyers' fees, registration charges, and press gazetting; obviously the charges will vary, depending on the size and type of business.

The two main limited liability structures are the *Aktiengesellschaft* (*AG*) a joint stock corporation, and the *Gesellschaft mit beschränkter Haftung, GmbH* a limited liability company. Other structures include Partnerships, Co-operatives, branches of foreign companies and Limited Stock Partnerships.

Aktiengesellschaft (AG)

Is the legal form of business used when funds are to be raised from the general public, shareholders are not personally liable for company debts. Five members are required to form an AG either private individuals or corporate bodies. On founding the company the contract and statutes must be signed in the presence of a notary. The formation documents must contain details of the founders' nominal value (in the case of corporations), the value of shares issued to each founder, the objects of the enterprise, the share capital and domicile (which must be in Germany) of the company. To found an AG a minimum share capital of €50,000 is required, this must be fully subscribed and 25% paid up at the time of formation. A management board legally represents the joint stock corporation.

Gesellschaft mit beschränkter Haftung (GmbH)

The GmbH is the most usual form adopted by foreign companies' subsidiary operations in Germany and for German family-run businesses. The legal format is simpler than for an AG and shareholders can control and instruct management directly .

The management structure and the method of operation of a large GmbH and an AG are broadly similar. However there are some differences in the start up procedure. A GmbH may be formed by a single shareholder and the minimum share capital requirement is €25,000, this capital must be expressed in Euros and be evenly divisible by 100 and at least half of this capital must be paid up when forming the company. A GmbH does not normally issue share certificates, but should it choose to do so, these must be registered and are not freely transferable. Share transfers may only be effected by notarised deed and can be made the subject of other restrictions similar to an AG. A GmbH can also issue different classes of shares and can take up loans. However, such loans are agreed by contract with the lender and therefore do not have the characteristics of debentures etc. which are capable of being traded on the money markets. As for an AG company statutes must be notarised.

In the case of a GmbH, the board of management is replaced by one or more directors (usually called *Geschäftsführer*). Unlike an AG there is no legal requirement for registered managers' meetings. A supervisory board (*Aufsichtsrat*) is not required if the regular complement of employees is fewer than 500 people.

Partnerships: As in other countries partnerships can take various forms:

Offene Handelsgesellschaft, OHG: A general partnership in which all general partners have unlimited liability for partnership debts. The firm name must include the family name of one of the partners with the addendum '& Co'.

Kommanditgesellschaft, KG: A limited partnership in which one or more of the active partners is liable without limit for the debts of the partnership and one or more limited partners is liable up to the amount of their capital input to the partnership as specified in the document drawing up the partnership. Authority to manage the partnership on a day-to-day basis is vested in the partner(s) with unlimited liability.

GmbH & Co Kommanditgesellschaft (GmbH & Co KG): This is a limited partnership with the GmbH as the general partner and individuals as limited partners. In such a structure the limited liability partners put up the whole share capital and form a GmbH to hold the general partnership and exercise managerial rights. In this way the company obtains overall limited liability which is worthless to a would-be creditor as its assets are restricted to a share in the partnership's capital which may be zero.

Gesellschaft des bürgerlichen Rechtes (GbR or BGB-Gesellschaft): This is a Civil Law Partnership and as such is not a legal structure, nor is it self accounting. Members of a civil law partnership agree to share the cost of running office premises but retain their own fees from their separate business pursuits. This structure is often used by groups of professionals, e.g. lawyers. It is not normally suitable for international corporations.

Stille Gesellschaft: This is a silent partnership of the usual kind where an unregistered person, in return for a share of company profits, participates in the business of another partner solely by making a capital contribution which becomes part of the business assets of the active partner. The active partner(ship) has sole responsibility for the running of the business. There is also an atypical silent partnership (atypische stille Gesellschaft) in which a contract is made with the silent partner to the effect that he or she has a stake in the net assets (including reserves) of the business and can influence managerial decisions.

Genossenschaft (Co-operative): A co-operative is a legal entity which may be limited, with the members' liability limited to the amount of capital stated in the articles of association needed for registration. Co-operatives can also be unlimited. This form is particularly suitable for where a large number of individuals need to benefit from financial support provided by a jointly-financed association. It is particularly useful for agriculturalists.

Einzelkaufmann: Sole trader or sole proprietor. This status is excluded from the legislation pertaining to the control of limited liability and partnerships and typically has unlimited liability. Einzelfirma make up 91% of enterprises and employ 35% of the workforce.

Niederlassung einer susländisch Gesellschaft: A branch of a foreign company which has to be registered in the commercial register in order to carry out the full range of business activities. This is known as an independent branch. If the branch is dependent (i.e. a representation office) it cannot be registered with the commercial register. In either case, the foreign organisation is fully liable for the debts of the branch. In the market place, the branch is sometimes seen as not carrying the same weight as a GmbH. Its chief advantage for the foreign company can be reduced taxation depending on the fiscal laws of the country of origin. Expert financial advice is therefore essential before establishing a branch.

IDEAS FOR NEW BUSINESSES

No budding Euro-entrepreneur can afford to overlook Germany, not least because, with a population of over 82 million, it constitutes the largest consumer market in the EC. In addition Germany (notably through Hamburg and Berlin) is rapidly becoming a springboard for access to the markets of Eastern Europe. Small businesses however should not try to cover too much ground at the beginning; by far the most challenging step is to establish yourself in the German market. The main problem here for foreign businesses is that the Germans are spoilt for choice: they are more widely accustomed than any other Europeans to high-quality goods and excellent services. The foreigner therefore has to offer a product at least as good and preferably better, or a service with better incentives and benefits. Various agencies in the UK including the DTI, the chambers of commerce in Germany and various EU organizations mentioned earlier in this chapter can help prepare you for starting business in Germany and carry out the necessary fact finding on your behalf for any of the suggested areas mentioned below. Thorough research is a prerequisite to entering the German market and you should also be prepared to make exploratory trips to Germany to make contacts and assess the competition and visit trade fairs. In some cases your research may involve buying the opposition's products and learning from them. There are a number of opportunities open to foreign entrepreneurs to provide goods and services to the Germans.

On the material side, Germans are interested in many types of quality wares and so businesses selling an exclusive range of products, particularly crafts from exotic countries are almost certain to find a market. In the services market there is an insatiable demand in Germany for translation services and this is one area in which British entrepreneurs have been exploiting their potential.

Whatever the aspirations of the Single Market to harmonise taxes and laws in individual member states, the existing bevy of variations belies the hope that this will actually happen in either the short or medium term. As far as business opportunities are concerned this is a possible goldmine for British enterprises providing consultancy services to Germans wishing to break into the UK market. Such services could be provided by lawyers and accountants with the relevant expertise, perhaps working with German partners. Other areas that offer scope are computer technology and language schools for teaching business English.

One of the main aims of the Commission is to see the establishment of a common market for services, even those which are traditionally government regulated like banking, transport and insurance. It is therefore envisaged that these will continue to be regulated by national authorities who will enforce certain rules of commercial operation whilst opening them up to companies from around the Community on an equal basis. Much of the legislation needed to make the financial services sector accessible to foreign companies has already been passed and in the case of banking is already well exploited.

Telecommunications: European telecommunications markets have been open to outside competition for several years now. At present the German telecoms market is worth around €40 billion, and while Deutsche Telekom has an effective monopoly, this can now be challenged by bulk phoneline handlers and cheap-rate operators. DT is also facing stiff competion in the mobile phone market.

The Internet: Whether the cabling you use to provide connections to users is supplied by Deutsche Telekom or not this is still an area ripe for exploration as the Germans are keen investors in modern technology and 'das Net' is no exception, either at work or in the home.

Shopping: Modern technology and fast transport methods now means that canny shop owners can set up shop in Germany. Good research on German shopping trends and customer requirements will pay dividends; as will having the right format, committed staff at all levels, a well identified target market and something new to offer shoppers.

Useful Publications

German Tax & Business Law Guide: In collaboration with the German law firm Boesebeck Droste, this is a one volume loose-leaf reporting service providing a concise yet comprehensive overview of Germany's business law and tax systems. The guide is a practical reference source for investors and company managers involved in doing business in and with Germany, and also for their legal, tax and financial advisers. Available from CCH Editions Ltd (Telford Road, Bicester, OX6 0XD; ☎01869-253300) for an annual subscription of £440 which includes six reporter updates and ten newsletters.

Mergers & Acquisitions in Germany: Written in 1995 by the German law firm Droste, this book offers information on the legal situation with an emphasis on the viewpoint of purchasers, and highlights the differences between German contract law and that of other jurisdictions. Available from CCH Editions Ltd (Telford Road, Bicester, OX6 0XD; ☎01869-253300) for £110.

Transactions in Real Property in Germany: Also written by the Droste law firm, this book is a practical guide, including bilingual sample agreements, to the legal and tax aspects of buying property in Germany. Also available from CCH Editions Ltd (Telford Road, Bicester, OX6 0XD; ☎01869-253300) for £110.

Department of Trade & Industry Publications: For more information contact the DTI Export Publications Unit; ☎020-7215 2470; fax 020-7215 2482; www.dti.gov.uk/publications.

Action Single Market Opens the door to Europe. A Guide for Business; ☎020-7215 4479.

Germany Your Business Partner: Published by the English German Office of Foreign Trade (*Bundesagentur für Aussenwirtschaft*), Agrippastr. 87-93, D-50676 Köln; ☎0221-205 1770; fax 0221-205 7212; www.bfai.de) this book summarises major trade and investment figures as well as providing an overview of German business types, taxes, incentives and the practical aspects of doing business in Germany. It also has a handy address list of all the major ministries and overseas offices related to trading with Germany, and a list of the ministries publications and reports including those published in English.

The German Office of Foreign Trade also publishes a wide range of industrial and business reports.

How to Do Business in Germany: Put together by the German American Chamber of Commerce of the Midwest (104 South Michigan Avenue, Suite 600, Chicago Illinois 60603-5978, USA), this booklet details the permits and regulations regarding businesses in Germany, as well as offering a breakdown of business types.

THE ENVIRONMENTAL FACTOR

Anyone contemplating starting a manufacturing business in Germany should be aware that Germany puts enormous emphasis on environmental issues and this is reflected in the extensive anti-pollution and anti-noise regulations. These include the following initial requirements:.

German Packaging Law: The Dual System

In pursuance of the above, the German waste recovery system as laid down in the German packaging/recycling law (*Verordnung über die Vermeidung von Verpackungsabfällen Verpackungs-Verordnung vom 27 August 1998*) is a measure aimed at the reduction and ultimately avoidance of packaging waste, this was based on estimates that showed German landfill capacity for waste disposal would be full by now. The Verpackungs-Verordnung obliges manufacturers to take back sales packaging or arrange for its collection and recycling by a third party. The object of the Verpackungs-Verordnung is to make all industrial producers responsible for the collection, disposal or recycling of the packaging of their products. The law also forbids the incineration of any items. The ambitious aim of the Verpackungs-Verordnung, is that it will embrace everything from a yoghurt carton to an automobile. These laws have seen the total tonnage of municipal waste collected in Germany drop while the amount of material recycled has risen. In 1990 less than 1 million tonnes of biodegradable waste was collected by 2001 this figure reached over 8 million tonnes.

The Dual System (*Duales System Deutschland*). Manufacturers and distributors of packaging materials may use third parties to fulfil their obligations under the above ordinance. These third parties are the Dual System with its Green Dot (*Grüne Punkt*) marking on packaging or the RESY company with its triple arrow logo. The Duales System was set up in 1990 as a non profit organisation (*Duales System Deutschland GmbH, Gesellschaft für Abfallvermeidung und Sekundärrohstoffgewinnung mbH*) by companies from the retail trade, consumer goods and packaging industries. The system has set up a nationwide collection system for sales packaging, thus exempting retailers and others from their obligation to take back packaging materials for recycling. The Dual System has ensured that the 78 kilos of waste packaging collected for every inhabitant (a total of nearly 6 million tonnes) at current figures, has been made from recyclable material, collected and re-used.

The DSD is also obliged to collect packaging from homes or collection points (see below), sort it, and forward the recyclable parts for recycling. This collection and sorting is financed by the licensing of the *Der Grüne Punkt*/Green Dot trademark. This indicates that the packaging in question is participating in the system and meets its requirements for recyclability (the same is roughly true of the RESY symbol, see entry below). The symbol may only be marked on materials if the licence fee has been paid, companies using the Green Dot without a valid licence contract will be prosecuted for violation of the trade mark law. The Green Dot is in use in 15 countries as financing mark for the collection, sorting and recycling of sales packaging.

The amount to be paid in Green Dot licensing is based on the material and weight and includes an item fee based on volume or area, fees in general being based on the overall costs for sorting and recycling.

In the year 2000, German consumers collected a total of 5,671,647 tonnes of used sales packaging manufactured from glass, paper/cardboard, plastics, tinplate, aluminium and composites in containers marked with the Green Dot. This corresponds to a collection quantity of 78.3 kilogrammes per person. In 2002 a new production facility for plastic bottles manufactured from recycled plastics went online.

In addition to this, as part of its mandate to organise the nationwide collection of recyclable material the DSD has harmonised its collection of waste with the systems operated by local authorities. In principal it offers two systems the 'kerbside collection' and the 'bring' system. In the former the lightweight packaging fraction (cardboard, plastic, aluminium, tin) is normally collected in yellow bags or bins from consumers houses by waste management companies. In the latter system people deposit used containers at collection points near their homes; these are not just bottle banks divided by colour but include card and paper banks.

In addition to these changes German packaging materials have gradually become lighter as manufacturers realise that there is a cost saving to be made with regard to the Green Dot licence fee, the current trend is towards refill packs and minimal packaging.

Packaging or industrial firms seeking to relocate to Germany may also wish to note that the Duales System has an annual Innovation Prize for Packaging (*Innovationspreis Verpackung*), with four categories covering various types of packing material and usage.

Useful Addresses

Der Grüne Punkt – Duales System Deutschland AG: Frankfurter Strasse 720-726, D-51145 Köln; ☎02203-9370; fax 02203-937190; www.gruener-punkt.de. The DSD is the main organization responsible for recycling sales packaging and the Green Dot recyclable mark.

RESY GmbH: Hilpertstr. 22, D-64295 Darmstadt, Germany; ☎06151-92940; fax 06151-929440. Is a firm created by the VfW (*Vereinigung für Wertstoffrecycling GmbH* see below), VDW (*Verband der Wellpappen-Industrie e.V.*) and the Paper Industry, to ensure the recycling of packaging made of paper or cardboard. Packaging firms can mark their cartons with the 'RESY' symbol under contract with the firm, the fee being based upon the total tonnage of shipping containers and packaging which contracting parties deliver for disposal each year. Packaging bearing the 'RESY' symbol is guaranteed to be collected and recycled by the German paper industry and VfW member companies.

ISD Interseroh GmbH: Stollwerckstr. 9a, D-51149 Köln (Porz); ☎ 02203-91470; fax 02203-9147394. Has 80,000 pick up points throughout Germany and in 2000 had a turnover of 772 Million DM for industrial packaging recycling. Interseroh's agreement with the DSD means that the firm recycles paper, cardboard, tin, steel, aluminium, and other materials for 4,300 companies through its pick up points to 600 raw materials companies.

Vfw Aktiengesellschaft: Postfach 400644, D-50836 Köln; ☎ 02234-95870; fax 02234-9587200; www.vfw-ag.de. The VfW is an association of 450 medium sized materials recycling firms and has 18 regional offices servicing 800 collection sites nationwide. This association accounts for the collection prior to recycling of 65% of the total amount of used paper in Germany. VfW firms can also ensure the recycling of pharmaceutical industry waste, sensitive industrial data and provide documentary proof of recycling should it be required.

Trade Partners UK, German Desk: Kingsgate House, 66-74 Victoria Street, London SW1E 6SW; ☎ 020-7215 4285; fax 020-7215 4765. Trade Partners UK distributes a free 'notes on the Gerrman packaging Ordinance' and details of the Duales System Deutschland. A list of recycling companies for different types of packaging is also included.

RUNNING A BUSINESS

Employing Staff

Germany has some of the strongest labour laws in the world, which many employers complain are too restrictive and work too much in favour of their employees. Amongst the battery of German legislation is the obligation for employers to have worker delegations participating in the decision-making in larger firms, and others that oblige management to seek consultation with their staff (through workers' councils) and obtain their approval before implementing a whole range of matters. Another set of laws fixes job security, welfare and fringe benefits, working conditions, and the procedures for collective wage bargaining. Whilst the spectrum of matters covered by labour legislation is not in itself unique to Germany, the precision and exactness with which the laws are set out, is.

The high level of skills and training amongst the German labour force is the object of envy throughout Europe. Over 70% of the workforce in western Germany is occupationally qualified compared with 30% in the UK. The availability of staff: managerial, skilled and unskilled, is generally good. However there is a shortage of specific skills in some areas (e.g. Information Technology). In eastern Germany there is high unemployment but the workforce there is retraining and willing to work.

When employing staff the following should be born in mind by the foreign employer:

○ Wage settlements are usually negotiated through agreement with trade unions.

○ Annual wage increases have tended to be above inflation rates.
○ Unit wage costs, which relate wages and productivity, are rising faster in Germany than in either France or the UK.
○ Hourly wages in Germany are now the highest amongst the world's leading economies including Switzerland.
○ Worker councils have a powerful voice in staff matters.

Workers Councils

The management of every business employing five or more staff over 18, must agree to the setting up of a *Betriebsrat* (Works Council) at the request of the staff. There is no legal obligation on the staff to have a Council if they do not wish to, but in practice they nearly always do. The Betriebsrat is elected by secret ballot and candidates may be either independent and/or union sponsored. However, the Betriebsrat can function entirely separately from the trade unions and many small companies whose staff are not unionised will still have a Betriebsrat. Depending on the size of the company, the Betriebsrat has an on-site office and one or more senior members who are occupied full-time in the execution of their Council duties whilst being fully salaried by the company. The Betriebsrat expects to be consulted by the management on a wide field of matters. For instance, legislation obliges the management to inform the Council regularly of any investment projects and financial plans for the company though it is not obligated to act on any suggestions put forward by the Council. In matters which concern the daily life of the staff, the boot is firmly on the Council's foot: safety regulations, installation of new equipment, catering facilities, working hours and holiday schedules all come within the Council's jurisdiction and the management is legally bound to seek the approval of the council before making any changes in these areas. The Betriebsrat can object and if no agreement can be reached with the management, the matter is taken before a labour court.

From the employer's point of view the works council system generally operates smoothly. However, over the past few years there has been a growth in friction particularly in the area of recruitment and dismissals, the introduction of flexible working hours and new technology. The works councils are inherently on the side of the employee and it can make dismissal for incompetence or lack of discipline very difficult for the employer to accomplish. As Germany has relatively high unemployment, the frictions between Councils and management generally are bound to be exacerbated. However, in smaller firms the system should continue to work smoothly and, as the majority of foreigners starting up businesses in Germany will be running SME's or tiny companies, the system should not prove a hindrance.

Co-Determination

An extension of the principal behind works councils, that everything a company does affects its employees, co-determination gives employees representatives on a supervisory board which oversees the company's activities. Companies not engaged in mining, or iron and steel production and which employ more than 2,000 staff fall within the scope of the 1976 Co-Determination Act. This specifies that companies should have supervisory boards made up of workers' and shareholders' representatives, at ratios of 6:6, 8:8 and 10:10 for companies employing up to 10,000, between 10,000-20,000 and over 20,000 staff respectively. Employees of joint stock company, a private limited company, a partnership limited by shares, a co-operative or a mutual insurance company can influence policy through the supervisory boards; including dismissing members of the management board (except in partnerships limited by shares).

Collective Bargaining

Wage settlements are agreed by the employers with the trade unions. Each employer is a member of the employers' federation for his or her particular industry. There is a branch of every type of employers' association in each of the Länder and collective bargaining therefore takes place on a regional basis. Generally, each employer comes within the ambit of a single trade union and the legally binding wage agreements apply to all the employees in a given place of work, regardless of whether or not they are union members.

Employee Training

Germany is a byword for youth vocational training (*berufliche Ausbildung*). The advantages of an overall vocational training system, whereby every employer from the Siemens corporation to the village baker pays for the apprentice scheme have been plain to see in Germany's abundance of highly-trained employees. The system is regulated at federal (*Bund*) level, but administration is handled at local level. Positions as trainees (*Auszubildende*) are provided annually for the majority of school leavers; usually around one and a half million take them up.

Trainees, known colloquially as *Azubis*, are given contracts for two or three-year courses on a dual training basis which means they spend two days a week at the *Berufsschule* (vocational school) and the remainder at the *Betrieb* (firm) learning a specific job. A formal training system covers a range of over 300 jobs and occupations ranging from bank clerk, to hairdressing or car mechanics. The Azubi takes examinations to continue as a journeyman (*Geselle*), assistant (*Gehilfe*) or Skilled Worker (*Facharbeiter*) and has his or her salary increased accordingly. The highest qualification is master craftsman (*Meister*) for which an exam must be taken after several years of practical professional experience. Another possibility after successful completion of basic trade training, is access to a specific *Fachschule* offering further training programmes and attendance at *Abendgymnasium* (Evening Grammar School) or *Kolleg* (special courses).

Almost all employers in industry provide training schemes for their employees. Training contracts are supervised by the local chambers of commerce in conjunction with local educational establishments. Many employers also encourage qualified employees to attend outside courses in order to ensure that their work keeps professionally up to date. Employees have a legal right to claim one week's paid training time a year in order to attend such courses, many of which are subsidised by the Government or trade unions.

Social Security Contributions

The German social security system is comprehensive and together with fringe benefits constitutes a considerable expense for employers. Social security consists of three main payment areas: old age pension insurance, unemployment insurance and health insurance. The contributions in each case are compulsory and are divided equally between employer and employee. Although some forms of social insurance are provided solely at the employers expense, such as the statutory occupational accident insurance. Exemption from German social security payments may be claimed by foreigners from countries (including the United States and Australia) with which Germany has a social security treaty; under this agreement they may work in Germany but still be registered with the social security system in their own country. More details on the responsibilities, exemptions and payments towards the social security system can be obtained from local chambers of commerce or the Federal Ministry for Labour and Social Affairs (*Bundesministirium für Arbeit und Sozialordnung:* Postfach 500, D-53105 Bonn; www.bma.de).

Pension Contributions. The national pension scheme requires contributions for practically all employees regardless of their salary level. The only exceptions are temporary staff from other countries (see above). For further information on pensions, see Chapter Six, *Employment.*

Unemployment Insurance. This covers all wage and salary earners. The contributions are 6.5% of income.

Health Insurance. This covers all employees and their families. The amount of the contribution is fixed by the respective sickness fund of which the employee is a member and is liable to variation between funds. The current rate for contributions is around 14% of gross wages. This applies to incomes below a set level, employees being paid above this ceiling can elect to pay voluntary contributions to the state system or to take out private health insurance. In either case they are still entitled to a tax-free contribution from their employer of 50% of the cost.

Occupational Accident Insurance (*Unfallversicherung*). The cost of this is borne by the employer through their payments to the employer's liability insurance funds. These premiums are based on the sum of wages paid each year and the risks to employees. The benefits provided by this are indefinite medical treatment, injury benefit (80% of lost wages) payable after six weeks, occupational assistance (for re-training), injury pension (if your capacity to earn is reduced by 20% or more), and funeral allowance and survivors pension (payable to dependants).

Other Employee Benefits

Quite apart from the contributions mentioned above, employers are also liable for other employee benefits, which can add considerably to labour costs:

Sickness benefit. A sick employee is entitled to receive a full salary for up to six weeks during his or her absence. For longer periods, the employee is paid out of the sickness fund.

Maternity leave. Working women are entitled to a fully paid maternity leave of six weeks before and eight weeks after childbirth. The health insurance fund pays a daily, tax-free allowance and the employer must pay the difference up to the employee's net salary of the last three months.

Parental leave. In addition to maternity leave, either parent may claim parental leave of up to three years following the birth. For six months the parents can each claim €300 per month after which the allowance may be decreased depending on the level of other income. The employer is obliged to resume the parent's previous employment after this period.

Bonuses. In common with several other European countries, companies in Germany pay their employees two extra months salary, one around mid-year and the other at Christmas.

Holidays. Although the minimum amount of paid holiday allowed per year is 24 days, many German employees are actually entitled (though binding agreements with trade unions) to as much as six weeks paid holiday a year.

TAXATION

Once a company has been registered notice has to be given to the tax authorities *(Finanzamt)* who will then allocate a tax number. Businesses in Germany used to bear one of the heaviest tax burdens in the EU these have been cut in recent years. The main taxes are as follows:

Municipal Trade Tax. Every business enterprise in Germany is liable for municipal trade tax at rates that vary between the municipalities. Trade tax is made up of two components, income and capital, the tax is calculated by applying a base rate of tax (5% of income and 0.2% of capital) and a local assessment rate (between 300 and 500%) to trade income and trading capital. There are allowances in the cases of individual traders and partnerships.

Corporation Tax (*Körperschaftssteuer*). The tax rate has been reduced to one flat rate of 25%, previously it varied according to how the profits were distributed.
VAT (*Mehrwertsteuer*) In Germany VAT is levied as in the rest of Europe on delivery of domestic goods and services and on the importation of goods. The standard rate is 16%, at present. On some goods such as groceries and books, VAT is at a reduced rate of this includes banking, insurance and medical services. From a business perspective, VAT is not an element of production cost as it is relayed on to the customer. Similarly, VAT paid by a company for goods and services received is reclaimable from the tax authorities.

Taxation Of Partnerships

Partnerships tend to be treated differently from AGs or GmbHs for tax purposes. They are subject to transaction taxes including VAT and trade tax, but not to income, corporation or net assets taxes. The nature of the partnership arrangement ensures that taxable income and net assets are shared amongst the partners who then become subject to corporation tax or if acting individually, to income tax (*Einkommensteuer*) and net assets tax in their own name.

PERSONAL CASE HISTORIES

ALAISDAIR HERON

Alaisdair is a Scot and has lived and worked in Germany as a Professor of Theology in the University of Erlangen (in the northern Bavarian region known as Franconia), since 1981.

How awkward was German red-tape in practice?
I was invited into the post by the Bavarian Ministry of Education and so had a much easier time, although my wife and I still had to register with the local authorities our initial residence permit was for five years which saved a lot of hassle. When it came to renew we were given the unlimited permit, and it struck me that they could have given us that one at the start, seeing as I was being employed by the state. However, there were different bureaucracies at work and that was part of the problem.

However, local registration meant that voting cards for the elections we were eligible to vote in, local council etc, came through automatically without us having to register to vote as you have to in Britain.

How crowded are German universities?
Well that depends on what you're studying some arts courses and even hard sciences like physics are short of students while finance and medicine are very busy. So much so that it seems that medical students are examined so heavily in the first two years that you'd think it was done to see if they'd give up.

What is German public transport/getting around like?
Well actually I don't use it much, Erlangen is rather flat and you can get around easily enough by bike so I do that mostly, or drive to go shopping and so on. When I do use public transport, it has always been very efficient and quite cheap.

Driving is a very nice experience in Germany but you do have to be on your toes at junctions and crossings, as the cyclists have a tendency to run the lights. Of course you have to bear in mind that cycle paths have their own traffic light at many junctions and these can allow them to cross your path legally. Mind you not many cyclists wear helmets so its worrying to see them ignore the rules, its getting a bit like Britain here in the way cyclists tend to think that the term one-way street doesn't include them. Cycle paths on pavements or at the side of roads are often marked with pink tiles or tarmac.

Were you given accommodation or did you rent a flat ?
Actually we were lucky in that a colleague in the department was leaving and we were able to arrange to take over his flat. When we first came here it was difficult, especially for foreigners, to find accommodation. Its a lot easier now, and there's less prejudice, but that doesn't mean 'none'.

How expensive is Germany?

Actually with wages being higher and most goods being cheaper Germany is a lot less expensive than Britain. Houses are a lot more expensive but people don't generally buy until they're a lot older. Certainly most household goods are cheaper and although petrol has risen recently its still a lot cheaper than in the UK or Holland. The euro has caused some price creep, especially as the mark went out overnight, which allowed shops to stop showing both prices. Mind you *Lidl* (a supermarket chain) are advertising goods as being cheaper than before the euro, although that's just a sales tactic, charging €2.96 for something that usually costs €2.98!

How good are the Germans at speaking English?

Bear in mind that Germany is bombarded with English 'pop-culture'. A great many Germans are taught it at the *Gymnasium* and many do courses in English literature at university. Generally the language is taught by thinking in German and translating that into English, rather than learning to think in English. This means that there's a tendency for the language to come across slightly stilted; as an anglophone you often find odd synonyms in use, purely from the absence of conversational English lessons in the teaching.

SARAH SIERRA

Sarah recently spent eight months in Regensburg at the university on an exchange trip studying German. We asked her:

How awful was German red-tape in practice?

Registering at the various places such as the Einwohnermeldeamt, the university and the DAK did not present too much of a problem as I and the other foreign students were given a lot of useful information from our home universities, and Regensburg has an induction programme designed for foreign students which was extremely helpful. I would describe the process as time-consuming rather than a nightmare. What I did find annoying was the fact that many offices closed at 11.30 am, and twice I found myself waiting in a queue for two hours only to be handed a form; which made getting all the red-tape over and done with in one day impossible.

Was it difficult to find work?

Although studying at university, I did do some part-time work as it happened upon arrival. I managed to get a job at 'Toys R Us', the application was a case of walking in and talking to the a manager, who was suitably impressed by the fact that I had worked for the company in England, and being offered a job. However, my advice to anyone seeking work in Germany would be to avoid shop work; the pay is quite low in comparison with average wages (which are a lot higher than in the UK), and shop staff seem to have no concept of customer service. Many of my friends (the other 'foreign' students) managed to find work in bars and restaurants during the summer, often by simply going in and asking for work as I had. English-speaking people seemed to be quite well accepted, although I would strongly advise people not to attempt work that involves dealing with the public or being under a lot of pressure without being at least 'A'-level standard in German. (As an example of the language problem even students can have at first, Sarah comments that) I found the atmosphere quite depressing and often got treated as if I was stupid because of not always understanding what people were saying to me, although I found out later that nobody realised that I'd only been in the country for a week.

Is the working environment pleasant?
One thing that was noticeable was that our German colleagues never seemed to socialise together after work, or even chat very much during breaks. All in all, I would say that working in a foreign country can be an enjoyable and challenging experience, and being from within the EU, there were no problems with visas. However, anyone intending to work with food in Germany has to pass a health test; the results of which can take three weeks to arrive.

How do you find the social life and the Germans?
I found socialising in Germany really enjoyable, for one thing the pubs stay open a lot later than in the UK; till 2 am, and on some occasions such as *Fasching* many stayed open all night. The atmosphere in pubs was generally relaxed – you could sit there as long as you liked with one beer without feeling pressured to buy another. It took some getting used to the fact that drinks are ordered from waiters rather than by queuing at the bar.

Initially I found making friends quite difficult, as the Germans tend to take friendship very seriously and do not have time for casual chit-chat, but with a little perseverance I gradually found myself being invited out. One thing I liked about the Germans was that they often organised small events in their own homes such as video evenings, parties and barbecues, which were enjoyable and a good way to get to know people. I found the Germans I met very helpful and trustworthy: at the beginning of my time in Regensburg I could hardly string a sentence together, yet they listened to me politely and gave me lots of encouragement.

What is German public transport like ?
Travelling in Germany is easy, due to the extremely efficient bus and train services. Prices on buses are fairly reasonable and although trains can be quite expensive, there are various offers to be taken advantage of, a 'Bahnkarte' is the equivalent of a railcard, and worth buying if you intend to travel a lot. The 'Wochenendkarte', which can only be purchased at the weekends is great, up to five people can travel anywhere in Germany. It does not allow you to travel on some trains, so long journeys can take hours due to your having to keep changing trains, but when you consider how cheap it is you can not complain.

Were you given accommodation or did you rent a flat ?
As an exchange student I was given a place in a university hall of residence, which was brilliant. My room, a reasonable size with ensuite shower and a balcony cost only €120 (DM235) per month, including heating and electricity. The kitchen was separate and shared with 10 other students. Regensburg university lets its unoccupied rooms out during the summer, as I imagine other universities do. So for anyone wishing to work in Germany over the summer it may be possible to arrange accommodation through the local university.

Have you any advice for anyone thinking of taking the plunge?
My advice to anyone intending to live or work in Germany would be to be prepared – find out as much as possible before you go, make sure that you have all the relevant documents, such as the E111 form, passport etc, and where possible arrange a job and accommodation before arriving in Germany. Do not get depressed about problems with the language, it gets easier as you go along. many regions have their own dialects – most notably *Bayerisch* and *Swäbisch* which are impossible for Germans to understand, never mind foreigners. I found that if I explained to people that I was English and did not understand what they were saying, then they were generally sympathetic and quite pleased that I was attempting to speak German at all. Making friends can be a slow process, as even the Germans themselves admit; they are not the most forthcoming or spontaneous people. But, if you persevere and show that you are serious about friendship then you will generally be treated very well. The cost of living is not a great deal higher than in Britain, in fact with the high pound many things are actually cheaper. Shops are generally similar to Britain but some of the supermarkets are awful.